Praise for _Chaucer, Ethics, and Gender_

'The effect is one of enriching a reading of the _Tales_, focussing attention upon what it means to face moral decisions, and contextualising those decisions within their contemporaneous ethico-moral discourses. . . . The study may profitably be read in conjunction with its author's previous extremely interesting work on Chaucer and gender. . . . I look forward to returning to it repeatedly with different questions and new curiosities.'
K. P. Clarke, _Review of English Studies_

'What is notable and useful about this book is the use of gender as a critical tool: Blamires proposes a new methodology, employing a gendered discussion of the presentation of ethics . . . to open up a new reading of Chaucer. . . it is the exploration of ethics and morality by reference to contemporary works such as the _Roman de la Rose_, Gower's _Confessio Amantis_ and the _Book of Vices and Virtues_ that I found particularly useful since it enables the reader to place Chaucer in his own moral environment. . . . what Blamires does that is new and interesting is to show how Chaucer's treatment of the vices and virtues does not always fall out along expected gender lines. Blamires challenges assumptions about medieval gender stereotyping by showing both how Chaucer sometimes attributes to women virtues normally characterised in medieval thinking as masculine, and how some virtues were, maybe against expectation, gendered feminine. . . . Blamires is at his best when he is engaging with "antique" and contemporary texts to throw light on the ethical dilemmas embedded in the tales.'
Cate Gunn, _Essays in Criticism_

'In each of these chapters, Blamires' analysis leads to rich, new, and often provocative readings of the tales or passages within the tales . . . _Chaucer, Ethics, and Gender_ richly demonstrates how generative it can be to read Chaucer's writings in dialogue with the ideas expressed in the moral and ethical treatises that inform the complicated world view of the late fourteenth century.'
Ann Dobyns, _The Medieval Revi_

Chaucer, Ethics, and Gender

ALCUIN BLAMIRES

OXFORD
UNIVERSITY PRESS

OXFORD

UNIVERSITY PRESS

Great Clarendon Street, Oxford OX2 6DP

Oxford University Press is a department of the University of Oxford.
It furthers the University's objective of excellence in research, scholarship,
and education by publishing worldwide in

Oxford   New York

Auckland Cape Town Dar es Salaam Hong Kong Karachi
Kuala Lumpur Madrid Melbourne Mexico City Nairobi
New Delhi Shanghai Taipei Toronto

With offices in

Argentina Austria Brazil Chile Czech Republic France Greece
Guatemala Hungary Italy Japan Poland Portugal Singapore
South Korea Switzerland Thailand Turkey Ukraine Vietnam

Oxford is a registered trademark of Oxford University Press
in the UK and in certain other countries

Published in the United States
by Oxford University Press Inc., New York

British Library Cataloguing in Publication Data
Data available

Library of Congress Cataloging in Publication Data
Data available

Typeset by SPI Publisher Services, Pondicherry, India
Printed in Great Britain
on acid-free paper by
Biddles Ltd., King's Lynn, Norfolk

ISBN 978-0-19-924867-4 (Hbk.)   978-0-19-953462-3 (Pbk.)

1 3 5 7 9 10 8 6 4 2

For my brothers
Gabriel, Cyprian, Benedict, Fabian

Abbreviations

ChauR	*The Chaucer Review*
EETS	Early English Text Society
ELH	*English Literary History*
FM	*Fasciculus Morum: A Fourteenth-Century Preacher's Handbook*, ed. and trans. Siegfried Wenzel (University Park: Pennsylvania State University Press, 1989)
JEGP	*Journal of English and Germanic Philology*
JW	*Jacob's Well*, pt 1, ed. Arthur Brandeis, EETS, o.s. 115 (London: Trübner, 1900)
MÆ	*Medium Ævum*
MLQ	*Modern Language Quarterly*
MLR	*Modern Language Review*
MP	*Modern Philology*
NML	*New Medieval Literatures*
PBA	*Proceedings of the British Academy*
PL	*Patrologia latina*, ed. J.-P. Migne, 162 vols. (Paris, 1857–66), cited by volume and column
PMLA	*Publications of the Modern Language Association of America*
PQ	*Philological Quarterly*
Riv.	*The Riverside Chaucer*, gen. ed. Larry D. Benson (Boston: Houghton Mifflin, 1987)
SAC	*Studies in the Age of Chaucer*
SN	*Studia Neophilologica*
SP	*Studies in Philology*
VV	*The Book of Vices and Virtues: A Fourteenth Century English Translation of the 'Somme Le Roi' of Lorens D'Orléans*, ed. W. Nelson Francis, EETS, o.s. 217 (London: Oxford University Press, 1942)

Contents

Acknowledgements

The concept of this book was developed through papers prepared for conferences, talks, and seminars spanning several years and several countries. I therefore owe many debts to the colleagues who took the risk of inviting me to speak, or who discussed ideas with me in panels and seminars, even if some of them might be surprised to discover here what edifice they unwittingly helped engineer. For me the book's chapters are alive with memories of the occasions that spurred them—from a St Hilda's conference on women and creativity to a session on Chaucer and ethics in the New Chaucer Society Congress at the Sorbonne; from a Lansdowne Lecture at the University of Victoria to a Fordham University symposium on polemic about women in the Middle Ages; from the 'Quid est amor?' conference in Dublin to research seminar presentations in Manchester, Canterbury, York, Cambridge, and Oxford. For these stimuli I am especially grateful to Thelma Fenster, Elizabeth Archibald, Norm Klassen, Jane Taylor and Lesley Smith, Paul Strohm, Andrew Butcher, Helen Cooney, Nick Havely, and Heather O'Donoghue. I am particularly beholden to colleagues who have allowed me to re-use or adapt materials originally published in volumes they edited. I gratefully acknowledge the permission of Oxford University Press and the editor Steve Ellis, to re-use in Chapter 3 parts of a contribution entitled 'Sexuality' previously published in *Chaucer: An Oxford Guide* (Oxford, 2005). To the publisher Palgrave Macmillan and the editors Thelma Fenster and Clare Lees, I am grateful for permission to re-use in Chapter 5 parts of an essay entitled 'Refiguring the "Scandalous Excess" of Medieval Woman: The Wife of Bath and Liberality', previously published in *Gender in Debate from the Middle Ages to the Renaissance* (New York, 2002). As for the encouragement of medieval colleagues propping up the present project in a more intangible but pervasive way, it is a pleasure to mention Helen Phillips, Bob Hanning, David Wallace, Stephen Knight, Alastair Minnis, Derek Pearsall, Larry Besserman, Julia Boffey, and Renate Blumenfeld-Kosinski. To Goldsmiths' University of London, I owe two periods of study leave during which portions of this book were written. The accumulated obligation to my parents and to my wife, finally, is somewhat beyond words.

Introduction

'The corruption of morals cannot be treated in a short article', John of Salisbury remarked in the twelfth century.[1] Indeed by the fifteenth century the bibliography of morality seemed to swamp the capacity of the individual researcher (predictably assumed to be male) to cope with it: 'ther beth so manye bokes and tretees of vices and vertues and of dyverse doctrynes, that this schort lyfe schalle rathere have an ende of anye man thanne he maye owthere studye or rede hem'.[2] There is therefore conspicuous temerity (or strictly *presumptio*, the attempting of some great work above one's powers),[3] in proposing to encompass the writings of Chaucer, their configurations of ethical and moral teachings, and associated genderings of these teachings, in one book.

Yet, in reading Chaucer's work, gender questions are frequently also moral questions. Does the Wife of Bath's discourse allege that women are mercenary, or generous, or profligate? What is the status of the friendship between Troilus and Pandarus in *Troilus and Criseyde*, what the value of brotherhood in 'The Knight's Tale'? If a female fortitude is projected in 'The Clerk's Tale', how much are we to admire it? Is Dorigen more sinned against than sinning, and is Arveragus's response to her acute dilemma ethically unsound in 'The Franklin's Tale'? Does 'The Pardoner's Tale' produce a coherent perspective (or any perspective at all) on homosexuality? Are the sexual adventures in 'The Miller's Tale' morality-free or morally significant? Does 'The Shipman's Tale' carry any critique of financial profit? These are the sorts of particular questions that readers find themselves asking when they encounter Chaucer's

---

[1] John of Salisbury, *Policraticus*, 2 vols., ed. Clement C. J. Webb (Oxford: Oxford University Press, 1909), vii.7; and *Policraticus: The Frivolities of Courtiers and Footprints of Philosophers*, trans. Joseph B. Pike (London: Oxford University Press, 1938), p. 325.

[2] From the 15th-cent. trans. of the *Horologium Sapientiae*, ed. K. Horstmann, '*Orologium Sapientiae* or *The Seven Poyntes of Trewe Wisdom*', *Anglia*, 10 (1888), 323–89 (p. 328).

[3] *ParsT*, x.402.

writing. The questions appear to flow, as one critic has observed, from a profound interest in dramas of personal morality—notably in how people behave when making and justifying their choices in sexual matters.[4] We might add, with another critic, that the narratives project questions more than answers, because Chaucer's creative energy goes into expressing how moral ideals conflict with numerous emotional or pragmatic or social or egocentric impulses that pull away from those ideals. The reader has to fulfil the narrative's potential by participating in the work of discerning and thinking through implied or possible moral choices in it.[5]

Shadowing the particular questions are the general: for instance, whether Chaucer implicitly critiques or endorses homosocial bonding; whether by often locating fortitude in women his moral design is culturally conservative or radical; whether indeed his writings leave moral stereotyping of the feminine and the masculine—e.g. in the domains of sexuality or materialism—where he found it, or whether on the contrary they destabilize it. (It will be seen that I do not scruple to ascribe certain perspectives to 'Chaucer'. Much criticism still searches endlessly for a degree of sophisticated distribution of independent points of view among narrators in Chaucer's works that far exceeds the merely impressionistic varieties of tone and social provenance he actually incorporated.[6] I shall emphasize conceptual continuity more than hypotheses of individuating dramatization in my consideration of questions structured in his writings.) In order to sharpen our sense of what the gender questions actually are and how they are addressed, we surely need to investigate among other things the embeddedness of these questions in the moral discourses with which Chaucer works. A new gender-aware study of his writings' engagement with those discourses is, in a nutshell, what this book undertakes.

---

[4] N. S. Thompson, *Chaucer, Boccaccio and the Debate of Love: A Comparative Study of 'The Decameron' and 'The Canterbury Tales'* (Oxford: Oxford University Press, 1996), pp. 226, 228, 270–1.

[5] George Kane, *The Liberating Truth: The Concept of Integrity in Chaucer's Writings*, John Coffin Memorial Lecture (London: Athlone, 1980), pp. 16–17. The questioning, exploratory character of Chaucer's texts is also cogently urged by Jill Mann, *Feminizing Chaucer* (Cambridge: D. S. Brewer, 2002), pp. xiv–xv and xvii (Preface to the revised edn of her *Geoffrey Chaucer*, London: Harvester Wheatsheaf, 1991).

[6] For a super-subtle example of such reading, see Lee Patterson, *Chaucer and the Subject of History* (London: Routledge, 1991), notably his claims for the Merchant's subjectivity at pp. 333–44. The more sceptical view was crystallized by Charles Muscatine, *Chaucer and the French Tradition* (Berkeley and Los Angeles: University of California Press, 1957), p. 172.

The undertaking is conceived against a background of by now formidably extensive discussion of gender issues in Chaucer's writings, never mind of gender theory. Although the present book espouses no one theory it acknowledges a spectrum of approaches to gender. (It owes least, perhaps, to psychoanalytical gender criticism.) The term 'gender' is not here shorthand for 'women', and the spotlight is on how ethical concerns feed into narrative construction of 'masculine' and 'feminine' behaviour.

The first round of book-length studies of gender in Chaucer up to 1992 offered capacious approaches signalled in titles like *Chaucer's Sexual Poetics*, *Chaucer's Women*, *Geoffrey Chaucer* (in a series of 'Feminist Readings'), and *Chaucer and the Fictions of Gender*.[7] Of course these sweeping titles concealed specific agendas. Characteristic of this phase was a debate about a putative 'feminization' of males in Chaucer's narratives, a concept most positively envisaged by Jill Mann, who proposed that Chaucer meant to break down prejudices by deliberately investing males in his texts with 'feminine' virtues. In subsequent years the focus of gender-based books on Chaucer narrowed, either to particular texts or genres, or to particular aspects of gender and sexuality.[8] What is now needed is a period of consolidation, defining gender formulations in Chaucer's poetry with greater precision in relation to the various medieval discourses through and against which his formulations are positioned.

Ideally such a book should include a historicization of its subject. However, in my view a prior objective is to identify and understand more about the doctrines applied (or knowingly misapplied) in his

---

[7] Carolyn Dinshaw, *Chaucer's Sexual Poetics* (Madison: University of Wisconsin Press, 1989); Priscilla Martin, *Chaucer's Women: Nuns, Wives and Amazons* (Basingstoke: Macmillan, 1990); Mann, *Geoffrey Chaucer* (1991); Elaine Tuttle Hansen, *Chaucer and the Fictions of Gender* (Berkeley and Los Angeles: University of California Press, 1992).

[8] See Margaret Hallissy, *Clean Maids, True Wives, Steadfast Widows: Chaucer's Women and Medieval Codes of Conduct* (Westport: Greenwood Press, 1993); Anne Laskaya, *Chaucer's Approach to Gender in the 'Canterbury Tales'* (Cambridge: D. S. Brewer, 1995); Susan Crane, *Gender and Romance in Chaucer's 'Canterbury Tales'* (Princeton, NJ: Princeton University Press, 1994); Angela Weisl, *Conquering the Reign of Femeny: Gender and Genre in Chaucer's Romance* (Cambridge: D. S. Brewer, 1995); Catherine S. Cox, *Gender and Language in Chaucer* (Gainesville: University Press of Florida, 1997); Florence Percival, *Chaucer's Legendary Good Women* (Cambridge: Cambridge University Press, 1998); Peter Beidler (ed.), *Masculinities in Chaucer* (Cambridge: D. S. Brewer, 1998); Robert Sturges, *Chaucer's Pardoner and Gender Theory* (New York: St Martin's Press, 1999). Gender discussion of Chaucer up to 2000 is incisively reviewed in Mann, *Feminizing Chaucer*, Preface.

works. Historicization can become more confident when that kind of groundwork is more fully established. Here, therefore, while ideas about localization of significance in the appropriate period will certainly be incorporated chapter by chapter, and while suggestions about the interplay between moral positioning in Chaucerian narrative and late fourteenth-century socio-political developments will be canvassed in my Conclusion, discussion is not fundamentally driven by a politically historicizing methodology.

There have of course been studies of Chaucerian narrative in relation to moral doctrine before. A colourful example is the robust disagreement between two eminent medievalists early in the twentieth century. In 1914 Frederick Tupper laid out an argument that the *Canterbury Tales* were designed as exemplifications of sins and virtues, each tale drawing on one of the 'strict categories' of traditional moral analysis. Where a tale had an analogue in Gower's contemporary poem, the *Confessio Amantis*, Gower's explicit moral identification of the story could be taken as a guide to a comparable identification in the *Tales*. 'The Parson's Tale' was a kind of matrix, and in many cases the tale-tellers 'incarnated' the sins that their tales actually condemned. Thus, 'The Wife of Bath's Tale' becomes a critique of the arrogance of a knight, while the Wife herself incarnates 'Inobedience', a branch of Pride; and 'The Man of Law's Tale' is based around 'Grucching', a branch of Envy, 'The Manciple's Tale' around 'Chiding', a branch of Wrath.[9] Almost as an afterthought, Tupper becomes terribly embarrassed about the straitjacket he finds that he has imposed. 'The moralization does not at all affect the story, but serves merely as a framework', he wriggles; and Chaucer escapes, with 'artistic dexterity', from the 'fetters of his formula'.[10] It is interesting to see this anxious resistance voiced against the threat of a far-reaching moral subtext in the *Tales*. Beguiled by the sometimes non-judgemental texture of Chaucer's writings, readers often want to rescue them altogether from the embrace of morality. Hence his writings have been held to transcend the moral imperatives of the age, and Chaucer is held to personify a universal principle: 'the artist is a humanist by profession'.[11] It has suited an era of pluralist and sceptical readers to suppose that Chaucer's only moral design is a design to destabilize categorical

---

[9] Frederick Tupper, 'Chaucer and the Seven Deadly Sins', *PMLA*, 29 (1914), 93–128.

[10] Ibid., pp. 127–8.

[11] Alfred David, *The Strumpet Muse: Art and Morals in Chaucer's Poetry* (Bloomington and London: Indiana University Press, 1976), pp. 3–6, 133.

morality ('the fetters of a formula'), a supposition so entrenched that readings affirming the opposite can appear self-consciously embattled.[12]

It was less Tupper's moral interpretation in itself than the viability of his sin-categorizations that drew a stern 135-page counterblast from John Livingston Lowes in 1915.[13] Lowes pointed out that medieval 'seven sins' paradigms with their subsets were in practice a maze of complicated interweaving, not reducible to the kind of synoptic grid offered by Tupper. As for the sins allegedly covered by individual tales, there were several objections. First, alternative affiliations could be advanced for every one of Tupper's examples: for example, 'The Man of Law's Tale' was surely about constancy, and the nub of 'The Manciple's Tale' seemed better defined as 'jangling' (garrulity). Second, the methodology was insensitive to the *breadth* of moral issues that might be observable in a given instance. Thus the Wife of Bath in her 'Prologue' couldn't just stand for 'inobedience'. Compounded of many morally nuanced impulses, she could not be 'cabined within the confines of a Sin'.[14] Third, following from that, and intended to bludgeon Tupper's entire thesis, there was the problem (naturally enough, since the doctrine of sins and virtues had been developed to cater comprehensively for the confessional interrogation of every parishioner) that the range of behaviour covered by the categorization of sins was so massively inclusive that 'if one is to tell tales at all, one is foredoomed to run into them'.[15]

Tupper was far from outgunned, and reinforced his moral analyses in a 1916 rejoinder.[16] For our purposes, three salutary warnings can be derived from the case of 'Lowes *vs.* Tupper'. First, Tupper was wrongly trying to read back into Chaucer an inherited technique of moral exemplification, still being applied by Gower with mixed success, but from which Chaucer was slipping away. Even in the *Confessio Amantis* the artificiality of the technique is made palpable because Gower consciously subjects it to such strain. Stories are corralled into signification in the domain of heterosexual love against the grain of their logical application, with the result that the reader's intellect is hard pressed to keep abreast of the exemplifying manoeuvres. Other

---

[12] J. Allan Mitchell epitomizes this 'embattled' status even as he urges a rethink, in *Ethics and Exemplary Narrative in Chaucer and Gower* (Cambridge: D. S. Brewer, 2004), pp. 1–21, 79–86.
[13] 'Chaucer and the Seven Deadly Sins', *PMLA*, 30 (1915), 237–371.
[14] *Ibid.*, p. 357.   [15] *Ibid.*, p. 258.
[16] 'Chaucer's Sinners and Sins', *JEGP*, 15 (1916), 56–106.

liminal modes of narrative exemplification are seen at this time in the poems of the *Gawain*-poet; 'liminal' in the sense that they seem on a threshold between stories of strict exemplification (of *trawthe, pacience, clannesse*) and stories which develop a momentum going way beyond that function. Chaucer appears to have stepped more decisively across that threshold: though quite how far, will be part of the business of this book to assess.

A second lesson from 'Lowes *vs.* Tupper' is that attempts to relate particular Chaucerian narratives to single vices or to their single contrary virtues are particularly vulnerable, though that has not prevented continuing experiments in this genre.[17] (Let me accordingly announce in advance a blanket proviso that, wherever Chaucer's works are discussed in terms of categories—e.g. 'Unshamefulness'—in the chapters of the present book, such categories are not advanced as the sole 'key' to interpretation.)

The third warning is that the medieval Christian discourse of virtues and sins was so encyclopedic, so all-encompassing, that hardly any story could avoid stumbling into the lexicography of sin. This problem has since been restated by Derek Pearsall. Analysing the ethos of the meditation on sufferance near the beginning of 'The Franklin's Tale', he suggests that the passage demonstrates how Chaucer 'struggles to disentangle a human truth from a vocabulary dominated by moral and religious ideas'.[18] Elsewhere Pearsall maintains, similarly, that we should not over-read confessional diction in *Sir Gawain and the Green Knight* because 'any attempt to talk seriously about human behaviour in late fourteenth-century English poetry is bound to take on a Christian colouring, since Christianity dominated the vernacular language of ethics'.[19] The implication is that a medieval writer wanting to analyse behaviour could not help hauling along a certain amount of superfluous Christian moral baggage. But this begs a large question. Should we deem a given passage innocent of doctrinal meaning until proved guilty, if its discussion of human behaviour uses vocabulary overlapping

---

[17] Denise Baker takes this risk by associating Griselda, for example, with Obedience (as a branch of Justice): 'Chaucer and Moral Philosophy: The Virtuous Women of *The Canterbury Tales*', *MÆ*, 60 (1991), 241–56.

[18] *The Canterbury Tales* (London: Allen and Unwin, 1985), p. 160.

[19] Derek Pearsall, 'Courtesy and Chivalry in *Sir Gawain and the Green Knight*: The Order of Shame and the Invention of Embarrassment', in *A Companion to the Gawain-Poet*, ed. Derek Brewer and Jonathan Gibson (Cambridge: D. S. Brewer, 1997), pp. 351–62 (p. 352).

with sins-and-virtues analysis? Or, is such a passage to be deemed resonant with doctrinal meaning unless self-evidently dissociated from that? These, indeed, are adjudications out of which major interpretative differences can arise.

I would rather start from the premise that if vocabulary is used that is reminiscent of the formal moral discourses of the period, we should not lightly unplug that vocabulary from its meanings in those discourses. 'Ethics in our time', as Patrick Boyde has commented, 'tends to be pluralistic, relativist, tolerant, and anxious to free itself from the preconceptions of the past.'[20] While a move in the direction of such pluralism is rightly considered one of the glories of Chaucer's writings, I shall hope to demonstrate how they everywhere interact profoundly with moral doctrine inherited by his period (which is not to say that they do so unquestioningly).[21]

As readers may by now be thinking, the terms 'ethics' and 'morals' are potentially troublesome. It will be necessary, so far as feasible, to sustain a distinction between them for the purposes of this study. (It should also be mentioned that although 'ethical' reading has been theorized in recent decades, contribution to such theorization is not the purpose of the present project.)[22] In general the term 'ethics' will be reserved for that part of the behavioural code that was inherited from antiquity and roughly associated, by the later Middle Ages at least, with the *Ethics* of Aristotle and with the Roman Stoicism which later succeeded it.[23] This is in line with David Burnley's use of the term 'secular ethics' to designate 'the ethical traditions descending by grace of the twelfth-century *ethici*

---

[20] Patrick Boyde, *Human Vices and Human Worth in Dante's 'Comedy'* (Cambridge: Cambridge University Press, 2000), p. 3.

[21] As Kane puts it, 'in [Chaucer's] historical circumstances considerations of morality were integrally a component of the truth of representation of a personality or an action', *The Liberating Truth*, p. 14.

[22] I have found more stimulus in Carol Gilligan's observations on psychology, morality, and gender difference: notably, her model of an 'ethic of justice' favoured by males as against an 'ethic of care' preferred by women: *In A Different Voice: Psychological Theory and Women's Development* (Cambridge, Mass.: Harvard University Press, 1982).

[23] Aristotle, *Ethics*, trans. J. A. K. Thomson (Harmondsworth: Penguin, 1953). The work was brought back into European consciousness after Grosseteste produced a full Latin translation in 1249, though a partial Latin translation was already in circulation in the 13th cent.: see *Ethica Nicomachea, Aristoteles Latinus*, ed. R.-A. Gauthier (Leiden and Brussels: E. J. Brill and Desclée de Brouwer, 1972). The medieval commentaries are reviewed in Georg Wieland, 'The Reception and Interpretation of Aristotle's *Ethics*', in *The Cambridge History of Later Medieval Philosophy*, ed. N. Kretzmann *et al.* (Cambridge: Cambridge University Press, 1982), pp. 657–72.

from the rational philosophy of the classical past'.[24] Chaucer may not have had first-hand knowledge of Aristotle's book, though he appears to identify it for its theory that behavioural ideals are the 'mean' between failings of excess or deficiency: 'vertu is the mene, / As Etik seith' ('Prologue' to *The Legend of Good Women*, 'ꜰ' text, 165–6).[25] The term 'morality' on the other hand will generally refer to the Christian moral schema, though this schema, it cannot be sufficiently emphasized, systematically sought to subsume antique ethics. Distinctions cannot be at all watertight. What I am referring to as Christian 'morality' is the more capacious descriptor, often encompassing or overlapping with what I am referring to as 'ethical' teachings, 'ethics' being the narrower descriptor. In a project of the present kind a residual sense of the distinction needs to be retained.

Burnley's *Chaucer's Language and the Philosophers' Tradition* is still the single most valuable contribution to the study of the penetration of Chaucerian vocabulary by ideas reaching back through ethical writings. Burnley organized his book around sub-themes of rulership and tyranny within both the political and psychological contexts. It was a structure conducive to tracing ethical and social themes across Chaucer's writings but it was less hospitable to extended comment on individual narratives and it only produced incidental insights into aspects of gender. Building on Burnley's work, a new approach will allow questions about ethical/moral issues and their gendering to be applied to a selection of Chaucer texts. What might particularly be expected of Chaucer, with his conspicuously eclectic tastes open to a mixed medieval-classicizing inheritance, is that he would be particularly interested in the accommodations negotiated between ethical concepts and the moral systems into which Christianity sought to assimilate them.

Reaching Chaucer partly as independent texts, partly through their assimilation into the pastoral literature, but partly filtered through other channels such as Macrobius's *Commentary on the Dream of Scipio*, Boethius's *Consolation of Philosophy*, and the *Roman de la Rose*, were

---

[24] J. D. Burnley, *Chaucer's Language and the Philosophers' Tradition* (Cambridge: D. S. Brewer, 1979), p. 9.

[25] For Chaucer's other references to the 'mean' see *TC*, 1.687–90, and *CYPr*, vɪɪɪ.645–6, 'That that is overdoon, it wol nat preeve / Aright . . . it is a vice' (cf. Aristotle, *Ethics*, ɪɪ.6, trans. Thomson, pp. 100–2). However, such summaries of the doctrine may have reached Chaucer as commonplaces, as the *Riv.* note to vɪɪɪ.645–6 suggests. All Chaucer quotations are from *The Riverside Chaucer*, ed. Larry D. Benson (Boston: Houghton Mifflin, 1987); The *Canterbury Tales* are cited by Roman numeral and line number in the body of my text.

readings and extracts from antique ethics, which means primarily Stoic ethics. Neo-Platonic ethical philosophy was also transmitted to the Middle Ages, and it too influenced Chaucer—perhaps most visibly in his early poetry and in *Troilus and Criseyde*. However, the Neo-Platonic strain is only incidentally glanced at in the present book, whose focus rests on practical ethics. The two most noted practical ethical writers from Latin antiquity were Seneca and Cicero. Cicero's *De officiis* ('On Duties'), Seneca's *Letters to Lucilius*, and his treatises on Favours, on Clemency, on Constancy, and on Wrath, were goldmines of ethical analysis and advice.[26] The Senecan *Letters* were probably the most widely available of these writings, though not often as a complete set until late in the Middle Ages.[27] Here in pleasantly digestible format were the hallmarks of Stoic ethical thought: ideals of self-sufficiency, magnanimous tranquillity of mind, and the elimination of fear and strong emotions. Whether Chaucer actually read whole 'works' of Cicero or Seneca is open to doubt.[28] Deschamps probably didn't imply that Chaucer had *read* Seneca when he hailed him as a new 'Seneca in morals';[29] it was just a grand compliment to a morally sophisticated

[26] Cicero, *De officiis*, ed. and trans. Walter Miller (Cambridge, Mass.: Harvard University Press, 1913) will be quoted in this book; I have also consulted Cicero, *On Duties*, ed. M. T. Griffin and E. M. Atkins (Cambridge: Cambridge University Press, 1991). For transmission of the text see N. E. Nelson, 'Cicero's *De Officiis* in Christian Thought: 300–1300', *Essays and Studies in English and Comparative Literature*, University of Michigan Publications (Ann Arbor), 10 (1933), 59–160. For Seneca's *Letters* see *Ad Lucilium Epistulae Morales*, 3 vols., trans. Richard M. Gummere (London: Heinemann; and New York: G. P. Putnam's Sons, 1917 [Letters 1–65], 1920 [Letters 66–92], and 1925 [Letters 93–124]). For Seneca's Dialogues and Essays see Seneca, *Moral Essays*, 3 vols., trans. John W. Basore (London: Heinemann; Cambridge, Mass.: Harvard University Press, 1928, 1932, and 1935); also consulted, *Senecae Dialogi*, ed. L. D. Reynolds (Oxford: Clarendon Press, 1977), and *Seneca: Moral and Political Essays*, trans. John M. Cooper and J. F. Procopé (Cambridge: Cambridge University Press, 1995).

[27] For summaries of the transmission of Seneca's *Epistulae*, see Beryl Smalley, *English Friars and Antiquity in the Early Fourteenth Century* (Oxford: Blackwell, 1960), pp. 153–4, and Jenny Swanson, *John of Wales: A Study of the Works and Ideas of a Thirteenth-Century Friar* (Cambridge: Cambridge University Press, 1989), pp. 29–33.

[28] However, Harry M. Ayres argues quite persuasively for the poet's direct knowledge of at least some of the Letters, 'Chaucer and Seneca', *Romanic Review*, 10 (1919), 1–15.

[29] In a *balade* (probably of the mid-1380s) entitled 'O Socrates plains de philosophie', heralding Chaucer as 'grant translateur': see Derek Brewer, *Chaucer: The Critical Heritage*, vol. I, *1385–1837* (London: Arnold, 1978), p. 40. Thomas Hoccleve hailed Chaucer as a modern Cicero in rhetoric and as 'heir in philosophie' to Aristotle (grandiose, but probably thinking of moral philosophy): *The Regiment of Princes*, ed. Charles Blyth, TEAMS Middle English Texts (Kalamazoo, Mich.: Western Michigan University, 1999), 2085–8.

writer. But in any case Chaucer could hardly avoid encountering Stoic ethics, because its propositions were endlessly cannibalized in medieval compilations.

Typifying those compilations were, firstly, numerous treatises and florilegia in circulation that marshalled discrete wise sayings with varying degrees of organizational rigour. Prominent among these were the sixth-century *Formula vitae honestae* and the twelfth-century *Moralium dogma philosophorum*.[30] Second, there were more ambitious compendia of antique story and aphorism brought together in order to create elaborate preaching aids, or even to amplify commentary on the Bible, by 'classicizing friars' in the generations before Chaucer. By such intermediaries Stoic ethical teachings passed through to the Middle Ages, often anonymized (or alternatively foisted on 'Seneca' as a likely authority even if not actually his work). Among yet other channels of transmission it should be added that even to read Augustine's *City of God*, one of the ubiquitous works of the Middle Ages, was to discover much about Stoic philosophy, as we shall see, through Augustine's careful positioning of Christian faith in relation to it.

In view of the present project it is natural to ask, was ethical teaching gendered? To give an interim answer, the facts are that Seneca addresses two of his consolatory ethical writings to women; and that he uses 'automatically masculine' language—but that this language need not (according to his translators) be taken as male-exclusive.[31] Yet women nevertheless seem to be disdained by their exclusion from discussion, since the business of life in which ethical choices are made is implicitly male. On the occasions when Seneca refers to women it is usually with

---

[30] Martin of Braga, *Formula vitae honestae* or *De quattuor virtutibus*, in *PL*, 72.21–8, a brief treatise on the cardinal virtues written as advice to a ruler, which remained popular throughout the Middle Ages, and of which a translation was issued in 1546 by Robert Whyttynton entitled *The Forme and Rule of Honest Lyuynge*. The *Moralium dogma philosophorum* is available in *PL*, 171.1007–56, entitled *Moralis Philosophia de Honesto et Utili*; and in a subsequent edn by John Holmberg, *Das Moralium Dogma Philosophorum des Guillaume de Conches* (Uppsala, 1929), which indicates that at least fifteen MSS in Latin and two in French survive in England. It is mainly a compilation of maxims from Cicero's *De officiis* and Seneca's *De beneficiis*: see Philippe Delhaye, 'Une adaptation du *De officiis* au xiie siècle: Le *Moralium dogma philosophorum*', *Recherches de théologie ancienne et médiévale*, 16 (1949), 227–58, and 17 (1950), 5–28; and Richard Hazelton, 'Chaucer's *Parson's Tale* and the *Moralium Dogma Philosophorum*', *Traditio*, 16 (1960), 255–74. For looser florilegia see *Florilegium gallicum*, ed. A. Gagner (Lund, 1936); and *Florilegium morale oxoniense*, ed. P. Delhaye and C. H. Talbot (Louvain, 1956). All translations of these are my own.

[31] Cooper and Procopé, *Moral and Political Essays*, p. xvii.

casual disrespect.[32] He genders magnanimity male and anger female, though conceding that men can catch anger from women.[33] Worse, the furthest that a (male) person could depart from the Stoic ideal of magnanimous unconcern, that is from the ideal of being impervious to attempted insults from any quarter, is to be affronted by the insult of a mere woman, who is an 'unthinking creature—wild and unrestrained in her passions' (though with the concessionary qualification, 'unless she has gained knowledge and had much instruction').[34]

The resources for studying moral doctrine (now turning to that more inclusive category) in the Middle Ages are vast. The disparate materials of the early Christian period were increasingly collated and systematized into *summa* form, and great quantities of 'maps' of the seven sins and seven virtues, their extended subsets, and associated schemata such as the five senses and the gifts of the Spirit, were produced and circulated, particularly from the early thirteenth century onwards as the later medieval church geared up to sustain a new policy of enabling the clergy to instruct the laity and to assist them in the requirement of making confession at least once a year.[35] The doctrines also seeped into other pastoral literature such as sermons and analyses of the Ten Commandments. St Thomas Aquinas (teaching in Paris in the 1270s) brought characteristic rigour and authority to moral analysis, and found a poet to match in Dante.

For present purposes the criterion of ready availability of moral concepts to an audience whom Chaucer is addressing in the vernacular has

---

[32] e.g. *Ep.* 63.13 (flippancy about widows' grief), *Epistulae*, vol. 1, p. 435; and *Ep.* 95.20–1 (women have even taken over conventionally masculine indulgences), *Epistulae*, vol. 3, pp. 70–1.

[33] *De clementia*, I.5.5, *Moral Essays*, vol. 1, p. 373; *De ira*, I.20.3, *Moral Essays*, vol. 1, pp. 160–1.

[34] '... inprudens animal est et, nisi scientia accessit ac multa eruditio, ferum, cupiditatium incontinens'; Seneca, *De constantia*, xiv.1, *Moral Essays*, vol. 1, pp. 88–9.

[35] For a late 14th-cent. paradigm of approved vernacular lay instruction, see Archbishop Thoresby, *The Lay Folks' Catechism*, ed. T. F. Simmons and H. E. Nolloth, EETS, o.s. 118 (London: Kegan Paul, Trench, Trübner, 1901). The centrality of sacramental absolution during the later Middle Ages may be among the reasons why Sins doctrine held sway against the competing catechetical lore of the Commandments, according to John Bossy, 'Moral Arithmetic: Seven Sins into Ten Commandments', in *Conscience and Casuistry in Early Modern Europe*, ed. E. Leites (Cambridge: Cambridge University Press, 1988), pp. 214–34. On the evolution of categorization of the Sins, see Morton W. Bloomfield, *The Seven Deadly Sins: An Introduction to the History of a Religious Concept* (Michigan: Michigan State College Press, 1952); and on the evolution of characterization of one Sin, see Siegfried Wenzel, *The Sin of Sloth: 'Acedia' in Medieval Thought and Literature* (Chapel Hill: University of North Carolina Press, 1960).

inclined me to draw particularly on two vernacular treatises (together with his own 'Parson's Tale'), which articulate in Middle English a substantial range of teaching available at the end of the fourteenth century. One is *The Book of Vices and Virtues*, an English translation made around 1375 of a heterogeneous work known as the *Somme le roi*. The *Somme* was compiled in 1279 in the same Dominican context at Paris that nurtured Aquinas, though the treatise reveals popularizing rather than academic aspirations. The *Somme* was translated all over Europe, and coexisted in several translations in England.[36] The other text is *Jacob's Well*, written a little later, in the first half of the fifteenth century, for sermon use.[37] Based on the graphic metaphor of scouring the human mind clean of the 'slime' of sin, it is superficially a more idiosyncratic text, but its doctrine is nevertheless unremarkable: its usefulness lies in its comprehensiveness. Both texts seem designed for lay consumption. In the *Book of Vices and Virtues*, the writer specifically emphasizes that the intended audience is the laity. The treatise is for 'lewede men' (not necessarily exclusively male) rather than for clerics, who have plenty of their own (Latin) books on these matters.[38] The lay ambience makes the two treatises particularly interesting as exemplars of such writing, presenting 'values and ideas in the midst of inculcation, at the very point at which they were being disseminated to the laity'.[39]

[36] *The Book of Vices and Virtues: A Fourteenth Century English Translation of the 'Somme Le Roi' of Lorens D'Orléans* [hereafter *VV*], ed. W. Nelson Francis, EETS, o.s. 217 (London: Oxford University Press, 1942), Introduction. Another Middle English translation (dated 1340) is Dan Michel, *Ayenbite of Inwyt, or Remorse of Conscience*, ed. Richard Morris, EETS, o.s. 23 (London: Trübner, 1866).

[37] *Jacob's Well* [hereafter *JW*], pt 1, ed. Arthur Brandeis, EETS, o.s. 115 (London: Trübner, 1900), Preface, pp. v–xiii. The remaining part of the treatise is currently unpublished.

[38] *VV*, pp. 38, 42.

[39] Jacqueline Murray, 'Gendered Souls in Sexed Bodies: The Male Construction of Female Sexuality in Some Medieval Confessors' Manuals', in *Handling Sin: Confession in the Middle Ages*, ed. Peter Biller and A. J. Minnis (University of York: York Medieval Press; in association with Woodbridge: Boydell, 1998), pp. 79–93 (p. 81). Among other vernacular vices–virtues texts consulted are: Robert of Brunne, *Handlyng Synne*, ed. Frederick J. Furnivall, EETS, o.s. 119 and 123 (London: Kegan Paul, Trench, and Trübner, 1901–3); *Speculum Christiani*, ed. Gustaf Holmstedt, EETS, o.s. 182 (London: Oxford University Press, 1933); Gower's *Mirour de l'Omme*, in *The Complete Works of John Gower*, vol. 1, *The French Works*, ed. G. C. Macaulay (Oxford: Clarendon Press, 1899), and trans. William Burton Wilson (East Lansing: Colleagues Press, 1992). Exposition of the moral tradition in a 14th-cent. preacher's handbook written by an English friar in Latin is conveniently accessible in *Fasciculus Morum* [hereafter *FM*], ed. and trans. Siegfried Wenzel (University Park: Pennsylvania State University Press, 1989).

People who have gone to these manuals before simply have not realized their power to stimulate concentration on knotty ethical issues. Consciously or unconsciously, the manualists draw attention to dilemmas. For instance: if Gluttony is defined as excessive consumption, does that mean that moderate (measured) consumption of expensive cordon bleu foods is acceptable, or that cordon bleu delicacies almost by definition entail excess? Can there be such a thing as a 'measured' consumption of delicacies? These problems are incipiently visible, but are not properly resolved, perhaps because they would be rather sensitive matters for some of a confessor's clients.[40]

The manuals are also significant indices of gender asymmetries lurking within church doctrine, as Jacqueline Murray makes us realize. She argues that the manualists do not sustain the theory propounded in Paul's idealistic letter to the Galatians, namely that differences of ethnicity, rank, and biological sex between individuals are erased by their faith and that in relation to Christ there is therefore 'neither male nor female' (Gal. 3: 28). By the thirteenth century the male-centred ideological framework was so entrenched, she suggests, that in confessional literature the notion of the soul as sexless before God was becoming a chimera. Murray shows how women emerge in the thirteenth-century manuals as a 'marked' category defined by their reproductive and sexual functions, viewed above all in terms of how their own sexual status (widow, wife, virgin, prostitute) contributes to the evaluation of males who commit sexual sin with them. They are constructed as sexually passive, and they are tacitly assumed to have no economic activity to be inquired into.[41]

Murray's verdict is somewhat less applicable, I think, to the later manuals since these make valiant efforts to be explicitly unisex.[42] But her diagnosis of the sexualized status of women in the manuals remains

---

[40] *JW*, pp. 141–7. Implicitly there is an attempt not to upset the aristocratic palate; e.g., it is argued that the *mesure* should be in the appetite of the person eating, not in the quality of what is eaten (p. 142); but this is contradicted by the statement that both eating 'ovyr-deynte' expensive food, and a 'habit' of seeking out 'delyces' are sinful in themselves (pp. 144, 146). The contradiction was already implicit in the divisions of Gluttony cited (via intermediaries) in *ParsT*, x.828–9 from a foundational list of sins in Gregory's *Moralia*.

[41] Murray, 'Gendered Souls'. See also Ruth M. Karras, 'Gendered Sin and Misogyny in John of Bromyard's *Summa Predicantium*', *Traditio*, 47 (1992), 233–57.

[42] Admittedly this is partly a matter of formulaic gender-inclusive phrasing: e.g. *VV* discussing how the Gift of Drede 'wexeth in a mannes herte or in a wommannes', p. 126, and cf. pp. 168, 179; and *JW* addressing both sexes at pp. 108, 159, 180.

valid (and we shall see subsequently how that helps us understand aspects of Chaucer's writings). It also remains true of the manuals that, for example, lists of activities that might be conducive to a certain kind of sin appear to aim themselves at males (for example, the sorts of preoccupations that the fiend uses to deflect the churchgoer's devotion).[43] One suddenly realizes that a thief is presumed to be male.[44] Medieval sin and virtue were not gender-neutral. That is partly why Chaucer can play off the Wife of Bath's version of herself against a range of gendered expectations, including expectations about ownership of 'goods' (material and sexual) and ethical/moral commentary on the proper retention or disbursement of those goods.

The ground that this pre-gendering of sin and virtue opened up for creative debate was appreciated by Chaucer, as it was by Christine de Pizan. Her writings, much more than his, unambiguously use formal argument to reclaim virtues (such as liberality) for women that misogynists allege women lack, as well as to suggest that what misogynists see as womanly 'vices' are, better considered, virtues. On the basis that misogyny was a form of indoctrination, I would name these moves 'redoctrination'. They 'redoctrinate' in that they up-end, or bracingly reverse, the 'normative' gender binaries of moral and ethical credits and deficits casually attributed to each sex.[45] Chaucer's forte is different in that he works through narrative and through juxtaposition of perspectives, not through a debating posture adopted in his own person. Yet, as will be urged later in this book, he too aspired to 'redoctrinate' readers in gender matters even if less directly and less radically than Christine.[46]

As we shall also note along the way, the repertoire of techniques at his command includes devious or comic misapplication of ethical or moral teachings. It is a distinctive feature of his art that he so often projects voices coolly misusing moral sentiments ('Take advice before doing anything' being a classic) in self-interested ways. The

---

[43] See *JW*, pp. 105 (list of idle pastimes), and 237–8 (list of preoccupations as distractions in church).

[44] See *JW*, p. 206 (addressing the thief regarding consequences for 'thi wyif').

[45] For a fuller discussion, see Alcuin Blamires, 'Refiguring the "Scandalous Excess" of Medieval Woman: The Wife of Bath and Liberality', in *Gender in Debate from the Early Middle Ages to the Renaissance*, ed. Thelma S. Fenster and Clare A. Lees (New York: Palgrave, 2002), pp. 57–78.

[46] See Chapters 5 and 8 below. Mann's case that Chaucer models 'active suffering' as a virtue for both sexes to aim at, transcending formerly gendered categories, exemplifies my concept of 'redoctrination'.

Host of the *Canterbury Tales* humorously epitomizes this tendency to 'embarrass the morality' of a tale 'by applying it eccentrically'.[47] We even find the morality of whole tales stood on end.[48] The mischievous misapplications sometimes yield a serious point. Sometimes they look like mere entertainment breaks in his writing, but this relaxation is not the same as triviality. Chaucer's levity, unlike that of some of his characters, is never the levity of moral indifference.

Let us return for a moment to the manuals and their organization. Although they aimed at a wholesale schematization of morality, in practice sub-categories of vice migrated alarmingly among the 'capital' vices or virtues. Writers were conscious of the fluidity. No sooner is *vilenye* identified in the *Book of Vices and Virtues* as the first branch of 'untrewthe' (itself the first branch of Pride) than *vilenye* is acknowledged to be a pervasive element in all sin: but the *vilenye* in this branch is defined as a type of prideful untruth that clerks call *ingratitudo*, known as 'unkyndenesse' in English (so why call it 'vilenye' in the first place?); and this is a forgetfulness of God, returning evil instead of thanks for good received.[49] Aspiring to precision, the treatises court muddle and overlap. There will be no point in building interpretations of Chaucer on the finer points of relationships within the mobile elements of these moral schemata: that way arise castles in the air. But the Chaucer student could already have gained insight from the tangle we have just reviewed. How much of that powerful significance of 'unkynde'—unnatural return of evil for good—subsists in the outwardly mitigating gesture in *Troilus and Criseyde*, where we are told that the fourth book will relate 'how Criseyde Troilus forsook— / Or at the leeste, how that she was unkynde' (*TC*, IV.15–16)?

The moral handbooks, as we have said, were also repositories of more-or-less assimilated antique ethics.[50] Specific acknowledgement of antique ethical teaching is intermittently voiced in the *Book of Vices and Virtues*, sometimes gracefully, or at least as a useful corroboration of Christian morals, more often with a colonizer's patronization (the natives got surprisingly far, considering), sometimes with the unattractively gloating

---

[47] Mitchell, *Ethics and Exemplary Narrative*, p. 84.

[48] In the case of 'The Clerk's Tale', probably as ironic corroboration.

[49] *VV*, p. 13. The Pardoner uses the word 'unkynde' in precisely this sense (*PardT*, VI.900–3).

[50] Scholastic writings took greater care to distinguish Christian from Aristotelian classification of the vices; Wenzel, *The Sin of Sloth*, p. 66.

consciousness of a faith revelling in its assumed superiority. Cicero's advocacy of 'common profit' is enthusiastically quoted to underpin the charitable imperative of loving one's neighbour.[51] On the other hand we are told that the antique moral philosophers wasted their time disputing what should be life's greatest good because it took a Saint Paul to explain that Charity constituted that good.[52] Seneca and St Gregory are found to have agreed on the Christian doctrine of loving the recalcitrant sinner even while hating the sin.[53] Again, it is suggested that antique authorities such as Seneca were right to define Magnanimity or 'Gretnesse' (first category of Prowess or Fortitude) as a kind of despising of superficially great things in a quest to undertake greater things; but, despite their recognition of an even more elevated concept of Magnificence, it is alleged that they could not push the virtue of Fortitude far enough, namely to the heights of Christian suffering which transcend the mere critique of vice and cultivation of virtue aspired to by the old philosophers.[54] All in all 'of the four cardinal vertues speken muche the olde philosofres, but the Holy Gost yeveth hem muche bettre', to quote one grudging observation.[55] Nevertheless *Piers Plowman* demonstrates the appeal of the Cardinal Virtues for a vernacular contemporary of Chaucer, since Langland, as Myra Stokes has explained, invokes them creatively in his efforts to articulate key questions about social justice.[56] Characteristically the difference again in Chaucer's case is that he uses stories rather than direct argument to raise the ethical/moral questions, and that he thereby ties the questions to dramas of human behaviour and to behavioural patterns in women and men.

Of all Stoic ethics it was self-sufficiency and governance of the self (of emotions as well as appetites) with which Chaucer most often engaged. These aspects of Stoic ethics are prominent especially in his shortest poems (the *balades*). In longer poems their presence is

---

[51] 'Do we than that that we be bore in this world fore and that kynde techeth us, and seche we al comune profight', *VV*, p. 146.

[52] *VV*, pp. 78–9.

[53] 'For, as Seneke seith and seynt Gregori, we mowe not helpe hem [sinners] up that ben falle, but we wole enclyne to hem how so it be', *VV*, p. 156.

[54] *VV*, pp. 164–9 (though a lacuna in the translation obscures the formulation of the last point, as clarified by the editor's note to 169/19 on p. 308).

[55] *VV*, p. 122. For illuminating discussion of the Virtues, see Rosemond Tuve, *Allegorical Imagery: Some Medieval Books and their Posterity* (Princeton, NJ: Princeton University Press, 1966), ch. 2.

[56] *Justice and Mercy in Piers Plowman* (London: Croom Helm, 1984), *passim*, but esp. pp. 66–8.

just as crucial but less acknowledged in criticism. Occasionally there is an eye-catching generalization. For example, Princess Canacee of 'The Squire's Tale', leaving a court banquet early to avoid morning blues, is described as 'ful mesurable, as wommen be' (v.362).[57] The action simultaneously fulfils criteria of moderation in consumption and of maidenly self-protection,[58] but the generalization stands out for its assertion that women are (we might say) constitutionally more moderate than men, against the grain of endemic disparagement of women's supposedly undisciplined 'appetites' in all manner of antique and medieval writings.

Minus the element of generalization, Chaucer often raids Stoic sources in order to extend or multiply questions about behavioural ideals. Another example will clarify this. In 'The Franklin's Tale' there is a celebrated statement of the paradoxical combination of service and lordship in the marriage of Dorigen with Arveragus, blending the social expectation that a husband exercises lordship, with romance assumptions of male deference to the wishes of the beloved. Editors always refer readers to comments by the 'Friend' in the *Romance of the Rose* about the folly of imposing marital *seignorie* on a relationship founded in love.[59] However, Chaucer's condensed paradoxes (e.g. 'Thanne was he bothe in lordshipe and servage. / Servage? nay, but in lordshipe above', v.794–5) are far more taut than the phrasing in the *Roman*: in fact they recall the tautness of a Senecan formulation that warns against intemperate exercise of power. Seneca juggles *servitus* and *imperium* as Chaucer juggles *servage* and *lordshipe*. Seneca's point concerns the exercise of political power, not heterosexual relations. Those in power have to restrain speech more than their subjects do, Seneca argues, since subjects can get away with a degree of obstreperousness that cannot be countenanced in rulers, the powerful being bound to behave with a gentle spirit by the constraints, the dignity, of their own power. The logic of this is that the ruler's position is more one of subjection than command ('Ista servitus est, non imperium'), and rulers should

---

[57] *Riv.* n. to 358–9 notes a possible debt to remarks about the temperance of Mongol women in a Missionary History possibly available to Chaucer (*Riv.*, p. 890), but this does not explain the element of generalization.

[58] Cf. Virginia, *PhysT*, vi.61–8; and on gluttony as consumption 'with-outyn temperure and mesure', see *JW*, p. 142.

[59] Guillaume de Lorris and Jean de Meun, *Le Roman de la Rose*, 3 vols., ed. Félix Lecoy (Paris: Champion, 1965) [henceforth *RR*], lines 9391–9443; *The Romance of the Rose*, trans. Frances Horgan, World's Classics (Oxford: Oxford University Press, 1994), pp. 144–5.

indeed be aware that in such a context sovereignty and servitude switch places.[60] This paradoxical dictum on 'servitude in power' lurks in the background of the Franklin's discourse.[61] It supplies a hint that the crux of the tale will be subjugation of 'lordship' by restraint of vengeful demeanour and speech, as we shall explore further in Chapter 6.

At the larger level it has to be said that Chaucer seems not to have had the inclination or the temperament to emulate the sort of ambitious syncretic project conceived by Dante: namely, an overarching work attempting to reconcile (along lines prompted by Aquinas) Christian morality with antique ethics.[62] Chaucer's broadest deployment of his eclectic knowledge of ethics is characteristically as a means of substantiating the lineaments of a roughly consistent pre-Christian fictional world, as in 'The Knight's Tale'. Thus Barbara Nolan argues that by furnishing these quasi-Stoic horizons he creates a novel kind of historical writing in English. More importantly, he creates a space in which to address moral questions 'without recourse to "higher" theological explanations' and even (as Spearing suggests) to open up Christian beliefs to surprising levels of interrogation.[63]

What Chaucer also scrutinizes is the awkwardness of the medieval patching together of ethical teaching and Christian morality. A sense of how unlike him Dante is in this respect arises from Patrick Boyde's eloquent figure for Dante's positioning. If, says Boyde, we imagine Aristotelian and Christian moral philosophy as two 'hemispheres', setting out from the contrary 'poles' of observable phenomena and revealed truth, Dante's position 'lies on the equator'.[64] Chaucer's positioning invites less grandiose analogy and manifests no equatorial clarity. If we envisage Stoic ethics as one sort of cloth and Christian

---

[60] Seneca, *De clementia*, I.8.1–3, in *Moral Essays*, vol. 1, pp. 376–9.

[61] Perhaps also in the *ClkT* (IV.113–15): 'Boweth youre nekke under that blisful yok / Of soveraynetee, noght of servyse', though here the paradox has absorbed also a biblical allusion to the 'yoke' of service (1 Tim. 6) as noted by Helen Phillips, *An Introduction to the Canterbury Tales: Reading, Fiction, Context* (Basingstoke: Macmillan, 2000), p. 118.

[62] Dante prepares himself for this aspect of the *Commedia* by working on Aristotle's ethics in *Il Convivio*; see *Dante's 'Il Convivio' (The Banquet)*, trans. Richard H. Lansing (New York: Garland, 1990), esp. Bk IV.

[63] Barbara Nolan, *Chaucer and the Tradition of the 'roman antique'* (Cambridge: Cambridge University Press, 1992), p. 352, n. 15; A. C. Spearing, *Medieval to Renaissance in English Poetry* (Cambridge: Cambridge University Press, 1985), esp. pp. 40–57; and see Alastair Minnis, *Chaucer and Pagan Antiquity* (Cambridge: D. S. Brewer, 1982).

[64] *Human Vices and Human Worth in Dante's 'Comedy'*, p. 77.

morality as another laid partly over it, Chaucer's narratives (I shall suggest) show creative awareness of ragged seams, and of overlaps where the nap of each cloth does not run quite in the same direction. In general it is my contention that hitherto we have only scratched the surface in discovering the extent of Chaucer's creative adoptions of ethical ideas or in discovering how they shape the questions he asks about women's and men's behaviour. It is not a matter of wanting to prove that Chaucer went off to recherché didactic sources (a few lines on lordship from a standard Senecan treatise do not qualify as recherché). It is a matter of realizing how the main written sources on the moral life, diffused widely through medieval culture and articulating what people understood of positive and negative behaviour, left scope for moral grey areas of the kind Chaucer found it congenial to cultivate.

Whereas the moral remedy in sin-vocabulary for the 'Presumption' initially detected in the present undertaking would be Meekness, the remedy in this project must instead be an element of selectivity. So far as assessment of Christian moral doctrine is concerned, vernacular medieval English treatises are here prioritized, though with many forays into their hinterland. For ethical doctrine (often partially visible in those treatises, as we have emphasized), Seneca and Cicero are particularly prioritized as contributors to Chaucer's thinking, on the basis that their ideas saturate the Middle Ages through a wide spread of routes. As for Chaucer, although all his writings have contributed to my conclusions, for reasons of space the book concentrates mainly on the *Canterbury Tales*, with intermittent attention to *Troilus and Criseyde* but rather less consideration of the dream poems. The methodology is theme-based. It cannot encompass all relevant dimensions of Chaucer's texts. (In particular, since *trouthe* and *gentillesse* have been extensively discussed in Chaucer criticism, they do not here have chapters to themselves, though they are far from being ignored.) In each chapter the aspiration is to produce readings of dimensions of texts, or of key passages in them, that emerge from the moral/ethical issues that the texts variously configure. Finally, the extent to which gendering of those issues can be determined fluctuates, and concentration on gender fluctuates in this study accordingly. The ethical or moral is generally the starting point. I hope it may come as an enjoyable surprise to the reader to discover how many fresh interpretative possibilities, not to mention insights into use of sources, can be opened up by this methodology, against the odds established by one hundred years of intensive Chaucer scholarship.

1

Fellowship and Detraction in the Architecture of the *Canterbury Tales*: from 'The General Prologue' and 'The Knight's Tale' to 'The Parson's Prologue'

Felaweshipe in 'The General Prologue'

In a notorious passage in the *Morte Darthur* following the news that two of Gawain's brothers have been killed by Lancelot during a skirmish at the Queen's threatened execution, King Arthur three times voices his forebodings for the loss of the 'fellowship' of knights that he has 'held ... together'. What is notorious is that the king expressly regrets the inevitable loss of the knightly fellowship more than the loss of his queen: 'for queens I might have enough, but such a fellowship of good knights shall never be together in no company'.[1] While there were urgent reasons for anxiety about a collapse of lordly cohesiveness in the later fifteenth century the valuation of aristocratic solidarity was nothing new, nor was the assumption that 'fellowship' was homosocial and might take precedence over the claims of a heterosexual relationship.

In this chapter we shall see how Chaucer dramatizes a traditional reverence for *amicitia* (friendship) and *societas* or *communitas* ('felaweshipe') as a primary glory and duty of humanity. In the *Canterbury Tales* he wills society into a fellowship ('General Prologue') but immediately strains the received ideal of homosocial friendship beyond its limit in 'The Knight's Tale', unleashing defamation or detraction as an alternative human drive in the following tales. Eventually, just before the Parson makes his bid to round off the story-competition, the competitive and

---

[1] Sir Thomas Malory, *Le Morte Darthur*, ed. Helen Cooper, World's Classics (Oxford: Oxford University Press, 1998), pp. 483–4.

defamatory impulse climaxes in 'The Manciple's Tale', which is both narrated in a context of blatant personal insult and also focused on the devastating capacity of verbal detraction (a category of both wrath and envy) to sever and destroy human bonds. In attending to this architecture in the *Tales* we shall need, in due course, to reckon with the formidable power, and the moral loathing, accorded to defamatory speech in the Middle Ages.

Sooner or later any medieval moral or ethical discussion turned to the subject of friendship. Friendship was a 'topic'—a matter for formal reflection—passed down from antiquity. Aristotle had assigned it a climactic position in *Ethics*, since he considered that ideal friendship presupposes probity, that it supports the community ideal of concord, and that it epitomizes justice: 'between friends there is no need for justice [. . .] indeed friendliness is considered to be justice in the fullest sense'.[2] Subsequently, Cicero was the chief Roman authority on the subject. He wrote of the 'principles of fellowship and society [*communitatis et societatis*] that Nature has established among men [*homines*, i.e. humankind]'; but of all the bonds of fellowship, he thought none more powerful than that uniting 'men [*viri*, i.e. males] of good character'.[3] We shall come back later to the implied partisan gendering of the inherited concept of friendship. Here we need to recognize that friendship and fellowship, while distinct from each other in some ways, were also a continuum. Fellowship, community, fosters 'the more intimate fellowship which is based on friendship'.[4] To offer friendship to another or others was to engage in fellowship with them.[5] One of Chaucer's earlier poems, *The Parliament of Fowls*, responds to these Ciceronian imperatives towards *communitas* by dramatizing through the oblique model of a bird-world council a vision of society and dissonance, of cordial governance and breach of accord that only resolves in a resort to the symbolic harmony of song. Already displaying interests that were to absorb Chaucer as they had absorbed Boccaccio, the poem is organized particularly around love's power to threaten fellowship through rivalry

---

[2] *Ethics*, VIII.1, trans. Thomson, pp. 258–9; see also VIII.9, p. 273.
[3] *De officiis*, I.16.50, 17.55, trans. Miller, pp. 52–3, 58–9.
[4] Seneca, *Ep.* 48.3, *Epistulae*, vol. 1, pp. 314–15.
[5] Thus Pandarus, speaking to Criseyde, praises Troilus as 'the frendlieste man / Of gret estat, that evere I saugh my lyve, / And wher hym lest, best felawshipe kan / To swich as hym thynketh able for to thryve', *TC*, II.204–7. Barry Windeatt translates 'the friendliest man . . . knows how to show the greatest friendliness': *Troilus and Criseyde: A New Translation* (Oxford: Oxford University Press, 1998).

as well as sustain it, and around the potential of group factionalism and competitiveness to wreck social harmony.[6]

If fear of God was the starting point for the Christian moral life, friendship was of primary significance for ethical behaviour.[7] Friendship in the wider sense, *societas* or 'felaweshipe', was conceived as a goal at which humanity naturally aimed. Conversely all impulses tending to division, disunity, were conceived as ethically and morally disreputable, if not downright destructive to civilization. Friendship or *amicitia*, and *societas* were ethical ideals that blended with the exalted Christian concept of love as *caritas*, but there were snags in that assimilation, as we shall see.

Malory's ideal fellowship is resolutely 'horizontal'. It envisages a set of ideals and prejudices among a socially exclusive caste of males: those beneath that caste, carters and suchlike, are menials only fit to be tossed aside. Some eighty years earlier, the ideal fellowships constructed in the 1380s and 1390s by Gower and Chaucer in the prologues to their most ambitious English writings were (in theory at any rate) more inclusive.[8] Gower's Prologue to the *Confessio Amantis* yearns for a monarch capable of tuning into harmony the various 'strings'—the diverse strata, commons and lords—of the harp that symbolizes political concord (*CA*, Prol. 1053–69).[9] Chaucer's 'General Prologue' tries to imagine a common purpose of pilgrimage bringing together into *felaweshipe* (a word used twice near the beginning, at 1.26 and 32) an assortment of figures of diverse social 'degree'. One acute reason why the cohesion that was yearned for at this time was socially 'vertical' instead of horizontal was the recent disaster of the Peasants' Rising and the continuing social unrest that followed it.[10] Of the two poets, Gower registers the impact of

---

[6] Chaucer accesses Cicero for this poem via the work of Macrobius (*c.*400): see *Commentary on the Dream of Scipio*, trans. William H. Stahl (New York: Columbia University Press, 1952).

[7] In the early 12th cent., Pedro Alfonso gives precedence to friendship in his *Disciplina Clericalis*: see *The Scholar's Guide, A Translation of the Twelfth-Century 'Disciplina Clericalis' of Pedro Alfonso*, trans. Joseph Ramon Jones and John Esten Keller (Toronto: Pontifical Institute of Mediaeval Studies, 1969).

[8] See esp. Paul Strohm, *Social Chaucer* (Cambridge, Mass.: Harvard University Press, 1989).

[9] John Gower, *English Works*, ed. G. C. Macaulay, 2 vols., EETS, e.s. 81–2 (London: Oxford University Press, 1900–1).

[10] 'The need for *trawpe*, for an enduring commitment to social bonds, will be felt most strongly in a society where the stability of these bonds can no longer be taken for granted. In late-fourteenth century England this was indeed the case': Ad Putter, *Introduction to the 'Gawain'-Poet* (New York: Longman, 1996), p. 44.

that uprising most despairingly. The *Confessio* Prologue is shot through with angst about social and political division. The word *divisioun* is obsessively used in it, and Gower conjoins images already used in his previous writings to utter a keenly felt need for social strata to unite in obedience to a strong charismatic sovereign steering the 'Ship of State' and capable of attracting the compliance of the 'limbs' of the body politic (*CA*, Prol. 151–3).[11]

Critics have not sufficiently acknowledged the overlap between Gower and Chaucer in their social Prologues. On the one hand Gower invokes diffuse concepts of 'love', 'charite', 'pes', and 'acord' as he meditates on social division; and he veils his concern for an effective monarchy under multiple symbols as he fantasizes about a return to 'obeissance / Under the reule of governance' (*CA*, Prol. 107–8). On the other hand Chaucer offers a beguilingly naturalistic pilgrim gathering at an inn to make an appeal in a different idiom (but not to a radically different end) for social 'felaweshipe'. In this case the role of monarch is assigned to a hotel manager who will be in charge of the speakers who will produce the poem. Political 'governance' and 'accord' are mediated to us through the expression of his self-appointment as marshal and manager of the company for the purposes of storytelling. At his suggestion the pilgrims make a show of taking counsel and of voting about whether they should agree to his rule, though not expecting to resist. The atmosphere is of political give-and-take, oaths are sworn, they consent to be 'reuled . . . at his devys', and are unanimously 'acorded to his juggement' (I.777–818). Accord, an option to take counsel and vote, a willingness to be ruled, and assent to the judgement of their governor—the configuration is that of a society functioning, in Robert Swanson's words, 'as a kind of monarchically governed unity',[12] just at a period in English history (1380s/1390s) when the power of monarchs to command the respect and assent of society reached a new low.[13]

Even before the Canterbury fellowship has formally constituted itself, its potential instability will be rather apparent to the reader. Friendliness,

---

[11] Gower, purportedly boarding the royal 'barge' at Richard's invitation, primarily enacts a symbolic co-operation with governance, whether or not this meeting on the Thames ever took place; *CA*, Prol. (first version) 35–56.

[12] Robert Swanson, 'Social Structures', in Peter Brown (ed.), *A Companion to Chaucer* (Oxford: Blackwell, 2000), pp. 397–413 (p. 404); and Alcuin Blamires, 'Crisis and Dissent', ibid., pp. 133–48 (pp. 143–6).

[13] As a Justice of the Peace for Kent during the post-Revolt period, Chaucer had reason to be exercised about this.

among the individual pilgrims gathered at the Tabard, is mainly a cloak for a profiteering or competitive instinct. The sweetness and pleasantness of the Friar is practised for cash; the Wife of Bath is an entertaining socializer but her 'charitee' collapses if the social precedence she claims is challenged. Where companionships are specified—Physician and Apothecary (I.428), Man of Law and Franklin (I.331), Summoner and Pardoner (I.669)—the relationships strongly imply venal alliance. Those who are credited with being 'good felawes' are fellows only in a mischievous sense, which shadows the whole concept of fellowship: they are socialites. 'For he that is a riatowre and a revelowre and a grete hawnter of the taverne or the alehowse, and a grete waster of his gooddys, then is he callyd a good felow', as the medieval moralist put it.[14] It is the devil's trickery to urge that we should sustain fellowship in this suspect sense, and party as others do if we would not be considered mean.[15] Although there are glimpses of more laudable fellowship in the 'General Prologue', even these barely come unqualified. That the Clerk prays for friends and others who support his studies is reassuring, but even he, with his need for books, has a tincture of grasping self-motivation, taking 'al that he myghte of his freendes *hente*' (I.299–300).

Yet the Host tries to weld the pilgrims into genuine fellowship, and his attempt is momentarily reinforced when the Knight starts the *Canterbury Tales* with a story of the two young cousins Arcite and Palamon united in lineage, sworn to brotherhood, and found lying wounded together after the conquest of Thebes by Duke Theseus of Athens. But of course it is to become a story of friendship going awry, portending the endlessly divisive pressures that will emerge in both frame and tales to afflict the Canterbury society and undermine its fellowship.

Friendship and its Discontents in 'The Knight's Tale' and *Troilus & Criseyde*

While 'The Knight's Tale' is focused on the fracture of a friendship, it nevertheless incorporates just one tantalizing benchmark of magnificent

---

[14] Quoted by Kathleen M. Ashley in her 'Renaming the Sins: A Homiletic Topos of Linguistic Instability in the *Canterbury Tales*', in *Sign, Sentence, Discourse: Language in Medieval Thought and Literature*, ed. Julian N. Wasserman and Lois Roney (Syracuse, NY: Syracuse University Press, 1989), pp. 272–93 (p. 275, and see also p. 286).

[15] *VV*, pp. 250, 244, 143.

amicitia when it refers fleetingly to another bond of affection, between Theseus and Perotheus. Duke Perotheus is described as 'felawe' to Theseus (1.1192) and it is by Perotheus's persuasion—as one who has known and loved Arcite as a friend—that Theseus releases Arcite from prison. As for the subsequent history of Perotheus and Theseus, we are told the old books say that when one of them died 'His felawe wente and soughte hym doun in helle' (1.1200). Chaucer pulls in this brusque Perotheus reference from an elaborately expansive discussion of friendship in the *Romance of the Rose*.[16] There the Lover's Friend speaks as one who tested the value of true friendship when he fell into poverty. He compliments the Lover on having sustained a loyalty to him such that either would live in the other's mind even if one of them were to die, just as Perotheus lived on after death in Theseus's heart and prompted Theseus's journey into the underworld in quest of him.

Tone and context have previously deflected critics from sensing the importance of this icon of friendship in 'The Knight's Tale'. Chaucer slots the reference in with a deadpan brevity that can be misconstrued as cajoling the reader into scepticism—into dismissing heroic death-defying friendship as a threadbare myth confined to 'olde bookes'. Yet the example is surely pointed, in a context which has painfully introduced us to a world where platitudes of eternal bonding cannot survive even the first flush of sexual competition between two youthful males. So far have the two Thebans lapsed from selfless friendship that the proverb cited by Arcite, 'at the kynges court [...] Ech man for himself, ther is noon oother' (1.1181–2), threatens to be a nail in the coffin of *amicitia* in the very first Canterbury tale. If shreds of knightly solidarity remain between them even while their jealousy explodes once both are out of prison, this only heightens the transformation of their bond of friendship into hatred. Each ritually helps arm the other, as if on chivalric autopilot, 'As freendly as he were his owene brother' (1.1652), but that is merely a calculatedly sarcastic reminder of what has just been destroyed amidst their hails of insult. Mutual altruism is at last so obliterated that when Theseus halts their deadly combat, Palamon not only blurts out their identity and demands death for himself but demands execution also for his 'fellow'. 'Sle my felawe eek', he urges, or (he corrects himself with startling ignobility) 'sle hym first' (1.1722–3), recapped at 1740). That afterthought is flatly antithetical to Theseus's altruism in refusing to lose Perotheus in death.

---

[16] *RR*, 8118–24, trans. Horgan, p. 125.

Chaucer has here driven the jealousy of the love-rivals to a pitch not found in his source text, the *Teseida*.[17] Indeed, the request 'kill him first' runs counter not only to the source text but also to a standard medieval exemplification of the heights of male friendship, through the story of a man who, reduced to despairing poverty, indicts himself for a murder he did not commit. His friend, recognizing him in court, then makes a counter-claim to be the murderer (though also innocent) so as to save him. In a tale of the tenth day in the *Decameron*, Boccaccio aligns this narrative of friendship with an act of altruism in love-rivalry, because the same man thus saved has, earlier in the narrative, ceded his fiancée to this friend. It is a narrative self-consciously designed by Boccaccio—almost as a rhetorical tour de force—to exalt the triumph of noble (male) friendship over all instincts of passion and self-interest.[18]

Not so in 'The Knight's Tale', where the hostility between Palamon and Arcite has brought the narrator to exclaim against Cupid for being a force so tyrannically incompatible with fellow feeling:

> O Cupide, out of alle charitee!
> O regne, that wolt no felawe have with thee!
> Ful sooth is seyd that love ne lordshipe
> Wol noght, his thankes, have no felaweshipe.
>
> (I.1623–6)

The aphorism about lordship and fellowship harks back to a proverb of Ennius, transmitted by Cicero: 'There is no fellowship inviolate, / No faith is kept, when kingship is concerned.'[19] Cicero, as we have noted, was profoundly concerned with the topic of friendship, both in its private dimension between individuals and in its public dimension

---

[17] *Teseida*, ed. A. Limentani, in *Tutte le opere di Giovanni Boccaccio*, gen. ed. V. Branca, vol. 2 (Milan: Mondadori, 1964), v.39–63 and 86–90; trans. N. R. Havely, *Chaucer's Boccaccio* (Cambridge: D. S. Brewer, 1980), pp. 119–21.

[18] Giovanni Boccaccio, *Decameron*, ed. Cesare Segre (Milan: Mursia, 1984), x.8; and *The Decameron*, trans. G. H. McWilliam (Harmondsworth: Penguin, 1972), pp. 776–94. On the story type to which Boccaccio's tale conforms and the significance of the departure from it in *KnT*, see further Robert Stretter, 'Rewriting Perfect Friendship in Chaucer's *Knight's Tale* and Lydgate's *Fabula Duorum Mercatorum*', *ChauR*, 37 (2002–3), 234–52.

[19] 'Nulla sancta societas / Nec fides regni est'; Cicero, *De officiis*, ed. and trans. Miller, pp. 26–7. Chaucer probably knew the proverb independently of Boccaccio's version of it in *Teseida*, v.13: 'signoria nè amore sta bene in compagnia'.

as a predisposition to *societas* or fellowship.[20] Suddenly, 'The Knight's Tale' clashes together the concepts of love, friendship, charity, so as to disclose the fissile nature of the ethical and moral ideals it is addressing. And the nightmare ripples outwards to subsume the planetary forces whose discordance of *compleccioun*, as Saturn observes when faced with strife between Venus and Mars over Arcite's apparent victory in the tale's tournament, routinely fosters 'divisioun' in the world (1.2475–6).

There is a broadening of horizons here towards the sort of panoptic spectacle of division threatening world, church, state, and individual that appalled Gower. But Chaucer, more than Gower, subdues the political to the ethical and the philosophical. If the antithetical poles of the narrative are on the one hand an ideal and perhaps even Christ-like sacrificial fellow feeling as exemplified by Theseus toward Perotheus, and on the other hand a pragmatic adage that holds both love and lordship to be incompatible with fellowship, the central ethical and moral problem to be negotiated must be the passion which most damages fellowship or, to apply a moral name to that, the sin of Ire or Wrath. So, while Barbara Nolan has used medievalized Stoic sources to comment persuasively on Theseus's role as a manifestation of Justice,[21] I would wish to add a complementary emphasis on the duke's concern to transcend and subdue Wrath.

As the tale proceeds, Theseus is heard trying to reduce malicious violence in the tourney by decreeing that none shall ride more than once against *his felawe* with an iron-tipped spear (1.2548). (This is an edict whose phrasing necessarily co-opts those on either side into fellowship.) Then he is heard spreading conciliation after the tourney, putting a stop to 'rancour and envye' (1.2732) by awarding honour to those on both sides equally, 'ylik as oothers brother' (1.2735). However, it is in the pivotal episode of his discovery of the cousins fighting in the grove that the ethical resonance of the tale in relation to wrath, and Chaucer's particular stake there in Senecan ethics, becomes most conspicuous.[22]

Recent criticism has emphasized the gender paradigm whereby, in the face of the defiance that the feuding cousins offer to his overlordship and in response to Palamon's acknowledgement that they both deserve

---

[20] Intermittently in *De officiis*, but see esp. Cicero, *Laelius, On Friendship, and The Dream of Scipio*, ed. and trans. J. G. F. Powell (Warminster: Aris and Phillips, 1990).

[21] Nolan, *Chaucer and the Tradition of the 'roman antique'*, esp. pp. 251, 261–6.

[22] Here I build on Burnley's analysis of Theseus, *Chaucer's Language and the Philosophers' Tradition*, pp. 25–7.

execution, Theseus's immediate impulse to sentence them to death is softened by the intercession of Emelye and other women who are present. The plight of the cousins prompts the women's 'pitee' and their tears out of 'verray wommanhede' (1.1748–57), and it is by their emotional pleading that the Duke's severity is initially relaxed. It is a moment that has been thought to epitomize a Chaucerian interest in borrowing from political and literary precedents for female intercession, in order to 'feminize' the male hero—to show the necessity of transcending gender polarities by redressing 'masculine' limitations with 'feminine' virtues.[23] In a different reading, this model narrative moment demonstrates, not that rigorous masculinity is in any way transformed by acceding to 'pitee', but rather that masculinity accommodates feminine sympathy within a dramatization of justice:

> The interceding women [...] resemble not agents of mercy but allegorical figures in a psychomachy of the ruler's decision making. [...] The scene locates pity in women as a way of describing the subordinate place it holds in the all-encompassing masculine deliberation.[24]

We may go even further and wonder whether (as I have suggested elsewhere) Theseus participates in a kind of ethical engineering that manages to sustain a male prerogative over anger by making women *responsible* for pacifying it.[25]

In any case, the melodrama of female intercession is quickly replaced by an internalized judicial debate, staged in the Duke's mind between Reason and Ire. Scholars might have devoted more attention to the way in which this passage goes on to disclose Chaucer building directly from antique ethics an ideal of rulership that restores fellowship. Seneca's essay *De ira* (*On Anger*) proves extraordinarily interesting as an antecedent here. Seneca highlights knee-jerk reaction, the temptation to respond to surface appearances, as the catalyst of anger; and he highlights restraint, reflection, and delayed response as important remedies. Even when a seemingly provocative action is actually witnessed, one should ponder its circumstances and understand how the status of the perpetrator—their

---

[23] See Mann, *Feminizing Chaucer*, pp. 165–85 (esp. p. 174); and Paul Strohm, 'Queens as Intercessors', in his *Hochon's Arrow: The Social Imagination of Fourteenth-Century Texts* (Princeton: Princeton University Press, 1992), pp. 95–119.

[24] Crane, *Gender and Romance*, p. 22, within an extremely thoughtful discussion of the episode's gender implications (pp. 18–23).

[25] Alcuin Blamires, *The Case for Women in Medieval Culture* (Oxford: Clarendon Press, 1997), p. 88.

youth, their sex, their authority or otherwise—has prompted it.[26] Seneca keeps returning to this. People characteristically overlook 'the intention of the doer', he observes, 'yet it is to the doer that we should give thought': what motive, what compulsion was there, what age are they?[27] We need to reflect that anyone can make mistakes. In fact, let us 'look back upon our youth and recall how often we were too careless about duty, too indiscreet in speech';[28] and let us 'consider the limitations of our human lot' if we aspire to wise judgement, for anyone who 'blames the individual for a fault that is universal' is hardly just.[29]

These are exactly the emphases that shape Theseus's thoughts as the anger he feels in response to the self-confessed guilt of the two Theban youths is 'excused' by his 'resoun' (i.1765–6). He recognizes the mitigating circumstance of human instinct: every person will try to help himself in love, and everyone will try to escape prison. He considers the intention of the doers and takes account of the youths' present attitude, one of frank acknowledgement, which lordly 'discrecioun' must properly distinguish from an attitude of arrogant hostility. He sees them as driven into their predicament by the power of love—and he is able to look back on his own youth ('I woot it by myself ful yore agon', i.1813) to reflect on his own former vulnerability to that power. The accompanying retreat from wrath is crowned by forgiveness. While Theseus graciously pretends to attribute this to the influence of the Queen and Emelye (i.1819–20), we have by now been privy to the interior ethical process that has led the Duke to this conclusion. And logically enough, the forgiveness is made conditional on the Thebans' agreement to be Theseus's 'freendes in all that ye may' (i.1824).

'The Knight's Tale' proceeds to enlarge this re-establishment of friendship by submerging the cousins' rivalry within the regulatory mechanism of tournament. On the face of it the event appears likely to augment their quarrel into something approaching organized warfare. However, Theseus wills no 'destruccioun of blood' (i.2564) and Susan Crane is therefore right to emphasize, to the contrary, how the Duke's solution of a tournament in a purpose-built stadium serves in effect to 'incorporate' the two knights' hitherto private antagonism safely

---

[26] *De ira*, ii.30.1–2, *Moral Essays*, vol. 1, pp. 230–3.
[27] *De ira*, iii.12.2, pp. 282–5.   [28] *De ira*, iii.25.2, pp. 316–17.
[29] *De ira*, iii.26.3, pp. 320–1.

into 'the chivalric community'.[30] Palamon and Arcite participate in a public spectacle of community and fellowship, which demonstrates their affiliation with all knights in subscribing to the overriding aristocratic values of that culture, whether in the colours of Mars or Venus. There is therefore the paradox that the spectacle of the two teams surging to and fro in their Olympic contest is also the quintessence of solidarity: every knight wished to be there (1.2111–14). This is not even the solidarity of knights only, because it is a microcosm of fellowship unifying society, by means of a public event within an arena that assimilates by the power of a ruler's edict all observers, participants, and even, so far as possible, implacable external forces.

For one exhilarating and optimistic moment, at the prospect of this grand benign tournament, 'the voys of peple touchede the hevene' (1.2561). Although the voice of the people is frequently a suspect voice in Chaucer,[31] this instance defies scepticism. Nolan has underlined that the successes achieved by Theseus against the encompassing forces of disorder and chance are 'provisional' and limited.[32] True, yet I do not think it an exaggeration to suggest that we have at this point in the first Canterbury tale, however temporarily and however much it is implicitly dominated by males, a pinnacle of emotive nostalgia for human community: complementing and supercharging the moment of fellowship contrived between Host and pilgrims in the 'General Prologue', it is meant to act as a beacon across the crevasses dividing individuals and groups that become visible as the tales proceed.

I am arguing that Theseus is ethically exemplary in his will to conquer wrath and reinstate fellowship. In a moment we shall consider how Chaucer concludes, as well as opens, the tale-telling with reflections on wrath and its resolutions. However, at this point we should begin to take stock of some gender implications in what has been discussed. Almost by default, the discourse of *amicitia* seems to encompass men more than women. The largely unspoken rationale for that, going back to the *Ethics*, was the assumed hierarchy between the sexes. Males were qualified to exercise the highest public virtues, hence male–male friendship constituted the highest reach of *amicitia*.[33] This

---

[30] Crane, *Gender and Romance*, pp. 34–5.

[31] For reasons explained in *Mel*, vii.1068.

[32] Nolan, *Chaucer and the Tradition of the 'roman antique'*, p. 250.

[33] Aristotle thought male–female friendship of a kind could occur within marriage (*Ethics*, viii.12, trans. Thomson, pp. 280–1) but did not see marriage as upholding the criterion of 'equality' in friendship (viii.7, trans. p. 269).

preconception was insidiously reinforced by the fact that 'brotherhood', as Barbara Newman emphasizes, was a substantial theme of formative medieval writing on the monastic life, whereas 'sisterhood' lagged behind.[34] In fact 'brotherly' love so much constitutes a yardstick of friendship in the Middle Ages that in Chaucer's *Book of the Duchess*, the heroine's generous non-sexual impulse of affection for all 'goode folk' has to be defined by it: 'She loved as man may do his brother' (*BD*, 892).

Nevertheless, Chaucer is conspicuously sceptical about ambitious forms of 'brotherhood'. As we have seen, he reduces this phenomenon to no more than flawed hyperbole in the case of Palamon and Arcite's brotherhood. The eventual softening of Arcite's stance, graciously commending Palamon to Emelye when he sees his own death imminent, is to my mind too belated a gesture of magnanimity to restore brotherhood in a profound way. Brotherhood fares little better in other tales.[35] It appears as the conjunction of opportunism and naïveté in the case of a monk and merchant in 'The Shipman's Tale', and as the conjunction of cool calculation and arrant folly in the case of the fiend and summoner in 'The Friar's Tale'. There are also three drunken thugs sworn to 'lyve and dyen ech of hem for oother' (except where inclined to murder by money) in 'The Pardoner's Tale' (vi.703). Their pseudo-brotherhood is mordantly contextualized by the sense the reader has that the Pardoner is very nearly excluded from all Christian brotherhood.

Richard Firth Green attributes the evident anxiety about commitment (*trouthe*) in human relations generally in writings of this time to the effects of a cultural shift from a society that had articulated people's commitments orally to one that increasingly expressed those commitments through written contract.[36] It is equally if not more likely that late-century anxieties about social cohesion accelerated by the Peasants' Rising and originating in the disruptive social consequences of plague caused Chaucer's poetry to be haunted by a blocked ideal of benign homosocial amity. He projects a male–male amity that is everywhere liable to be twisted by deception and collusion. Troilus and Pandarus constitute the most interesting test case, in a poem that offers

---

[34] Barbara Newman, *From Virile Woman to Woman Christ: Studies in Medieval Religion and Literature* (Philadelphia: University of Pennsylvania Press, 1995), pp. 34–5.

[35] Cynical elaborations on this theme are surveyed in Jean Jost, 'Ambiguous Brotherhood in the *Friar's Tale* and *Summoner's Tale*', in Beidler (ed.), *Masculinities*, pp. 77–90.

[36] Richard Firth Green, *A Crisis of Truth: Literature and Law in Ricardian England* (Philadelphia: University of Pennsylvania Press, 2002).

many reflections on friendship. We hear Pandarus air the doctrine that a friend is a comforter in times of difficulty (*TC*, I.593–5); we hear of a category called 'love of frendshipe' (*TC*, II.371, that is, affection between friends, something that can accommodate female–male relationships that are not sexual, or can disguise those that are sexual; and that can constitute the residue that is left when such a relationship has lapsed, *TC*, v.1080).[37] We are also hugely aware of Pandarus's ceaseless effort in pursuit of his friend's, and in his own eyes of his niece's, welfare.

How untrammelled, though, is the 'friendship' between Pandarus and Troilus? It is a question that has long tantalized readers of Chaucer. There comes a crunch moment where Pandarus himself puts it to Troilus as his 'brother deere' (*TC*, III.330) that for Troilus's sake he has become a culpable intermediary in their affair, and that the guile he has used in making Criseyde receptive would, if known, be perceived as outright treachery to his own niece (253–5, 274–8). Troilus responds, with self-conscious sensitivity, that there should be no question of construing as 'bauderye' what Pandarus has actually done 'for compaignie' (395–7). Proper distinctions must be made. Whatever it might be *called* if a person were a go-between in an amorous affair for reasons of profit, 'this that thow doost, calle it gentilesse, / Compassioun, and felawship, and trist' (400–3).

The sentiment seems logical and reassuringly noble, and it is substantiated by inviting us to remember Pandarus's desire to rescue Troilus from the mortal pangs of his initial passion (415); but the language is nevertheless quite disturbing. As Allen Frantzen puts it, Troilus 'demonstrates how words can change the perception of a morally ambiguous act'.[38] In fact, Troilus is here uncomfortably close to a recognizable medieval patter of sin-mitigation. To rationalize sin into an adjacent sociable virtue—to 'call' one thing the other—was the oldest trick in the book (in fact a trick remarked upon at least as far back as in Seneca's Letters).[39] The devil would tempt to gluttony on the pretext of

---

[37] Burnley connects 'love of frendshipe' with Aquinas's rather more exalted concept of *amor amicitiae* (disinterested affection): *Chaucer's Language and the Philosophers' Tradition*, pp. 137–8.

[38] Allen Frantzen, *Troilus and Criseyde: The Poem and the Frame* (New York: Twayne, 1993), p. 87.

[39] 'Vices creep into our hearts under the name of virtues; rashness lurks beneath the appellation of bravery, moderation is called sluggishness, and the coward is called prudent', writes Seneca in a critique of verbal quibbling: *Ep.* 45.7, *Epistulae*, vol. 1, pp. 294–5.

calling it fellowship; sexual satisfaction could be rationalized as natural solace. 'Thus the devil and his minions conceal sins beneath attractive words.'[40]

So, to 'call' Pandarus's behaviour *compassioun* and *felawship* and to claim thereby to cancel all moral equivocation attaching to that behaviour is to beg a large question.[41] More than Boccaccio, Chaucer has brought to awkward attention the question what to 'call' Pandarus's actions.[42] At a critical juncture we are being obliged to face the difficulty, not the easiness, of accepting the unscrupulous things done in the name of that medieval *amicitia* that ostensibly inspires a male–male relationship. In fact, Cicero's considerable authority was behind the principle that friends must ask only honourable things of each other, and that asking for help 'in illicit pleasures' was inimical to friendship.[43] Although we saw that Chaucer can gesture towards something noble in the case of Theseus and Perotheus, he certainly seems to find it hard to imagine how male friendship can fully attain the affecting ethical quality envisaged for it by Cicero.

How do women fit into this fictional world obsessed with failure and self-delusion in male fellowship? Feminist criticism sometimes implies that in Chaucer's writings as in some other medieval literature, women are implicitly projected as that which impedes or upsets male–male

[40] Bromyard, *Summa predicantium*, quoted by Ashley, 'Renaming the Sins', p. 275. The *TC* example is not discussed by Ashley. See also *JW*, p. 143, and examples in Anne Hudson, *Selections from English Wycliffite Writings* (Cambridge: Cambridge University Press, 1978), pp. 81, 179.

[41] The question seems enforced by the way Troilus goes on to call his love-suit 'this grete emprise' (III.416). In any case, a contrary move in *MancT*, IX.207–22 assures us that terminological distinctions can be hypocritical, as discussed in Chapter 8 below.

[42] Boccaccio's Troiolo urges Pandaro not to 'give yourself such a vile title [of 'procurer', *mezzano*]', arguing that Pandaro has done what he has done to help a friend in torment: *Teseida*, III.48, trans. Havely, *Chaucer's Boccaccio*, p. 48. John Fleming's discussion of the episode describes Troilus as committing an act of 'creative philology' that makes the moment sound 'even sleazier' than it is in Boccaccio: *Classical Imitation and Interpretation in Chaucer's 'Troilus'* (Lincoln: University of Nebraska Press, 1990), pp. 165–71 (p. 170). Defenders of Troilus point out that Troilus is reciprocating Pandarus's own earlier sweeping gesture (*TC*, 1.860–1) that he would help obtain the woman causing Troilus's distress, even if she were his own sister. See John Hill, 'Aristocratic Friendship in *Troilus and Criseyde*: Pandarus, Courtly Love and Ciceronian Brotherhood in Troy', in Robert G. Benson and Susan J. Ridyard (eds.), *New Readings of Chaucer's Poetry* (Cambridge: D. S. Brewer, 2003), pp. 165–82; Leah R. Freiwald, 'Swych Love of Frendes: Pandarus and Troilus', *ChauR*, 6 (1971–2), 120–9; Robert G. Cook, 'Chaucer's Pandarus and the Medieval Ideal of Friendship', *JEGP*, 69 (1970), 407–24; Alan Gaylord, 'Friendship in Chaucer's *Troilus*', *ChauR*, 3 (1968–9), 239–64.

[43] *Laelius, On Friendship*, ed. Powell, XIII.44 and IX.35.

friendship and solidarity.[44] Yet we only have to think of the modifications he made to Emelye's role in 'The Knight's Tale' (where by contrast with Boccaccio's Emilia, coquettishly flirtatious towards the imprisoned cousins, Chaucer's heroine is unconscious of their longing, an unwilling object of desire) to realize that Chaucer resists straightforward invitation to represent woman as the actively disruptive gender.

Besides, as we have already noted and as will be further explored in Chapter 3, Chaucer's writings inscribe empathy and a pacifying spirit, impulses of conciliation which ease rather than endanger fellowship, as an especially feminine virtue. That does not mean there are no dissonant displays of female wrath, though it does mean that such displays tend to be flagged as transgressively shrill, out-of-gender behaviour. This is seen, for example, in the sequel to 'The Tale of Melibee'. Perhaps Chaucer assigned 'Melibee' to be his 'own' tale as Canterbury pilgrim because it promoted a tolerance that he held especially valuable. It contrasts a wife's calm and pacific reasoning with the rancorous vengeful instincts of her nobleman husband against enemies who have raided his property and attacked his family.[45] However, the exposition of Dame Prudence's tolerance is immediately qualified by the Host's vignette of his own allegedly spitfire wife, Goodelief. Her style as he represents it is of a kind to unsettle community harmony: she reacts angrily to presumed social insults, taunts her husband for not standing up for his or her 'rights', and eggs him on to a violence she considers properly masculine. She threatens to swap her distaff for his knife ('Prologue to the Monk's Tale', vii.1891 ff.). At first sight the passage implies that the gendering of tolerance and pacific tendencies in 'Melibee' as feminine does not take account of the behaviour of 'real women' like Goodelief. On second thoughts, since Harry Bailly says he wishes that his rampantly aggressive wife had heard 'Melibee', there is a possible hint of a very modern idea that culture genders mildness feminine as a form of social indoctrination, in order to *contain* assertiveness in women. In any case the bottom line is that the gender template that Mrs Bailly keenly invokes is actually one in which women expect their *men* to be belligerent and wrathful.

However, the 'Goodelief' interlude is tonally teasing. In part it is a *jeu d'esprit*, meant to defuse the moral strenuousness of Geoffrey's

---

[44] e.g. Laskaya, *Chaucer's Approach to Gender*, p. 81.

[45] See esp. David Wallace's analysis of the crucial role of Prudence's 'household rhetoric': *Chaucerian Polity: Absolutist Lineages and Associational Forms in England and Italy* (Stanford: Stanford University Press, 1997), pp. 212–46.

preceding tale through the fun of caricature, jestingly aired by a self-styled hen-pecked husband. We are in the territory of a particularly shrill misogynous cliché holding that nothing is more incendiary than a provoked woman—none so 'cruel' when 'she hath caught an ire', especially with husband or lover, as an obnoxious friar claims in 'The Summoner's Tale' (III.1986–2003). This friar borrows the topos from Jean de Meun, who borrowed it from Ovid.[46] Since the tale goes on to focus on ire in a series of *men*, culminating in the tooth-grinding rage of the friar himself as he tries to make a public issue of the affront he receives from the very villager he has lectured on wrath, the misogynous allegation hangs somewhat futilely in the air. We are aware both of the friar's intellectual caprice and of a characteristic Chaucerian u-turn that undoes gendered moral stereotyping the minute it has been uttered.

The one Chaucerian context in which the claim of women's susceptibility to a distinctively cruel anger seems to be most pressing is 'The Man of Law's Tale', though not formally identified as 'ire' in the tale itself. Here the Sultan's mother is the culprit, her particular viciousness shown in plotting extreme retaliation against her son for his conversion and betrothal to a Christian, and even more in her savage gloating over the font-ful of water that will be needed, she suggests, to wash away the blood of the massacre she plans at the wedding feast (II.353–7). For this the Man of Law luridly condemns her as 'serpent under femynynytee' and (in her malice against innocence) 'feyned womman' (II.360, 362). Some have wondered whether she earns that last epithet because she presumes to take action, or because she aims to usurp male rule by assuming power (II.434).[47] To me it seems more likely that it is her calculated malice against innocence (II.362–3) and against her own kin, destructive of elementary bonds of fellowship and therefore defying the supposed social normativity of 'feminine' compassion, which brings the accusation of displaced gender.[48]

The most remarkable instance of anger in a woman in the *Tales* both invites empathy and remains brilliantly ambivalent, and this is the Wife of Bath's reaction to her fifth husband's subjection of her to nightly

[46] *RR*, 9761–76, trans. Horgan, p. 150; *Ars amatoria*, II.376–8.

[47] Laskaya thinks the Sultaness is called unfeminine because acting independently of men: *Chaucer's Approach to Gender*, p. 144. Martin attributes the allegation to wholesale inversion by the Sultaness of 'all the decent roles available to women': *Chaucer's Women*, p. 134.

[48] In Hoccleve's *Regiment*, where a mother's desire to avenge a trivial affront to her daughter provokes the comment, 'certes in that she lakked wommanhede' (3446).

readings from his antifeminist anthology. The sheer remorselessness of this provokes her both into tearing pages from the book, and striking him on the cheek so that he falls back into the fire (III.788–93). Since he responds in kind, we are soon in the realms of what the British police euphemistically call 'a domestic'. Chaucer's skill lies in the implication that misogyny's mental brutality *causes* the wifely reactiveness which misogyny then pillories.[49] Beyond this, Alisoun's physical raid on the book is a 'direct action' means of eliminating the offensive clichés of misogyny and continues her protest at the male monopoly of literary representation, but only at the risk of reminding the medieval reader of another critique of women; that they are impassioned beings not susceptible to the rational complexities of the written word.

Whatever the effect of this unique moment, the broader evidence suggests that Chaucer's writings largely affirm 'sociable' feminine impulses and inscribe men as authors of angry violence.[50] At the same time Chaucer reveals little interest in projecting women engaging in strong friendships with each other. Both the 'Prologue' to *The Legend of Good Women* and 'The Wife of Bath's Tale' loosely articulate female solidarity—women encountered in groups, acting in concert—but not female friendship. In her 'Prologue' the Wife of Bath has a network of close friends named as gossip, niece, another wife (III.530–9), but their companionship seems represented as abrasively indiscreet and conspiratorial, an alliance energized by genial contempt of men. One episode in *Troilus and Criseyde* gives Criseyde a chorus of city women friends, only to demean their well-meaning 'wommanysshe' comment (*TC*, IV.680 ff.). Not knowing of her secret love of Troilus, they cannot offer relevant comfort concerning her departure from Troy. They 'misunderstand Criseyde crucially when most she needs their wisdom', as one critic puts it; the same critic notes how Criseyde, motherless and sisterless, 'has no recourse to nurturing female figures'.[51]

There are some other instances of female–female friendship, of which that between Hermengyld and Custance in 'The Man of Law's Tale' has perhaps the most impact (II.535–67); but the intimacy of these two is required by the plot in order that Custance can be held suspect for

---

[49] Mann, *Feminizing Chaucer*, pp. 66–7.

[50] This view was to be directly articulated by Christine de Pizan: see Alcuin Blamires, with Karen Pratt and C. W. Marx (eds.), *Woman Defamed and Woman Defended* (Oxford: Clarendon Press, 1992), pp. 285–6.

[51] Nicky Hallett, 'Women', in Peter Brown (ed.), *A Companion to Chaucer* (Oxford: Blackwell, 2000), pp. 480–94 (p. 487).

Hermengyld's murder, and the source material is little developed. In the case of Philomela and Procne, and Ariadne and Phaedra in *The Legend of Good Women*, and of Criseyde and her 'niece' Antigone in *Troilus*, or Dido and her sister Anne, the relationships are somewhat determined by the obligation of kinship. So, despite other vague hints of companionship between noblewomen and their 'ladies' in Chaucer,[52] we look in vain for substantial personal alliances between women, even though these are celebrated elsewhere in medieval literature.[53] Paradoxically, the most promising female–female friendship in the *Tales* is that between princess Canacee and a desolate female hawk on whom she takes pity in 'The Squire's Tale'. Whether or not (as Gavin Douglas famously wrote) Chaucer revealed himself 'ever woman's friend', he did not much represent women as women's friends. Probably because his imagination was swayed by the concept of isolated and victimized women, by Heroidean heroines as modelled by Ovid, his writings sustain the male-specific tendency of much medieval discourse on *amicitia*.[54]

A Design of Defamation and Conciliation

Let us return now to the extraordinary prominence given in the *Tales* to key impulses that damage fellowship, particularly to the defamation that anger breeds. This phenomenon has often been commented on by critics through reference to Chaucer's vocabulary of 'quiting' ('matching'; or more aggressively 'retaliating; getting even with') that accompanies it. We should equally attend, though, to the vocabulary of defamation and slander, the ruthless insistence on 'not sparing' one's target, that also surrounds the motif of retaliation. Here we are in the realms of what is not just technically a sin but actually something taboo, deeply disturbing to the community consciousness of the Middle Ages.[55]

When the drunken Miller threatens to 'quite' 'The Knight's Tale' by telling of a clerk who hoodwinked a carpenter, the Reeve objects

[52] e.g. May in *MercT*, IV.1933; Canacee in *SqT*, V.382 f.

[53] e.g. Laudine and Lunete, and Fenice and Thessala, in Chrétien's *Yvain* and *Cligés* respectively; Melior and Urrake in *Partonope of Blois*; and several instances of female bonding in the *Lais* of Marie de France.

[54] On Chaucer and the exclusion of women from male canons of 'trouthe', see Richard Firth Green, 'Chaucer's Victimized Women', *SAC*, 10 (1988), 3–21.

[55] Carl Lindahl, *Earnest Games: Folkloric Patterns in the 'Canterbury Tales'* (Bloomington: Indiana University Press, 1987), pp. 79–96. For extensive discussion of defamation, see Edwin Craun, *Lies, Slander, and Obscenity in Medieval English Literature* (Cambridge: Cambridge University Press, 1997).

that it is 'a synne and eek a greet folye / To apeyren any man, or hym defame' and to bring wives into ill 'fame' (1.3146–8). The Miller goes on regardless, and refuses to restrain his speech: he 'nolde his wordes for no man forbere' (1.3168). That speaking ill of another is a 'sin' is perhaps an alien thought today, but easily confirmed from that period. 'Missaying' of another, 'to apeire hym ne his good name' is a breach of the commandment not to bear false witness and is a deadly sin, declares the *Book of Vices and Virtues*; and clerks call it detraction.[56] Detraction is naturally prominent in the affiliated sin category of 'sins of the tongue'. It also comes up as a regular branch of 'envy'. To speak with malice in a way that brings another person 'out of charity' is to sow discord and it is sharply prohibited.[57]

This was not merely a matter for the conscience of the individual. We learn in the first section of *Jacob's Well* that defamation is a serious contravention of moral law punishable in the church courts and ultimately by the Great Curse of excommunication itself.[58] Defamation cases constituted, in fact, one of the largest categories of offences dealt with by the medieval ecclesiastical courts.[59] The antidote to it was a form of 'restitution', a restoration of the good name that one had impugned, and this was to be effected with conspicuous attention to the equilibrium of the relevant community, that is, among the very people and in the very place where the defamation has been uttered, acknowledging the lies and falsehood one had spoken against the victim.[60] No reader of Richard Green's book on law and literature in the Middle Ages can be left in doubt of the community detestation (not to mention, in the early Middle Ages, the savage punishments by mutilation) reserved for those who damaged the standing of others in the community by false allegations against them.[61]

It is surprising how rarely critics think across from the motif of defamatory speech that is announced in the first fragment of the *Canterbury Tales* (and as we shall see deliberately sustained throughout the work), to the comprehensive exploration of defamation that Chaucer develops in the *House of Fame*. The date of that extraordinary poem is debated. If as early as some say, it attests a lifelong anxiety about the fallibility of speech and the fallibility of the reputations speech

---

[56] *VV*, p. 5.   [57] *JW*, p. 83.   [58] *JW*, p. 15.

[59] R. N. Swanson, *Church and Society in Late Medieval England* (Oxford: Blackwell, 1989), pp. 167–8.

[60] *JW*, p. 200.   [61] Green, *Crisis of Truth, passim*.

engenders;[62] if as late as some say, it reinforces Chaucer's particular anxiety with these issues precisely in the period of the inception of the *Tales*. The *House of Fame* prompts horror (not eliminated by this poem's prevailing good humour) at the *process* of defamation. Fame, in the sense of bad repute, is particularly figured throughout in the image of blasts of noise. The blast from the foul trumpet of slander is like a pellet fired from a gun (*HF*, 1642–3); the noise of Rumour is like the whistling of a missile let fly from a siege-engine (*HF*, 1933–4); it is the fire bursting out from a spark, to burn up a whole city (*HF*, 2078–80). These formulations disclose a sense of the vicious annihilating power of defamation. Small wonder the meta-story of Aeneas inherited from antiquity begins, in this dream, with Sinon the Greek by whose 'false forswerynge' the treacherous horse was brought into Troy (*HF*, 151–6). And the most memorable victim is female. Dido imagines the power of 'every tonge' manufacturing a 'wikke fame', presuming to judge her so that she is for ever disgraced by her affair with Aeneas (*HF*, 345–60). Of course, goddess Fame herself is represented as a 'femynyne creature' (*HF*, 1365). The poem owes it primarily to Virgil, Ovid, and the accident of grammatical gender that Fame is a female deity. Perhaps something is made of this gendering in the poem's emphasis on the unstable physical form of Fame and the caprice of her judgements, reminiscent of slogans about women's instability and unwisdom. At the same time it is another deity, Eolus god of the wind, who actually does the damage by broadcasting slander.

Moralists regarded defamation as a worst-case version of unguarded or misdirected speech, and such speech constituted a human failing they persistently warned against. It is in the indiscreet speech of individuals, sounding off and (to use an insistent phrase in the *Tales*) 'not sparing' either their words or other people's sensitivities, that Chaucer articulates breaches of those tolerances that sustain social life. The conviviality of fellowship is projected as persistently threatened by anger and by audacious or reckless speech, which I have described elsewhere as a facet of Chaucer's own 'risk-taking' as a writer.[63] Combat-by-tale is famously fought in the case of Miller and Reeve, and subsequently of Friar and Summoner. The animosity between the latter two is such that the

---

[62] The dating problem is summarized by Helen Cooper, 'The Four Last Things in Dante and Chaucer: Ugolino and the House of Rumour', *NML*, 3 (1999), 39–66 (p. 59).

[63] Alcuin Blamires, *The Canterbury Tales* (Basingstoke: Macmillan, 1987), pp. 70–2.

pilgrim Summoner is quivering with wrath by the end of 'The Friar's Tale', indeed standing up in his stirrups in his desperation to retaliate with his tale of a friar who himself will be consumed with wrath.

Whether because work on the headlinks remained in progress, or by strategic avoidance, Chaucer did not present conciliation or resolution in these two quarrels. However, attempts to perform conciliation do appear later in the frame of the *Tales*. The first is at the conclusion of 'The Pardoner's Tale'. The Pardoner has disclosed a deeply vengeful spirit, a readiness to spit out poison with his tongue to defame opponents (VI.412–22), which seems indeed an apt correlative to the travesty of fellow-feeling whereby one of the revellers in his tale describes himself as doing a good turn ('a freendes torn') to his comrade when he broaches the plan to murder the third of their group (their 'felawe', VI.810–15). The Pardoner's own ingratiation with the company thinly conceals an underlying manipulative contempt. Chaucer is perhaps not as eager as some of his readers are to derive this contempt from homophobic provocation by the pilgrims, though the Host addresses him with a likely sneer as 'beel amy' (VI.318). Eventually the Pardoner, congratulating the company on having him there as a spiritual insurance in their fellowship (VI.938), recklessly taunts the Host; he identifies him as the most steeped in sin of all the pilgrims and challenges him to open his 'purse', to come forward with an offering and kiss his relics. Goaded, and taking advantage of available genital puns in 'relics' and 'purse', the Host's retort about cutting off the Pardoner's testicles reduces that normally expert purveyor of speech to speechless wrath (VI.957).[64]

There is now a moment of crisis because, as Helen Cooper has said, on every level the Pardoner 'threatens the harmony of this pilgrimage'.[65] The Host accordingly moves to ostracize the Pardoner, declaring that he will 'no lenger pleye' with such an 'angry man' (VI.958–9). It is a double-edged threat. On one hand it attributes corruptive *danger* to the Pardoner's wrath, by recalling a warning in Proverbs 22: 24–5: 'Make no friendship with an angry man [...] lest thou learn his ways, and get a snare to thy soul.'[66] On the other, in terms of the

---

[64] For discussion of the gender issues, see below, Chapter 3.

[65] Helen Cooper, *The Canterbury Tales*, Oxford Guides to Chaucer (Oxford: Oxford University Press, 1989), p. 271.

[66] This resonance, and a parallel (though milder) warning against dealing with 'angry folk' in the *Romaunt of the Rose* (3265–8), are noted by J. D. Burnley, 'Chaucer's Host and Harry Bailly', in *Chaucer and the Craft of Fiction*, ed. Leigh A. Arrathoon (Rochester, Mich.: Solaris Press, 1986), pp. 195–218 (p. 213).

commitment of the pilgrim company to conviviality on their journey, the Host's declaration threatens to pronounce social exclusion against the offender, in effect a kind of excommunication. In the event the Knight intervenes, urging the Pardoner to regain good humour and 'drawe [. . .] neer', thus repairing the social fracture that has just distanced him; and urging the Host to offer a kiss of peace (rather than a 'relic-kiss') to the Pardoner (VI.960–8). Although it has been suggested that the Knight is thereby 'imposing' social harmony, in a move that arrests social tension without acknowledging or addressing it,[67] I would not underestimate the community significance of that kiss.[68] The Kiss of Peace that is in Chaucer's mind was and remains a powerful performative gesture of fellowship amongst congregations in the liturgy of many churches.

Before the work's last drama of fellowship, a variation is included whose logic will now be clear. This is the case of the Canon and his servant (Yeoman) who catch up with the pilgrims on the road. As the Host questions the newcomers, he wonders particularly at the inconsistency between the high powers the Yeoman ascribes to the Canon, and the Canon's dirty, unkempt clothing. The Yeoman begins to let slip his scepticism about his master's alchemical practice, a disclosure that the Canon tries to stall by complaining that it amounts to slandering him (VIII.695). This is enough for the Host to encourage the Yeoman to talk freely. The result that the reader might predict from the familiar sparking of hostilities is that a satirical 'Yeoman's Tale' is imminent and will duly be countered by a 'Canon's Tale'. Instead the Canon flees, to avoid discomfiture. This variation complements the case of the Pardoner. He was nearly expelled from the fellowship: the Canon all but joins it. The Canon's self-exclusion is itself revelatory of something profoundly asocial about him and corroborates his practice (which the Yeoman is now able to describe unsparingly) as a despicable but secretive figure operating from the margins of society to draw people away from spiritual to delusory material goals. His flight, as Muscatine rightly suggests, symbolizes 'an apostasy from the human congregation' represented by the pilgrims—though the 'sluttissh' clothing (VIII.636) of one who has been on the verge of joining the pilgrim company also makes the episode interestingly reminiscent of the man disqualified

---

[67] Phillips, *An Introduction*, p. 156.

[68] Alfred David calls it 'a meaningful reassertion of the brotherhood of man': *The Strumpet Muse*, p. 204.

from the biblical wedding feast (allegorically, from heaven) because he is improperly dressed (Matt. 22: 11–13).[69]

The tale that was probably planned as the penultimate in the Canterbury collection, the Manciple's, notoriously rehearses questions about unchecked speech and verbal restraint in a puzzlingly self-mocking way. Chaucerians have so picked over the ironies and subversions with which discretion in speech is handled that there is a danger of inferring that no sensible person, let alone Chaucer, could have taken the topic seriously. However, before we discuss that let us assess the last of the headlink explorations of professional animosity and conciliation, in 'The Manciple's Prologue'.

The fragility of the pilgrim society appears once more in the spectacle of the Manciple's sneering attack on the Cook, who is drunk. In an oblique hint at what is to come, the Manciple demands that the drunkard should *close up* his reeking mouth with its infectious breath, only to be warned by the Host of the risk of retaliation that he himself runs by indulging such 'open' reproof (IX.37–9, 69–75). What with the Cook's lolling, speechless, contagious mouth, his loss of control—falling from his horse, he emblematizes a complete failure of rationality and is literally a burden to companions who must lift him back up—and the Manciple's raucous enthusiasm for condemning him, the scene is a veritable tableau of un-restraint and its dangers. The mode of conciliation is at first by retraction: the Manciple disclaims any wish to anger the Cook, and pretends he was only joking (IX.80–1). Then, for a laugh ('a good jape', IX.84), the Manciple supplies the drunkard with more drink, upon which the Cook duly thanks him, so far as his wits are able to. The Host marks the moment and delivers a mock encomium on the power of drink, a veritable deity able to 'turne rancour and disese / T'acord and love' (IX.95–101).

The general hypothesis of the *Tales* is that it takes considerable skills of ethical governance (like those displayed as if miraculously by the untutored Griselda in 'The Clerk's Tale') to convert rancour into peace and to bring together people filled with wrath (IV.431–7). With animosity flaring up yet again it is as though the obstacles to human fellowship are despaired of at this stage of the *Tales*. The last refuge is the oblivion of inebriation. This precisely complements the last safeguard

---

[69] Muscatine, *Chaucer and the French Tradition*, p. 221; Lynn Staley, 'The Man in Foul Clothes and a Late Fourteenth-Century Conversation About Sin', *SAC*, 24 (2002), 1–47 (esp. pp. 38–9).

against provocative speech that the tale is about to announce: the oblivion of silence.

The ensuing tale grows obsessive about the problem of the uncalculated effects of speech. Restraint of all that which Nature imparts to creatures (from mobile sexual desires to the mobile tongue) is judged well-nigh impossible. The action presents a brilliant convergence between metaphoric and literal modes of un-restraint that centres on the destructive power of the tongue, though this is not well understood in Chaucer commentary.[70] In the story, Phebus Apollo's pet crow considers itself bound to report to Phebus (but abrasively, in a harsh and exultant kind of 'singing') the infidelity of Phebus's wife. Since Phebus reacts with such angry impetuosity that he shoots his wife dead with an arrow, it becomes a lesson in a matter of great import in the Middle Ages: the devastating power of indiscreet words.[71]

While there is extraordinarily interesting resonance in the fact that Phebus proceeds to 'break his minstrelsy' (does Chaucer imply that ill-judged speech, or even truthful speech, may spell the end of poetry?), our focus here is on the fracture of social bonds wrought by speech. Among the dogged moralizations with which the tale ends, we hear that a rash tongue 'kutteth freendshipe al a-two' (IX.342) like a sword. Moreover, once you have uttered something, you can't recover it because 'forth it gooth' (IX.355). Implicit here is a connection between indiscreet speech and not only swords but also arrows, for once fired, they too are not to be recalled. Both sword and arrow were standard biblical figures for defamation, since they were found together in a verse in Proverbs: 'A man that beareth false witness against his neighbour is a maul, and a sword, and a sharp arrow' (Prov. 25: 18).[72] The arrow duly turns up as an emblem of detraction in Gower's *Mirour de l'Omme*, which likens words launched by a malicious tongue to arrows penetrating and injuring soft flesh: they are retractable only with pain.[73] In 'The Manciple's Tale',

---

[70] The exception is Wallace, *Chaucerian Polity*, pp. 253–4.

[71] On the period's anxiety about the risks of 'speaking out', the dangers of unwary speech in a lord's household, and commendations of 'a policy of judicious silence', see Nicholas Perkins, *Hoccleve's 'Regement of Princes': Counsel and Constraint* (Cambridge: D. S. Brewer, 2001), pp. 12–24.

[72] The verse, but not its connection with the action of the *MancT*, is noted by Craun, *Lies, Slander, and Obscenity*, p. 199.

[73] 'Just as the arrow from the hand of a strong archer easily enters the flesh, which is tender and soft, but can be drawn out backwards only with great pain and danger, so in the same way goes the word that flies from an evil tongue: it easily injures the name of a man, to whom it cannot afterwards make amends': *Mirour*, 2833 ff., trans. Wilson,

Phebus kills his wife with an arrow in an act of reckless anger, which, with hindsight, he himself sees as a lapse of 'discrecion'. The fiction, that is, *enacts* the destructive metaphorical impact of verbal attack (the injurious arrow) through Phebus's literalization of it. The 'arrow' *is* the 'tongue'.[74]

We shall return to questions about propriety of speech in this and other tales in Chapter 8. For the present we can note how the paradoxes of the tale are such that Phebus's consequent remorse is skewed, from the reader's point of view, because it grows from supposing the crow's truth (which is true so far as we know) to be a mere dubious allegation. Phebus becomes, like January in 'The Merchant's Tale',[75] an epitome of credulity in love, eventually taking refuge in supposing his wife innocent and the crow defamatory for reporting truth about her.

Phebus has nevertheless murdered his wife in a rash fit of ire (ix.265) resulting from a misuse of speech by the crow. It hardly strikes us as 'misuse' now, but the advice of Loyalty in such a case, according to one thirteenth-century arbiter of ethics, Brunetto Latini, would be: 'if you have known the truth of a fact, and by speaking of it quickly you gave birth to great trouble, certainly if you kept silent—even if you were reproved for it—you would be defended by me'.[76] Climactically, near the conclusion of the *Tales*, Chaucer produces an object lesson in the disastrous impact of words, which (given the crow's tactlessly gloating way of informing Phebus that he has been cuckolded) amount to a sin of chiding, open revilement, and slander. In the idiom of 'The Parson's Tale', such words strike 'grete woundes' and they *'unsowen the semes of freendshipe* in mannes herte' (x.621, my emphasis). The pilgrimage began with good intentions of amity and accord. We have watched the seams of friendship being frayed and torn by verbal aggression during the pilgrimage. The tale-telling promotes competition and, as if incited by the breach of friendship between Palamon and Arcite within the very first tale, it veers away into discord. It provokes individuals not to 'spare' each other. That audacity does creatively invigorate the pilgrims' social and narrative belligerence, at the same time as it keeps threatening their

---

p. 43. See also Brunetto Latini, *Il Tesoretto (The Little Treasure)*, ed. and trans. Julia Bolton Holloway (New York: Garland, 1981), lines 1603–9. Cf. also *VV*, pp. 63–4.

[74] Wallace suggests that 'Phebus himself has been struck by arrows, fired by the crow', linking this to a comment in Albertano of Brescia's *De arte loquendi et tacendi*, I.v, 'words are like arrows, easy to shoot off, hard to retrieve': *Chaucerian Polity*, pp. 253–4. I see as central to the tale the perception that Wallace relegates to a footnote—that 'this commonplace metaphor' is 'painfully literalized by the Manciple' (p. 462, n. 23).

[75] See Chapter 2 below.   [76] *Il Tesoretto*, lines 1888–94.

fellowship. But Chaucer allows a last perspective on it and a counter to its divisiveness in the Parson's intention to 'knytte up al this feeste' (x.47), with a summoning to spiritual objectives. Where the words of others have threatened to unsew the seams of fellowship, his doctrine belatedly aspires to knit up. The whole poem's concern with fellowship and friendship determines that structure. It remains to be seen whether the structuring of other ethical concepts in Chaucer's writings offsets the pessimism he communicates on the subject of *amicitia* in his time.

2

Credulity and Vision: 'The Miller's Tale', 'The Merchant's Tale', 'The Wife of Bath's Tale'

The real voyage of discovery, thought Marcel Proust, consisted not in seeking new landscapes but in having new eyes. For Chaucer, writing about what the physical or mental eyes could see or foresee seems to have held a particular fascination. His work is shot through with acknowledgement of the limitations of vision of the here-and-now, let alone the limitations of pre-vision. Partly the limitation is registered as a relief. Individual perception is paltry—but in compensation there are immense resources of books and faith to supplement that paltriness: 'God forbede but men shulde leve / Wel more thing then men han seen with ye!' ('Prologue', *Legend of Good Women*, 'F' 10–11). Unaided human sight being such a fragile and feeble thing in relation to (for example) the solar system, it is expedient to place a certain trust in those who have been privileged to report back on things (*House of Fame*, 1012–17). But at the same time, if their vision-claims (founded in turn on potentially flawed vision) are likely to condition our own perception, there can be no complacency about the reliability of human vision.[1] By what empirical perception or on the basis of what authoritative insight can 'true' knowledge be obtained and 'true' reportage circulate?

The two dream poems just mentioned make palpable for the reader some of these problems of distinguishing the more plausible from the less. What or whom to trust, and the mind's infinite receptivity to suggestion: these are impulses that energize Chaucer's narratives again and again. This chapter will read three of the *Canterbury Tales* to consider

---

[1] Chaucer, as dreamer on a voyage through space in the *House of Fame*, 'sees' the world diminished to a pinprick, as he has read that it should be, but wonders alternatively whether the thickness of intervening air is affecting what he can see (*HF*, 904–9).

how, by emphatic narrative exploration of credulity and of delusions of foresight—by exploration, especially, of human readiness to believe, on weak or insufficient evidence, in the possibility of anticipating providential events—Chaucer cajoles readers into fresh appreciation of impediments to ethical wisdom. It is a gendered context because in the misogynous culture of the period women are sometimes held to act as decoys, disabling the faculty of prudence that should transcend credulity. Nevertheless one may argue that in Chaucer's writings it is also frequently women, precisely because they are so often the objects of the male gaze, who can enable men to 'see' better.

Foresight Mocked: 'The Miller's Tale'

The Miller lets slip in his 'Prologue' that his story will be of a clerk's victory over a carpenter and his wife, and immediately has to defend himself against the accusation that he is a defamer of wives and men. He therefore hastens to add that not every wife makes her husband a cuckold: he would not wish to take such a burden on himself as to 'demen' that he were a cuckold himself; 'I wol bileve wel that I am noon' (I.3160–2). He then elevates this voluntary credulity into a celebrated aphorism ingeniously (or perhaps drunkenly) muddling unquestioning Christian faith with unquestioning sexual trust:

> An housbonde shal nat been inquisityf
> Of Goddes pryvetee, nor of his wyf.
> So he may fynde Goddes foyson there,
> Of the remenant nedeth nat enquere.
>
> (I.3163–6)

Although there is much to unpack in these lines, it is their intimations of credulity that will especially concern us here—and the associated questions about believing counsel and giving counsel that subsequently arise in the tale.

That husbands should not 'inquire' into what wives might do with (as it were) surplus sexual capacity is a viewpoint also jocularly argued by the Wife of Bath. Somewhere in the background are two traditional convergent ideas, capable of both positive and cynical application. One is that love is instinctively credulous. The lover (assumed male, in the case sarcastically envisaged at the end of the *Roman de la Rose*) is unwilling to believe that others will succeed with his mistress: 'no-one lightly suspects a beloved object'.[2] Another idea, stemming from Stoic commendation of indifference to actual or imagined insult or injury, is the suggestion that it is noble and magnanimous to transcend suspicion.[3] In 'The Franklin's Tale' Arveragus is perhaps represented exercising precisely such magnanimity in his refusal to speculate about any approaches to Dorigen in his absence: 'he noght entendeth to no swich matere' (v.1094–7). By contrast in 'The Miller's Tale' old John is introduced as a husband who clearly does not display the statutory husbandly credulity (which is, in any case, a sort of *knowing* credulity). Full of jealousy, he guards his wife closely and deems himself vulnerable to cuckoldry (I.3226). Of course his possessiveness is no safeguard against a seducer's plots; and that is partly because John cannot distinguish between when credulity is appropriate and when it is not. He is especially in a muddle over *Goddes pryvetee*, a muddle that discloses once again those slippery compromises that were perceptible between antique ethics and Christian morality and which are the subject of this book.

Chaucer's comic narrative engages, in fact, with a nexus of inconsistent moral and ethical commonplaces associated with trust, credulity, and counsel, which the many critical discussions of this tale's *pryvetee* motif have not fully recognized. For sure, it has been remarked that the injunction the Miller utters against inquiring into God's private business derives from standard doctrine holding that humans should accept their intellectual limitations in the face of divine mystery. A classic statement of this in the *Book of Vices and Virtues* explains how, thanks to the Spiritual Gift of *Scientia* or 'Cunnynge', the human reason is able to attain a proper relation to faith, defined as follows:

To beleue wel is whan a man bileueth sympeliche or sengeliche al that God comaunded and without to moche askynge and sechynge the counseil or pryuete of God and the deepnesses of his iugementes and highenesses of his gretnesses and the resounes and skilles of the sacramentes.[4]

The carpenter of the tale mutters an abbreviated elementary form of this—'Men sholde nat knowe of Goddes pryvetee' (I.3454)—when faced with the spectacle of Nicholas gaping crazily upwards in a pseudo-contemplative trance as the clerk embarks on his plot. The

---

[2] *RR*, 21630–7, trans. Horgan, p. 333; see also *RR*, 9695–9702, trans. Horgan, p. 149.

[3] This is a ubiquitous theme of Seneca, *De constantia*, summed up in the aphorism 'no wise man can receive either injury or insult' (II.1), *Moral Essays*, vol. 1, p. 51, and grounded in the virtue of 'magnanimitas' (XI.1), p. 81.

[4] *VV*, p. 150.

familiarity of the prohibition could be rehearsed from a wide number of sources.[5] God's simple word was to be respected without delving into it. People should learn to distinguish the strictly reserved business of divine prerogative from more 'open' categories of knowledge, as explained in a traditional way by the mystic Julian of Norwich. One category of understanding concerns what is necessary to our salvation, and this is 'opyn and clere and plentious'. The other category concerns what is extraneous to human salvation: it is 'our lords privy councell', and it is usually hidden and barred from humans because 'it longyth to the ryal lordship of God to have his privy councell in pece, and it longyth to his servant, for obedience and reverens, not to wel wetyn [not to know thoroughly] his conselye'.[6] By the end of the fourteenth century, clerical authority was beginning to be particularly anxious about those—especially women—who claimed access to God's privy counsels. It is not surprising that for Margery Kempe early in the fifteenth century, the question whether or not to 'give credence' to the 'prevy cownselys' seemingly bestowed by God on oneself was a high drama of serial doubt quashed by affirmation.[7]

Nicholas's great triumph, of course, is to make John suppress his own orthodox instincts on this matter. But after all 'Maister' Nicholas is a clerk, and some right was conceded to trained clerks to push inquiry further, to know all that can be known, on condition that they did not confuse the ordinary laity.[8] It only requires one imposing speech about the imminent apocalyptic flood allegedly revealed to clerk Nicholas by 'Cristes conseil' (1.3504), embroidered with strategic mystification where inspiration fails (as to the fate of John's servants, Nicholas 'wol nat tellen' *all* 'Goddes pryvetee', 1.3558), and John's imagination is overwhelmed.

---

[5] e.g. Ecclus. 3: 22. The author of *JW* states that the virtue of 'meknesse' should induce trust in God rather than a 'sekynge of resouns' concerning his word, p. 245; echoed in *VV*, p. 132; Hoccleve (with specific reference to Lollard debate about the Eucharist) reproves the 'presumpcion' of inquiry into God's business, which is 'hid': *Regiment*, 281–94, 330–71.

[6] Julian of Norwich, *A Revelation of Love*, ed. Marion Glasscoe (Exeter: Exeter University Press, 1976), ch. 30 (p. 31).

[7] *The Book of Margery Kempe*, ed. Barry Windeatt (Harlow: Pearson, 2000), 1.59 (pp. 281–4).

[8] Preachers 'schulde nought prechen to the lewyd peple the heyghe thingis and the preuyte of the godhed', according to the Longleat Friar quoted in H. Leith Spencer, *English Preaching in the Late Middle Ages* (Oxford: Clarendon Press, 1993), p. 46.

Over John's head, what the tale ingeniously exploits is the interface between the ethically aware person's appropriately analytical response to human advice, and the model Christian's properly unanalytical, uncritical response to divine mysteries. John has been brought up to cultivate simple faith rather than meddle in mysteries: 'blessed be alwey a lewed man / That noght but oonly his bileve kan!' (I.3455–6).[9] But his ability to find refuge in uneducated faith is vitiated by two things. One is that it is a faith quaintly mingled with superstitious folk gibberish; the other is the debilitating extent of his ignorance, for he has forgotten God's most important comment on the Noah deluge, which, if the carpenter could but remember it, was a promise never to repeat the event.

John is bamboozled because Nicholas's fiction of God's *pryvetee* is made to sound bewilderingly like familiar faith or *bileve*. Moreover, 'John' happens to be the propitious name for someone destined to receive divine secrets. St John the Evangelist was identified rather emphatically as the disciple to whom Christ displayed special grace by 'schowyng of hys pryuetee'. Both the book of the Apocalypse itself of which St John is the assumed author, and various miracles performed by St John, were said to be the result of 'reuelacyon of the priuetye of God'. This association between the name 'John' and divine secrets provides one of several witty substrata to the tale's comedy.[10]

In any case Nicholas presents himself as a clerkly adviser, cajoling John to accept his 'good conseil' in such a crisis (I.3527–31). Within the blarney about counsel, Chaucer is reminding readers of standard ethical protocol on advice and on what degree of credulity to bring to it. If 'simple belief' is what Christian morality lays down in relation to God's law, an opposite wariness is what ethical wisdom lays down as an appropriate response to other people's advice. Immediately following the recommendation quoted above from the *Book of Vices and Virtues* not to ask any questions about the counsel of God, comes a recommendation (without the slightest recognition of inconsistency) to follow an altogether more wary middle way when responding to human counsel:

---

[9] On this see Alan J. Fletcher, 'The Faith of a Simple Man: Carpenter John's Creed in the "Miller's Tale"', in his *Preaching and Politics in Late Medieval England* (Dublin: Four Courts Press, 1998), pp. 239–48.

[10] On Christ's 'pryuyte' dispensed to St John, see *Mirk's Festial*, pp. 31–4.

Wel bileuyng is that a man leue not to soone ne to late ne to euery wight ne to no wight, for bothe that on and that other is euel and vice, and Senek seith.[11]

This nugget of wisdom had proverbial status. It was familiar to Chaucer, as demonstrated by Pandarus's adaptation of it when trying to persuade lovelorn Troilus to trust him. It is equally a vice, Pandarus protests, to mistrust everyone or believe everyone: but there is a middle way whereby trusting *some* people can be a demonstration of loyalty.[12] Clearly Pandarus perceives himself to be working against the grain of circumspection here, however, and circumspection more than readiness to trust was what ethical tradition most urged. Thus, the same *Vices and Virtues* treatise returns to the folly of credulity and the necessity of wariness in a section on Counsel as the fifth Gift of the Spirit. The standard injunction to do nothing without good counsel means, we are told, always being ready to ask advice, though preferably not from the young. However, it also means pondering critically, with *auysement*, whatever counsel is received, and not too lightly believing the word of one or two people:

For Senek seith that a wise man wole examyne his counseil and leeue it not to lightliche. For he that leeueth lightliche fynt alday who bigileth hym.[13]

Seneca does indeed strenuously urge the danger of credulity and the necessity of circumspection, particularly in his essay *On Anger*, with which Chaucer seems to have been familiar. Seneca sees anger as being the consequence of facile response to apparent injuries. But appearances are often misleading: 'credulity is a source of very great mischief'.[14] This emphasis was channelled to the Middle Ages also through accounts of prudence, as in the pseudo-Senecan ethical piece called the *Formula vitae honestae*. Here we are told that the characteristic of the prudent person 'is to ponder counsels, not to fall readily into false conclusions by over-hasty credulity'. Delay and reflection are necessary to disentangle truth and falsehood, which often look like each other. But a prudent person 'can't be deceived'.[15]

---

[11] *VV*, pp. 150–1.

[12] *TC*, 1.687–90, a commonplace, ultimately from Seneca, *Ep.* 3; see *Riv.* note to these lines.

[13] *VV*, p. 189.

[14] 'Plurimum mali credulitas facit': Seneca, *De ira*, ii.22.2–24.1, *Moral Essays*, vol. 1, pp. 215–17.

[15] *PL*, 72.23–4 (my translation). Boccaccio, drawing on Seneca, represents the prudent person weighing another's words 'like a mental watchtower': Giovanni Boccaccio, *The Fates of Illustrious Men*, trans. Louis Brewer Hall (New York, 1965), p. 24 (*De casibus*, i.ix.3–5).

In Christian thought the properties of prudence are replicated besides in analysis of the gift of *Scientia* or 'Cunnynge' (knowledge or understanding). It is the gift that ideally enables people to see clearly into things all around them; it makes the heart 'so bryght on alle sides that he may not be deceuyed ne bigiled of no man'.[16] But Chaucer's carpenter is not prudent and he has no understanding; his 'wit' is 'rude' (1.3227). In fact, he is pointedly characterized in the story as prey to superstition and to *affeccioun*, a quality glossed as 'emotion' in standard editions. Almost certainly Chaucer is thinking of a classic assumption that human reason is constantly in danger of being overwhelmed by passions (*affectus*). The danger in these *affectus*, according to Seneca, lies not just in being 'moved' by chance 'impressions' presented to the mind, but in actually 'surrendering' to them and acting on them.[17] In those whose minds are not under their own control, the *affectus* are often deeply resistant: or, as 'The Miller's Tale' puts it, 'which a greet thyng is affeccioun!' (1.3611).[18] Thanks to emotion and ignorance and naïve faith John fails to observe the rules on advice that we have noted: he does not 'examyne' Nicholas's 'counseil', he believes it too 'lightliche' and becomes exposed to one 'who bigileth hym'.[19]

Nicholas, for his part, creatively exploits the role of adviser. He perverts the normative social duty that everybody should help neighbours with advice. (It is a principle of 'rightwysnesse' or Justice 'to yelde to thi neyghbour that thou owyst hym, that is, loue & good counseyl'.)[20] Doubtless Chaucer has partly in mind the issue of institutional clerical control, able to exploit through rhetoric the credulity of the simple and unlettered. This phenomenon had been brought provocatively to notice in fourteenth-century Italian culture, and it had been taken up by (among others) Boccaccio.[21] Boccaccio, as Michaela Grudin observes, 'returns repeatedly and directly to the issue of credulity',[22]

---

[16] *VV*, p. 149.   [17] *De ira*, II.3.1, *Moral Essays*, vol. 1, pp. 170–3
[18] *De beneficiis*, II.18.4; see also a comment at II.14.1 that humans often desire what is actually harmful to them because judgement is obstructed by *affectus*: *Moral Essays*, vol. 3, pp. 86–9. The difficulty of controlling the *affectus* or 'passions' is discussed in *Ep.* 71.37; 75.12; 85.6–12; and 92.8.
[19] Admonitions against hasty credulity were also characteristic of the wisdom books in the Bible: see e.g. Prov. 14: 15 and Ecclus. 33: 3.
[20] *JW*, pp. 287–8.
[21] Michaela Paasche Grudin, 'Credulity and the Rhetoric of Heterodoxy: From Averroes to Chaucer', *ChauR*, 35 (2000–1), 204–22.
[22] Ibid., p. 212.

both in narratives of satirical exploitation in the *Decameron*, and in passages of specific ethical comment elsewhere. Boccaccio incorporates a whole excursus 'De credulitate' in the *De casibus illustrorum virum.* He highlights both the folly and danger of credulity. 'Nothing is more foolish than a credulous mind'; for the 'deceptive tongue believed too easily' brings down the credulous and can destroy cities and nations.[23]

Of course in 'The Miller's Tale', the tale positions the reader to relish rather than frown upon Nicholas's intellectual control and his breathtakingly impudent stratagem. Conversely, whatever touches of warmth and solicitude appear in the dull-witted carpenter tend to be contaminated by his lumbering conceit. Nicholas inevitably exerts strong narrative appeal as inventor of the comic script that John is persuaded to act out. The imaginative appeal of this clerkish script is enhanced by its brilliant parody of biblical morality: Noah's flood, that was intended to eliminate the world's promiscuity, is redesigned in order to supply a triumphant night of adultery, supplanting 'Noah', as it were, in his own bed.

I am emphasizing the centrality of Nicholas's intellectual reach for two reasons. One is that Alisoun has too often wrongly been read as the crucial centre and symbol of this fabliau's meaning, whereas her presence and contribution, in comparison with the clerk's, carry certain important limitations. The other reason is that Nicholas lapses from his prudential foresight in the plot when he tries to imitate Alisoun, and thereby makes both of them vulnerable to a quasi-apocalyptic catastrophe.

Alisoun is a female figure about whom critics (especially male critics) have enjoyed writing. They have responded delightedly to the associations with attractive natural phenomena that are invoked within her description—milk, apples, sweet pear-tree, swallow, sheep, calf, colt, primrose. Without denying that the passage is full of affectionate buoyant zest (she is not only like a colt, but 'wynsynge' like one; not just tall, but 'long as a mast' (1.3263–4)), we might remind ourselves just how absolutely the description fixes her as a physical sex-object suited for male consumption or handling, whether casually by lord or in wedlock by yeoman. She is a shiny new coin ready for circulation, fruit ready to taste, a 'blisful' sight to see: and sight is accordingly

[23] Boccaccio, *Fates of Illustrious Men*, trans. Hall, pp. 24–6 (*De casibus*, 1.ix).

invited, down and up her body, concluding at those shoes laced suggestively 'on hir legges hye' just as our inspection began at the pleats that cover her thighs. For all the rush of descriptive adrenalin, the description creates for Alisoun no sense of a person with any talents, no sense of what she does in the workaday life of which the reader catches one glimpse (I.3311). She exists absolutely as a sensuous conglomeration, a creature of animal energy joyously decked out in fetching clothes: a brilliant evocation of scarcely contained vigour, a tour de force of burlesque rhetorical medieval feminine description, and no implied function other than availability. And it is all done with a dash of condescension that notes the flirtatious eye of 'swich a wenche', the purse at her middle, the coin-like shine, the overdone brooch.

Nicholas, by contrast, is defined in terms of accomplishments. There is condescension here too, at his pride in wooing skills and at his exaggerated spicy 'sweetness'. There is also the implicit comfortable superiority of a broadly read clerk (Chaucer) over the beginner, a student who has veered off the curriculum into the charms of astrology and the lure of weather forecasting and other prognostication. Yet in this the description nevertheless inscribes the youth's skills. It focuses on the books he uses, the astrological equipment carefully laid out, and the psaltery on which he accompanies himself when he sings. Here is intellect and talent to be reckoned with (competitive ones in fact), as the development of the Noah's Flood play-within-a-tale is to confirm.

The gender contrast implied here is one that ought to be more objectively viewed by critics, and its implications ought to be more carefully tracked through 'The Miller's Tale'. Anne Laskaya is one who has noticed the contrast, for she discusses how it inscribes the tale's exploration of subject and object gender positions.[24] I would give more emphasis to moral and ethical currents in the gender contrast, but Laskaya's approach is illuminating so far as it goes. Her subject/object contrast can be substantiated, for instance, in the *rime riche* of the lines that herald Nicholas's 'wooing' of Alisoun. He accosts her with the alleged wiliness of his male profession—'As clerkes ben ful subtile and ful queynte'—whereas she is not 'wily' in that mental sense but simply *has* the secreted wily body part he desires: 'And prively he caughte hire by the queynte' (I.3275–6). Alisoun is duly won over by Nicholas and has only a small scripted part to play in the clerk's fiction, a part mainly

[24] Laskaya, *Chaucer's Approach to Gender*, pp. 90–1.

narrated through reported speech (1.3412–18, 3604–6). She is allowed to speak only four pre-arranged lines, appealing to John to 'save' their lives (1.3607–10).

In considering her subsequent role we should keep in mind the emergent antithesis between 'intellectual' clerk, his mind dwelling on the future outcome of devious planning, and sprightly sensual 'wenche'. That contrast is not lodged in the tale to create a proto-Laurentian tribute to untrammelled Nature in antithesis to intellectual or social artifice. In so arguing, I shall diverge here significantly from much received opinion, which is extravagantly and even patronizingly committed to the hypothesis that the tale, in its natural and animal imagery, constructs a completely morality-free zone. V. A. Kolve is among the subtler proponents of this view.[25] Thus according to Kolve this is a tale in which 'potentially moral notations [...] are not allowed to signify' (p. 164). The figurative context of 'a country landscape' of 'young animals—charming, instinctual, untamed', endows the characters with energies seeming to originate 'outside of any moral system' (pp. 165, 170). Kolve trawls encyclopedic lore to affirm that the coltish animal spirits of Alisoun yield 'no lesson' because they express the sheer energy of youth (pp. 177, 181). It is a view of the tale that surely inclines towards academic sentimentalism: human actions are deemed as free of moral meaning and 'weighty consequence' as 'those of the birds, beasts, and flowers of the English countryside' (p. 215).[26]

One cue for a reading less sentimentally favourable to volatile teen-age Alisoun actually lurks in the negative insinuation in her 'colt-like' prancing. This comparison is repeated from her initial description ('Wynsynge ... as a joly colt', 1.3263) to the later description of her rebounding from Nicholas's first opportunistic grab (1.3282) like a colt in the 'trave'—usually glossed as 'a frame for holding a horse', perhaps to be shod. But the colt was used in moral discourse as a symbol of the adolescent will, that requires taming once and for all. By analogy moral-ists urged that a tight hold should be kept over youngsters, to discipline

---

[25] *Chaucer and the Imagery of Narrative* (London: Arnold, 1984).

[26] Cooper continues this line of thought, maintaining that the association with 'spring and youth [...] deflects moral comment towards a reading of [Alisoun] as part of the natural resurgence of the world': *The Canterbury Tales*, p. 211. Mark Miller claims that the Miller *means* his tale to be 'a celebration of the blessed natural state of the human animal' in a world of plenitude, only to disclose problematic philosophical consequences of 'the attempt to think this way': *Philosophical Chaucer: Love, Sex, and Agency in the 'Canterbury Tales'* (Cambridge: Cambridge University Press, 2004), pp. 44, 50.

them to keep their chastity and avoid bad company that might lure them into 'harlotrie' and sexual gropings.[27] To quote Gower, 'What the colt receives in training will last it all its life'; hence 'the lechery to which a young woman becomes accustomed in youth will last her into old age. The young woman will take delight in wantonness as long as she can.'[28]

Alisoun escapes some of the moralizing force of such analogy in so far as she is a 'joly' colt whose friskiness expresses a healthy bounce proper to youth. Nevertheless in constructing her Chaucer may come closer to a dismissive view of recalcitrant sexualized female 'animality' than has mostly been recognized.[29] One critic who does suspect this is Elaine Tuttle Hansen, who remarks of Alisoun that 'her animality is all there is; it is not worth examining a woman's moral or spiritual qualities, the tale implies'.[30] The tale is doubtless not as dismissive as is Seneca who, as we saw in the Introduction, writes off a woman as a wild and imprudent animal, 'unrestrained in her passions'.[31] Yet while Alisoun's contribution to the plot is not subjected to hostile comment, it contrasts absolutely, and in a way suggestive of the *inprudens animal*, with Nicholas's carefully orchestrated plan.

How should we describe her contribution? When she and Nicholas are together in John's bed while John snores in his improvised dinghy in the loft, exhausted by his exertions in fulfilling Nicholas's boat-preparation scheme, Alisoun notoriously decides to deal with an interruption by rival suitor Absolon by offering him, through the dark window space, her arse to kiss. This is a sublime moment of grossness, laid on as a jest for Nicholas (and the reader) to relish. Yet, if we look backwards

---

[27] See the discussion of Chastity in *VV*, pp. 243–4: 'for as men seith that techeth a colte in dauntyng tyme, that is whan he cometh first to honde, right as thou wolte haue hym for euere-more after, the whiles he lasteth'; the colt analogy is similarly used at p. 200. The importance of taming a colt once and for all had the force of rhyming proverb in French: 'quaprent poulain a donteure / tenir le veut tant comme il dure': *VV*, p. 310, n. to 200/5–7.

[28] *Mirour de l'Omme*, 9445 ff., trans. Wilson, p. 130 (in a section concerning Wantonness, the 'fifth daughter of lechery').

[29] Another knowing hint comes through the remark that 'she hadde a likerous eye' (1.3244): cf. ' "impudici cordis impudicus oculus est nuncius"—the leccherous eyghe is the signe of an unclene herte', *JW*, p. 158.

[30] Hansen, *Chaucer and the Fictions of Gender*, p. 225. This hardly warrants Hansen's ensuing argument that Alisoun's sexuality is blurred with 'dirt' and anality. On the other hand Janette Richardson is representative of many critics in uncritically assuming the animality to be positive: *Blameth Nat Me: A Study of Imagery in Chaucer's Fabliaux* (The Hague: Mouton, 1970), p. 160.

[31] *De constantia*, xiv.1, *Moral Essays*, vol. 1, pp. 88–9.

in medieval culture, a story about a woman who bared her behind in court is used in misogynous discourse to justify the exclusion of women from public speaking. A certain Cafurnia was supposed to have exposed herself in this way when pleading a lawsuit; and thus she disqualified women from judicial office ever after. So claimed the thirteenth-century misogynist Matheolus and his fourteenth-century translator Jean Le Fèvre in the *Lamentations of Matheolus*.[32]

Whether Chaucer knew this particular gem from Le Fèvre or not, the analogy helps us to sense the demeaning implication of a 'Miller's Tale' moment which criticism usually evaluates with unqualified enthusiasm, for its brilliant demolition of Absolon's fastidious love-posturing. The brilliance should not blind us to the potentially misogynous element within the hilarity of the gesture. Moreover if that misogynous element is agreed, we would need to consider what is implied when, at Absolon's return, Nicholas thinks he will improve the jest, resorting to the same naked-arse trick in Absolon's face, with the added insult of a thunderous fart.

Nicholas has committed himself to detailed forward planning in his elaborate adaptation of the Noah story to the carpenter's household. There is a hint, it is true, that his foresight reaches a premature vanishing point in that it tends to vagueness concerning what lies beyond the hypothetical achievement of the projected night with Alisoun. He tells John to equip each of the impromptu tub-boats with provisions sufficient just for a day: 'fy on the remenant!', for the flood will subside 'the nexte day' (1.3551–4). From the Miller's use of the same diction in the headlink to describe matters best not looked into ('Of the remenant nedeth nat enquere', 1.3166) we recognize that Nicholas, sniggering carelessly about that next day, is being optimistically negligent. In this respect he is less in overall control than appears: he only half-sustains the ethical principle that 'if you want to be prudent, stretch your vision into the future and lay out in your mind everything that can happen'.[33]

Worse than this, in the relaxation of post-coital lassitude, Nicholas proceeds to deviate from his plan (such as it is) when he attempts

---

[32] For the whole passage see *Lamentations*, II.177–200, trans. in Blamires, Pratt, and Marx (eds.), *Woman Defamed and Woman Defended*, pp. 183–4.

[33] *Formula vitae honestae*, PL, 72.24. I do not think it matters that, by the strictest standards, only 'false' prudence could be found in such a plan as Nicholas's in any case: on *prudentia falsa* see John Burrow, 'The Third Eye of Prudence', in *Medieval Futures: Attitudes to the Future in the Middle Ages*, ed. J. A. Burrow and Ian P. Wei (Woodbridge: Boydell, 2000), pp. 37–48 (pp. 40–1).

to join in the arse-mischief. *And* he deviates in a way that, as we have implied in discussing Alisoun's part, could be deemed to lower him from a 'masculine' rationality to an imprudent 'female' animality. Alisoun's trick has already endangered Nicholas's plan, which did not accommodate negotiations with a thwarted midnight serenader. And now Nicholas himself, by giving in to the temptation to double the physical insult to the Cloten-like intruder, abandons foresight altogether. In the consequent unforeseen attack he endures from Absolon's branding iron is a configuration that has various sexual implications depending on how you read it—but among which is certainly that of a sodomitic act. Nicholas lets out his famous scream for water, whence the flood materializes in the carpenter's mind, and the fabric of the clerk's ingenious but makeshift plan collapses in a heap. A Noah's flood of the imagination has been triggered (like its prototype) by a sequence of sexual antics increasingly deviant from what the church would have called 'natural'.

Besides the complications of sex and gender arising here, which we shall consider in Chapter 3, there flows from this comic reversal an important consequence for the kind of statement the tale finally makes about human intellect. Nicholas's foresight has not been (can anybody's be?) up to the standard set by ethical instruction. The commonplace standard is, 'Let nothing be "sudden" for you, but see it coming at your leisure. The prudent person does not have cause to say, "I had not thought this would happen." '[34] We are accustomed to scoff at the arrant miscalculations of Absolon, whose itching mouth combined with his deductions from John's absence cause him to mis-project a scenario of amorous kissing with Alisoun; but providence trips up *both* clerks. Human foresight and 'deeming' is hilariously demonstrated to be way short of genuine providential planning.

It is worth emphasizing this because an influential view articulated by Marsha Siegel holds that the tale dedicates itself to physical and psychological causality, and celebrates the power of human intelligence to comprehend and manipulate that causality—by contrast with the metaphysically enigmatic world of 'The Knight's Tale' where all is full of chronic unpredictability. Siegel eventually has to concede that the

---

[34] *Formula vitae honestae*, PL, 72.24. See also Seneca, *De beneficiis*, IV.34.4: the wise man anticipates; he 'has presupposed that something might happen to thwart his designs'; he 'weighs uncertain outcome against his certainty of purpose', *Moral Essays*, vol. 3, pp. 276–7.

causality of the denouement in 'The Miller's Tale', while explicable, is not actually predictable.[35] But against her overall emphasis, I am arguing that the tale demands interpretation as a witty demonstration of the *limitations* of human capacity to calculate the future.[36]

'The Miller's Tale' plays out a drama of providence. Although the audience is granted insight into the causality produced by human actions in the tale, what this insight demonstrates is the impossibility for humans to anticipate or match God's secret plans. That, moreover, is precisely the deduction that would have been primarily associated in Chaucer's mind with the concept of both deluge and lifeboats because (though scholarship routinely neglects this important point) in the *Roman de la Rose* the question of human independence and moral responsibility in relation to providence and fate is elaborated precisely through meditation on the limited human capacity for predicting heaven-ordained floods or for escaping from them by strategically preparing ships in which to flee.[37] The relevant passage is a crucial spur to Chaucer's conception of 'The Miller's Tale'. The connection offers another reason for qualifying the Kolve-esque view that the tale is hermetically sealed, 'uncomplicated by transcendent idea or ideal' (pp. 214–15).

In the *Roman* the personification, Nature, maintains that there is wisdom in using a ship to escape a flood when forewarned. The context is a discussion of the efficacy of free will, despite the astrological influences that 'incline' individual behaviour. The will's power to resist such forces is compared with the human power to prepare for catastrophe. 'If we could predict what heaven had in store for us, we could do something about it.' If humans knew there was to be a flood they could run to higher ground 'or build ships strong enough to save their lives when the great flood came', like Deucalion and Pyrrha. These 'acted wisely in thus using a ship to escape the flood; in the same way, anyone who was forewarned of such a flood could escape it'. Similarly one could plan to counter the extremities of all sorts of weather.

[35] Marsha Siegel, 'What the Debate is and Why it Founders in Fragment A of *The Canterbury Tales*', *SP*, 82 (1985), 1–24.

[36] In this perspective the tale can be aligned with *Troilus and Criseyde*, if Monica McAlpine is right in her conclusion about that poem's attitudes to the future, i.e. that it manifests at the same time an 'extraordinary interest' in preventive anticipation of future disaster, and a fear that foreknowledge may 'distort ethical judgment': 'Criseyde's Prudence', *SAC*, 25 (2003), 199–224 (p. 224).

[37] *RR*, 17549–17620, trans. Horgan, pp. 271–2.

However (and here Nature somewhat muddles the point of her digression), 'without some miraculous vision or oracle sent by God [. . .] no one unfamiliar with astronomy' and all its multifarious complexities could anticipate such natural disasters so accurately as to plan for them.[38] Nature reflects, then, on the tremendous reach of human strategic planning at the same time as she admits how the taxing specialized science involved, along with its inexact results, erode the power of foresight. Chaucer's 'Miller's Tale' magnificently embodies and dramatizes all this. The tale confirms the clouded foresight even of a student of astrology, with a reputation for storm-forecast, whose plans have precisely been to contrive shipping in which to 'escape' a 'flood' of whose coming he has hypothetically been forewarned by divine communication.

Moreover, the centrality of the 'flood' in the tale takes us to probable further dimensions of providence in this narrative that have gone unnoticed. Since the plot invokes the idea of global deluge it invites description in terms of pseudo-eschatological or pseudo-apocalyptic design. This apocalypticism is reinforced, I think, in two ways.

First, is there an allusion, through the concept of the deluge, to the Last Judgement? The faithful were often reminded that the universal Doomsday would be preceded by fourteen days of cataclysmic terrifying signs. These would commence with a flood: the sea was to rise forty cubits higher than any hill, though it would remain standing, towering within its shorelines, rather than immersing the land. On the 'second day' this uncanny sea-flood, portending the end of the world, would collapse (a notion that assumes particular interest in view of Nicholas's claim that the Oxford deluge will subside around Prime on its second day, 1.3553–4). The prophecy of this doomsday flood is rehearsed in pastoral writings at the end of the fourteenth century.[39]

Second, there is another way in which apocalypticism is invoked— precisely through the text's harping on God's *pryvetee*. Here we need to remember that what is now called the Book of Revelations, some-times referred to simply as the 'Apocalips' in Middle English, was just as often referred to as the 'Book of God's Pryvetees'. It is so named in the treatise *Dives and Pauper*, for instance, as also in other moral treatises and sermons, notably (three times) in a sermon contemporary

---

[38] *RR*, 17663–72, trans. Horgan, p. 273.
[39] See e.g. *Mirk's Festial*, p. 2, and *Dives and Pauper*, viii.14, ed. Barnum, vol. 1, pt 2, p. 247.

with the *Tales* ascribed to Thomas Wimbledon.[40] *Pryvetees* and apoca-
lypse were, then, somewhat interchangeable terms. It is worth pausing
over the Wimbledon sermon, in that it expresses the apocalypti-
cism of the age, harping on biblical nightmares about the decline
of man and the end of the world. Wimbledon computes the date
of the coming of the 'abomination', i.e. Antichrist, as 1400, and
supplies a date of composition of 1387 by adding that this is just
under twelve and a half years ahead.[41] Like John Gower, embark-
ing on his *Confessio* at about this time, Wimbledon sees around
himself the tokens of the collapse of the world as forecast in Mat-
thew's gospel.

While the apocalyptic strain was intermittently heard throughout
the Middle Ages, it seems to have become suddenly more urgent in
the Ricardian period. Yet Chaucer, at least so far as explicit allusion is
concerned, is something of an exception, and the scarcity of apocalyptic
material in his writings has been discussed by Russell Peck—though
mainly with specific reference to material from the Book of Daniel.[42]
It is a very significant measure of the difference between Gower and
Chaucer that the only memorable invocation of the idea of eschaton in
Chaucer's poetry is his burlesque of the deluge.[43] In 'The Miller's Tale'
the poet reveals himself as interested in apocalypse—in the ultimate
judgemental forces hidden in God's design—only as a comic measure
of the weakness of human foresight. Nicholas the not-so-arch-schemer
is caught out by a witty providence that cuts short and transcends his
own little game with *Goddes pryvetee*. Chaucer here recognizes the sense
of apocalyptic crisis touted by others writing at the time, but refuses to
join credulously in their hysteria. His poetry does engage with personal
judgement, personal destiny in heaven or hellfire, as in Pardoner's and

---

[40] *Wimbledon's Sermon, 'Redde rationem villicationis tue': A Middle English Sermon
of the Fourteenth century*, ed. Ione Kemp Knight (Pittsburgh, Pa.: Duquesne University
Press, 1967); see especially the final section on the 'vniuersal' reckoning of Doomsday. Six
of the sixteen extant MSS are reckoned 'late 14th century or *c*.1400': see Nancy H. Owen,
'Thomas Wimbledon's Sermon: "Redde racionem villicacionis tue" ', *Mediaeval Studies*,
28 (1966), 176–97 (p. 176, n. 3).

[41] *Wimbledon's Sermon*, p. 116.

[42] Russell A. Peck, 'John Gower and the Book of Daniel', in *John Gower: Recent
Readings*, ed. R. F. Yeager (Kalamazoo: Western Michigan University, 1989), pp. 159–87
(p. 165).

[43] I am thinking of reference to Doomsday, as opposed to references to punishment
in hell (of which there are many). Arguably, however, Fame's judgements in *The House
of Fame* constitute a parody of the Last Judgement.

Friar's 'Tales', but it does not engage solemnly with universal doom. He prefers to weave stories around prudence and the folly of credulity.

Rebellion against Counsel: 'The Merchant's Tale'

'The Merchant's Tale' is most often analysed in relation to the Clerk's and Franklin's 'Tales' as an exploration of marriage. In the present book some analysis of its exploration of ideas of pleasure and sexuality will be found in Chapter 3. Here it is juxtaposed with 'The Miller's Tale' instead, in order to draw attention to further ethical dimensions of Chaucer's sustained interest in credulity and delusion.

John the carpenter is not alone in the *Canterbury Tales* in 'falling readily into false conclusions by over-hasty credulity', to recall our earlier quotation on the dangers of credulity. Right at the end of 'The Merchant's Tale', the blind old knight January is given back his sight just in time to watch with horror as his wife May and his squire Damyan copulate in a tree. There ensues an outrageous comedy of vindication as May plucks from nowhere (or from her patroness Proserpyne) the sensationally implausible explanation that under best medical advice she was 'struggling' with a man in a tree to *make her husband see* (iv.2374). To her husband's protest that what he saw was Damyan's penetration of her, she responds that the cure cannot yet be complete: 'Ye han som glymsyng, and no parfit sighte' (iv.2383). As January's certainty falters, May builds on her brainwave. Whatever he thinks he saw, she says that in recovering from blindness he is just like someone waking from sleep, who does not immediately focus properly. His sight may therefore 'beguile' him for a couple of days (long enough for some other sexual escapade to be got away with perhaps). Let January be careful, she concludes:

> Ful many a man weneth to seen a thyng
> And it is al another than it semeth.
> He that mysconceyveth, he mysdemeth.
>
> (iv.2408–10)

Other than noting the possible sexual mischievousness of *mysconceyveth* in the coital context, editors are silent about the resonance of these lines, but to me it seems beyond doubt that they are a further evolution of Chaucer's fascination with the Stoic advocacy of prudential wariness. To prove that we are in the territory of inherited ideas on credulity and prudence, a passage that we have already glanced into from the *Rule for Honourable Living* is worth rehearsing at length:

The characteristic of a prudent person is [...] not to fall readily into false conclusions by over-hasty credulity. Do not make deductions about uncertain matters; suspend your judgement. Don't affirm anything unproven, since not everything that looks true actually is, and similarly very often what first looks incredible is not necessarily false. Indeed, truth frequently bears the appearance of a lie, and a lie concealed under the appearance of truth. Just as a friend displays a heavy expression and a flatterer displays a soothing one, so too truth may assume a likeness under which it may deceive or creep.[44]

While the convergence here with the tale's focus on counsel, flatterers, truth, and falsehood is striking, the immediate point is that May is brilliantly manipulating the central adage. Truth (she agrees with Stoic tradition) may be other than superficially appears; but she is brazenly applying this to a situation in which on the contrary truth, in the sense of what is going on in front of January's eyes, is *exactly* what it seems.

Seneca as we have mentioned was quite preoccupied with such problems, and he engaged with them in terms of both internal and external deception. Internal or self-deception he expressed in the metaphor of a 'blockage of the eye'. Showering somebody with precepts was no use, he maintained, if they had an inadequate grasp of good and evil. Such a person needed not 'precepts' in order to 'see', but more radical treatment for the 'curing of eyesight'. In this extended metaphor of vision—rather pertinent to January's case—the role of precepts is supplementary to the substantive cure. Only when the cataract of fundamental ethical ignorance is peeled away might precepts help with the process of adjusting the perception to bright daylight. Precepts may also help someone who theoretically understands ethical obligations, but does not 'see with sufficient clearness' what they are.[45] Seneca was equally concerned with external deception. He warned that because falsehood can have the look (*species*) of truth, we are easily misled into becoming angry with those who are innocent. He thought suspicion was such a virus that ideally we should 'believe only what is thrust under our eyes and becomes unmistakable'.[46]

In January's garden, all this is turned topsy-turvy. The truth is unmistakably beheld under the eyes, and it incites anger, which is

---

[44] *Formula vitae honestae*, *PL*, 72.23–4 (my translation).
[45] *Ep.* 94, *passim*, but esp. paragraphs 18 and 32, *Epistulae*, vol. 3, pp. 22–3, 32–3.
[46] *De ira*, II.22.2–4 and 24.1–2, *Moral Essays*, vol. 1, pp. 215, 217–19.

promptly parried on the basis that the eyes only half saw, and that the viewer has believed appearances true that were false (except that they were true). We are perhaps in the realms of the opinion of the Jealous Husband of the *Roman de la Rose*, that men seem often to view women with 'disordered vision' so that lies cannot be distinguished from truth, sophistry cannot be unravelled.[47]

What would Seneca have advised? Not much. At one point he confronts the problem of knowing whether someone's expression of gratitude for a favour might be only a deceitful semblance of the real thing. The appearance in which we 'trust' (*credidimus*) may be deceptive. Seneca can only shrug. If there is nothing else to guide opinion, then we shall have to ponder these unreliable 'traces' of truth as best we can and—the watchword of Stoic caution—not be too hasty in believing. We shall have to be content with the truth so far as we can determine it on best evidence.[48] In any case he knew that 'seeing properly' was as contingent on the sight of the viewer as on the nature of the object viewed. Something straight that is half submerged in water can look bent or fragmented to the human eye, he observed: 'it matters not only what you see, but with what eyes you see it'.[49]

Senecan determination to persevere nevertheless in trying to see truth and in making wary deduction despite the odds contrasts significantly with 'The Merchant's Tale''s preoccupation with self-delusion and chronically flawed vision of all sorts.[50] Delusion, sight, and blindness in this narrative have been much explored by critics, so there is no need for me to dwell on many of the nuances. January's physical blindness, afflicting him after years of sexual indulgence and a hasty ameliorative marriage, is rhetorically presented as a dramatic reversal of fortune. However, quite apart from the medieval medical opinion that too much sexual activity might drain a man's vigour to the point of literally causing blindness,[51] January's affliction cries out to be read also as the physical

[47] *RR*, 8885–8900, trans. Horgan, p. 137.

[48] *De beneficiis*, IV.34.1–2, *Moral Essays*, vol. 3, pp. 274–5.

[49] *Ep.* 71.24, *Epistulae*, vol. 2, p. 89.

[50] For a recent account see Angela Lucas, 'The Mirror in the Marketplace: Januarie Through the Looking Glass', *ChauR*, 33 (1998–9), 123–45 (esp. pp. 138–40). On the tale's power to lure even its readers into self-deluding complacency, see Jay Schleusner, 'The Conduct of the *Merchant's Tale*', *ChauR*, 14 (1979–80), 237–50.

[51] Lechery 'diminishes the strength of the body' and 'blinds the clear eye': Gower, *Mirour*, 9685 ff., trans. Wilson, p. 133; and see Danielle Jacquart and Claude Thomasset, *Sexuality and Medicine in the Middle Ages* (Cambridge: Polity Press, 1985), p. 56.

symptom of his mental and spiritual self-deception.[52] His blindness is in part the blindness to the reality of his own relationship with women, and perhaps the general blindness of both courtly idealization and misogyny.

But the blindness gestures also towards homiletic commonplaces about metaphorical blindness, for example that Christ came to heal and 'enlighten' not so much the blind in body as the blind in soul, those 'combryd wyth derkeness of synful lyuyng [. . .] and nomely [especially] of syn of lechery'.[53] Moralists argued that corporeal sight should be matched by the 'eye of discernment'. This is specifically urged in 'The Canon's Yeoman's Tale', in a context riddled with visual deception (a fraudulent alchemist using sleight of hand to deceive his victim by switching metals in the alchemical furnace). That tale warns, 'If that youre eyen kan nat seen aright, / Looke that youre mynde lakke noght his sight' (VIII.1418–19).[54] Moralists claimed that lechery in particular makes one 'blynd in mynde'.[55] To protect oneself there was 'Equite', a virtue associated with the eye of discernment: it fostered an individual's 'clere syght' in numerous ways, for instance by enabling one to see properly into one's own conscience.[56] Equite is linked with the spiritual Gift of Understanding, a gift which neither John the carpenter nor January the knight seems able to receive. Yet this is the gift they need, for it makes people 'wel to loke forth', removing impediments to inner sight so effectively that they 'seen al clerliche into here hertes and al aboute hem' with penetration and foresight. Furthermore, this gift is linked with the Beatitude 'Blessed are the clean in heart, for they shall see God': such bliss for the clean in heart actually begins in this world because 'thei ben clensed of derkenesse and errour' as regards the understanding, and of the contamination of sin as regards the will.[57]

Nothing could be pointedly further from January's pornographic mind and gross egotistical imperceptiveness than the clean heart and clear moral sight hailed in such doctrine. But the way in which Chaucer conceptualizes the old man's self-delusion does not place such doctrine

---

[52] In another perspective it is the objective correlative of the conventional 'blindness' of love.

[53] *Mirk's Festial*, p. 23 (emending 'leuyng' at line 30 of the edition to 'lyuyng' on the basis of the expression 'synful lyuyng' at line 31).

[54] For useful discussion of the eye of the mind, see Theresa Tinkle, 'The Heart's Eye: Beatific Vision in *Purity*', *SP*, 85 (1988), 451–70.

[55] *JW*, p. 162. [56] *JW*, pp. 273–4. [57] *VV*, pp. 148–9, 221, 270.

altogether in the foreground. Rather, he foregounds a misconception about what constitutes 'secure' happiness, as will be discussed in Chapter 3. January has indeed a 'glimpsing' (as May calls it), an intimation of beatitude and salvation, but the impediments to his vision cannot be removed by the return of mere physical vision.[58] What the tale suggests as the cause of January's misconception is that it is rooted in his egotistical resistance to the advice of others. While this possibly appears a self-explanatory feature of the tale, it is another case where Chaucer proves to be writing within a precise moral framework that warrants a little more scrutiny than it customarily receives.

In the Middle Ages the protocols of counsel were discussed with a zeal which may seem odd nowadays except in so far as they anticipate obsessions with interpersonal and consultation skills in modern management training. The prerequisites of giving advice were assumed to be of rather general application because counsel was thought a universal obligation: 'of conseil and of help been we dettours / Eche to other, by right of brethirhede', as Hoccleve writes.[59] Yet naturally the topic was especially rehearsed in 'Mirror for Princes' texts for rulers, such as Hoccleve's *Regiment* itself, which incorporates a whole section on counsel (4859 ff.). The emphases here are that rulers should listen to others without disclosing their own opinion; they should listen to the poor as well as the rich, and should test the reliability of advisers, eschewing flatterers and the greedy. One should act on the counsel of wise and preferably seasoned heads, not fools or the young.

Chaucer found himself reproducing a similar map of dos and don'ts about counsel in 'The Tale of Melibee'. When Prudence is faced with her husband Melibee's hastily convened meeting from which he draws support for his impetuous desire to avenge his family on those who have raided his household, she dictates (i.e. prudence dictates) that prior to consulting with advisers one should first appeal to God and second take counsel with oneself, eliminating any anger, greed, or impulsiveness from the heart and trying to determine one's own thoughts about a potential strategy. Prudence sets great store by not revealing such thoughts when approaching advisers. To disclose them to others is to give them a basis for responding flatteringly, merely mirroring the

---

[58] January's 'intimations' concerning spiritual life are the subject of Gertrude M. White, ' "Hoolynesse or Dotage": The Merchant's January', *PQ*, 44 (1965), 397–404.

[59] *Regiment*, 2486–7. For further comment on counsel as a necessary form of human benevolence, see Ch. 5 below.

strategy one has disclosed: for 'the conseillours of grete lordes [. . .] enforcen hem alwey rather to speken plesante wordes, enclynynge to the lordes lust, than wordes that ben trewe or profitable' (vii.1151). Then, in actually taking counsel, the priorities are to consult initially with a select group, identifying the wisest, truest, and most mature of one's friends as advisers, and rejecting the 'swete' words of flatterers in favour of the 'egre' or sharp words of the true friend (vii.1174–6). The final consideration is to reflect carefully on the advice received. Her own husband's botched attempt at consultation has failed Prudence's criteria so badly that she describes it as not 'conseil' but a 'moving of folly'. His counsellors have been an indiscriminate rabble, with whom he initiated counsel in an inexpedient state of anger and 'hastifnesse'. He has committed the cardinal error of revealing to them his own vengeful inclination, and he has not pondered the advice in a discriminating way (vii.1235–56).

'The Merchant's Tale' systematically invokes the same imperatives of prudential counsel by travestying them. When January calls advisers concerning his marriage plans, he announces at once his foregone conclusion—'th'effect of his entente' (iv.1398)—that he will marry and that he would like to hear no argument against it.[60] Concerning the actual choice of a wife he pretends to defer to the bride-hunting skills of his advisers, only to disclose his strong feelings in that matter too; he asserts his own odious preconceptions about the age and sex-appeal of a candidate necessary to ensure procreation, and he concludes by urging them to assent to his will. Moreover the protocols of deliberation here give way to precipitate haste, for his proposal is to marry 'al sodeynly' (iv.1409).

The stage has been set, and Chaucer obliges with a set piece of polarized advice. This part of the tale is somewhat protracted for modern taste, but I think we have to recognize both that counsel *mattered*, and that there was a corresponding medieval enthusiasm for such sagas of counselling. Probably Chaucer's elaboration of the episode also addresses the fact that the appointment of suitable advisers and the proper use of counselling machinery were notoriously sensitive matters in the time of Edward III's declining years and in much of Richard II's reign.[61] But in any case, 'counsel dramas' had been long cultivated

---

[60] Noted by Burnley, *Chaucer's Language and the Philosophers' Tradition*, pp. 49–52.

[61] See Judith Ferster, *Fictions of Advice: The Literature and Politics of Counsel in Late Medieval England* (Philadelphia: University of Pennsylvania Press, 1996).

by predecessors such as Chrétien de Troyes, who in *Yvain* constructs a rigged counsel, which is likewise called to 'discuss' a pre-decided marital intention, namely Laudine's intention to marry Yvain.[62]

In January's case, two figures emerge from a vague larger group to debate January's marriage, Placebo and Justinus. From the names alone, the reader's legitimate but not altogether accurate expectation is that one of them is going to be 'wrong' and the other 'right'. Certainly Placebo is a timeserver, a blatant caricature of the sort of flatterer who (as Prudence urges) will mirror his lord's inclinations once those have foolishly been revealed.[63] Placebo delivers unctuous platitudes about 'working by counsel', while not actually offering any on the grounds that January's own counsel is already so wonderful. Placebo extravagantly (though not without betraying sarcasm) epitomizes Prudence's caricature of the courtier bent on speaking 'plesante wordes, enclynynge to the lordes lust'.

In Justinus's speech we hear a countervailing warning against that impatient hastiness which January has displayed. Justinus five times repeats that January should 'avyse' himself, take careful thought, over such a momentous thing as marriage and the choice of a partner (IV.1524–31, 1555). Justinus's counsel of wariness focuses on the problem of determining the personality of the potential spouse, but his cynical vision reduces the process of finding a wife to something hardly more savoury than it is for January: given that one can't find any human or beast that 'trots' perfectly in every respect, says Justinus, one may have to be satisfied with more good 'thewes' (traits) than vices in a wife. The ambience is of horse purchasing, and there is no recognition that a vicious husband might be in prospect for the bride whose character is to be so scrutinized.[64]

More subtly, Justinus's ethic of prudential deliberation is undercut when he cites his own bitter experience of marrying a wife who was popularly held to be steadfast and meek but who, he claims, has been toil and trouble to himself. Such information either erodes the possibility that deliberation can really detect a prospective spouse's 'thewes', or alternatively proves that the good traits associated with her might not in

[62] *Yvain*, 2070–2147, trans. D. D. R. Owen, in Chrétien de Troyes, *Arthurian Romances* (London: Dent, 1987), pp. 309–10.

[63] For the stereotype to which this figure belongs, see *VV*, p. 58.

[64] That Justinus's views do not amount to 'the moral orthodoxy of the poem' is emphasized by J. D. Burnley, 'The Morality of *The Merchant's Tale*', *Yearbook of English Studies*, 6 (1976), 16–25 (p. 18).

themselves guarantee a harmonious marriage. Indeed the tale's healthy concern for sensible advice does not suppress a contrary hint that the verbiage of counsel may be beside the point. After all the guff the tale piles up about marriage—about what January's wife should or shall be, from tender veal to the bride celebrated in the Song of Solomon—May simply obtains what sexual solace she can find outside her unlovely bond.

Before that she has to be 'chosen', however, and we need to finish the saga of January's consultation. January's response to Justinus's strictures is explosive:

> 'Wel,' quod this Januarie, 'and hastow ysayd?
> Straw for thy Senek, and for thy proverbes!
> I counte nat a panyer ful of herbes
> Of scole-termes.'

> (IV.1566–9)

This has that ring of gutsy realism that readers prize in Chaucer, but at the same time it articulates an impatient rejection of counselling that was familiar and nameable in medieval moral discourse. January makes a pretence of preferring 'wiser' counsel than Justinus's but is in fact preferring his own opinion when he states that people wiser than Justinus have assented to his 'purpos' (IV.1569–71). Moralists called the type of dismissive arrogance shown by that (and by sweeping 'Senek' aside) 'rebellioun' or 'contrariouste'; this was manifested where someone oblivious to his own faults rebels against those who are trying to do him good: 'yif men chastise hym, he is wroth; yif any man counseileth hym, he leueth no man but his owne witt'.[65]

January is clearly in the state of imperviousness against which those 'precepts' Seneca himself speaks of—or what January calls 'proverbes' and 'scole-termes'—are useless unless a fundamental change of perception is achieved. The denouement of the tale enacts an officious attempt by a male 'guardian' power (Pluto) to effect such a change by restoring January's sight, countered by the efficacy of May's female guardian power (Proserpyne) in apparently explaining away the moment of 'truth' enabled by such retrieval of sight. The scenario finally identifies January as projecting a recalcitrant male fantasy that actually *does not wish to see* since it would rather go on cherishing its illusions.[66] 'You ought always

[65] *VV*, p. 18, and see also p. 66.
[66] A. C. Spearing comments on January's preference for a world of solipsistic sexual fantasy: *The Medieval Poet as Voyeur* (Cambridge: Cambridge University Press, 1993),

to believe [your sweethearts]' as the *Roman de la Rose* instructs male lovers, with a nod and a wink; 'believe them as you would a *paternoster*, and never abandon that belief'.[67]

Moreover, the implied gendering identifies May as embodiment of a form of instantaneous female quick-wittedness, something that according to the tale's foundational myth is to be characteristic of 'alle wommen after' (IV.2267) in order to reinforce the male fantasy. (Elsewhere it is Venus who stands as a similar foundational figure for gendered quick-wittedness. In the *Roman*, amidst a large meditation on credulity, on distorting mirrors, and sight problems, Venus trapped in bed with Mars epitomizes an alleged female ability to 'prove' the contrary of what has happened, to oblige a husband to 'believe that [adultery] never happened' or that if he had seen it with his own eyes 'his sight was dim and disturbed'.)[68]

It is worth noting that the mental resilience conferred on May by Proserpyne corresponds to a gender typology that Chaucer seems aware of, and which in various medieval contexts tended to distinguish female discernment from the full foresight of prudence. The stereotype is actually enunciated in *Troilus and Criseyde*, for it is there, amidst the impending crisis of the heroine's departure from Troy in exchange for Antenor, that Pandarus suggests to Criseyde that her wits may somehow find a way out of the problem because 'Women ben wise in short avysement' (*TC*, IV.936). Windeatt translates this 'Women are clever at quick thinking'.[69] Criseyde seems to accept this construction of herself, since not long afterwards we find her saying that the ideas she puts to Troilus are those of 'a womman [...] avysed *sodeynly*' (*TC*, IV.1261–2, my emphasis).[70] It is interesting that Caxton, probably under Chaucer's

pp. 171, 176. See also Peter Beidler, 'Chaucer's *Merchant's Tale* and the *Decameron*', *Italica*, 50 (1973), 266–84 (p. 271).

[67] *RR*, 15721–34, trans. Horgan, p. 243: the twist in this context is that Adonis *should* have believed Venus's warnings about hunting.

[68] *RR*, 18075–93, trans. Horgan, p. 279.

[69] *Troilus and Criseyde: A New Translation*, p. 107. The notion of ingenuity as a characteristically feminine facility for thinking on one's feet is found in the plots of Chaucerian and Continental fabliaux. Lesley Johnson describes it as women's 'striking ability to turn a dangerous situation [...] to their advantage': 'Women on Top: Antifeminism in the Fabliau?', *MLR*, 78 (1983), 298–307 (pp. 299–300). After Chaucer, the formulation 'Women are wise in short advisement' became proverbial, according to B. J. and H. W. Whiting, *Proverbs, Sentences, and Proverbial Phrases from English Writings Mainly Before 1500* (Cambridge, Mass.: Harvard University Press, 1968), W531.

[70] The self-construction is nevertheless tempered by evidence of her thoughtfulness at, for instance, *TC*, II.1726 and III.157.

influence, reproduces a similar stereotype in his rendering of *The Game and Playe of Chesse*: 'verily hit cometh of nature oftentymes to women to gyve counceyll shortly and unavysedly to thynges that ben in doute or perillous and nedeth hasty remedye'.[71] Significantly we can detect from this that the phenomenon of thinking on one's feet that both writers refer to can be described positively as a product of *short/sodeyn avysement* ('urgently thought up'), yet can equally be described negatively as something *unavysed* ('not pondered').[72] Clearly quick-wittedness is held to imply as flip-side a possible lack of skill in deliberative long-range planning. In fact that is precisely what Criseyde accuses herself of afterwards amidst her isolation in the Greek camp. She theorizes that she has always understood past and present but has lacked foresight, the third component of *prudentia* (*TC*, v.744–9).[73]

Ready answers, clever quick thinking, are not the sorts of skills advocated by the medieval discourses on prudence and counsel: instead those discourses prioritize careful reflection and leisurely selection of a course of action.[74] As I have elaborated elsewhere, moral-philosophical writings conspired to construct the female intellect to be suited to the quick or ephemeral and unsuited to the leisurely or reflective.[75] The scholastics found that Aristotle had deduced from the 'softness' of female skin that in theory women should characteristically be more prudent than men, since he held that the human intellect improved in proportion to the sensitivity (literally the soft receptivity) of the body. Moral philosophers such as Albert the Great and John Buridan drew on humoral theory to head off this gender heresy. They attributed female softness to a negative and debilitating 'humidity' rather than to a positive abundance of blood.[76] They resolved that any quickness

---

[71] *Caxton's Game and Playe of Chesse, 1474, A Verbatim Reprint*, intro. William E. A. Axon (London: Elliot Stock, 1883), iii.4, p. 115.

[72] The latter infringes the moralists' insistence on reflection before speech: 'man sholde hym avyse what he speke' (*MancT*, ix.324). See Craun, *Lies, Slander, and Obscenity*, p. 205.

[73] McAlpine curiously attempts a revisionary view of this self-indictment in her article 'Criseyde's Prudence'.

[74] Hence the implicit commendation of the duke's opening of the Athenian parliament in 'The Knight's Tale': '[. . .] Theseus abiden hadde a space / Er any word cam fram his wise brest' (i.2982–3).

[75] 'Women and Creative Intelligence in Medieval Thought', in *Voices in Dialogue: Reading Women in the Middle Ages*, ed. Linda Olson and Kathryn Kerby-Fulton (Notre Dame, Ind.: University of Notre Dame Press, 2005), pp. 213–30.

[76] Albertus Magnus, *Quaestiones super de animalibus*, xiii, q. 3 ('Whether a softer heart is better') and xv, q. 9 ('Whether the body of the male is softer than that of

in sense-perception and hence agility of mind in women would be offset by the disadvantage that because the female constitution was more 'humid' (as well as colder) than the male constitution, women's minds would not *retain* what they received. Humidity entailed slipperiness; thus, although women's minds might excel in ephemeral short-term intellectual receptivity they would not easily support the sustained cogitation associated with prudence.[77] Physiological lore, as often, served misogyny.

By such wizardry, Albert thought he could prove that women are not as prudent as men, for in women prudence slips towards 'astuteness' (*astutia*) and ingenuity, which concentrates on pragmatic and material ends and is a lesser form of wisdom according to the Bible. Here, then, was the academic and 'scientific' rationale for the dictum about quick female wit trotted out in *Troilus* and given a mythic 'origin' in 'The Merchant's Tale'.

Chaucer does not challenge the received scholastic framework on its own terms. Christine de Pizan provides a contrasting model in that respect. In the *City of Ladies* she engages in an extensive modification of Boccaccio, upgrading the 'astuteness' that he attributes to some of the women he writes about into 'prudence', and pointedly insisting on the *retentive* powers of the intellects of many women. Christine scholars have not fully realized, I think, the dialectical scholastic penetration implied by such adjustments as these. At the same time, she is content to take the ingenuity or agility of intellect ascribed (albeit somewhat condescendingly) to women by previous writers, and commend it as an important human talent by which the amenities of civilization have been enhanced.[78]

We do not find Chaucer engaging in this type of polemical reconstruction, even in 'Melibee', and even in that part of 'Melibee' where Prudence defends women from her husband's misogynous clichés (vii.1069–1110). Chaucer's Prudence never fashions any academic argument in support of a gendered claim for women's deliberative

---

the female'); *Opera omnia*, vol. xii, ed. Ephrem Filthaut, OP (Aschendorff: Monasterii Westfalorum, 1955).

[77] Albertus Magnus, *Quaestiones super de animalibus*, xv, q. 11; and cf. John Buridan, *Quaestiones in octo libros politicorum Aristotelis* (Oxford: Turner, 1640), iii, q. 5, pp. 122–4 (esp. p. 124). The conclusion becomes axiomatic in such statements as: 'a woman ought naturally to be subject to a man because she is naturally inferior to the man in prudence'; quoted from Aegidius (*De regimine*, i.2.65) by Nolan, *Chaucer and the Tradition of the 'roman antique'*, p. 169.

[78] Blamires, 'Women and Creative Intelligence', pp. 220–4.

capacity. She simply, but powerfully, offers an object lesson in prudential management of the incitement to war that the household faces. However, there is one place in the *Tales* where it can be argued that Chaucer comes back to the gendered issue of discernment and prudence and offers a fascinating counterbalance to the conclusion of 'The Merchant's Tale', and that is in 'The Wife of Bath's Tale', though characteristically he prefers narrative drama rather than para-scholastic debate to make the point.

Insight Un-Curtained: 'The Wife of Bath's Tale'

If 'The Merchant's Tale' comments on a male egotism that is only too ready to prefer its self-indulgent fantasy to the possibility of permanently peeling away impediments to perception of the truth, then the configuration of pig-headed knight, woman-as-educator, and intervening curtain in 'The Wife's Tale' is a suggestive alternative. The tale quietly keeps vision and vision's uncertainties in mind. For instance, there is the teasing substitution whereby, to the rapist knight's sight, twenty-four dancing ladies become nothing but one seated ugly woman when he approaches them. Among ways in which this might be interpreted, one is surely that the knight's problem with women is that there is a gap between the alluring fantasies he creates about them at a distance, and the loathing he feels when encountering them close up.

Then, in the old woman's speech on their wedding night, correcting the knight's prejudices about nobility and birth which make him horrified to have to marry her, the example she uses to urge that moral nobility is not 'planted naturally' in aristocratic dynasties is that if this were the case every descendant of such families would manifest nobility, just as fire goes on burning brightly wherever it is put. Shut fire away in a benighted house halfway to the Caucasus mountains, and it will still burn inside as if 'twenty thousand men myghte it biholde' (III.1134–43). This fire analogy was, as Chaucer had reason to know, a favourite philosophical proof of the continuity of a species behind superficial difference.[79] More significantly still, the analogy was also

---

[79] The analogy would have been most immediately known to Chaucer through *Boece*, III pr. 4: 'Certes yif that honour of peple were a natureel yifte to dignytes, it ne myghte nevere cesen nowhere amonges no maner folk to don his office; right as fyer in every contre ne stynteth nat to eschaufen and to ben hoot.' The principle goes back to Aristotle's observation—even closer to the old woman's formulation—that 'a natural law is immutable and has the same validity everywhere, as fire burns both here and in Persia': *Ethics*, v.7.2–3, trans. Thomson, p. 190.

recognized by academics in the Middle Ages as a way of demonstrating that men and women, being companions and equals, should have the same opportunities. (In the fourteenth century John Buridan notes in his commentary on Aristotle's *Politics* an argument that women as well as men should be able to be judges, since men and women are companions (*socii*) and companions are said to be equal. Moreover they are of the same species and should function alike: 'this is clear from the case of fire, which burns the same whether here or in Persia'.)[80] To revert to the case of the old woman in 'The Wife's Tale', since she is actually protesting her own capacity for moral nobility despite 'low' birth, there is an interesting implication that the knight is the one trying to 'close doors', trying not to behold possible truths about women. Then, once more, she invokes sight as a metaphor for understanding when she goes on to discuss poverty and describes it as a 'spectacle' through which someone may 'see' his genuine friends (III.1203–4). Meditating the same topos elsewhere, Chaucer wrote that misfortune made hyena's gall superfluous as the medicine for disclosing true friends and for clearing the darkened eyes of those who had been 'in ignoraunce'.[81]

The comments on sight that we have so far examined in the old woman's speech on 'gentillesse' and poverty, by which she tries to educate her unenlightened bridegroom, are cumulatively noteworthy as pointers to a fundamental aspect of the tale's climax, namely enlightenment through altered *perception*. Accordingly, the moment when the knight has deferred to the old woman's judgement and placed her future in her own hands, yielding choice to her in the matter of what wife she is to be (where previously in the act of rape he had erased all female choice), is fittingly rendered as a moment when a *curtain* is pulled back. 'Cast up the curtyn, looke how that it is', she says, and with that the knight *'saugh verraily* al this'—truly saw her beauty and her youth (III.1249–50). This is not just the curtain around the bed in which they lie, which must be raised to let in light and make her beauty visible. Nor in my view is conventional critical wisdom right to suppose that the 'truth' the knight sees is only what the male (even Chaucer) wishes to see, a masculine fantasy of compliant young female sexuality. Nor even, in a tempting elaboration

<hr>

[80] *Quaestiones in octo libros politicorum*, III.26 (p. 175). Sheila Fisher is unaware of this dimension in her otherwise useful discussion of the fire analogy as a means of analysing 'value' or 'intrinsic worth': *Chaucer's Poetic Alchemy: A Study of Value and its Transformation in 'The Canterbury Tales'* (New York: Garland, 1988), pp. 40–3.

[81] In the dialogue poem 'Fortune', 33–7.

of that, should we necessarily suppose that the business of the curtain anticipates modern theory on the male gaze, the gaze that Luce Irigaray describes as intent on 'knowing' women and as being obsessed with veiling or unveiling, as if Woman is to be ever defined as a mystery.[82]

Rather, crowning the cumulative emphasis produced by the preceding figurations of ways of seeing, this action symbolizes the *removal* of impediments to sight, specifically in this instance impediments to male sight. The curtain—or in Stoic thought the cataract—which formerly prevented the knight from 'seeing' women aright, which caused him to perceive ugliness where truly ('verraily') nobility and beauty lay, is drawn aside.[83] Bernard Levy was on the right track when he suggested long ago that 'the transformation is the natural consequence of [the knight's] own corrected vision and insight'; the loathly lady 'has been truly beautiful and truly *gentil* all along; the knight had previously failed to perceive this truth'.[84] It is a narrative realization of the theory of knowledge Chaucer read in Boethius, whereby the extent of what can be known about something is not determined by the 'strengthe and ... nature' of that thing, but by the 'faculte (that is to seyn, the power and the nature) of hem that knowen'.[85] At its most miraculous, this produces a notion of perception whereby those endowed with particular faith literally 'see' phenomena (for instance, in 'The Second Nun's Tale', angel and crowns) that are denied to those without the faculty of that faith.[86]

What happens to the 'loathly lady' is metaphorically akin to, but an inversion of, what happens to the Siren in Dante's *Purgatorio*, Canto

[82] Luce Irigaray, *This Sex Which Is Not One*, trans. Catherine Porter with Carolyn Burke (Ithaca: Cornell University Press, 1985), p. 210.

[83] Cf. Melibee's apology to Prudence for his angry, therefore ignorant and imperceptive speech: 'the prophete seith that "troubled eyen han no cleer sighte" ', *Mel*, VII.1700.

[84] Bernard S. Levy, 'The Wife of Bath's *Queynte Fantasye*', *ChauR*, 4 (1969–70), 106–22 (p. 109). Mann similarly affirms that 'the point of the story is the transformation of the *knight* ... female deformity is the accurate reflection of the deformity of male desires': *Feminizing Chaucer*, p. xvi. Richard Neuse rightly states that 'purging of vision (or its failure)' is 'a recurrent theme in the *Canterbury Tales*': 'Marriage and the Question of Allegory in the *Merchant's Tale*', *ChauR*, 24 (1989–90), 115–31 (p. 127).

[85] *Boece*, v pr. 4.130–40.

[86] See *SNT*, VIII.253–9, and analyses by Bruce A. Rosenberg, 'The Contrary Tales of the Second Nun and the Canon's Yeoman', *ChauR*, 2 (1967–8), 278–91 (pp. 282–5), and Robert M. Longsworth, 'Privileged Knowledge: St. Cecilia and the Alchemist in the *Canterbury Tales*', *ChauR*, 27 (1992–3), 87–96.

19. It is only the male human gaze that converts the Siren into a 'false' image of the good, as Love would prefer to see her. St Lucy, patron of sight standing at Dante the dreamer's side, restores true 'sight' by ripping the Siren's garments open and sharply awakening the pilgrim Dante to the horror of the Siren's true nature.[87] These myths show a woman both as object of male sight (or 'decoy' as I said earlier) and also as agent of transformation in the male. Dante's Siren is the classic misogynous projection: women are perceived as superficially attractive but underneath, morally repulsive.[88] The Wife of Bath's is an alternative projection: women are casually disdained by men as vile and untouchable, but with prejudice removed, seen to be agents of a wisdom which is also beauty.[89]

In the delightful interplay of the Canterbury stories it seems to me that the ending of 'The Wife of Bath's Tale' links particularly provocatively with that of 'The Merchant's Tale'. January the knight is a marital rapist and an outrageous egotist whose only chance to be brought out of moral blindness is through the shock-tactic of seeing what May is and what manner of sexual partner—not himself—is appropriate to her. He passes up the opportunity because in his preference for mere 'glimpsing' he proves unreformable. In 'The Wife of Bath's Tale', despite the rape of a girl outside marriage (far more of a sin and crime in the medieval context than adultery), the nameless knight proves educable,[90] first by a court of women and then more intimately by a nameless wise woman who can be all sorts of woman, both old and young. While 'Melibee' is often thought of as the most allegorical narrative Chaucer wrote and concerns an emblematic woman's systematic re-education of the aggressive male, it cannot match the intense allegorical power of moral discovery and of revised perception of the Other engineered in an Everyman by an Everywoman in 'The Wife of Bath's Tale'.

---

[87] *Purgatorio*, xix.7–33; and see Boyde, *Human Vices and Human Worth*, pp. 162–3.

[88] The classic figure is the one used by the Jealous Husband in the *Roman*, comparing outwardly beautiful women with flower-adorned dunghills: *RR*, 8859–99, trans. Horgan, pp. 136–7.

[89] This seems to me a more logical reading than to take *both* representations of women—ugly and beautiful—as equally 'masquerades', with Crane, *Gender and Romance*, pp. 85–92.

[90] Many critics would disagree with this emphasis, but Fisher is an instructive exception: 'if [the knight's] crime is underplayed, it is because the tale's purpose is not vindication, but education', *Chaucer's Poetic Alchemy*, p. 84. Peggy Knapp also comments on the tale's cultivation of insight: 'Alisoun of Bath and the Reappropriation of Tradition', *ChauR*, 24 (1989–90), 45–52.

Although the Wife of Bath herself does not let the grander implications of the tale go unscathed (she is unmistakably heard adding a raucous coda relishing meek young husbands and cursing old miserly ones), the 'loathly' woman's reform of the knight, rooted in moral egalitarianism and drawing on longstanding ethical investigation of the problem of perception, stands as the most eloquent exploration in the *Canterbury Tales* of a strikingly gendered way out of credulity and towards beneficial prudence.

3

Sex and Lust: 'The Merchant's Tale',
'The Reeve's Tale', and other *Tales*

Late classical Stoic writers took up a position critical of sexual pleasure, lumping it together somewhat disdainfully with other sensual pleasures or *voluptates*. This ethical suspicion of sex was redoubled within emergent Christian morality. Under the massive influence of St Augustine, the arbiters of medieval religious doctrine relentlessly promulgated a view that having sexual intercourse for sheer enjoyment was a sin. The fundamental reason given was that sexual excitement and climax obliterated rational faculties and rendered the mind oblivious to God.[1] Doubtless an underlying function of the doctrine was to reinforce the church's concern to enforce celibacy amongst its religious orders, as well as (eventually) amongst its pastoral clergy. Beyond that, a doctrine of sexual repression may have served fluctuating socio-economic ends.[2] However, the remarkable continuity with which the teaching on the underlying sinfulness of sex was sustained across many centuries remains an impediment to arguments for localized historical causation. Except amongst medical authorities, which tended to take the more 'modern' view that timely intercourse promoted health, formal analysis of sex was persistently dominated by assessment of its sinfulness. The sin was worse if the context was 'fornication' (a broad category including sex between unattached consenting adults); and the sin became more and more extreme if the context was adulterous or same-sex coupling.

---

[1] Echoed in *ParsT*, x.904–6. Augustine frowns upon the 'almost total extinction of mental alertness' in intercourse: *The City of God*, xiv.16, trans. Henry Bettenson (Harmondsworth: Penguin, 1972), p. 577.

[2] James Brundage notes that fifteenth-century statistics, at a time of reinforcement of repressive sexual mores, give evidence of delayed marriage and a high proportion of single people in urban contexts: *Law, Sex, and Christian Society in Medieval Europe* (Chicago and London: University of Chicago Press, 1987), pp. 494–5.

Hypothetically even within marriage it was difficult to get away with sex without incurring at least minor sin.[3] Marital intercourse became less culpable only to the extent that it met one or more of three criteria: that it was performed with the conscious objective of having a child; that it was performed in order to pay the conjugal debt (i.e. to satisfy a spouse's request for sex); or that it was resorted to as a 'remedy for fornication' (in effect, as an outlet preventing the sex drive from having to be satisfied some other way). Even marital sex that fulfilled these criteria was supposed to be self-regulated, for moralists constantly warned against 'extraordinary voluptuousness' in marriage.[4] It seems that by this they especially meant the use of aphrodisiacs, too-frequent intercourse, and experimentation with different coital positions.

James Brundage's capacious survey of the legal and doctrinal literature on all this introduces us to a world of theories that can seem bizarrely removed from the relaxed attitudes that characterize much of Western thinking on sex today. 'Marital sex was free from sin only so long as no one enjoyed it', is his laconic summary at one point; again, 'if the couple went to bed solely in order to conceive and "endured" the pleasure because it was unavoidable, their act was not sinful and might be meritorious'.[5] Although these views were sometimes muted or challenged, they present themselves in Chaucer's writing when the Parson (after identifying the three criteria mentioned above which reduce the sin of intercourse) rebukes married couples who 'assemble oonly for amorous love and . . . for to accomplice thilke brennynge delit, they rekke nevere how ofte. Soothly it is deedly synne; and yet, with sorwe, somme folk wol peynen hem moore to doon than to hire appetit suffiseth' (i.e. they go beyond meeting basic sexual needs; 'Parson's Tale', x.942). The Parson reminds his audience, too, of a doctrinal claim that a man's excessively ardent lovemaking with his own wife can amount to 'adultery': it is a sort of spiritual suicide, killing himself with his own 'knife' (x.859).

Outside the Parson's sermon, how do the established moral constraints on sex fare in Chaucer's writing? With regard to the embattled moral status of sexual love, it is clear that Chaucer expects readers to appreciate

---

[3] An instructive guide to variations of emphasis in this regard (from 'rigorist' to 'moderate') among canon lawyers and theologians is Henry Ansgar Kelly, *Love and Marriage in the Age of Chaucer* (Ithaca: Cornell University Press, 1975), ch. 10.

[4] Brundage, *Law, Sex, and Christian Society*, pp. 285–7, 367.

[5] Ibid., pp. 429, 449.

instantly the force of the Wife of Bath's exclamation, 'Allas! allas! that evere love [i.e. sexual love] was synne!' ('Wife of Bath's Prologue', III.614). But one of the fascinating questions in study of Chaucer is precisely whether he expects us to keep on importing this generalized moral judgement as a rod with which to beat every manifestation of erotic relations in his narratives. Troilus and Criseyde provide the classic instance. The consummation of their love is celebrated by Troilus with apostrophes to 'benigne Love', 'holy bond of thynges' (*TC*, III.1261), and orchestrated by the narrator with dangerous but passionate emotional empathy. 'Why nad I swich [a night] with my soule ybought!' (*TC*, III.1319), the narrator exclaims, and is in awe of a happiness that surpasses what can be described or even thought (*TC*, III.1688–94). My own position would be that while such idioms jar us into reflecting that souls probably should not be sold to achieve erotic fulfilment, or that it ought to be divine love not sexual ecstasy that passeth human understanding, an option is left for the reader *not* to intrude ready-made judgements. As we shall also see in a discussion of 'The Merchant's Tale', the moral brake on celebration of fulfilled sexual love in Chaucer arises more typically and persuasively from the circumstances of transience that so often beset it in his narratives. But before coming to that, it will be useful to consider further the Chaucerian engagement with the specifics of church teaching on sex within marriage.[6]

The first thing to say is that one context in which the requirement of a procreative intention in intercourse is specifically ignored, and two contexts in which it is specifically championed, would equally prompt readers of Chaucer towards scepticism about that part of the doctrine. The requirement is ignored by, of all people, a cockerel, since it is Chauntecleer whom the Nun's Priest hails in his tale for exerting himself primarily in the service of the love-goddess Venus, 'moore for delit than world to multiplye' (VII.3345). The effect is to expose the doctrine to irreverent laughter, and to remind us how much more attractive it might be to aim at delight first and at multiplying the world second. As for the two Chaucerian champions of procreative sex in marriage, one, January in 'The Merchant's Tale', odiously congratulates himself about his virility (IV.1441–60); and the other, Queen Cenobia in 'The Monk's Tale', is made to seem eccentric in her

---

[6] Still useful is Joseph J. Mogan, 'Chaucer and the *bona matrimonii*', *ChauR*, 4 (1969–70), 123–41.

punctilious observance of the church's doctrine—including elaborate precautions not to have intercourse if she *might* be pregnant already (vii.2279–86).[7] More insistently than the procreative trope, Chaucer's texts make use of the moral resonance of the concept of conjugal 'debt'. He may have been particularly aware of the way exposition of this concept actually rested on an assumption that women preferred not to express sexual desire—indeed, that their desire had to be intuited *for* them by male partners. Outwardly the conjugal debt was an 'equal opportunity' concept developed by early Christianity from a famous biblical passage (1 Cor. 7: 3–4), which declared that control over the wife's body belonged not to her but to her husband; and conversely that control over the husband's body belonged not to him but to his wife. Moreover neither was to 'defraud' (or 'starve') the other except by mutual consent (1 Cor. 7: 5). This was taken in sexual terms to mean that there was reciprocity of sexual obligation within the marriage bond; each spouse 'owed' a debt of sexual satisfaction to the other.

The doctrine is easily mistaken as a site of gender equality, exceptionally preserved in a period which otherwise so often endorsed the domination of women by men.[8] In the period itself the doctrine generally takes for granted its own even-handed status. Thus, when the topic is introduced in the *Book of Vices and Virtues*, sexual intercourse is defined as a mutual yielding of the 'debt' on the same basis as distributive justice, whereby one gives to another what is due to them.[9] It is possible to speculate that such a validation of sex-on-demand was not really equitable but biologically and psychologically prejudicial to the wife.[10] We may detect a gender imbalance concealing a form of

---

[7] On prohibition of sexual relations during pregnancy (a doctrine in decline by the late Middle Ages), see Brundage, *Law, Sex, and Christian Society*, pp. 91, 156, 198–9, 451–2, 508.

[8] See Pierre Payer, *The Bridling of Desire: Views of Sex in the Later Middle Ages* (Toronto: University of Toronto Press, 1993), p. 92. While Payer's analysis of theological and pastoral literature on sexual matters does not probe gender issues far, his work is deeply informed concerning medieval exposition of the 'debt'. For another discussion see section 5 of Alcuin Blamires, 'Sexuality', in *The Oxford Guide to Chaucer*, ed. Steve Ellis (Oxford: Oxford University Press, 2005).

[9] *VV*, p. 246. For a summary discussion of distributive justice see Baker, 'Chaucer and Moral Philosophy', pp. 243–5.

[10] Dyan Elliott, 'Marriage', in *The Cambridge Companion to Medieval Women's Writing*, ed. Carolyn Dinshaw and David Wallace (Cambridge: Cambridge University Press, 2003), pp. 40–57 (p. 51).

coercion of wives towards intercourse, expressed even within the heart of the doctrine itself.

The truth is that the small print of the doctrine assumes that husbands will be likely to have to take an interventionist sexual role more than wives. A husband should be on the alert to satisfy a wife's 'right' to sex even when it is only requested 'bi signe, as many wommen don that ben schamefast to aske suche thinges'.[11] (This projects the husband into a position of determining when his wife, in her modesty, might be tacitly hoping for him to render the sexual debt.) The same psychology applied to the idea that a sexually active marriage was a 'remedy for fornication', an outlet for the sexual drive. This was occasionally interpreted bluntly to mean that 'wives should function as safety-valves for their husbands' libido'.[12] More insidiously, it was interpreted along the lines of the husband 'remedying' *the wife's* unspoken sexual drives. Intercourse was a remedy for a wife's allegedly characteristic sexual reticence, whereby the husband, realizing that 'sche wolde neuere bidde here lord' for sex, must be vigilant to anticipate her unspoken desire, and must demand sex in order to prevent her falling into unspecified sin (masturbation? adultery? same-sex activity?).[13]

Here, then, we have a rooted hypothesis of female sexual diffidence that specifically authorizes male sexual intervention. Embarrassment in one of the sexes, the gender typology which constructs verbal confidence as masculine and constructs indirect bashful communication *by signs* as feminine,[14] prevents the supposedly reciprocal debt from being discharged in an openly reciprocal way. And lurking behind this, at least for St Thomas Aquinas, was a qualitative asymmetry in the sex act itself:

> The husband, because he has *the more noble part* in the conjugal act, *is naturally more disposed than his wife not to be ashamed* to ask for the debt. Consequently the wife is not bound to pay the debt to her husband who does not seek it, in the way the husband [is bound to pay it] to his wife [who does not seek it].[15]

---

[11] *VV*, pp. 246–7.

[12] Jacqueline Murray, 'Gendered Souls in Sexed Bodies', p. 90.

[13] This has a pedigree in confessional theory analysed by Payer, *Bridling of Desire*, p. 94, but is here cited from *VV*, p. 247.

[14] Nicky Hallett points out how frequently in Chaucer's writing male tutelage obliges women to resort to the subaltern power of 'signs' (for example, in the case of May motioning to Damyan, *MercT*, iv.2150): 'Women', pp. 490–2.

[15] Payer, *Bridling of Desire*, p. 95, citing Aquinas's article on 'Whether husband and wife are equal in the marriage act' (emphasis added). The argument is reinforced in an accompanying article on 'Whether a husband is bound to pay the debt if his wife does

In an optimistic reading we can say that Aquinas is advocating a husbandly sensitivity that circumvents a wife's inhibitions.[16] In a more sceptical reading, doctrinal sophistry is used to reassure husbands that fulfilment of their own 'nobler' sexual demands can always be rationalized as a 'remedying' of their wives' instinctually repressed desires. We are not very far from a legitimation of marital rape.

Returning to Chaucer's writings with all this in mind, we are better equipped to understand the partisan colouring of the comment on the sexual debt in 'The Parson's Tale', where we hear that 'she hath merite of chastitee that yeldeth to hire housbonde the dette of hir body, ye, though it be agayn hir likynge and the lust of hire herte' (x.940).[17] In tune with this are three notable passages in the *Tales* that quizzically define female sexual submission to husbands as a kind of necessary evil, a compulsory feature of the marital deal to be taken 'in pacience at nyght' by wives who must 'leye a lite hir hoolynesse aside, / As for the tyme, —it may no bet bitide'. That is Custance's situation in 'The Man of Law's Tale' (ii.708–14), as it threatens also to be Cecile's in 'The Second Nun's Tale' when night comes and 'to bedde moste she gon / With hire housbonde, as ofte is the manere' (viii.141–2). Chaucer appears to have embroidered his source with the generalizing 'as ofte' clause here, linking Cecile forward from sub-Christian Rome to a continuing present of wifely obligation.[18] And then there is the moment in 'The Franklin's Tale' when Dorigen protests at Aurelius's folly in wooing the wife of another man 'That hath hir body whan so that hym liketh' (v.1005).

Of course each passage has its own dynamic. The assertion of the necessity of sexual compliance that enfolds Cecile is but prelude to its successful challenge, as she invokes the power of celibacy. In the case of Custance the Man of Law's patronizing way of dwelling on her descent from holiness into the marital bed rebounds on the

not ask for it': *The Summa Theologica of St Thomas Aquinas*, trans. Fathers of the English Dominican province, pt iii, vol. 19, *Quaestiones XXXIV–LXVII* (London: Burns Oates and Washbourne, 1922), q. 64, art. 2 and art. 5, pp. 315, 320.

[16] Further confirmation of this thinking is offered by Brundage, *Law, Sex, and Christian Society*, pp. 426–7, citing the *Summa summarum* of William of Pagula (*fl.* 1314–31).

[17] Significantly, the gendering of this in the chain of sources leading to the *ParsT* was originally the other way around (the husband having merit despite being obliged to yield the debt): Kelly, *Love and Marriage*, p. 263.

[18] For the comparable text in the *Golden Legend*, see Sherry L. Reames, 'The Second Nun's Prologue and Tale', in Robert M. Correale and Mary Hamel (eds.), *Sources and Analogues of the Canterbury Tales*, vol. 1 (Cambridge: D. S. Brewer, 2002), p. 504.

speaker, not on the character. In Dorigen's case we may suppose that her comment on marital possession is offered as a strategic put-off: she 'refers to herself as a body that is the property of someone else' as protection against an unwanted suitor, not as a literal description of her own marriage.[19] Even if we take the apparently contrasting case of the merchant's wife's burst of enthusiasm for paying the marital debt at the end of 'The Shipman's Tale' ('For I wol paye yow wel and redily / Fro day to day'), it is interesting how an awareness of potential husbandly sexual coercion lurks within her accompanying witticism: should she fail to pay him, 'I am youre wyf, [you have a right to] score it upon my taille' (VII.413–16).[20]

A seemingly contrary example is the Wife of Bath, an individual who knows her conjugal rights and intends to exact them. Her husband is to be 'dettour' and he will be obliged to 'make his paiement', and accordingly she articulates the biblical doctrine of mutual sexual obligation as though it actually envisaged one-way traffic: 'I have the power [...] Upon his propre body', with no mention of the reverse ('Wife of Bath's Prologue', III.129–32, 149–61). It is nevertheless instructive that she does not unambiguously (to adopt the moralists' verb) 'bidde' her husband for sex. She will 'use' her 'instrument' generously, for sure, but where her elderly husbands are concerned she thinks in terms of doing so reactively, whenever he should 'come forth' to pay his debt (III.153); indeed (in a searing literalization of debt for debt) she means to 'suffre' his attentions only when a ransom is offered by him first (III.409–12). Her most sexually assertive idiom—'Myn housbonde shal it have bothe eve and morwe' (III.152)—does not so much express a request for sex as transform the sort of passive construction that medieval writing associates with female desire into a threat of relentless availability. I propose in Chapter 5 that the Wife of Bath's famous 'liberated' sexuality is most productively understood as a brilliant representation of liberality. For now, we can see that the Wife's sexual assertiveness, notable though it be, is not totally inconsistent with the moralists' hypothesis that husbands have to urge the debt because wives won't *ask* for sex.

[19] Francine McGregor, 'What of Dorigen? Agency and Ambivalence in the *Franklin's Tale*', ChauR, 31 (1996–7), 365–78 (p. 374); but Hansen takes Dorigen's words as her statement of the 'actual position': *Chaucer and the Fictions of Gender*, pp. 275–6.

[20] Thompson is too ready to take the language of the conjugal debt here as evidence of 'a plea for women's rights': *Chaucer, Boccaccio and the Debate of Love*, pp. 211–12, 219.

In fact, despite traditional misogynist cant about female lust and insatiability, the female sexual drive was generally characterized as passive.[21] This assumption provided a robust moral argument against the complaint that women's artillery of beauty amounted to an incitement of male lust, simply by virtue of looking at men.[22] Men were not to deny their free will so lightly; and their own onerous moral responsibility was proven by the fact that, since men 'do' the deed in sex and pursue women, then women are recipients not agents where sexual activity is concerned and cannot therefore be held as culpable as men.[23]

It is interesting that Chaucer radically disrupts the passive/active assumption in the scenes of the courtship of Criseyde, without really broaching that argument of moral responsibility. Here and elsewhere, the form of sexual responsibility that most insistently absorbed him was the responsibility for an unsullied reputation, constitutive of a woman's 'honour' in particular. This imperative is noted everywhere in medieval writing.[24] Since there was a moral edge to the social delicacies involved here, a woman's moral repute hung on every decision to concede amorous 'routhe' or 'grace'. If she misapplied the concession her entire social and psychological stability might be threatened.[25] Yet the exercise of her 'pite' was at the same time required by what the culture persistently identified not only as a characteristic of fine

[21] Murray states that in confessional literature, the words used to denote sexual intercourse in the confessors' manuals all reinforce the passive role of women. 'Men know women, have them, deflower them, use them, or abuse them ... but women are known by men or are approached by men ... Thus, women's nature, while inherently sexual, was also perceived to be sexually passive': 'Gendered Souls', pp. 85–6. A rare exception found in the poem *Cleanness* (line 705) hints at mutuality of sexual initiative: see Elizabeth B. Keiser, *Courtly Desire and Medieval Homophobia: The Legitimation of Sexual Pleasure in 'Cleanness' and its Contexts* (New Haven: Yale University Press, 1997), pp. 137–8.

[22] 'She shall be rightly responsible before God for all the souls she deceives, for by her glance she touches the will, which is the mental equivalent of committing the sin itself': *Mirour*, 9349–60; *VV*, p. 44. For the counter to this see *Dives and Pauper*, VI.11–12, ed. Barnum, vol. 1, pt 2, pp. 84–90.

[23] A conventional argument vigorously put e.g. in Christine de Pizan's *L'Epistre au Dieu d'Amours*; and in *The Southern Passion*, 1923–59, ed. O. S. Pickering, in 'The "Defence of Women" from the *Southern Passion*: A New Edition', in *The South English Legendary: A Critical Assessment*, ed. Klaus P. Jankovsky (Tübingen: Stauffenburg, 1992), and trans. in Blamires, *Woman Defamed*, pp. 245–6.

[24] An unmarried girl who loves a man 'peramoure' (i.e. is having an affair) reckons herself 'a-schamyd as sone as sche wott that ony man perceyuyth it', according to *JW*, p. 246.

[25] See e.g. *Anelida & Arcite*, 344–5.

behaviour generally, but more specifically as a key 'womanly' virtue. To have compassion for someone's distress was a mark of 'verray wommanly benignytee' ('Squire's Tale', v.484–6).[26] This gendered ethic therefore defined women in terms of the very 'virtue' whose unguarded exercise most dangerously exposed them to chasms of moral disrepute. Even more insidiously, as Felicity Riddy has emphasized, the central love poem of the era, the *Roman de la Rose*, dramatically depicted the opposite behaviour in a woman—an uncompassionate, distancing response—as something uncouth, ugly, vulgar, and *male*: this was the 'vilain' Dangiers.[27]

In the sexual domain, then, the courtly ethics that Chaucer adopted modelled for women a cautious, slow-release responsiveness to male entreaty. Only momentarily does Chaucer ever project a woman able to abstract herself from the usual constraints, neutrally, as a kind of free-roaming sexual being. (I say 'neutrally' because the Wife of Bath's determination to go 'walkynge out by nyghte' (III.397) is wittingly transgressive.) This is Criseyde's famous reflection beginning 'I am myn owene womman', and going on, perhaps even more significantly, '... and stonde unteyd in lusty leese' (*TC*, II.750–2). The analogy of an untethered horse roaming free in rich pasture that she is using here is surely prompted by a memory of Jean de Meun's use of the same analogy in the *Roman de la Rose*, where it figures pre-civilized unrestrained natural sexual appetites:

... if a black mare were not held back, she would come running to a black horse, or indeed to a sorrel or grey, just as her desire prompted her. The first one she found would be her husband, for she ... would have looked no further than to see if she found them *untethered*.[28]

In Criseyde's case the analogy appears to me morally neutral, configuring a remarkable sense of cherished sexual freedom which is actually the precise antithesis of the entrapment of coltish vigour that constitutes

---

[26] Hence Pandarus reassures Troilus that there must be 'pitee' among the qualities of a lady who is 'vertuous', like Criseyde (*TC*, I.897–900).

[27] Felicity Riddy, 'Engendering Pity in the *Franklin's Tale*', in Ruth Evans and Lesley Johnson (eds.), *Feminist Readings in Middle English Literature* (London: Routledge, 1994), pp. 54–71 (pp. 58–9). On further social complexities of the role of Dangiers see Sarah Kay, *The 'Romance of the Rose'* (London: Grant and Cutler, 1995), pp. 109–10.

[28] *RR*, 14023 ff., trans. Horgan, pp. 216–17 (my emphasis).

Alisoun's jealously guarded situation in 'The Miller's Tale'.[29] Criseyde's self-understanding here is also anticipated by the way she is represented when Troilus first sets eyes on her in the temple, free-standing and affirming her independent presence (*TC*, i.282–92).

Nigel Thompson, comparing Chaucer with Boccaccio, goes so far as to suggest that the two writers are alike unusual at that epoch in particularly acknowledging the naturalness of female as well as male desire.[30] Whatever the truth of that, Chaucer's writings do avoid projecting women as voluptuaries—as morally suspect orchestrators of sensuality. Rhetorical portrayals of Venus are his nearest approach to that. Yet Venus in the *Parliament*, or in her oratory in 'The Knight's Tale', seems to stand not so much for what women want to be, as what men's fantasy wants them to be.[31] While there are women (Alisoun) with a 'lecherous eye' and women (the Wife of Bath, Phebus's wife in 'The Manciple's Tale') who decidedly follow sexual appetite, Chaucer's arch voluptuary, for whose sexual mores he reserves the greatest sarcasm, is male: the old lecher January in 'The Merchant's Tale'. In January we can see an implicit gendering of dedication to sensuality as a vice proper to the male. We shall devote the centre of this chapter to analysing the moral and ethical grounding of that.

'The Merchant's Tale': The Voluptuary Quest for Sanctioned Sex

'The Merchant's Tale''s analysis of voluptuary obsession and sexual fantasy relentlessly unmasks an old man's misconception about what constitutes 'secure' happiness. It is on this facet of the tale that we shall first concentrate here, one that presents a notable spectacle of moral and ethical trajectories zig-zagging complicatedly.[32] Although I shall not be the first to emphasize January's pursuit of secure pleasure—of 'delit' with 'sikernesse'—I shall suggest new ways in which the currents of

---

[29] Hallissy strains to attribute such features of Criseyde's stance (that of 'natural woman') to non-Christian and rather self-concerned ethical criteria less demanding than those that the text expects the reader to adopt: *Clean Maids*, pp. 149–50.

[30] Thompson, *Chaucer, Boccaccio and the Debate of Love*, pp. 193, 200–1.

[31] Chaucer's Venus does not dwindle into the debased originator of female promiscuity projected in Gower, *CA*, v.1388–1431.

[32] It is more usual to note the elusiveness of a moral foothold in the tale, but see Burnley, 'The Morality of *The Merchant's Tale*', on allusions to the liturgy of the sacrament of marriage as one fundamental norm.

antique ethics and Christian doctrine interweave and produce gendered effects in the narrative of this pursuit.

Human longings for sanctioned sensual happiness are satirically exposed in the tale's prominent attention to the concepts of *sikernesse* and *felicitee*, together with a constellation of associated concepts such as *ese*, *delit*, and *honest* lifestyle. From early in the tale an exaggerated and systematically ironized hypothesis is set up that whereas a career of extramarital sex has ephemeral rather than secure foundations (IV.1279–80), acquisition of a wife establishes a man's life in 'sikernesse', on a solid footing. With manifest tongue in cheek, marriage is heralded for lay folk as the 'sure' way (IV.1355, 1390). Chaucer's point of course is not that marriage cannot be a happy, securely sanctioned institution; rather, that January's motive in aiming for it is cynical and his predictions of guaranteed bliss are naïvely outlandish. The trail of suggestion concerning 'sikernesse' that is begun early in the tale is capped by the comment in the description of January's wedding, that the priest performed the routine rites and 'made al siker ynogh with hoolynesse' (IV.1708). January's fantasy of guaranteed bliss is, as it were, sealed with a psalm.

In the meantime January claims to feel his conscience 'pricked' by a worry concerning the legalized erotic delight, the 'parfit felicitee' of honourable 'ese' that is his belated objective in life (IV.1642–7), because he has heard tell that none can have bliss twice, both on earth and hereafter.[33] January soon drops the question, but of course it is more than gratuitous material for his conceit. Clearly, among other things it is a spur to readers to think about what the world's 'felicitee' is and how assured it can ever be. The same issue is broached elsewhere when the narrator of *Troilus and Criseyde* suggests that the word 'felicite' can barely suffice to describe the inexpressible joy of Troilus and Criseyde's mutual love. Yet next minute he is admitting that felicity, other than temporary, would not actually be a satisfactory term for their love, because it is only by Fortune, and for a while, that the lovers are

---

[33] See Kenneth A. Bleeth, 'The Image of Paradise in the *Merchant's Tale*', in *The Learned and the Lewed: Studies in Chaucer and Medieval Literature*, ed. Larry D. Benson (Cambridge, Mass.: Harvard University Press, 1974), pp. 45–60 (pp. 46–7). *JW* (p. 104) warns it is unlikely that a person can proceed from 'delytes' in this world to 'delytes' in the next, referring to Jerome's aphorism 'de deliciis ad delicias difficile est transire': *Ad Julianum*, VII (*PL*, 22.965). See also Passus 'B' XIV.139–43 in William Langland, *The Vision of Piers Plowman: A Complete Edition of the B-Text*, ed. A. V. C. Schmidt (London: Dent, 1978).

'led' in fulfilment (*TC*, III.1716). That their bliss is at the mercy of fortune is the nub of their tragedy. Their relationship cannot attain the certainty they wish for it—as, for example, in Criseyde's reassuring words to Troilus, 'lyve in sikernesse', when they exchange oaths of fidelity (*TC*, III.1513). The poem locks this yearning for stability within a dialectic that keeps registering an alternative view of sexual love (and this, the reader remembers, is extramarital sexual love) as a state of inevitable brittleness.

In 'The Merchant's Tale', *sikernesse* and *felicitee*, with heavier irony, intertwine spiritual and ethical facets of the narrative. Given the specifically Christian context, the certainty that matters most here is the *securitas* of personal salvation. January admits at the outset that he has jeopardized that assurance up to now by foolishly 'expending' his body as a libertine (and we might remember that in the Middle Ages the male body was indeed thought to be literally expended, drained, by unrestricted sexual activity).[34] Having been obliged at last to think 'somwhat'—a telling diminutive—about his soul, his scheme is that marriage will provide a last-ditch salvific haven on the brink of death. 'Blessed be God that it shal been amended!' (IV.1400–6).

It is no coincidence that the crux in the most authoritative source concerning late repentance was *sikernesse*. One vernacular moralist explains that 'tarrying', or the temptation to defer repentance throughout one's lusty youth, is distinguished as a category of Sloth impeding 'amendment' of life. The writer then translates some of Augustine's words on the matter, from the relevant section of canon law on penitence:

I dar noght seyn, [Augustine] seyth, that a man schal sykerly be sauyd, yif he take his sacramentys in his ende & deth, wyth repentauns, that has usyd his synne whyl he myght, & wolde neuere leve tyl sykenes of deth com. We mowe gyue hym penaunce, he seyth, but we mowe noght gyve him sykernes to be sauyd. Therfore, thou synnere, forsake thi synne, & do penaunce, whil thou art hool, & tarye noght . . .[35]

The Augustinian paragraphs of the section in the *Decretum* about the deadline for penitence from which this is extracted disclose an extraordinary emphasis on *securitas* and *securus*. The newly baptized, Augustine writes, depart life *securus*; the faithful who live good lives

[34] See e.g. Albertus Magnus in *Quaestiones super de animalibus*, xv, q. 2, where the idea that a woman is less 'debilitated by coitus' than a man is applied to explain why women, despite being physiologically inferior to men, often outlast them.

[35] *JW*, pp. 107–8.

depart life *securus*; those living good lives after mid-life penitence depart *securus*. But as for those who delay penitence to the very end, Augustine is not 'sure' (*securus*) whether they are *securus*. 'When I am sure, I say so and give assurance; when I am not sure, I can give penitence but I cannot give assurance.'[36]

January, looking for perfect felicity and *sikernesse* on his 'pittes brynke' in a marriage that is supposed to constitute some sort of 'amendment', both debases the idea of spiritual assurance into (as it were) saved sex, and runs the gauntlet of specific canonical warnings against overestimating the security of delayed reform.[37] He is a hilarious but grimly plausible example of ignorant cocksure spiritual calculation. The grim plausibility has to do not only with the sense we have of a recognizable human predilection for having it both ways and for short cuts (sex plus last-minute salvation); it has to do also with the way that January's simplification concerning the route to salvation echoes the crude simplifications actually found in medieval Christian discourse. Admittedly they might be presented as venal perversions. Thus a friar wheedles Lady Mede for money in *Piers Plowman* on the basis that if she will but sponsor the glazing of a window in the friary church, 'Sykur sholde thi soule be hevene to have.'[38] On the other hand there is the earnest encouragement of the sermon-writer that a man's last-minute almsgiving '*makyth hym sykur* ayens the day of dome'.[39] January is a selective, naïve, and over-literal listener to a simplifying tendency in the popularization of salvation doctrine.

---

[36] 'Agens penitenciam ad ultimum, et reconciliatus, si securus hinc exit, ego non sum securus. Unde sum securus, dico, et do securitatem; unde non sum securus, penitenciam dare possum, securitatem dare non possum': Aemilius Friedberg (ed.), *Corpus iuris canonici*, pt 1, *Decretum Magistri Gratiani* (Leipzig: Tauchnitz, 1879), *Decretum*, pt 2, c. 33, q. 3, dist. vii (headed 'The time for penitence is right up to the ultimate moment of life'), cols. 1244–7 (here 1245).

[37] Admonitions—and occasionally reassurances—about delayed repentance are legion in medieval religious writing. Exempla showed that deathbed 'repentance' might not work if, like January's, it was motivated more by fear of hell than genuine contrition (*JW*, pp. 176–7); and that it was likely to be prevented by despair (*Mirk's Festial*, p. 91). But some latecomers might be unexpectedly saved through the 'pryuete of Godis dome' (*Mirk's Festial*, pp. 74–5).

[38] 'B' III.48–50.

[39] *Mirk's Festial*, p. 105. However, the narrative has elaborated the sincerity of the dead man's belated turn to almsgiving; and, in a contrasting vein, another sermon in the collection declares that Christ's advocacy after one's death is the real guarantee of 'sycurnes' to all humankind: p. 153.

At the same time, I should like to suggest, Chaucer puts us in mind of another pervasive use of the concept of 'security', one that is found in antique ethics. Here, as often, Seneca will prove a most pertinent guide. 'Tranquillity' might be described as the common denominator of the cluster of qualities that Stoics prized as possessions of the 'wise' person. Rising above passion and turmoil, transcending affronts, such a person was to cultivate 'secure' forms of happiness. Particularly antithetical to such security were the 'voluptuary' sensual pleasures that drew one into dependence and cravings, inimical to the crucial virtue of self-control. Genuine joy was a stern interior business, not to be confused with the transient *voluptates* of the body; only virtue provided a joy that was *securus*.[40] Solid assurance, *solida securitas*, was not to be attained by seeking physical pleasure all over the place, for 'we Stoics hold that pleasure is a vice' ('vitium esse voluptatem').[41] In one of Seneca's essays this thinking crystallizes into quotable aphorism: assurance 'is the peculiar blessing of the wise man' ('securitas autem proprium bonum sapientis est').[42]

Although in our own time 'security' has become a term redolent of nervous personnel with body-armour and helmets rather than redolent of serenity, the concept was the hallmark of ultimate untroubled happiness in the Stoic strand of late antique thought transmitted to the Middle Ages. One key area of debate, though, concerned the status of 'pleasure' within that assured happiness. The Epicureans were vilified for supposedly defining *voluptas* as beatitude. This was not strictly true because Epicure himself exalted above all the absence of pain and effort: sensual pleasure itself was not necessarily always the highest good in his philosophy, as Seneca noted, since such pleasure might sometimes cost far more effort to achieve than a meagre lifestyle. Seneca himself argued firmly that people needed to have the courage to make the move from worldly ease to the 'felicity' and 'security' of simple fare: there lay the pleasure of the highest good.[43]

A habitual simplification of Epicure's position resulted in him being nicknamed the 'Professor of Pleasure', *magister voluptatis*. Thereafter

---

[40] Seneca, *Ep.* 23 and 27, *Epistulae*, vol. 1, pp. 158–64, 192–5.

[41] *Ep.* 44.7, and 59.1, *Epistulae*, vol. 1, pp. 290–1 and 408–9; cf. *De beneficiis*, VII.2.2–3, *Moral Essays*, vol. 3, pp. 460–1 (proper 'voluptas' is not bodily indulgence but freedom from perturbation).

[42] *De constantia*, XIII.5, *Moral Essays*, vol. 1, pp. 88–9.

[43] *Ep.* 21, *Epistulae*, vol. 1, pp. 140–9.

texts as influential as Augustine's *City of God* asserted that Epicurean philosophers 'live by the rule of the flesh since they place the Highest Good of man in physical pleasure'.[44] Hence, again, the 'General Prologue''s sketch (in the Franklin portrait) of Epicure as one who 'heeld opinioun that pleyn delit / Was verray felicitee parfit' (1.331–3). It has been suggested by Paule Mertens-Fonck that in this description Chaucer *knowingly* parodies Epicure's belief, as if it meant little more than dedication to food.[45] To my mind she is off the scent in attributing detailed knowledge of Epicurean thinking to Chaucer. His knowledge in that respect is filtered through commonplaces (encouraged by such remarks as Augustine's) and through Stoic commentary.

While Seneca himself remained ambivalent about Epicureanism, he certainly attacked it for making virtue the servant of pleasure.[46] Dedication to pleasure was not consistent, he argued, with what is 'honourable' (*honestum*). With this Cicero, too, strenuously agreed in his book on moral duty. For Cicero the whole point of 'moral rectitude' (*honestas*) or of what is 'honourably good' (*honestus*) is that it is the antithesis of sensual pleasure (*voluptas*). In the Ciceronian view the dignity of human nature is betrayed by abandonment to 'excess and luxury and voluptuousness', whereas it is more honourable (*honestus*) to live in 'thrift and sobriety'.[47]

Now January is clearly represented as an Epicurean in all but name:

> Somme clerkes holden that felicitee
> Stant in delit, and therfore certeyn he,
> This noble Januarie, with al his myght,
> In honest wyse, as longeth to a knyght,
> Shoop hym to lyve ful deliciously.
> His housynge, his array, as honestly
> To his degree was maked as a kynges.
> Amonges othere of his honeste thynges,
> He made a gardyn . . .
>
> (IV.2021–9)

---

[44] Augustine, *City of God*, XIV.2, trans. Bettenson, p. 548.

[45] Paule Mertens-Fonck, 'Le Franklin et la doctrine d'Epicure dans les *Contes de Canterbury*', in *Etudes de linguistique et de littérature en l'honneur d'André Crépin*, ed. Danielle Buschinger and Wolfgang Spiewok, Wodan, band 20 (Greifswald: Reineke, 1993), pp. 273–80.

[46] Augustine also transmits this Stoic critique in *City of God*, V.20, trans. Bettenson, p. 214.

[47] *De officiis*, I.30.106, trans. Miller, pp. 108–9.

January's plans for living a life of utter pleasure ('deliciously') are introduced here with a peculiar and decidedly mocking threefold iteration of the suitability of such a lifestyle: it is pursued 'in honest wyse', 'honestly', by means of 'honeste thynges'. Rosalind Field calls this 'one of the most sustained passages of sneering in the tale', particularly in the way it 'devalues' through ironic repetition of 'honest'.[48] Commentators have not made much of the point, but this is a Latinate vocabulary calculatedly drawn and debased from the Latin ethical tradition.[49] January is making nonsense of ethics not only by mistaking voluptuous pleasure as the route to 'sikernesse' but also by seriously imagining that it is 'honeste' to cultivate *delit*.

In fact January implicitly travesties the meaning of *honeste* (or more strictly the Merchant narrator travesties it for him) and debases it to the level of aristocratic consumerism. January's sumptuous household is 'honourable' only in the sense that it projects his status.[50] The Middle English adjective can stretch in meaning to encompass the morally honourable at one end of the spectrum and the merely socially impressive (like January's lifestyle) at the other. In this cheap, status-obsessed use of 'honest' we are miles from the idealistic reverence for *honestas* in Cicero and Seneca.[51] The significance of the concept in antique philosophy was known to medieval vernacular moral literature, where we hear that some 'old philosophers' located the highest good in 'delyt of body', but others in 'honeste lyvynge'.[52] For January, by contrast, honourable living has become confused with the 'delit' of suitably fine apartments and a luxury garden. By his own estimate it also implies *ese* (IV.1628, 1633): a word very suggestive of leisured sensual gratification and hence readily aligned with sloth.[53]

---

[48] 'January's "honeste thynges": Knighthood and Narrative in the *Merchant's Tale*', *Reading Medieval Studies*, 20 (1994), 38–49 (p. 42). Field detects (p. 44) the envious malice of the 'new' man (the Merchant) against 'old' money (January as knight), but this presumes, I think, an unrealistically sustained reader awareness of the narrator's status.

[49] Neuse rightly suggests that the Merchant 'calls up a key term of Stoicism' by using the word 'honeste', but my deduction from this differs from his: 'Marriage and the Question of Allegory in the *Merchant's Tale*', p. 122.

[50] *MED* 'honest(e', sense 2(b). The word's large medieval semantic field, by contrast with its modern 'narrow ethical meaning', is well discussed in Keiser, *Courtly Desire*, pp. 27–8.

[51] It is a keystone of Senecan ethics that 'the honourable and the good are identical' ('idem est honestum at bonum'): *Ep.* 87.25; cf. *Ep.* 71.4, 74.1, and 74.10; *Epistulae*, vol. 2, pp. 336–7; pp. 74–5, 114–15, and 118–19.

[52] *VV*, p. 78.   [53] *JW*, p. 103.

Sloth, voluptuous *delit*, fine housing, and a garden—the picture of a morally and ethically unpardonable Epicurean is complete. No reader is fooled by the narrator's pretence that January lives like this *because* 'Somme clerkes holden that felicitee / Stant in delit'. January has not been converted to Epicureanism by taking private tuition in antique philosophy: rather, the availability of a simplified philosophical justification is a stick-on validation for his sensual indulgence. But the garden, it should be added, contributes to January's 'Epicurean' stance more knowingly than most Chaucerians recognize. Commentators have naturally taken up the allusions by which Chaucer connects it with the Garden of Deduit (Pleasure) in the *Romance of the Rose*, also with the Garden of Eden, and with garden metaphors for the beloved in the biblical Song of Songs.[54] Yet, coming as an alleged effect of January's compliance with Epicurean ideas of 'felicitee', the garden may be seen to invoke that sect very directly. Seneca caricatures Epicureans as cultivating a version of *securitas* that is more like torpor while, 'in the secret retreats of [their] gardens', they stuff their bodies with food and drink.[55] Why the reference to gardens? The answer is that Epicure taught followers in a garden in Athens, whence the Epicurean school immediately acquired the nickname 'The Garden'.[56] Knowledge of this passed to Chaucer's period through negative allusions in Jerome's treatise *Adversus Iovinianum* and in John of Salisbury's *Policraticus*.[57] January's garden is therefore more than a place for recreation and sexual delectation, it *is* the body of thought that, in the popularized view of Epicureanism, prioritizes such things.[58] 'Honest', in its fully ethical sense, is precisely the wrong word to apply to the garden. Chaucer's passage displays a brilliant sarcasm that skewers January's value-system

---

[54] For a summary see White, ' "Hoolynesse or Dotage" ', p. 398; more elaborately, Bleeth, 'The Image of Paradise', pp. 50–4, 56–9.

[55] *De beneficiis*, IV.13.1–2, *Moral Essays*, vol. 3, pp. 230–1.

[56] For information about Epicure's school, see e.g. Howard Jones, *The Epicurean Tradition* (London: Routledge, 1989), 16–20.

[57] Jerome mocks Jovinian as 'our Epicurus in his garden among his little disciples'; John of Salisbury contrasts the garden of wisdom with the garden of the Epicureans 'which has as its source lust': respectively, *Adv. Iov.* II.36; and *Policraticus*, VIII.16, trans. Pike, p. 396. See Emerson Brown, Jr, 'Epicurus and *Voluptas* in Late Antiquity: The Curious Testimony of Martianus Capella', *Traditio*, 38 (1982), 75–106.

[58] Neuse anticipates me in noting the possible connection with Epicureanism in the tale through its garden: 'Marriage and the Question of Allegory', p. 122. Mertens-Fonck posits an implausible association between the garden of the *Franklin's Tale* and Epicure: 'Le Franklin', p. 278.

by attributing the honourableness of his erotic garden project precisely to the 'wrong' philosophy.

The Senecan passage about Epicurean gardens is also helpful to us in two other ways. First, it reminds us that Epicureanism values inertia (Greek *apatheia*), and this links with the cumulative atmosphere of sloth in 'The Merchant's Tale'. The tale eschews action. January sleeps much (IV.1854, 1926, 1957) and sits in the hall (1895). He 'works', paradoxically, only at the business of 'ese', because the *voluptas* of sexual activity is a serious labour for him; but even there his policy as a 'werkman' is to do things slowly, 'at leyser' (IV.1832–4). At one point (IV.1914) he very nearly extends himself to perform a Work of Mercy (visiting the sick), but on second thoughts he sends May off instead and goes for a rest (IV.1926). Even Pluto and Proserpyne, in this relaxed ambience, have no more to do than to sit on a turf bench.

The second reminder is that Epicureanism is strongly associated with consumption of food and drink. The interesting thing about January's representation is that gourmandize is mainly transferred into the sexual domain as metaphor. We don't see him devouring food and drink, only taking wines and spices as aphrodisiacs before sex, and afterwards a 'sop in fyn claree' (IV.1843). We hear of no table piled with delicacies in his house. Most memorably, January grades female sexual eligibility by reference to hierarchies of food (pike, pikelet; old beef, tender veal: IV.1419–20). Chaucer has here creatively adapted a culinary metaphor used in an oppressive passage near the end of the *Roman de la Rose*. There the Lover discusses the pros and cons of older and younger women; he advises those desirous of young women to adopt a try-any-once policy. The male should be like a connoisseur who frequents the kitchen to taste meat every which way—boiled, roasted, marinated—in order to cultivate a discriminating palate.[59] This process, we are told, is analogous to the doctrine of contraries whereby a person learns what is 'good' by experiencing 'evil'. January stands revealed as precisely such a sexual gourmet, obsessed (like l'Amant) with the advantages or disadvantages of a prospective partner's age (IV.1415–32). The suggestion in both texts is not so much of a gross, inflamed sexual predator as of an egotistical sexual connoisseur bent on cultivating an appetite dedicated to 'deyntee'. At the same time January tacitly emulates the Lover in travestying the doctrine of contraries. Priding himself on judicious

---

[59] *RR*, 21515–52, trans. Horgan, p. 332.

powers of sexual appraisal, he has precious little idea where sin ends and moral amendment begins.

As critics increasingly point out, the impression of January's experienced appetite is unexpectedly complemented in the case of our reading of May, for she too, when we are allowed behind the bland exterior that January sees, turns out to have incipient criteria of performance appraisal: 'she preyseth nat his pleyyng worth a bene' (IV.1854).[60] May's sexual appetite is imagined as evaluative, and proactive to some extent. Instead of being wax to be plied by her husband, she proves to be a *user* of wax against him, in order to duplicate the key to his garden (IV.1429–30, 2117). We read that such 'love' for Damyan is incited in her that she must either die or 'han hym as hir leste' (IV.2095). The evidence has been taken to show that she 'begins to take control of her own sexual desires',[61] Clearly she expresses this desire, that impels her to make strategic arrangements to couple with Damyan, both through sign-language—the gesture of twisting his hand on his sickbed (IV.2005)—and through verbal indirection by speaking to January (in Damyan's hearing) of her 'appetit' for 'fruyt' (IV.2336). However, her desire is otherwise reported primarily as a wish to pleasure Damyan, to *serve* her lover's satisfaction: to 'doon hym ese' and 'unto his lust suffise' (IV.1981, 1999). Thus while May, escaping from her unlovely marriage, proves less inhibited and less passive than many Chaucerian women, the vocabulary in this pseudo-courtly fabliau still inclines to render her role as sexually passive. In the event, what she euphemistically describes to January as reciprocal activity between herself and Damyan in the tree ('struggling' with a man) is more one-sidedly presented to the reader as a drastic invasion of May's body by the squire: 'in he throng' (IV.2353).

If we were not persuaded that this precipitousness was something wished for by May after enduring January's protracted labourings, we might wonder how far it is distinguishable from rape. In bringing this chapter towards a close we shall turn to consider the specific case of sexual violence in rape. Having looked at the orientation of this topic to perception and credulity in 'The Wife of Bath's Tale', I have chosen

[60] 'Chaucer's good wives would never indulge in such implied comparisons, or cash valuation, of sexual experience': Cooper, *The Canterbury Tales*, p. 210. *Preyseth* here means 'appraises' or 'evaluates', not 'praises', despite the contrary conviction of many critics.

[61] Susan K. Hagen, 'Chaucer's May, Standup Comics, and Critics', in Jean E. Jost (ed.), *Chaucer's Humor: Critical Essays* (New York: Garland, 1994), pp. 127–43 (p. 139).

to discuss 'The Reeve's Tale' because of its manipulation of moral ideas on the subject.

'The Reeve's Tale': Rape as Theft

'The Reeve's Tale' is Chaucer's Measure for Measure, a tale grounded in the Old Testament morality of an eye for an eye, a tooth for a tooth.[62] It both executes and is structured by the intention stated by the Reeve in his Prologue, to retaliate against the Miller in his own 'cherles termes': 'For leveful is with force force of-showve' (1.3917, 3912). This legalistic maxim[63] is pointedly echoed in modified form in the tale by Aleyn when he and his fellow clerk have been discomfited by the trick Symkyn the miller has played with their horse in order to steal some of their corn, and when they have been further humiliated by having to stay the night in the thief's own quarters. Aleyn, thinking in legal terms of what 'esement' (remedy) the law might afford them, cites a law 'That gif a man in a point be agreved, / That in another he sal be releved' (1.4179–82). The reason why they cannot actually take an eye for an eye and must find compensation by analogy instead of compensation in kind, is that they know they cannot quantify their loss; indeed the stolen corn (as the reader knows) is already metamorphosed into a cake.

Aleyn's *esement* puns wickedly on the 'ese' of the sexual satisfaction he anticipates. Manipulating another neat double entendre, he aims to make the Miller's family pay for the defrauded flour by taking from them the sexual flower of the daughter's virginity: then the household will have the 'flour of il endyng' (1.4174).[64] Patternings of various kinds in the tale have been well observed in Chaucer criticism.[65] What appears more neglected is the rationale of the specific concept of retaliation, 'point' for 'point', which is carried through by the clerks' joint sexual

---

[62] Paul Olson, 'The *Reeve's Tale*: Chaucer's *Measure for Measure*', SP, 59 (1962), 1–17.

[63] Some manuscripts include as a gloss the commonplace Latin maxim 'licitum est vim vi repellere'.

[64] 'Taking' women, indiscriminately ('what thing comth next to honde') like a cock among hens or a stallion in the fens, is Gower's characterization of the untamed sex drive that the church tries to restrain: *CA*, VIII.148–63.

[65] e.g. by Janette Richardson in *Blameth Nat Me: A Study of Imagery in Chaucer's Fabliaux* (The Hague: Mouton, 1970); and by V. A. Kolve, *Chaucer and the Imagery of Narrative* (London: Edward Arnold, 1984) who discusses the moral significance of the 'unbridled horse' as a correlative of the clerks' libido: pp. 236–52.

revenge on the Miller, though it is absolutely central to the legalism of the plot: namely, the compensation of theft by theft.[66] The essential connection to make here is with moral doctrine on both rape and adultery. Let us take the case of rape first. One underlying commonplace here held that virginity was a 'treasure': it was therefore something that was ever in danger of being 'robbed', to the delight of the fiend.[67] Accordingly when Gower comes to focus on rape in the *Confessio Amantis*, the sin-categories under which he includes it are two not very discrete branches of Avarice called 'Ravine' and 'Robberie'. The example of the latter clearly, and in uncomfortable detail, demonstrates the doctrine in action. Neptune is a prowler on the beach who finds the maid Cornix walking there alone and resolves to take 'pilage' from her. Seizing her, he

> ... putte his hond toward the cofre
> Wher forto robbe he made a profre,
> That lusti tresor forto stele,
> Which passeth othre goodes fele
> And cleped is the maidenhede,
> Which is the flour of wommanhede.
>
> (*CA*, v.6176–82)

In one sense it is the woman herself, in this and other adjacent examples, from whom are stolen the 'goods' which, writes Gower, every good woman desires to keep (*CA*, v.6345–7). However, Gower's text also preserves some awareness of the technical sense in which the virginity that is stolen belongs to another *man*, the virgin's father or other male guardian.[68] Hence Gower introduces the 'robbery' that rape constitutes with reflections on the mentality of thieves who 'robbeth mennes good aboute' and will take a woman no matter whom, 'for other mennes good is swete' (where *mennes* is probably not used in a gender-neutral way; *CA*, v.6106–18). Indeed if we are unaware of this

---

[66] The key role of compensation by theft is missed altogether by Joseph A. Hornsby, *Chaucer and the Law* (Norman, Okla.: Pilgrim Books, 1988), pp. 115–21. Conceivably Chaucer intends a link not only with the thievery of a miller but also with hints in the *Gen Prol* that the Reeve himself is a covert or 'pryue' thief, as it is asserted that reeves typically are in *VV*, p. 33.

[67] *VV*, p. 252.

[68] The various senses in which canon law defined *raptus* as 'theft' are clarified by Corinne Saunders, *Rape and Ravishment in the Literature of Medieval England* (Cambridge: D. S. Brewer, 2001), pp. 76–87. Saunders also shows how pastoral writings slowly shifted attention towards violation of consent (pp. 99–119).

conceptualization we shall encounter puzzling moments in medieval literature: as for instance in the romance of *Amis and Amiloun* where Amis, a youth in the patronage of a duke, is spied on in bed with the Duke's daughter and reported to the Duke. 'Mi lord the douke', states the steward informant, 'In thi court thou hast a thef', that is, a traitor who has taken his daughter's virginity.[69] The crux is, of course, that 'in medieval literature, the marriageable young virgin and her valuable chastity belong to the father and are given by him to a husband'.[70]

Safely hoarded for such eventual transference, female virginity both constituted a value in itself and also secured the bloodline. This helps explain why there is such mischievous emphasis in 'The Reeve's Tale' on the exotic plans of Malyne's grandfather (a priest who has sired her mother illegitimately) for the girl's future, fantasizing that he will 'bistowe' her, by courtesy of diversion of some church assets, into aristocratic stock (1.3980–2). Readers universally respond to the mocking humiliation of Symkyn in his realization that by sleeping with her Aleyn has socially debased ('disparaged') the daughter he considers so well bred (1.4271–2). But we need to be equally alert to the understated point that what Gower would call her 'flour of wommanhede' has been stolen from her thieving father and hence stolen from the would-be dynasty launched by her corrupt grandfather, during Aleyn's all-night sexual labour with her. It is to underline that implication, I believe, that in her sentimental leave-taking from the clerk in the morning she motions him to the hidden cake made with the flour that she helped her 'sire' to steal (1.4240–6). Having committed herself retrospectively to her violator she transfers back the material flour, to complement the sexual flour she has had to yield to him.

There is yet to be considered the aggressive adventure of clerk John, who joins in the campaign for *esement* and pounces on Symkyn's wife. This too is an act of rape (though the wife's level of awareness of it as such is carefully blurred by the Reeve's suggestion that no such 'myrie fit' was ever to be had with her husband) but it is not a theft of virginity. No matter, any 'adulterous' sexual act involved an element

[69] *Amis and Amiloun*, 787, ed. Jennifer Fellows in *Of Love and Chivalry: An Anthology of Middle English Romance* (London: Dent, 1993).

[70] Hallissy, *Clean Maids*, p. 43; see also Kathryn Gravdal, *Ravishing Maidens: Writing Rape in Medieval French Literature and Law* (Philadelphia: University of Pennsylvania Press, 1991), pp. 6, 8–9.

of theft too. Again it is theft of the woman's body, this time from her husband's ownership.[71] Other writers confirm that adultery was condemned as a theft that was substantially worse than ordinary theft, because in ordinary theft an irrational thing was taken, but in adultery a rational being was taken:[72] as the preacher Jacobus de Voragine put it, an adulteress commits 'a greater theft than if she filched money from her husband and gave it to the adulterer'.[73]

The logic of theft for theft that we have been pursuing tends in practice to reduce the women to 'irrational things' precisely through the materiality of flour for flower. The tale concedes little autonomy to either of the women: they are, as we have seen moral-physiological lore insisting that women were in the sex act, categorically the 'passive' figures, the ones to whom something is 'done'.[74] Yet Chaucer (some would say, the partisan Reeve) introduces just enough ambiguity to cloud the circumstances. Malyne is not conscious of the approach of Aleyn until it is allegedly 'too late' for her to scream (1.4196). Saunders argues that the girl's sleeping state counters a cynical reading of the moment, though I would note that the pretext of 'too late' seems to be a deposition of which medieval rape law is unaware.[75] Then, in a trice, 'they were aton'—a way of putting it that further confuses the reader's perceptions.[76] 'Now pley, Aleyn', urges the narrator, cajoling

[71] Gower writes of the evil committed by an adulterous wife who 'gives herself and the property of her husband to her paramour': *Mirour*, 8929–30, trans. Wilson, p. 123. See also *ParsT*, x.877.

[72] *FM*, p. 681.

[73] David D'Avray and M. Tausche, 'Marriage Sermons in *Ad Status* Collections of the Central Middle Ages', *Archives d'histoire doctrinale et littéraire du moyen âge*, 47 (1981), 71–119 (p. 89). It is notable that the moralists harp on the responsibility of the woman, not the man, for this 'theft'.

[74] As we have seen, this gendering of active and passive is transmitted from Aristotelian physiology by such academics as Albertus Magnus. By contrast the Galenic 'two-seed' theory of conception, also available in the Middle Ages, credited women with a more 'active' sexual role, as Carol Everest reminds us with reference to the question of May's possible pregnancy, in '"Paradys or Helle": Pleasure and Procreation in Chaucer's "Merchant's Tale"', in Muriel Whitaker (ed.), *Sovereign Lady: Essays on Women in Middle English Literature* (New York: Garland, 1995), pp. 63–84.

[75] *Rape and Ravishment*, p. 299. Medieval rape law required the victim to signal non-consent by resisting and by protesting audibly: Brundage, *Law, Sex, and Christian Society*, p. 396; but the law struggled to define the degree of resistance necessary to verify rape, Brundage, pp. 470 and 532.

[76] Chaucer could, however, have read in John of Wales's *Communiloquium* that a woman remains chaste within rape 'for two bodies cannot become as one if the limbs are intertwined while the spirits are not': Swanson, *John of Wales*, p. 125. Cf. Augustine's celebrated discussion of the rape of Lucretia, *City of God*, 1.19, trans. Bettenson, p. 29.

the reader to conspire with the intruder's point of view on this sexual escapade (1.4197–8).

By the end of the night Malyne is making the best of things, ready to reciprocate the intruder's sweet farewells. Given that Symkyn's wife meanwhile experiences her 'myrie fit' from John's torrid thrustings, there is little scope for a reader to suppose that the clerks enjoy their 'pley' and their 'joly lyf' (1.4198, 4232) utterly one-sidedly, except to the extent that we can stand aside from the controlling view of the narrator. Although such an argument is hugely provocative in a twenty-first-century context, I would deduce that Chaucer wants us to envisage daughter and wife as at least part-collaborators in their own 'theft', and that in fact this is essential to increase the cumulative fabliau humiliation of Symkyn, a man who deserves to be derided with the title 'patriarch' if ever anyone did.

The tale ends with summary comment on how the false proud miller's fate, with his wife and daughter both 'swyved', confirms the adage 'A gylour shal hymself bigyled be' (I. 4321). Langland reminds us how such thinking is characteristic of an Old Testament dispensation when he writes a dense passage on Christ's use of guile (through human disguise in the Incarnation and Passion) to defeat the consequences of Satan's guile (through disguise as a serpent in Eden). 'Thefliche thow me robbedest', Christ declares to Satan; 'the Olde Lawe graunteth / That gilours be bigiled ...' (*Piers Plowman*, 'в' xviii.339–40). But Christ adds that he also *transcends* the ethic of measure for measure, since the 'grace' of his salvific act now 'destroys guile' (xviii.348). I mention this Langlandian use of the same adage that closes 'The Reeve's Tale' precisely because it is a powerful reminder that Chaucer's tale remains wrapped up in an 'old dispensation' ethic.[77] No grace deflects or softens the tale's retaliatory regime, unless it be Malyne's moment of morning-after tenderness. Because fabliau in general favours paradigms of requital and one-upmanship, the genre does not offer fertile ground for acts of grace. 'The Reeve's Tale', with its brilliant wordplay, its boisterous horse-chase and its 'fits' of sexual energy, is a more joyous fabliau than received criticism often claims, yet it locks its comedy within a model of theft-for-theft in which women's bodies are reduced to vessels in which masculine *esement* is found for an afternoon of grievance and a cake's-worth of flour.

---

[77] Robert W. Hanning prefers to emphasize the comedic potential for the tale implicit in the paradigm of the devil as the trickster tricked: ' "Parlous Play": Diabolic Comedy in Chaucer's *Canterbury Tales*', in Jost (ed.), *Chaucer's Humor*, pp. 295–311 (p. 308).

Same-Sex (Mis)Representations: 'The Pardoner's Prologue' and 'Tale'; 'The Miller's Tale'

Not much space is left in this chapter for discussion of Chaucer's projection of moral issues around same-sex relationships. The reason for this is that no such issues are unequivocally broached in the writing. Some critics have built complex sexualizations around the companionship of Pandarus with Troilus in *Troilus and Criseyde*, where there is no specific cue. More plausibly the narrator's conjecture in the 'General Prologue' that the Pardoner *might* be a 'geldyng or a mare' based on such evidence as his concern to be fashionable, his hair worn long, and his high-pitched (goatish) voice, has prompted elaborate deductions about eunuchry or homosexuality, or hermaphroditic possibilities, in 'The Pardoner's Prologue' and 'Tale'.[78]

Since the moralists rated sodomy as an 'unspeakable' sin and wrote only very cagily about it (as witnessed by 'The Parson's Tale', x.909), there is warrant for wondering whether Chaucer carefully encodes in the Pardoner a response to the outcast moral status attributed by medieval doctrine to homosexual acts. For a queer reading to work, however, the Pardoner's affirmations of heterosexuality in his 'Prologue' require to be taken as a 'front'; his reference to the possibility that members of his typical rustic audience have committed a sin that cannot be spoken (vi.377–80) requires to be taken as a reflexive allusion to what he cannot mention about himself; and the invitation, or challenge, to the Host to come forward to offer to his 'relics' at the end of the tale requires to be taken as a bisexual or gay man's attempt to confront the intuited homophobia of the company's most self-consciously macho male.[79]

The trouble with argument founded on what cannot be spoken is that it can't be proved either. In moral propaganda of the period, unbelief and heresy were linked with sodomitical practice.[80] Yet the Pardoner, a self-confessed hypocrite reneging on Christian faith, is only

---

[78] For an overview see Sturges, *Chaucer's Pardoner and Gender Theory*. Earlier criticism mainly considered the implications of the Pardoner's putative eunuchry. An alternative hermaphroditic implication is gaining ground, particularly in light of evidence that worldly churchmen were satirized by Lollards as hermaphrodites: Alan Fletcher, 'Chaucer the Heretic', *SAC*, 25 (2003), 53–121 (pp. 82–3).

[79] Monica E. McAlpine, 'The Pardoner's Homosexuality and How it Matters', *PMLA*, 95 (1980), 8–22.

[80] *VV*, pp. 14–15, 39, 132–3.

faintly interpretable within that frame.[81] In the absence of the way other medieval texts flag up potential homosexuality in characters (e.g. by alleging fondness for boys), there needs to be an *a priori* case that the 'Prologue' and 'Tale' don't make sense without sexualized interpretation. The claim, for example, that when the Pardoner preaches about avarice as 'root of evil', this is a displacement of his perception of a supposedly underlying sin which is the 'root' of his own predicament in society,[82] seems a figment of the imagination.

On the other hand there is no doubting the unexpectedly gendered, personalized violence of the Host's retort when the Pardoner unadvisedly picks on him. The Host is here invited to open his 'purse', make an offering, and kiss the Pardoner's relics. This is sexually suggestive because in the *Roman de la Rose* 'purses' have phallic innuendo and 'relics' are associated with genitalia.[83] The Host reacts violently against the (literal) prospect of kissing fraudulent relics, which might in reality be nothing but a pair of smelly breeches. He swears pointedly by the cross that St Helena found (i.e. by the 'true' cross), that if he had the Pardoner's testicles in his hand he would have them cut off, to be shown as the man's relics instead (vi.946–55). That oath draws attention to the problem of acute inauthenticity that the Host detects in the Pardoner's status—but which status, that of profession or gender?

Moreover, it is well known that the prospective metamorphosis of testicles into relics recalls some wry observations by Reason comparing the words 'testicles' (*coilles*) and 'relics' in the *Roman de la Rose* when she defends the *nameability* of testicles against the Lover's prurience.[84] But can such an echo amount to a statement about the Pardoner's own sexual status, and/or can the Host's threat of castration be made to cohere with a systematic reading of the Pardoner as being already a 'geldyng' (eunuch, or castrate)? David Burnley, normally sceptical about psychoanalytical

---

[81] Lee Patterson, combating anachronistic Freudian readings and citing reformist critiques of simoniacs and false preachers, finds symbolic sterility—a failure in the efficacy of spiritual 'seed'—to be the referent for what is revealed of and by the Pardoner: 'Chaucer's Pardoner on the Couch: Psyche and Clio in Medieval Literary Studies', *Speculum*, 76 (2001), 638–80 (esp. pp. 664–8).

[82] As argued by McAlpine, 'The Pardoner's Homosexuality'.

[83] From shape and because slung between the legs, purses were sometimes associated with the female vulva, but in the *Roman de la Rose* decisively with the phallus: see *RR*, 19637–8, trans. Horgan, p. 303, where the curse pronounced upon sodomites is that they should lose the 'purse and testicles that are the signs of their manhood'; cf. the Wife of Bath's reference to her husband's 'nether purse' (iii.44b).

[84] *RR*, 7076–88, trans. Horgan, p. 108.

readings of Chaucer's characters, sees the allusion to the discussion in the *Roman* as demonstrating Chaucer's willingness to entertain a coterie audience over the head of the innkeeper's 'character', and finds reference to sexual proclivities here: Chaucer takes 'an irresistible opportunity for wittily allusive play upon the topic of spurious relics in the context of the Pardoner's implied deficiencies'.[85] It remains to be shown exactly how his testicles, severed by the Host and coated in hog-shit to be carried forth by the Pardoner as quasi-relics, constitute a statement about supposed sexual 'deficiencies'. This only works if the inauthenticity that the testicles would have if they were presented as relics, by a process of back-formation makes us suppose they are fraudulent (inefficacious) *in situ* on his body as well: as Alfred David puts it, the Host 'humiliates the Pardoner with a cruel jibe about another pair of false relics that the Pardoner is doomed to carry with him'.[86] An alternative is to read the lines, as they primarily demand to be read, as scatological insult.

By contrast a more cogent allusion to sodomy becomes a salient function of the comic catastrophe of 'The Miller's Tale'. Here it is a case of the destination of the heated ploughing implement wielded by Absolon, the unsuccessful clerk who has been tricked into kissing the arse of the girl of his dreams. That anal kiss cures him, we are told, of his malady of love 'paramours' (I.3754–9). It also inaugurates a crescendo in the tale of what moralists would have termed 'unnatural' sex (i.e. any sexual activity other than 'missionary position' heterosexual intercourse). Absolon's expectation, returning outside the window which was the scene of his humiliation, is to do violence to Alisoun's arse with the 'plough' weapon borrowed from the smithy—a phallic weapon, clearly, that we may well interpret as a counterfeit, his own virility having been called in question by the humiliation of Alisoun's trick and his displacement by his rival Nicholas. Since the actuality turns out to be that it is Nicholas's bottom that is now presented to him in the darkness, Absolon's thrust with the red-hot plough acquires considerable sexual ambiguity. On one hand the action could be taken to re-gender Nicholas from male clerk to female body,[87] implying that he has conformed himself to Alisoun's mode of bodily behaviour. On the other, in that we are perfectly aware of the switch of bodies,

---

[85] Burnley, 'Chaucer's Host and Harry Bailly', pp. 212–13.

[86] *The Strumpet Muse*, p. 203.

[87] Hansen writes subtly of the patterns of sex- and gender-confusion implicit in this incident: *Chaucer and the Fictions of Gender*, pp. 231–3.

Absolon's action is transformed in our minds into a quasi-sodomitic attack, causing Nicholas's famous scream for 'water' and the imaginary onset of the awaited deluge.

All this cunningly befits the tale's burlesque of Noah's Flood, an event popularly supposed to have been caused precisely by humanity's lapsing into 'unnatural' sexual acts.[88] Chaucer's modern fourteenth-century pastiche, not only of the flood, but also of sexual sins held to have triggered it, leaves us amused but, so far as moral overtones are concerned, reeling. Perhaps one thought that could be pinned on the action would be a version of the medieval moralists' old chestnut that frustration of a person's (in this case Absolon's) presumed 'natural' heterosexual desires may cause a diversion of sexual energy in another 'unnatural' direction. However, on the whole, although Chaucerian representation in 'The Miller's Tale' of a quasi-sodomitic act as a misfire arising from thwarted yearning for a woman might seem fleetingly to promote that view, the speed and blandness of the tale's denouement inhibits the attempt to pursue such reading strenuously. Same-sex relations and their morality are therefore at most only lightly touched on by Chaucer.[89]

Summarizing what has otherwise been observed in this chapter about sex, gender, morality, and ethics, we can see that Chaucer's texts treat the moralization of sex quizzically so far as formal doctrines on procreation and the conjugal debt are concerned. He calls the church's bluff by disclosing how male-centred the 'debt' proves to be. In his writings sexual relations sometimes disrupt, sometimes substantiate binary views of 'active/passive' sexes, but not with moral effect. Social mores come more into play chiefly as a function of women's dispensation of 'pitee' to their suitors. Rape, even in fabliau, is not severed from *implicit* moral scrutiny, but the moral dimension of sexual matters in Chaucer's writings is especially located in marital interaction, or otherwise in the question of loyalty to one's partner. Simultaneously there is acute awareness of

---

[88] e.g. *Mirk's Festial*, p. 72.

[89] Gower by contrast shows significant interest in 'near-miss' same-sex unions, even to the extent of encompassing moments of 'sexual indeterminacy' in the participants: see Rosemary Woolf, commenting on Achilles as Deidamia's playmate, 'Moral Chaucer and Kindly Gower', in *J. R. R. Tolkien: Scholar and Storyteller*, ed. Mary Salu and Robert T. Farrell (Ithaca: Cornell University Press, 1979), pp. 221–45 (p. 224). For further discussion of the 'sexual/ethical confusion' of the fictive world of *Confessio Amantis* see Diane Watt, *Amoral Gower: Language, Sex, and Politics* (Minneapolis: University of Minnesota Press, 2003), pp. 71–81.

the arbitrariness of libido. Perhaps the poetry emphasizes male perfidy in particular (though I tend to take the blatant 'misapplication' to males of an example in 'The Manciple's Tale' seemingly confirming the sexual unreliability of females, to be confirmation that '. . . and vice versa' is the rule in these matters; ix.187–95). If there is resort to an Augustinian perspective on 'blynde lust', as a deflection of human attention away from the afterlife, this is less prominent than the emphasis on the melancholy transience of sexual passion, considered in the context of longer vistas (*TC*, v.1823–5). Ethical tradition supplies a powerful pragmatic Stoic reinforcement for this anxiety about eros, exposing in particular the folly of dedication to voluptuary life, even while the narratives persistently acknowledge the sheer power of the erotic impulse. For Chaucer the unacceptable voluptuary is male (January) more decisively than female (Wife of Bath), and he is not as disposed as Gower to trace degenerate voluptuary instinct to a foundational female origin in Venus. Overall in Chaucer's presentation, the element of ethical or moral critique has to contend with a strong current of emphasis upon the yearning and pain, or the cruelty and ugliness, associated with the sexual drive.

4

The Ethics of Sufficiency: 'The Man of Law's Introduction' and 'Tale'; 'The Shipman's Tale'

A characteristic Hocclevian moment in the poem *The Regiment of Princes* by Chaucer's junior contemporary Thomas Hoccleve occurs in the midst of the disconsolate poet-narrator's preliminary dialogue with an old man. In response to the narrator's moaning about lack of remuneration and the arrears in payment of his annuity, the old man utters predictable exhortations. Indigence is no excuse for grumbling. 'God thanke always of thyn ese and thy smert', for neither should one revel in prosperity nor complain at adversity: grace is to be gained by accepting adversity in 'pacient souffrance' (1061–71). The old man's view is that, in any case, the narrator's residual annual income of six marks constitutes not serious need but beneficial moderate poverty, the kind of threshold income which moral tradition would applaud as sufficient for life's necessities and would thus see as protecting one from the moral risks arising equally from wealth or destitution. But 'Hoccleve' is unimpressed and digs his heels in. To accept a diminution of well-being to that extent, if other resources fail him, would require more 'perfection' than he possesses. Six marks are just too insufficient to sustain the responsibilities he has (1198–1225).

I call this a 'characteristic' Hoccleve moment because it is typical of him, though of few other medieval writers except perhaps Langland, to strike that kind of gruff note, making moral platitude squirm on the nail of quotidian circumstance. Is six marks a viable income—and for whom? What livelihood *is* 'enough'? How much destitution *should* imperfect humanity be prepared to thank God for?

We shall investigate the medieval parameters of 'enough' presently. The more immediate point to make is that in Christian moral writing the specific question of achieving a right attitude to the adequacy of one's means is often subsumed within the wider question of acceptance of whatever God 'sends' in life. Sometimes that is a matter of relative amounts of wealth. Thus the cardinal virtue of Fortitude is heralded as a virtue that 'strengthens' a person to respond resiliently to whatever God 'sends' to chastise or test an individual, whether riches or afflictions or poverty.[1] It is also a facet of Lowness or Meekness to suffer deprivation gladly and patiently and to find 'grace' in whatever God sends.[2] Conversely—a warning issued almost ad nauseam—there must be no begrudging the mysteries of God's grace that make one person rich and another poor.[3] Those who begrudge deprivation are guilty of one sin in particular. Their reaction 'ayens goddys sonde [against God's sending, what God endows them with]' signifies wrath, whether as a sin of the tongue or more culpably as angry objection that God 'werkyth unryghtfully'.[4] Such complaint amounts to asserting one's personal judgement over God's and (in the dramatic words of the *Book of Vices and Virtues*) to singing the devil's paternoster: not 'Deo gracias; God worth thanked of al that he doth us and sent us' but a song of hell.[5]

In view of the uses of the expression that we are about to notice in Chaucer, it is worth emphasizing how habitual in medieval writing is deference to what God 'sends' or to *goddes sonde* in the context equally of tribulations and unexpected benefits.[6] But the cliché was most often resorted to for its gnomic reassurance in adversity.[7] Chaucer, giving prominence to precisely this formula of response in 'The Man of Law's Tale', thereby taps into a central current of moral discourse. The sheer repetition in the tale is notable and it constitutes a thread that Chaucer draws out from the merest hint in the Anglo-Norman 'Life of Constance' from which he works.[8] After the heroine Custance is set adrift at the mercy of the sea by pagans opposing the marriage arranged by her father between herself and the Sultan of Syria, her boat eventually goes aground on a sandbank on the Northumbrian coast. Rescued and

---

[1] *JW*, p. 300; cf. *VV*, p. 123, and *PPl*, 'в' xix.291–6.   [2] *VV*, pp. 133, 201.

[3] *Mirk's Festial*, pp. 86–7.   [4] *JW*, p. 91; see also pp. 94, 100, 155.

[5] *VV*, pp. 65–6.   [6] *Mirk's Festial*, pp. 69–70, 184, 222.

[7] Thus Bors responds to Lancelot's warning of imminent war: 'Sir [. . .] all is welcome that God sendeth us [. . .] we will take the woe with you as we have taken the weal', Malory, *Morte Darthur*, ed. Cooper, p. 474; see also p. 428.

[8] Trevet's 'Life of Constance', in W. E. Bryan and Germaine Dempster (eds.), *Sources and Analogues of the Canterbury Tales* (Chicago: University of Chicago Press, 1941), pp. 165–81. Trevet speaks of God's *volunte* (p. 167) but that does not match the nuance of the ME *sonde*. Priscilla Martin, among others, has noted that 'sending' is a key concept in the tale: *Chaucer's Women*, p. 138.

brought ashore by the constable of the nearby castle, she 'kneleth doun and thanketh Goddes sonde' (II.523). Later when she bears a son by King Alla of Northumbria while the king is absent, and the king's mother Donegild sends Alla an evil report that the son is a misbegotten fiend, the king responds to the news with model acceptance: 'Welcome the sonde of Crist for everemoore', putting his will in Christ's 'ordinaunce' (II.760–3). Donegild tries again, fakes another letter back from the king as if his response had been horror, commanding the constable to put Custance and the child back to sea. Hearing of this command, Custance echoes her husband as she conforms herself again to Christ's will: 'Lord, ay welcome be thy sonde!' (II.824–6).[9] This time, by way of counterpoint and to underline her acceptance, the tale voices through the constable the sentiments of doubt and objection that would have constituted a less perfect reaction (one more like that of a Dorigen, for example, or of the dreamer in *Pearl*). Since God is reckoned a rightful judge, the constable wonders, 'how may it be' that God 'wolt suffren innocentz to spille?' (II.813–16).

Once alerted to the motif of *goddes sonde* and its iteration (II.902, 1041–3, 1047–9, 1160–1), the reader is justified in being sensitized to all instances of sending and their consequences in the tale. Mere human 'sending' (if we try for a moment to distinguish it from God's) scores little success. At the outset Custance is 'sent to strange nacioun', and the Sultan 'sente his sonde' (message) to his mother and throughout his lands, spreading the news of his wedding (II.388–92): the result is a bloodbath. Custance herself at last wryly draws a line under the inefficacy of human sending when she and her husband, reunited in Rome, meet her father again. Reminding him how he first sent her to Syria, she urges 'Sende me namoore unto noon hethenesse!' (II.1108–12). It is a rare moment of reproach from a woman who began as archetype of virgin-as-gift, and whose body has intermittently been shuttled around the seas ever since.[10] Perhaps she says this now because she thinks there is no longer a danger of being 'sent' anywhere else; but also because she is a tired woman who is visibly reaching the limit of her capacity to endure.

---

[9] In the Trevet 'Life', Constance expresses at this point her acceptance of divine and royal will: 'puis que a dieu plest e a mon seignur, le rois, moun exil; *a bon gree le doys prendre*, en esperaunce qe dur comencement amenera dieux a bon fyn, e qil me porra en la meer sauuer' (Bryan and Dempster (eds.), *Sources and Analogues*, pp. 174–5; my emphasis).

[10] Martin represents this as the only moment when Custance's 'natural feelings break out': *Chaucer's Women*, p. 139.

Critics have often been suspicious of the tale's obsession with submissive acceptance and suspicious of the thick flights of rhetoric with which the Man of Law orchestrates the miraculous preservation of the submissive heroine from the hostility both of the elements and of malicious oppressors at every crisis. Ruggiers detected a 'facile' affirmation of 'sublime resignation' (though one might be confused by the notion of facile sublimity) in the tale's attempts to justify providential suffering. Like other readers, he suspected that the tale is to be contrasted unfavourably with 'The Knight's Tale' on the grounds that the latter develops a more philosophical questioning of human tribulation and its relation to divine necessity.[11] Helen Cooper modifies but continues this vein of response, finding it 'hard to credit so serious a thinker as Chaucer [. . .] with believing that the naïve folk piety of the *Man of Law's Tale*, with its miracles provided to order, answered any serious questions'. Cooper reverts to the solution of a pairing with 'The Knight's Tale'—the latter a pagan tragedy, the former a hagiographical exploration of 'unmediated divine intervention'. Neither 'reading of life', she suggests, has ultimate validity, for they are relative to each other (though Cooper has made clear her sense that 'The Man of Law's Tale' falls shorter in terms of 'serious' reflection).[12]

Two reservations can be set against such sceptical views of 'The Man of Law's Tale'. The first, simply, is that it is precisely in relation to a narrative such as this, relentlessly dedicated to human submission to the divine, that our own cultural concern for personal autonomy and for liberated personality is most at sea. Chaucer actually appears to have gone out of his way to empty Custance of elements of what we would call agency. As Laskaya exasperatedly emphasizes, Chaucer eliminates from the story what few traces of an 'active quality of mind' had been associated with the heroine by Trevet in terms of educational accomplishments and the mental powers she exerts in her acts of conversion. By comparison the Man of Law's Custance attains—or sinks to—a more radical condition of 'self-erasure'.[13] Presumably Chaucer knowingly inscribes this even more extreme, quasi-ritual suppression of self in submission to the divine. It respects that enormously powerful current of doctrine we have looked at, which encourages grateful responsiveness to *Goddes sonde*. If the tale's strident rhetoric makes this current seem sometimes

---

[11]　Paul Ruggiers, *The Art of the Canterbury Tales* (Madison: University of Wisconsin Press, 1967), pp. 170–3.

[12]　*The Canterbury Tales*, pp. 131–2.　　[13]　*Chaucer's Approach to Gender*, p. 152.

suspect as well as sometimes 'sublime', the reason for that is probably that Chaucer intermittently emulates here a preacherly and morally hectoring manner because the sermon is, after all, the classic medium through which this current is disseminated. The preacherliness does not have to be presumed to contaminate altogether the vision of providential purposes that the tale unfolds.

A second reservation I have about the scepticism, which as we have seen tends to be expressed through comparisons with 'The Knight's Tale', is that the emphasis of 'The Man of Law's Tale' is more immediately to be seen in contrast not with other tales but with its own Prologue. Just as 'The Clerk's Tale' is thrust against (and defined further by) an epilogue that sarcastically pretends to recommend a loudly militant alternative to its ethic of obedience, and just as the cynicism of 'The Merchant's Tale' is in tension with (and defined further by) the mocking eulogy of marital bliss offered by an elusive voice as the tale begins, so 'The Man of Law's Tale' exists in tension with a prefatorial voice that pretends to repudiate the very acceptance of providence which the tale will describe. Whereas part of Ruggiers's objection to the tale was that it shows no *process* of accommodation to providence because the human will is '*correctly oriented* [. . .] *from the outset* in a wholly salutary trust in the Lord',[14] I would argue that the Prologue is there precisely to highlight dialectically 'at the outset' the ever-present possibility of rejection of providence; perhaps literally the present temptation for the audience of the tale to judge the uncompromising ethos of the tale against more expedient standards.[15]

To pursue this line of thought we need to emphasize that although the Prologue ostensibly focuses more on the ills of poverty and the tale focuses more widely on victimization by intrigues and afflictions, the ground of providence is common to both. In any case the tale certainly does not overlook the problem of destitution and material sustenance. At Custance's second exiling we are told that her boat was well stocked with food; and 'othere necessaries that sholde nede / She *hadde ynogh*', thanks to God's grace (ii.869–72, my emphasis). Similarly the narrator, reflecting on Custance's first ordeal at sea, asks 'how lasteth hire vitaille?'

[14] *Art of the Canterbury Tales*, p. 173 (my emphasis).
[15] A partial statement of this view is offered by Helen Phillips: 'The Man of Law's observations about poverty could be seen as both congruent with the tale's theme of earthly adversity and loss, while voicing through the fictional rich lawyer a completely contrasting . . . this-worldly approach to them', *An Introduction*, pp. 79–80.

and answers, with a glance at Christ's miracle of the feeding of the five thousand, 'God sente his foyson at hir grete neede' (II.498–504).

To these reassuring reciprocities of human need and divine sufficiency, the tale's Prologue opposes cynical discontentment. Using a favourite medieval source on the miseries of human life it begins by lambasting poverty as a condition of deprivation and humiliation, where stark 'nede' will betray the hidden anguish even of those too embarrassed to beg (II.99–105). From here the speaker dwells on the bitterness of the poor, their rancour against what they deem divine injustice, their grudge against better-off neighbours, their self-consoling 'sinful' vindictiveness, which relishes the thought of hellfire awaiting such neighbours for not being generous to the needy:

> Thow blamest Crist, and seist ful bitterly,
> He mysdeparteth richesse temporal;
> Thy neighebor thou wytest synfully,
> And seist thou hast to lite, and he hath al.
> 'Parfay,' seistow, 'somtyme he rekene shal,
> Whan that his tayl shal brennen in the gleede
> For he noght helpeth needfulle in hir neede.'
>
> (II.106–12)

The moral positioning here is complex. Condemnation of one's neighbour is specifically tagged 'sinful', as the victim of poverty is imagined gloating maliciously and punningly over the prospect of the better-off neighbour's tally stick (but also 'tail', nether parts) consumed in ashes at a Gothic Reckoning.[16] Yet the encompassing denunciation of God's distribution of wealth is of course doctrinally speaking equally sinful because it constitutes blasphemy, another division of Wrath: 'that is, whanne thou grucchyst or spekyst ayens god in tribulacyoun [. . .] demynge that god is unryghtfull or unmyghtfull, for he grauntyth the noght thi wyll anon at thi luste; & whanne thou demyst that god yevyth the more wo and lesse wele than thou were worthy to have'.[17]

---

[16] Chaucer's puns on *taille, tayl,* and *taillynge* have several times been explored in relation to 'The Shipman's Tale'; e.g. Albert H. Silverman, 'Sex and Money in Chaucer's "Shipman's Tale"', *PQ*, 32 (1953), 329–36 (pp. 329–30); Gerhard Joseph, 'Chaucer's Coinage: Foreign Exchange and the Puns of the *Shipman's Tale*', *ChauR*, 17 (1982–3), 341–57 (pp. 349–51 and references in n. 25). Cf. *PPl*, 'в' xv.105.

[17] *JW*, p. 94. Tupper links the Prologue's postures with a description of 'murmuracion' in *ParsT*, x.498–9 (including grievance against poverty and against the prosperity of others): 'Chaucer's Sinners and Sins', pp. 90–1.

And yet the Prologue proceeds as though there is nothing wrong with despising poverty, uttering more imprecations and sayings against it on the grounds that it withdraws respect and incites disdain (II.113–21). Quite different, the speaker concludes, is the situation of wealthy merchants, 'noble' and 'prudent' in this *cas*—in this aspect of fate or chance or luck. Their bags are not full of losing throws of the dice but winning ones, that run well for their 'chaunce'. They are 'wise folk' who know the world, its kingdoms, its tidings; and such a merchant's tale it is that the speaker will now tell (II.122–33). The 'wele' and the alleged 'prudence' of merchants, in this arch summary, appear to be identified as an effect of good luck won in the lottery of life, a lottery that, from the viewpoint of losers, Christ appears to run as a travesty of fair distribution. But where is this discourse going? At the last minute the speaker seems to salvage relevance from his cynical review of poverty by straining to see a literary usefulness in merchant adventurers, for they know a story or two and he will now tell one.

Critics have found this Prologue puzzling and have laboured ingeniously over it.[18] They have wondered why Chaucer substitutes praise of riches, in that concluding stanza, for Pope Innocent III's denunciation of riches at the end of the passage from which Chaucer is borrowing in the *De miseria condicionis humane*.[19] Why preface a narrative lauding a heroine's deprivations in this way? Kolve argues, I think wrongly, that there is 'nothing suspect' about the Prologue's disprase of involuntary poverty, a poverty that 'damages the spirit', though he does sense something 'implausible' in the 'complacent praise of wealth as a kind of bliss'. His better instinct detects in the voice of the Prologue a morally undermined voice, one which acknowledges how lawyers or others 'seldom prefer poverty over prosperity'.[20] This is the type of reading that I would wish to reinforce.[21]

The point of the Prologue seems to be to set up a quasi-normative, unreformed, sceptical estimate of poverty, a state that sufferers (like the 'Hoccleve' persona) naturally resist, blaming Christ and reproaching the rich in a mood of embittered alienation. The focus is entirely on

---

[18] See Patricia Eberle's notes in *Riv.*, p. 856.

[19] See e.g. R. E. Lewis, 'Chaucer's Artistic Use of Pope Innocent III's *De miseria humane conditionis* in the *Man of Law's Prologue* and *Tale*', *PMLA*, 81 (1966), 485–92, which interprets the passage as a dramatization of the Man of Law's interest in wealth.

[20] *Chaucer and the Imagery of Narrative*, p. 478 n. 78, and p. 295.

[21] Tupper demonstrated something of this thematic interplay between 'Prologue' and 'Tale' in 1916: 'Chaucer's Sinners and Sins', p. 91.

negatives, and on the conviction that the wealth of the so-called 'prudent' is really no more than a lucky throw in life's roulette. This is a mood of cynical anger and envy, dangerously given to ideas of arbitrariness and implicitly contemptuous of providence: it is not the sort of mood that makes virtue of necessity or endures the 'adversitee of Fortune'. It is not the contented frugality whereby the widow in 'The Nun's Priest's Tale' reconciles herself to living on an egg or two, managing to sustain herself 'By housbondrie of swich as God hire sente' (vii.2828). Rather it is the opinion that if God hasn't sent much then God is an unjust bungler. But in the tale of Custance, the central thrust is of course to assert the opposite, that God can be trusted to throw a lifeline to need, rescuing, feeding, manifesting his 'myghty werkis' in the individual (ii.478), and generally working towards his ends in ways 'ful derk' to human wit because that wit is too ignorant to discern 'his prudent purveiance' (ii.483). Such emphases tacitly rebuke those of the Prologue. Even the Prologue's claim that the poor become totally friendless is countered in the tale, for when Custance is framed for murder and 'Fer been [her] freendes at [her] grete nede!' (ii.658), a divine voice intervenes to champion her. Even the constable's near-protest at providence in the tale is as we have seen predicated on an assumption, countervailing that of the Prologue, that God must be 'rightful'.

To sum up, where the Prologue insinuates that need is an evil social stigma perversely imposed on the poor by a denial of fair chances, the tale counters with demonstrations that God sends 'enough' to those who patiently trust—sends even an abundance ('foyson') by which to survive in moments of direst need. This matter of need and enough and surplus is a topic that is close to Langland's heart too, and it is Langland who can help us appreciate its moral urgency in an epoch always vulnerable to famine and plague.

Langland's poem is hypersensitive to disparities and frictions between poor and rich, played out within a framework of various absolutes, of which one is the belief that absolute need must fight for the means to live however it can,[22] and another is the conviction that the ever-looming nemesis of spiritual reckoning is liable to catch out the ungenerous rich. Several times *Piers Plowman* focuses particularly sharply on neediness and sufficiency. The first occasion is prompted by the problem of beggars,

---

[22] The rights of the needy to sustain life are prominently but ambiguously discussed (as a way of 'excusing' one's actions) in 'в' xx.6 ff. For a fine analysis, see Robert Adams, 'The Nature of Need in *Piers Plowman* xx', *Traditio*, 34 (1978), 273–301.

raised uncompromisingly when society ploughs the half-acre: they are described as being mostly excluded from the 'pardon' subsequently given to Piers. Illicit begging is defined as begging without 'nede'. Need in turn is defined as deficiency of enough: but that only raises (as we saw in Hoccleve) other problems of definition, for what *is* enough? An answer is sought in an adage from Jerome that identifies what we would still call the 'breadline' as the crux: 'he hath ynough that hath breed ynough, thogh he have noght ellis' ('ʙ' vɪɪ.84).[23] Yet Piers goes on to try to transcend this practical hypothesis in a sudden switch of emphasis from the economic to the spiritual. He will no longer be so 'bisy' about the claims of the body ('ʙ' vɪɪ.118–19). Perhaps the best 'bread' one can 'eat' is in the shape of penance, as the Psalm has it.[24] We are moving towards a hypothesis that God will always provide enough sustenance for those who put morality, penitence, and prayer before preoccupation with provision.

It is this emphasis that prevails in further discourses on poverty and sufficiency in Passus XIV. 'Enough' of a livelihood will somehow come to those true in faith, claims Patience, though the 'livelihood' he is touting shrivels on inspection to nothing more than a phrase of the paternoster: 'thy will be done'.[25] At its most idealist the argument soars into mysticism, alleging that just as God's word (his 'breath') created everything, so by God's 'breath' people should live ('ʙ' xɪv.62). At a more pragmatic level the speaker Patience tries to sort out whether the spiritual chances of someone with legitimate riches who spends them reasonably can match those of someone patiently poor. The verdict is: barely. The poor always have the advantage that they can claim compensation in the afterlife for deprivation, the rich always the disadvantage that they appear to have been rewarded once already, and what is worse, that they are burdened with superfluities that they should have used to help the needy. Langland's attempts to view wealth with benignity are those of someone leaning over backwards at an acute angle to be positive about something he deeply distrusts. On the other hand he is extremely receptive to the received commonplaces about benefits of poverty, especially its alleged freedom from worry on the grounds that the poor person has nothing to be stolen and no business ventures

---

[23] Cf. 'ʙ' xɪv.314, where patience is described as 'bread' for the poor; and 'ʙ' xv.315–17.

[24] 'My tears were bread for me, day and night', Ps. 41: 4 (Vulg.), 42: 3 (AV).

[25] For assurance of a sufficiency for those who fear and love God, see also *VV*, p. 232.

to go wrong. Augustine and Seneca rub shoulders as authorities on this. For Augustine, poverty is *felicitas* (bliss) without *sollicitudo* (anxiety), 'a blessed lif withouten bisynesse'; for Seneca, poverty is a narrow path travelled without *sollicitudo*, 'a path of pees' ('в' xɪv.316–18; 301–6).

Chaucer was also receptive, though to a lesser extent, to these patterns of thought. While it is not like him to explore with as much vehemence as Langland the *polarity* of wealth and poverty, 'The Man of Law's Tale' palpably promotes the hypothesis that God sustains the faithful, and there is in Chaucer's work a current of sympathy with Stoic claims that freedom from anxiety and contented fulfilment thrive on minimal sustenance.[26] This current has been noted by David Burnley and Patricia Kean.[27] It comes out rather forcefully in Chaucer's shorter poems, especially in 'Fortune' ('he that hath himself hath suffisaunce', line 26) and 'Truth' ('Suffyce unto thy good tho it be smal', line 2).[28] Seneca never stopped harping on the theory that natural needs are satisfied with little, and on the argument that contentment depends on separating oneself from possessions because they are sources of worry and subservience. We are to forget Hocclevian 'excuses' about needing to acquire more in order to have enough.[29] Since true virtue takes pleasure in what it has and does not crave what it has not, 'whatever is enough is abundant in the eyes of virtue': consequently 'enough' is not some kind of knife-edge amount, it is a limit state which really constitutes fullness in the person who is content with what life brings.[30]

As we move from 'The Man of Law's Tale' to 'The Shipman's Tale' we shall see how these two Chaucer texts make antithetical allusion to the trails of moral and ethical thought we have uncovered so far in this chapter: to the problem of responding to what providence 'sends', to the calibration of what is 'enough' wealth, to the problematic anxious

---

[26] Jill Mann calls attention to a definition of felicity as *sufficientia* in the medieval Latin version of the *Nicomachean Ethics*: 'Satisfaction and Payment in Middle English Literature', *SAC*, 5 (1983), 17–48 (p. 39).

[27] Burnley, *Chaucer's Language and the Philosophers' Tradition*, pp. 72–3, 78–9; P. M. Kean, *Chaucer and the Making of English Poetry*, 2 vols. (London: Routledge, 1972), vol. ɪ, pp. 38–42.

[28] However, it is not commonly remarked how oddly the example from 'Truth' is phrased: not in terms of goods sufficing the individual but of the individual sufficing the goods.

[29] *Ep.* 17.5, *Epistulae*, vol. 1, pp. 110–11; cf. *Epistulae* 4, 8, 15, and 25.

[30] *Ep.* 74.12, and 85.22–3, *Epistulae*, vol. 2, pp. 120–1 and 296–9. Cf. *Boece*, ɪɪɪ pr. 2.90, defining 'blisfulnesse' as a condition 'that ne hath nede of noon other thyng, but that is suffisant of hymself unto hymself'; developed in pr. 3.40 ff.

'bisynesse' of entrepreneurial preoccupation. I am juxtaposing the two tales precisely because they, and their heroines, beg to be juxtaposed in their articulation of the age's characteristic concern with God's *sonde*.

'The Shipman's Tale': What is 'taillynge ynough'?

The wife of the St-Denis merchant in 'The Shipman's Tale' directly raises the issue of the sufficiency of God's provision when she complains at her husband for secreting himself in his office, where he has gone to ponder 'his nedes' (vii.76), and reproaches him for poring over his accounts, thereby delaying dinner so that the household and their guest John the monk are all kept 'fasting':

> Quod she; 'what, sire, how longe wol ye faste?
> How longe tyme wol ye rekene and caste
> Your sommes, and youre bookes, and youre thynges?
> The devel have part on alle swiche rekenynges!
> Ye have ynough, pardee, of Goddes sonde;
> Com doun to-day, and lat youre bagges stonde.'
>
> (vii.215–20)

The note of righteous reproof that she strikes, redolent of a hundred moral treatises, condemns the businessman's concentration on worldly 'reckonings' on three counts. One is that she insinuates a spiritual peril in them. (Her actual words are a curse, 'may the devil have a part in such reckonings', but the curse can hardly be uttered without at the same time fleetingly invoking the moral platitude that the fiend *may* have a part in monetary reckonings, and perhaps that one is better advised to anticipate the soul's last reckoning.) Another is that the merchant should not need to dwell on his accounts so, because he has 'enough' wealth, enough of *Goddes sonde* already. A third is that his studious accountancy imposes antisocial fasting upon his household and guest.

The morality is all mockingly diminished, of course. Latent spiritual threat reduces to casual domestic curse. The sufficiency of providence dwindles into an argument for hastening the next meal; and as for that pretext, we know that the guest is a monk, who might have some duty to fast. In any case we are aware that the speaker has just concluded a financial and sexual negotiation with their guest precisely on the pretext that she herself does not have enough money, with a strong insinuation that she might not be getting 'enough' in bed either.

Clearly we are in a world of parody, a fact most drastically signalled
in the arch Resurrection allusion earlier in the tale whereby it is on 'the
third day' of the monk's visit that the merchant 'up ariseth' to see to his
accounts (VII.75).[31] The tale's appropriation of the ethical and moral
injunction to be content with 'enough' likewise keeps on pushing it in
delightfully parodic directions. Does that mean that moral judgement is
irrelevant? For sure, such a fabliau 'expresses a licensed, fictional revolt
against orthodoxies and social morality'—but we need not rush to the
totalizing conclusion that the tale 'provides no moral parameters',[32] any
more than we need resort heavy-handedly to the sort of moral criterion
that finds the merchant 'doomed' in blind substitution of materialistic
values for spiritual truth.[33] Even Jill Mann (a subtle commentator on
usage of 'enough' in Chaucer and the *Pearl*-poet) seems to join in the
either/or view of 'The Shipman's Tale' by relegating it to a 'coda' to her
discussion, as a merely comic transformation of the 'serious concept' of
sufficiency.[34]

Yet it is worth combing the tale's usage to test what 'seriousness' might
still be lurking within the traditional vocabulary. Its initial appearances
seem incidental. The first is little more than a narratorial cliché to hasten
description ('Na moore of this as now, for it suffiseth', VII.52). A second
occurs when the monk manoeuvres his morning conversation with the
wife flirtatiously by suggesting that five hours of sleep 'oghte ynough
suffise' a man, at least ought to be enough for a man not subjected to the
nightly physical exertions of marriage (VII.100–1). While this remark
has its part to play in the developing sexual innuendo of the scene, it
comes up unexpectedly, and thus draws attention to itself: it announces
off-key the tale's focus on what 'suffices'.

After the wife's reproach to her husband that he 'has enough' wealth,
the next occurrence is in the merchant's reply to her. He concludes
this reply with news that he is to go on business to Flanders, adding a

[31] One may doubt how far this strategy of religious allusion 'sanctifies a life centred
on [...] pursuit of economic profit', as argued by David Aers: 'Representations of the
"Third Estate": Social Conflict and Its Milieu around 1381', *Southern Review*, 16 (1983),
335–49 (pp. 342–3).

[32] John Finlayson, 'Chaucer's *Shipman's Tale*, Boccaccio, and the "Civilising" of
Fabliau', *ChauR*, 36 (2001–2), 336–51 (pp. 348–9). For another representative
assertion of the 'absence' of moral values from the tale, see Joerg O. Fichte, *Chaucer's
Frame Tales* (Tübingen: Narr; and Cambridge: D. S. Brewer, 1987), p. 55.

[33] Janette Richardson, 'The Façade of Bawdry: Image Patterns in Chaucer's *Shipman's
Tale*', *ELH*, 32 (1965), 303–13.

[34] 'Satisfaction and Payment', p. 45.

flurry of devastatingly ironic bits of advice concerning what he expects of her in his absence. This includes his misplaced assurance, 'Thou hast ynough [. . .] / That to a thrifty houshold may suffise' (VII.245–6): misplaced, not necessarily because there is not literally 'enough' to run the household,[35] but because we are aware of her claim to the monk that she has run up a one-hundred-frank debt. (I call this a 'claim' because it has no independent corroboration in the text. The reader infers at the end that she has repaid such a debt with the money she receives in return for sex with the monk, but it would not be inconsistent with the tale's gyrations if we were to conjecture that the debt were her invention and the money still with her at the end.)

The narrative now seems to leave the topic of sufficiency behind for a while, though I would argue that it is present by association in the report that the merchant goes 'aboute his *nede*' in Bruges, buying and borrowing on credit (VII.302–3): for, once the question of God's provision and sufficiency has been raised, 'need' inevitably becomes, as demonstrated in *Piers Plowman* and 'The Prologue to the Man of Law's Tale', a charged concept. (Riches, sufficiency, and need were inextricably linked, particularly to anyone who had read Boethius.)[36] The merchant's need is, so to speak, extremely relative. Equally, the earlier bland-sounding statement that the merchant was pondering 'his nedes' while looking at balance sheets in his office, is interpretable as a veiled critique: these are *nedes* comfortably removed from the Stoic and Langlandian thresholds of austerity.[37]

In any case we return explicitly to sufficiency, though in a displaced way that recalls Daun John's initial use of it, in the comic finale. There the merchant, who has arrived back after concluding his successful deal, makes repeated sexual demands on his wife. In response, she

---

[35] The fact that the tale has assured us that the merchant is popular for the 'largesse' of his 'worthy hous' (VII.20–2) balances out the wife's insinuations of his 'nigardye' (VII.172), which, as Finlayson notes, we do not have to believe: 'Chaucer's *Shipman's Tale*', pp. 343–4.

[36] See *Boece*, III pr. 3, where *nede* or its cognates are used 14 times, *richesse* or its cognates 13 times, *suffisaunce* or cognates 5 times, and *inoghe* twice. On *nede* as part of the lexical constellation to which 'ynogh' belongs, see Mann, 'Satisfaction and Payment', p. 19. The same constellation is in evidence in the *Romaunt*, 5579–5708, 5769–98. Need was much discussed by the scholastics as a way of defining an acceptable extrinsic criterion of economic value, as shown by Patterson, *Chaucer and the Subject of History*, pp. 353–4, and by Lester Little, *Religious Poverty and the Profit Economy in Medieval Europe* (London: Elek, 1978).

[37] This is not to deny that Chaucer can use this phraseology neutrally, as when John packs off his servants 'upon his nede', *MillT*, I.3632.

good-humouredly transfers to the sexual domain her previous reproach concerning sufficiency in the financial domain: ' "Namoore," quod she, "by God, ye have ynough!" ' (vii.380). That she says this in jest is made clear from the line that follows: 'And wantownly agayn with hym she pleyde.' A moral precept apt for the mercantile context is being knowingly extended by the speaker—and presumably knowingly understood by her husband to be extended—to the sufficiency of sexual provision coming to him through *her*; a sexual provision described elsewhere in the *Tales* as 'Goddes foyson' (i.3165). But when she discovers that the hundred franks she gained from John has originated as a loan from her husband that has ostensibly been repaid to her, her ruse is to resort to a parodic form of the currency conversion by which her husband himself (using bills of exchange) has made his profit.[38] She converts her ability to supply sexual solace into a capital resource for the repayment of the money, switching in the process into double entendres on the sexual 'debt' between wife and husband (vii.413). He is to 'score' the debt upon her 'taille'—famously, on her sex organ as if on a 'tally stick' or account record (vii.416). The narrative is rounded off with a sort of prayer pointedly and triumphantly muddling up the various senses in which *Goddes sonde* might be conferred on 'us' (shipmen, husbands, merchants, wives, readers; take your pick) in a glorious sufficiency of tallying: 'God us sende / Taillynge *ynough* unto oure lyves ende' (vii.433–4).

At this point we might pause to collect some gender implications in the tale's discourse on sufficiency. In the sexual domain, the discourse is asymmetrical for it primarily projects the woman's body as a form of commodity, one that can be a source of deficiency or satiety, as well as sufficiency, for the male.[39] It is the woman who determines what is enough of this supply, and it is she who proposes to release the commodity on an instalment basis. Worse (from the point of view of transactional ethics), the commodity which she thus trades is not quantifiable and cannot ever be owned by any male who supposes he purchases it with gifts. Considered as a tradable resource its aberrant character is that it is not finite and that hypothetically, in the colourful phrase of a misogynous dictum from Proverbs, the mouth of a woman's

---

[38] Helen Fulton, 'Mercantile Ideology in Chaucer's *Shipman's Tale*', *ChauR*, 36 (2001–2), 311–28 (p. 318).

[39] The opposite, the male as source of extravagant sexual activity, is imagined by the monk in terms of a husband 'labouring' a wife (vii.108).

vulva might never shout 'enough'.[40] This gendered element in the tale's comedy precisely evokes a rueful and misogynous analysis of 'Venus's trade' in the *Roman de la Rose*. The tell-tale link here is provided by the monk's pointed reference to livestock or *beestes* as euphemism for the sexual gratification he intends to purchase with the money he borrows from the merchant. In the *Roman*, Amors, the God of Love, describes transactional 'love', a woman's sexual compliance purchased through Venus without Love's involvement, as mere merchandising; a one-hundred-pound purchase, like buying a horse. But Amors corrects himself. Sexual trade is not as equitable as horse-purchase because the investor parts with money without ever owning the commodity purchased: he cannot be 'master of the goods', cannot prevent others from possessing what he has 'bought'. To engage in such trade is foolish merchandising.[41]

In 'The Shipman's Tale' the monk knows all this for he is an expert operator in Venus's trade. He therefore substitutes another's money while pretending to buy 'livestock', and he plans no long-term ownership, because he does not intend to fall into the trap detected by Amors; the trap of losing both the sum paid *and* the thing purchased.[42] The wife also plays with the transactional ethics we have glimpsed. She pretends that she will merge a financial with a marital (sexual) 'debt', and that she will thereby equitably refund the sum she finds she owes her husband. The reader knows, of course, that the husband has no more ownership now of the sexual commodity thus proffered than he has had all along. A major part of the tale's comedy resides in these 'unethical' or asymmetrical transactional configurations centred on the analogy between female sexual favour and commodity, familiar to the Middle Ages not only through the *Roman de la Rose* but also John of Salisbury's *Policraticus*.[43]

In the material domain the gender pattern is also asymmetrical. When the merchant's wife asserts that in material terms her husband has enough

---

[40] Prov. 30: 15–16.   [41] *RR*, 10735–96, trans. Horgan, pp. 165–6.

[42] The monk is a variant of the sexual rival imagined by Amors, who may not even need to pay the woman for possessing what the first purchaser wants to possess; the rival 'may have such a way with words that he receives all for nothing': *RR*, 10779–80, trans. Horgan, p. 166.

[43] *Policraticus*, VIII.3, trans. Pike, pp. 301–5. The passage bewails the injustice of a 'market at which a thing once bought does not profit unless it continues to be bought'. In John of Salisbury's mind are the sexual favours of the Terentian courtesan Thais, favours which are 'bought' for three days but which she then bestows elsewhere.

of what God has sent, she is invoking the commonplace as it applies to a male envisaged as the household's primary recipient of prosperity or disaster (through the risk-taking of trading in this instance). That is the most common application in the moral treatises. By contrast, as we have seen, the sufficiency that is associated with Custance in 'The Man of Law's Tale' either designates survival-provisions during her exile, or concerns her resignation to crises that afflict her through the agency of enemies. When it is the merchant's wife's turn in 'The Shipman's Tale' to be told by her husband that she has enough to 'suffise' for running the household fittingly during his absence, it is clear that this really means something more ordinary—an allowance or sufficiency of provisions and cash, estimated by himself in proportion to the outgoings. Here we are not in the realms of 'Goddes sonde'.

In what is still one of the most interesting readings of 'The Shipman's Tale', John Scattergood draws attention to intimations of a traditional medieval opposition in the tale between 'wasters' and 'winners', and argues that the merchant is constructed to be a surprisingly positive version of the 'winner' stereotype in that his honest and serious dedication to his profession is rendered with unusual respect, even though ultimately the tale obliges us to disparage him for his 'literal-mindedness'.[44] To me, however, this appears an over-genial estimate. In my view the questions about what is 'enough' for humanity are meant to stick. It is true that they are brought obliquely into the narrative and that they are mostly uttered with coolly unscrupulous intent. The merchant's wife, who utters them twice, is something of a direct antithesis to Custance. She is 'bold' (VII.401) and assertive where Custance is mild and obedient. Her use of the language of sufficiency is manipulative rather than a matter of belief as it is with Custance. Yet although this tempts the reader to discount the possibility that the moral dicta have serious relevance to the merchant household, significant features of the merchant's talk reinforce a moral thrust that is still latent, I suggest, in the reference to *Goddes sonde*.

When his wife chides him for his preoccupation, he retorts that she can't really grasp the 'curious bisynesse' of the merchant profession; the high risk of failure behind the façade of success, the need for astuteness in what is a 'queynte' world. Doubtless here is one of the numerous double entendres that the reader sees recoiling on the merchant, for we

---

[44] V. J. Scattergood, 'The Originality of the *Shipman's Tale*', *ChauR*, 11 (1976–7), 210–31 (esp. pp. 225–6).

are bound to read him as foolishly incautious about a more intimately *queynte* world than the one he apparently refers to. But in his own terms, which we should not lose sight of amid the mischievousness of the punning irony, what he is expressing is the anxious vulnerability—as preachers customarily saw it—of the life dedicated to trade. In fact he finishes his appeal for understanding precisely in the language that would have serious negative valence for the moralist:

> For everemoore we moote stonde in drede
> Of hap and fortune in oure chapmanhede
>
> (vii.237–8)

This rehearses the bleak anxieties of the merchant's life identified by Reason in the *Roman de la Rose*.[45] There, Reason's critique is reinforced by a stoic idealization of contented sufficiency and by emphasis on the fear that the insecurity of wealth induces.[46] In the Middle English translation, precisely the vocabulary used by the Shipman's merchant is deployed to question the merchant life. Whereas the poor can be rich in the abundance of 'suffisaunce' (*Romaunt*, 5689–90) merchants experience woe in acquiring, *drede* in guarding, and *bisynesse* in increasing their goods (5593–6); always on edge, they '*never shal ynogh* have geten' in their dread of becoming 'nedy' (5698–5703).[47] In a similar vein is the sketch of covetousness associated with Haukyn's coat of sin in *Piers Plowman*. Covetise is momentarily imagined as a merchant, for whom loss of goods eradicates all thought of penance from the mind, and who is consumed with anxiety when his servants are in Bruges or Prussia on business—to 'maken here eschaunges' for instance. In such a case the merchant would get no comfort from hearing mass or from anything else, because his 'mynde was more on [his] good in a doute [in anxiety] / Than in the grace of God' ('B' xiii.383–98).

---

[45] *RR*, 4945–60, esp. the last few lines: 'he continues to fret about increasing and multiplying [his pile], for he will never have enough, however much he manages to acquire', trans. Horgan, p. 76; see also 5041–50, trans. p. 77. The woes of wealth are enumerated at 5160–84, trans. pp. 79–80.

[46] *RR*, 5227–36, trans. Horgan, p. 80. What Thompson doubts readers should suppose (*Chaucer, Boccaccio and the Debate of Love*, pp. 211–12) is precisely what I am affirming that they should suppose—namely that 'the merchant should stand "in drede" of God more than the "hap and fortune" of business'.

[47] 'Besynesse' and 'dred' (along with 'trauayle') are again the clichéd accompaniments of the life devoted to wealth, in *Dives and Pauper*, ix.9 (in a section on factors that should temper anyone's 'covetise'), ed. Barnum, vol. 1, pt 2, p. 273.

Chaucer had seen how Boethius balanced the 'angwyssous' effects of riches against the ideal of sufficiency in the *Consolation of Philosophy* (III pr. 3). There Philosophy obliges Boethius to concede that even amidst the abundance of riches he was 'alwey in angwyse of somwhat', and that 'thanne mai nat richesses maken that a man nys nedy, ne that he be suffisaunt to hymself'. Wealth, which people imagine will provide sufficiency, actually creates further need, if only through the anxiety to protect it. In 'The Shipman's Tale' Chaucer, using an oblique technique that we recognize from its deployment in his 'General Prologue', has arranged for the anxiety, the 'drede' or 'doute' thus associated with wealth in the moral and ethical tradition, to be described by his representative merchant *as if it were morally neutral*, indeed as if it were a ground for positive sympathy.[48]

By comparison with *Piers Plowman* the effect is further muted by the absence of any victims of the wealthy and acquisitive, the absence of the suffering poor who clamour at the edges of discussion of the rich everywhere in Langland. Although we are assured in general of the largesse of the merchant and we hear of the monk's strategic gifts even to the humblest servant in the merchant's household, the destitute are beyond the vision of the tale. Yet Chaucer is surely closer to the Langlandian moral perspective than most readers intuit. Evaluation should not confine itself to analysis of the technical legitimacy of the merchant's specific credit transactions in the tale. Although such analysis can yield a conclusion that he 'seems to fit the scholastics' qualifications for the ethical businessman',[49] I believe the ethics are to be judged on a larger canvas. The 'bisynesse' of the merchant is not the enterprise of a bold competitor heroically combating fortune in an emergent world of finance;[50] nor is it the ideal frank industriousness of someone intent on avoiding sloth and on social altruism. Instead it is an intricate ('curious') alertness and it fosters perpetual fear of loss. Because his manipulative

---

[48] Such intimations of moral neutrality have encouraged critics, of whom Lee Patterson is the most suasive, to read the tale as a legitimation of commercial life: *Chaucer and the Subject of History*, pp. 349–66. William E. Rogers and Paul P. Dower find critical response to the moral status of wealth in the tale dependent on whether money is perceived as a 'measure of value' or as a 'medium of exchange': 'Thinking about Money in Chaucer's *Shipman's Tale*', in Benson and Ridyard (eds.), *New Readings of Chaucer's Poetry*, pp. 119–38.

[49] Fisher inclines to this view in her discussion in *Chaucer's Poetic Alchemy*, pp. 109–11.

[50] Thompson (drawing on Branca's estimate of the *Decameron*) explores, though he does not fully endorse, this view: *Chaucer, Boccaccio and the Debate of Love*, pp. 218–19.

and apparently amoral wife is the one who jibes that he has wealth enough we probably feel that we can ignore the moral and ethical hint: *this* manipulative woman as the conscience of the tale—what a thought! But the tale, with its quiet reminders of the relevant moral discourse, keeps in play the suggestion that the merchant epitomizes misdirection of attention and that he may indeed have more than 'enough'. Nor is it a coincidence that in the sequel to the merchant's speech a merely routine mass is 'hastily' dispatched (vii.251). Mass is as negligible to the merchant's preoccupation as it is to Haukyn's stereotypical Covetise. Actually we should have been expecting stereotyping of the kind after the tale's second line stating that because the merchant was rich 'men helde hym wys'. This was a cliché of moral discourse: in Langland's formulation, those who have 'welthe of this world and wise men ben holden' will still have to settle their spiritual account at doomsday.[51]

Successful though he is—and the huge round figures, a twenty thousand shields' loan, a clear one thousand franks' profit, give a sense of substantial risk and impressive returns—this merchant represents a commitment of anxious effort to chance ('hap') of a sort that is cynically caricatured in 'The Man of Law's Prologue' and opposed by the emphasis on simple reliance on God's 'sending' in 'The Man of Law's Tale'. David Burnley follows through the question of 'wisdom' raised in the second line of 'The Shipman's Tale'. He concludes that no one whose skill is limited to *marchaundysyng* 'can appear truly wise to Chaucer'.[52] This type of generalization antagonizes some critics because of its insinuation that 'commercialism as a whole is under attack in the tale, as if Chaucer were simply toeing the moral line of the church'.[53] I agree that the tale should not be appropriated as evidence of blanket attack on the merchant community, any more than of blanket enthusiasm for that community. What Chaucer effects is a narrative in which a benign merchant's uneasy moral status is here and there measured in an understated but precise way, against concerns about acquisition of wealth expressed in the jostling Stoico-Christian vocabulary of the Middle Ages. Lee Patterson supposes that what he calls 'judgmental readings' work against the evidence of the tale's investment in exchange of all sorts (including semantic exchange through wordplay)

---

[51] *PPl*, 'b' vii.186–9; cf. 'He that hathe wyt to gete goode, he ys holden a wyse man': *Mirk's Festial*, p. 159.
[52] *Chaucer's Language and the Philosophers' Tradition*, p. 59
[53] Fulton, 'Mercantile Ideology', pp. 314–15.

by invoking 'an extratextual norm of rectitude'.[54] It will be apparent that in the present discussion the ethical and moral signals, though unobtrusive, are not reckoned 'extratextual'.

There is yet another self-betraying dimension to the merchant to be mentioned, an ethical one that derives specifically from Stoic thought, though this has never, I think, been perceived before. It shows Chaucer actively blending (rather than receiving ready-blended) his received ethical and moral ideas.

As we have noted, Seneca had plenty to say against committing oneself to the anxieties of money-making. He also had much to say, in a treatise thoroughly respected and extensively plundered in the Middle Ages, on the granting of gifts or 'favours'. Many of the emphases in this treatise are rehearsed (though without attribution) in the *Roman de la Rose*.[55] Now the loan requested by the monk and granted by the merchant in 'The Shipman's Tale' is not strictly a favour (*beneficium*) by Seneca's definition. But because the tale dwells on the spirit in which the loan is granted and also on the problem of what the merchant considers to be a misunderstanding concerning the calling-in of the favour, it nevertheless invokes quite decisively key parts of the Senecan discussion on favours.

The monk approaches the merchant for the favour of the loan with a flurry of prefatorial manipulation ranging from a show of candid solicitude for his impending trip, to an effusive promise to do anything for his friend that lies in his power. John then requests the hundred-frank loan, using as we have seen an outrageous but allusive sexual double entendre concerning the 'beestes' he must buy in order to 'stock' a place that is 'oures' (the wife's body considered as joint property).

What of the merchant's response? In the ethics of the bestowal of favours, the first test is the manner in which a favour is bestowed. Ideally it should be given gladly, promptly, unhesitatingly,[56] and indeed even anticipating the request if possible so as to obviate the embarrassment associated with the asking.[57] If the need for the favour cannot be anticipated and it does have to be requested, the best response is extreme readiness, implying that the giver was on the point of acting anyway,

---

[54] *Chaucer and the Subject of History*, p. 362.

[55] *RR*, 2237–52, 4679–4722, 8025–68, trans. Horgan, pp. 35, 72–3, 124.

[56] As emphasized by Dante in his discussion of generosity in the *Convivio*, i.8, trans. Lansing, pp. 19–20.

[57] *RR*, 8025–38, trans. Horgan, p. 124.

coupled with a friendly rebuke for the asker's tardiness in asking.[58] The merchant's response to John is at first exemplary: 'Now sikerly this is a smal requeste'—his gold is his friend's, let him take whatever he wishes (vII.282–6). Almost immediately, however, the fine impression is undermined. He adds the rider that merchants cannot do without cash, it is their 'plough', the very instrument of trade: so the favour will be decisively a loan, one to be repaid 'whan it lith in youre ese' (vII.291).

I do not doubt that, apart from inviting us into further sexual ironies surrounding the merchant's financial 'fertility', Chaucer here measures him negatively against the ethical discourse governing favours. That would also explain something which is rather conspicuous later in the narrative, and which seems surprisingly diversionary in a tale otherwise quite brisk, namely the detail lavished on the visit to the monk made by the merchant when he goes to Paris to obtain credit as part of the deal he is making.[59] According to the narrator the merchant drops in on John out of friendship and fellow feeling, not for any financial reason. But when the merchant mentions that his deal is going well and requires only a large loan to sew it up, John sees an opening to make airy remarks about how generously he would himself help his friend if he had the wherewithal, and to state that he has already repaid the hundred franks previously lent to him. John then concludes the conversation in a coolly peremptory way. Subsequently the merchant complains to his wife of the 'straungenesse' that he feels has come between John and himself over this matter of the loan, protesting that he never intended to imply he had gone to John for repayment, and urging his wife to be sure to tell him of any repayments of 'debts' in his absence (vII.383–99).

Here the confluence of financial and sexual 'debts' is ingenious and hilarious. But there is another reason why Chaucer is elaborating the sensitivity surrounding the merchant's conversation with John, and it derives from Seneca *On Favours*. The model for favours is that the giver should immediately seem to forget giving. Seneca rules that one should never remind anyone of a favour bestowed on them, since to remind the

---

[58] 'He should not wait to be asked for help', *RR*, 4680–1, trans. Horgan, p. 72. Seneca, *De beneficiis*, II.1.1–II.5.4, *Moral Essays*, vol. 3, pp. 50–9. Advice on promptness of response is among a clutch of citations from Seneca's essay in the *Florilegium morale oxoniense*, ed. P. Delhaye and C. H. Talbot, vol. ii, *Flores auctorum*, pp. 152–6 (p. 155).

[59] The 'apparent supernumerary detail' in the episode functions, according to Finlayson, to emphasize that the merchant is a 'sympathetic victim': 'Chaucer's *Shipman's Tale*', pp. 345–6.

beneficiary 'is to ask him to return it'.[60] The merchant contrives retro-
spectively to protest his own innocence in this regard and to shuffle blame
off on his wife. Yet the fact is that he has blundered into precisely the faux
pas of 'reminding' the recipient that Seneca warns against, and that he
has done so in a context where he allegedly meant to make no reference
to the loan at all (so that the question of whether it had been repaid or
not would not be particularly material, despite his criticism of his wife).

In one sense this is an object lesson in how not to behave where favours
are concerned—even when they are loans. The merchant stands revealed
as too short on delicacy; too ponderous; socially and conversationally
inept. In another sense the episode suggests that merchants, ever involved
in complex ('curious') transactional processes, are readily subject to
misinterpretation. The reader of this tale can easily be lured into a
satirical perspective on the merchant by a line such as 'Ful riche was his
tresor and his hord' (vii.84), or by the wife's allegation of his miserliness.
The wife's ostensible predicament at the start, that she owes money for
clothes bought for her husband's 'honour' (vii.179, echoing a remark in
a passage mimicking wifely self-justification with which the tale begins,
vii.12–13), equally lures us into a caricaturing view of her. In fact the
tale's world, besides being shot through with the instability of wordplay,
is also explicitly a world of temporarily deceiving stereotypes. The monk
misleadingly stereotypes the sexual exhaustion of husbands: the wife
contrasts the allegedly miserly and sexually deficient merchant with a
stereotype of the 'ideal' husband. Yet the stereotypes are double-edged or
are found to be qualified during the evolution of the tale. For one thing,
wives really were encouraged to believe that it was appropriate to dress
lavishly for the honour and pleasure of their husbands. For another, the
tale proves the merchant to be virile and moderately generous, even if
he is less than generously altruistic in the way he harps on the necessity
for repayment when he first lends the monk money.[61]

More subtly, misrepresentation is recognized by the merchant him-
self to be the foundation of his occupation. Members of this profession

[60] ii.10.4–ii.11.2; see also vii.23.2; *Moral Essays*, vol. 3, respectively pp. 66–7 and
508–11. Evidence that this model became associated also, ideally, with loans as well as
favours is in Generosity's advice to a knight not to delay if asked for a loan, and then
'not to cause such pains that the gratitude is lost before the loan is restored': Brunetto
Latini, *Il Tesoretto*, ed. Holloway, lines 1819–24.

[61] On the narrative's contradiction of the wife's insinuations, see Peter Beidler,
'Contrasting Masculinities in the *Shipman's Tale*: Monk, Merchant, and Wife', in
Beidler (ed.), *Masculinities in Chaucer*, pp. 131–42 (pp. 136–8).

must 'make chiere and good visage' whatever their anxieties; they can borrow on credit while they 'have a name', a reputation for solvency (VII.230, 289). Their wives participate in supporting this façade of creditworthiness, since they know that they must be dressed and access-orized so as to corroborate the standing of the husband (VII.12–13). Chaucer has already identified the reliance on misrepresentation as the prop of commercial creditworthiness, in the 'General Prologue'. There the pilgrim Merchant is a marvel of imposing dignity, solemn in dis-course, emphasizing his profitability, and, no one knew him to be in debt (whether he was or wasn't), 'So estatly was he of his governaunce' (I.270–81). There is, apparently, a presupposition that the true *estaat* of a merchant will be ever a private matter (VII.232); the merchant's business and household (the latter designed to support the former) are, in short, staged.

If 'The Shipman's Tale' catches the reader out in premature and mis-guided interpretations, and if in some sense it makes misinterpretation the focus of the narrative, does that suggest that its ostensible concern with sufficiency, with what is 'enough', also holds no solid signific-ance—is merely (to borrow an idiom used in the tale) a shadow on the wall? This seems to me the wrong deduction. Amidst the triumphant cynicism and egotism of the story, the motif of sufficiency sustains a meaningful presence. Despite (or even because of) its being mischiev-ously misapplied or applied for ulterior purposes, it inevitably reminds the reader of a traditional moral critique of the merchant's profession. Nevertheless there is no simple animus against wealth. The merchant's life in the tale seems half-protected by the same kind of moral opacity that we find identified in *Piers Plowman*: there Langland worries about the way Christianity, especially in its mechanisms of confession, is being subverted by 'colours' (rhetoric) and 'sophistrie', to the extent that Conscience can neither tell Christian from non-Christian, nor whether a merchant who deals in money may be profiting 'with right, with wrong or with usure' ('B' XIX.347–53). In the case of the Shipman's merchant Chaucer projects a world of dealing that easily covers itself in analogous moral obliquity. Given the absence of lepers begging at this merchant's gate, and in the light of the general decency of this merchant's behaviour, Chaucer disables the more raucous possibilities of the critique of wealth: but he by no means eliminates the critique altogether. What constitutes 'taillynge ynough', in the material as well as the more obvious sexual sense, actually is the underlying question posed by 'The Shipman's Tale'.

5

Liberality: 'The Wife of Bath's Prologue' and 'Tale' and 'The Franklin's Tale'

The monologue and tale assigned to the Wife of Bath constitute a delightfully multivalent and wittily nuanced discourse. For so rich a textual experience and for such a widely debated creation it would be particularly provocative to peddle a moral interpretation as if it were a magic key, though that has not prevented such approaches in the past.[1] My more limited aim is to show that it can be beneficial to realize what part is played in these texts by the ethical and moral resonance of 'liberality' or 'largenesse'—a surprisingly complex ethical/moral ideal upon which Chaucer seems to draw here, even though the signposts to it have eluded modern criticism. Among the rewards for investigating this resonance, I shall suggest, is a solution to one of the evergreen puzzles of Chaucer scholarship, namely the question of what underlying principle unifies 'The Wife of Bath's Prologue' and 'Tale', so often regarded as divergent or even contradictory.

We shall come to that shortly, but a logical starting point is in some writings by Boccaccio that could have prompted Chaucer's interest in liberality since he probably based 'The Franklin's Tale' on one or both of them. The jury is still out on the question of whether that tale is an adaptation of a story from Boccaccio's *Il Filocolo*, or of the fifth tale on the tenth day in the *Decameron*, or of both.[2] For my purposes the uncertainty does not matter. Both of these 'Franklin's Tale' analogues give emphasis to *liberalità*. In the case of the *Filocolo* the story's conscious function is to provide a stimulus to a debate on precisely this topic. Tarolfo is the courtly suitor who undertakes an 'impossible' task to win

---

[1] e.g. Bernard Huppé, *A Reading of the Canterbury Tales* (Albany: State University of New York Press, 1964).

[2] See Robert R. Edwards, 'The Franklin's Tale', in Correale and Hamel (eds.), *Sources and Analogues*, vol. 1, pp. 212–17.

the lady he desires, but then perceives that it would be reprehensible of him to act ungraciously to a man of such *gran liberalità* as her husband. The magician who has enabled Tarolfo to fulfil the wife's rash promise decides to sustain the same *liberale* standard of behaviour, and the company goes on to discuss which character showed most *liberalità*.[3] In the case of the *Decameron*, the context is a systematically competitive climactic day of stories all on this same topic, namely on actions done *liberalmente* or *magnificamente*, whether in the cause of love or otherwise.[4] In Book X there are not just one but two stories in succession about lovers relinquishing to the woman they desire the rights they hoped they had gained over her. The second of these (x.5) is the analogue to the Franklin's narrative. Again the husband's 'liberality' is the catalyst to resolution, and brief comments on the tale by its teller Emilia and by the rest of the company harp further on the same concept.[5] It is notable that the very last in this series on generosity that closes the *Decameron* is Boccaccio's version of the Griselda story.

One way or another it seems likely that Chaucer's attention was drawn to 'liberality' by his Italian reading. Given that most of these demonstrations centre on instances of male liberality, we should note that offsetting the example of generosity to be provided by Griselda is a jibe (or perhaps a piece of irony) offered in passing by the female narrator Elissa, insinuating that generosity is a virtue not common among women. She says that her story is to concern a generous priest, which is a miracle because priests are 'so incredibly mean that women are positively generous by comparison'.[6]

Elissa here tweaks a vein of conventional medieval misogyny in relation to the medieval concept of liberality and the gendering issues that surround it. In order to take up these issues as they emerge in the Wife of Bath's discourse, we shall need to clarify the virtue of liberality or 'largenesse' or 'largesse'. *Liberalitas* and *largitas* were, it must be emphasized, interchangeable names in the Middle Ages for the virtue of generosity: 'another word for liberality [*liberalitas*] is

---

[3] *Tutte le opere di Giovanni Boccaccio*, gen. ed. Vittore Branca, vol. 1 (Milan: Mondadori, 1967), *Filocolo* (pp. 47–970), ed. A. E. Quaglio, IV.31–4, pp. 396–410; extracts in *Chaucer's Boccaccio*, trans. N. R. Havely (Cambridge: D. S. Brewer, 1980), pp. 154–61.

[4] *Decameron*, IX.9 (Conclusion), trans. McWilliam, p. 731.

[5] For a convenient recent summary and analysis, see Thompson, *Chaucer, Boccaccio and the Debate of Love*, pp. 251–62.

[6] *Decameron*, x.2, ed. Segre, p. 957; trans. McWilliam, p. 737.

bountifulness [*largitas*]'.[7] Because *largesse* is familiar to medievalists as a defining feature of elevated social class, it is also important to mention at the outset that largesse/liberality was not class-exclusive but had a wide moral scope, and was discussed as much in pastoral instructional literature as in romance.

Within the Aristotelian ethical paradigm that the Middle Ages received from antiquity, we have seen that excess was the malfunction of a given virtue in one direction, while deficiency was the malfunction in the other direction. Liberality was thus a virtue delicately poised between parsimony (deficient liberality) on one hand, and prodigality (excess liberality) on the other:

> Tak Avarice and tak also
> The vice of Prodegalite;
> Between hem Liberalite,
> Which is the vertu of Largesse,
> Stant and governeth his noblesse.[8]

But the first point to notice is that misogyny faulted women in both directions where the functions of giving or retaining were concerned. Boccaccio himself in his book on famous women parallels the hostile remark just noted in the *Decameron* with a supposition that women are innately parsimonious with material goods, even while he enthuses over exceptions. (The moderate liberality of a woman who used her own resources to prop up a defeated legion, he claims, was splendid precisely because it went against the grain for a woman: 'women have habitual, even innate frugality and very little generosity'.)[9] Similarly at an earlier date, in the notoriously misogynous last section of Andreas Capellanus's *De amore*, there is the allegation that women are driven by *rapacitas*, addicted to gain, to the extent that they consider it a virtue to hoard whatever they get and to give it (*largiri*) to none.[10] However, contrasting

---

[7] St Thomas Aquinas, *Summa theologiae*, IIa IIae q. 117 on Liberality, in *Summa Theologiae*, gen. ed. Thomas Gilby, OP, 60 vols., vol. 41, *Virtues of Justice in the Human Community*, ed. and trans. T. C. O'Brien (London: Blackfriars, in conjunction with Eyre and Spottiswoode; and New York: McGraw-Hill, 1972), pp. 224–5. See also *ParsT*, x.464, where among signs of *gentillesse* is 'to be liberal, that is to seyn, large'.

[8] Gower, *CA*, v.7644–8.

[9] *De Mulieribus claris*, ed. Vittoria Zaccaria, in *Tutte le opere*, vol. 10 (Verona: Mondadori, 1970), pp. 274–8; *Concerning Famous Women*, trans. Guido A. Guarino (New Brunswick, NJ: Rutgers University Press, 1963), pp. 150–1.

[10] *Andreas Capellanus On Love*, ed. and trans. P. G. Walsh (London: Duckworth, 1982), pp. 310–11.

with the deficiency of generosity shown in this alleged material avarice (and also relevant to the way liberality will emerge in the Wife of Bath's discourse) women are equally held to display a contrary excess of sexual generosity: for they are 'unable to deny' their bodies and are so driven by lust that no man could satisfy their libido.[11] A further classic allegation of boundless excess in Andreas concerns speech. It is the complaint that women can't keep quiet. Secrets burn them up inside: women cannot restrain their tongues from talking.[12]

The allegation of material 'hoarding' was surely a reflex of an ostensibly more neutral medieval assumption that womanly virtue lay especially in guarding or keeping, not giving. It was a social hypothesis of ancient origin, still urged by Christine de Pizan at the start of the fifteenth century, that while a man's role is to acquire goods for the household, a woman's is to 'conserve' such goods through prudent domestic management (Latin *conservare*, Middle English *kepen*).[13] The ideal wife steers prudently between parsimony and wastefulness: in the bland platitude of 'The Merchant's Tale', she 'kepeth [her husband's] good, and wasteth never a deel' (IV.1343). This division of functions appropriated to men the prerogative of conspicuous material liberality[14] and therefore the charisma of what was often reckoned a particularly fine virtue of humanity.[15] Conversely, it was axiomatic that in the case of a lord who abandons largesse, 'negardship exilith ientilesse'.[16] Even the world of literary courtship in which generosity served to distinguish noble from *vilein* behaviour tended to reinforce an insinuation that

---

[11] *On Love*, pp. 318–21. Andreas thus articulates a view that women 'exhaust' men's substance both in the financial and physiological domains, since physiologically they deplete men's bodies by intercourse: *On Love*, pp. 304–5, and cf. *ParsT*, x.147.

[12] *On Love*, pp. 316–19.

[13] 'It is the duty of the man to acquire all the necessary provisions [. . .] Likewise the woman ought to manage and allocate them with good discretion [. . .] without too much parsimoniousness, and equally she ought to guard against foolish generosity [. . .] She should understand that nothing must be wasted, and she should expect all her household to be frugal': *Le Livre des trois vertus*, ed. Charity Cannon Willard and Eric Hicks (Paris: Champion, 1989), III.1, p. 173, and *The Treasure of the City of Ladies*, trans. Sarah Lawson (Harmondsworth: Penguin, 1985), p. 146.

[14] This explains the gendered expression in *ShipT*, VII.43: 'Free was daun John, and manly [*Riverside* edn, though 'namely' in the earlier Robinson edition] of dispence'.

[15] 'Largesse maketh folk cleer of renoun' (translating 'Largitas maxime claros facit'), *Boece*, II pr. 5.10. 'Generosity [*largesce*] is the mistress and queen that gives lustre to every virtue', *Cligés*, 188–90, ed. Alexandre Micha (Paris: Champion, 1978); and *Arthurian Romances*, trans. Owen, p. 95.

[16] John Lydgate, *The Fall of Princes*, III.372–5, ed. Henry Bergen, EETS, e.s. 122 (London: Oxford University Press, 1924).

largesse was masculine. The *Romance of the Rose* commands male lovers to give 'largement'.[17] The lover in Gower's *Confessio amantis* fanatically complies: he would shower his lady with gifts if she would let him — 'Als freliche as god hath it yive, / It schal ben hires' (*CA*, v.4769–70). Giving as lavishly as God has given: this is a resonant formulation, as we shall see.

The patterns of thought that we are following constituted a disincentive for women to aspire to the prerogative of practising liberality and an incentive for them to be thrifty with goods and money. Negative and simplistic allegations easily flowed from that, and Christine de Pizan was stung into repudiating misogynous charges of female greed, arguing in her *City of Ladies* that one could readily demonstrate the endless *largesces* and *liberalités* of women, who are only too happy to see money used with wise generosity rather than hoarded away in some chest by a (male) miser.[18] In this respect, Christine makes the classic reactive move against misogyny: she recovers for women a virtue which the other side alleges they lack. This is an example of the gender 'redoctrination' strategy outlined in my Introduction, whereby the gendering of vices and virtues is challenged.[19] Christine offers a further form of redoctrination by arguing that in any case the imputed female vice of 'avarice' should really be reckoned a virtue. Thriftiness is not a symptom of avarice or greed, but is 'a sign of their great prudence'. Christine is aware that many women are not in a position to practise the virtue of liberality because they are kept on a tight rein financially by miserly husbands. They 'hang on to the little they have' for the sake of the household, she suggests, but their reward is perverse; they acquire a reputation for graspingness.[20] Christine knew already what modern commentators have subsequently deduced, which is that stereotypes of womanly 'greed' derived from women's financial dependence on men, which kept women permanently in the position of begging men for money.[21]

---

[17] *RR*, 2201–3, trans. in the *Romaunt* (2331–3) as 'Resoun wole that a lover be / In his yiftes more large and fre / Than cherles that can not of lovyng'.

[18] *Le Livre de la cité des dames*, ed. Maureen Curnow, Ph.D. dissertation, Vanderbilt University (1975), Xerox University Microfilms (Ann Arbor), II.66.2 and 67.2, pp. 963–5; *The Book of the City of Ladies*, trans. Rosalind Brown-Grant (Harmondsworth: Penguin, 1999), pp. 192–4.

[19] This phenomenon is more complicatedly identified by Anne Clark Bartlett as 'regendered counter-discourse': *Male Authors, Female Readers: Representation and Subjectivity in Middle English Literature* (Ithaca: Cornell University Press, 1995), ch. 11.

[20] *Cité*, II.66.1, ed. Curnow, pp. 962–3, trans. Brown-Grant, p. 193.

[21] Andrée K. Blumstein, *Misogyny and Idealization in the Courtly Romance* (Bonn: Bouvier, 1977), p. 7.

Small wonder that wives are heard in the *Canterbury Tales* insisting that one of the top seven qualities women want in husbands, is that they be generous ('free') and 'no nygard'.[22] But, however generous a husband might be, a wife was supposed to 'conserve' her husband's goods on his behalf just as she conserved her body on his behalf (since her body constituted another category of his 'goods'). This principle of double conservation can be seen to be reinforced by wordplay. In Latin, a woman is to be both 'servatrix pudicitiae' (guardian of her sexual modesty), and 'servatrix thesaurum' (guardian of the family treasures).[23] In English, it is a matter of 'keeping'. (Thus in Chaucer's 'Shipman's Tale', the merchant urges his wife to 'kepe oure good' scrupulously, just when she has in fact decided to trade a sexual part of it elsewhere (vii.241–3).) Generosity in a woman carried a certain danger. There should be some keeping in a lady's giving. Some lines in Gower's *Confessio* labour to express the balancing-act that this requires: 'Sche takth and yifth in such degre, / That as be weie of friendlihiede / Sche can so kepe hir wommanhiede / That every man spekth of hir wel' (*CA*, v.4753–7).

As this implies, while some cultural impulses favoured a feminine generosity that was scrupulously calibrated, other cultural impulses constructed the feminine to be a beneficent, abundant source of bounty and radiance. Deriving from sources such as Pseudo-Dionysius,[24] the Neo-Platonist tradition envisaging divine love as a sun-like irradiation, received by all according to their capacity to receive, was developed as a means of exalting femininity in medieval lyric tradition. It provided a way of associating the courtly beloved with liberality or grace, and Chaucer reaches for it when he wants to eulogize Duchess Blanche in his elegiac poem *The Book of the Duchess*. In this text, the Black Knight eventually describes his dead duchess as a paradigm of beneficence. True, he has to work through more inhibiting feminine virtues before fully unfolding that thought. He assures us that Blanche's charismatic

---

[22] *NPT*, vii.2913–17, and *ShipT*, vii.172–7.

[23] Boccaccio, *De Mulieribus claris*, ed. Zaccaria, pp. 410–12; trans. Guarino, p. 228.

[24] Pseudo-Dionysius offers the following definition of divine goodness: 'the Essential Good, by the very fact of its existence, extends goodness into all things'. Like the sun, which 'gives light to whatever is able to partake of its light', the originary principle of Good 'sends the rays of its undivided goodness to everything with the capacity ... to receive it': Pseudo-Dionysius, *The Divine Names*, in *The Complete Works*, trans. Colm Luibheid (London: 1987), pp. 71–2. Dante adapts the same figure in *Il Convivio*, iii.7, trans. Lansing, pp. 106–7.

and magnetic look was consistent with 'mesure'; it was never 'foly sprad' (*BD*, 874) and it bespoke a 'brotherly' love for decent folk. In *this* asexual sibling sort of love 'she was wonder large' (marvellously generous, *BD*, 891–3).

The Knight finally gives free rein to the discourses of Neo-Platonism and liberality. When Blanche relaxed, he says,

> ... she was lyk to torche bryght
> That every man may take of lyght
> Ynogh, and hyt hath never the lesse.
> Of maner and of comlynesse
> Ryght so ferde my lady dere;
> For every wight of hir manere
> Myght cacche ynogh, yif that he wolde,
> Yf he had eyen hir to biholde.

(*BD*, 963–70)

Here are the familiar Neo-Platonist rays of goodness (in Blanche's case, her 'manere'), which can be received by every person with the capacity to do so ('Yf he had eyen ...'). But here also is a simile complexly associated with liberality, which offers a connection with the Wife of Bath: the simile of a distribution of fire or light from a source, in this case a torch, which remains un-impoverished by such distribution.

This analogy goes back to (and beyond) a passage in Cicero's ethical treatise on duties. Cicero finds the elementary principle of *liberalitas*—what he calls 'common liberality'—enshrined in the offering of common property for the common benefit. For example, 'to give directions to another who's lost, is to light another's lamp by one's own: no less shines one's own lamp after lighting another's'. The principle is extended in the maxim 'let anyone who will take fire from fire'. Other maxims reinforcing the point are, that water should be freely given from a flowing source; and (something we shall also come back to in relation to 'The Wife of Bath's Tale') that one should give good advice to anyone in doubt. Cicero goes on to claim that ideal liberality with *private* property actually conforms to the same principle as he observes in these instances: that is, what is given away should not seriously deplete one's means, otherwise liberality drains away the basis for further liberality.[25]

Here straight away in this caveat was a latent discrepancy between antique ethics and Christian morality. By the third century the early

---

[25] Cicero, *De officiis*, I.16, trans. Miller, pp. 52–6.

Christian writer Lactantius was attacking the Ciceronian view that generosity should be applied with rational caution; Lactantius objected that the principle of giving should simply be to give as much as possible, out of humanity and empathy.[26] On the basis of biblical citations, moral treatises in the Middle Ages went on to repeat that if you have much, you should give lavishly, mindful of the largesse of God to humanity. In a discussion of Mercy, *The Book of Vices and Virtues* notes the 'grete largenesse' of God who gives generously to all '& maketh his sonne schyne vpon the goode and vpon the schrewen, as he seith in the gospel'. Since God is so 'large' to us, giving us 'alle the goodes that we haue, we schulde be large and curteis eche of vs to other' as urged in the gospel, 'Beth merciable, as youre fadre is merciable'.[27] Divine abundance is itself memorably imagined by the writer of the Middle English *Pearl* in terms of water poured out of a bottomless gulf.[28] Alternatively, writers used the analogy of a great 'comune' wine-cask of God's love in eternity, giving forth so generously and inexhaustibly that everyone is filled as if to drunkenness; or, the analogy of God's wisdom flowing so copiously from the master's mouth as nearly to 'drown' his followers.[29] God's largesse was the model of boundless selfless giving, of utterly *un*-calculating charity; and although definitions of liberality overlapped considerably with those of charity, the overlap was therefore often uncomfortable. The moral imperative of giving uncalculatingly might be said to have been always in tension with the received reverence for liberality as a rationally guided mean. In a later period Sir Francis Bacon knowingly put in a nutshell the contradiction between Aristotelian and Christian understanding when he wrote, 'In charity, there is no Excesse.'[30]

The hypothesis expressed by Bacon could be propped up by an act of faith holding that if you emulated unrestrained divine abundance, God would enhance your resources to sustain such generosity. Guillaume de Lorris writes of Largesse in the *Roman de la Rose* that 'God caused her

[26] See Burnley, *Chaucer's Language and the Philosophers' Tradition*, pp. 135–6.

[27] *VV*, p. 193. Under Cupidity, *JW* discusses *nygardschippe* and urges 'yif thou haue myche, gyue thou plentyuously; yif thou haue lytel, gladly geue thou part therof to the poore'; a later section on Poverty of Spirit and *Largitas* cites Christ as outright exemplar of generosity, his arms symbolically open on the cross: *JW*, pp. 121–2, and pp. 307–11.

[28] 'For the gentyl Cheuentayn is no chyche, [. . . He] lauez hys gyftez as water of dyche, / Other gotez of golf that neuer charde. / Hys fraunchyse is large': *Pearl*, 605–9, ed. E. V. Gordon (Oxford: Clarendon Press, 1953).

[29] Respectively *VV*, pp. 274–5; and Horstmann, '*Orologium*', p. 327.

[30] Essay XIII, 'Of Goodnesse, and Goodnesse of Nature', in Sir Francis Bacon, *The Essayes or Counsels*, ed. Michael Kiernan (Oxford: Clarendon Press, 1985), p. 39.

wealth to multiply, so that however much she gave away, she always had more.'[31] But despite the delightful hypothesis that human generosity might optimally accelerate, as it were, the divine supply, it was more normal to advise that liberality should be restrained according to the ethical golden mean. To reiterate, the right use of riches meant avoiding excess or 'fool-largesse' on one side and parsimony on the other.[32] The crux was the first of these: a self-impoverishing generosity was not largesse: it was prodigality.

The wonder of Chaucer's Blanche is that her personality is a torch-like phenomenon which is at once private yet *un-depletable*. She herself, or her radiant personality, is (in modern idiom) a sustainable resource. What I should like to argue now is that the Wife of Bath models herself, or is modelled, in much the same way.

Chaucer's Wife of Bath explicitly (though not consistently) advocates a policy of bodily largesse, and she formulates this by drawing upon the mixed ethical and moral discourses of liberality. Liberality, after all, is about the right use of riches. Everyone, she recalls from Scripture, has some special gift from God (III.103–4). Adapting the sorts of argument found in moral exhortations to generosity and charity, she proposes to utilize whatever bountiful sexual resources she has received. 'So bids St Peter', as the *Book of Vices and Virtues* puts it, 'that the graces that God hath lent us, that we should deal forth to our neighbours', in the interests of common profit.[33] The underlying moral principle was that whatever superabundance some people have, they have in order that they can gain the merit of 'dispensing it well'.[34] It is in this spirit that the Wife of

---

[31] *RR*, 1134–6, trans. Horgan, p. 18.

[32] Riches are to be used 'in swich a manere that men holde yow nat to scars, ne to sparynge, ne to fool-large' (*Mel*, VII.1596–1600). The exposition of the use of riches at this point derives from a brief hint in chapters 43 and 45 of Albertano's treatise, and takes up the invitation there to draw on a chapter 'De acquirendis et conservandis opibus' in his *De amore et dilectione dei et proximi et aliarum rerum et de forma vitae*. See Albertano of Brescia, *Liber consolationis et consilii*, ed. Thor Sundby, Chaucer Society, 2nd ser., vol. 8 (London: Trübner, 1873); and Bryan and Dempster (eds.), *Sources and Analogues*, p. 563.

[33] *VV*, p. 146; see also the treatise's further discussions of 'largenesse', pp. 193 and 212–16.

[34] Aquinas invokes Ambrose on the point that *superabundantia* is bestowed upon some so that they can gain the merit of good stewardship whereby the *liberalis* spends on others more than self: *Summa theologiae*, IIa IIae q. 117, art. 1, on 'whether liberality is a virtue'. For similar statements see *Boece*, II pr. 5; *Dives and Pauper*, ed. Barnum, vol. 1, pt 2, p. 160. For a survey of the doctrine of wealth as stewardship, see Miri Rubin, *Charity and Community in Medieval Cambridge* (Cambridge: Cambridge University Press, 1987), ch. 3, 'The Idea of Charity Between the Twelfth and Fifteenth Centuries', pp. 54–98.

Bath sees herself as using what she calls her 'instrument' as 'frely' as God has given it (III.149–50): indeed, she says she uses it without fastidious concern for her partner's size, colour, degree of poverty, or humble social status (III.622–6). In the same spirit she represents herself bestowing her body as refreshment, so as to emulate the Lord's own miracle of supplying five un-depletable barley loaves that could feed five thousand.

She brings this vocabulary of liberality into sharp focus when she wittily adapts the old analogy of the lantern and candle. Declaring that women desire to be free and expansive ('at oure large', III.322) she argues that husbands should be content with a sufficiency from wives, and generous-minded about any surplus:

> Ye shul have queynte right ynogh at eve.
> He is to greet a nygard that wolde werne
> A man to lighte a candle at his lanterne;
> He shal have never the lasse light, pardee.
> Have thou ynogh, thee thar nat pleyne thee.
>
> (III.332–6)

Probably Chaucer picked up this knowingly sexual application of the 'torch' image from one of his favourite authors, Ovid in *Ars amatoria* or Jean de Meun in the *Romance of the Rose*: the latter suggests that such an application is notorious.[35] One's first thought may be that it is a wicked manipulation of the aphorism; a naughty travesty of the social imperative of generosity, indeed a travesty of the warming radiance that was admired in Blanche. Blanche, of course, radiates her charisma unselfconsciously, in a stringently *involuntary* way,[36] which corresponds rather precisely with the Pseudo-Dionysian notion of goodness as a source exerting ray-like beneficence by virtue of its sheer existence, not as a matter of active choice. By contrast the Wife flaunts her bountifulness self-consciously, lacing it with a mischievous

---

[35] *RR*, 7379–84, trans. Horgan, pp. 113–14: Jealousy is berated for greediness: 'It is foolish to hoard such a thing, for it is the candle in the lantern, and if you gave its light to a thousand people, you would not find its flame smaller.' Cf. Whiting and Whiting, *Proverbs, Sentences, and Proverbial Phrases*, c24, 'One Candle can light many'. The antecedent is in Ovid, *Ars amatoria*, III.88 ff.: 'That part [the female pudendum] endures, and has no fear of loss. What forbids to take light from a light that is set before you, or who would guard vast waters upon the cavernous deep?'; in *The Art of Love, and Other Poems*, ed. and trans. J. H. Mozley, 2nd edn revised by G. P. Goold (Cambridge, Mass.: Harvard University Press; and London: Heinemann, 1979), pp. 124–5. For an extended discussion of the Ovidian link, see Michael Calabrese, *Chaucer's Ovidian Arts of Love* (Gainesville: University Press of Florida, 1994), pp. 81–111.

[36] Martin, *Chaucer's Women*, p. 25.

nuance of threat ('ye shul have ynogh'). This is the side of 'The Wife of Bath's Prologue' that prompts even well-disposed critics to splutter censoriously about the Wife's 'theatrical exaggeration of female sexuality', her 'licentious charity', and her 'false analogies', which 'pervert' orthodox positions.[37]

More sophisticatedly, R. W. Hanning links her refusal to let her sexuality be privatized with her refusal to privatize speech—rather, she will disclose anything and everything to her group of intimates. These impulses to pour out rather than to hold in contribute, Hanning suggests, to a dramatization of tensions between telling and not telling in a still oral but incipiently literate culture, a dramatization that drives the whole project of the *Tales*. In Hanning's words, the side that she stands up for (in terms of the evidence that I have so far considered) is an imperative 'towards gratuitous outpouring, towards undamned, unrestricted giving of words or of self'.[38]

Absorbing though Hanning's proposition is, the discourse of liberality, not utterance itself, seems to me to be the primary referent for the arguments we have identified in her Prologue. Moreover, as will be explained in a moment, it is teaching on liberality that most immediately explains the conjoining of 'giving of words' and 'giving of self', without resorting to a quasi-allegorical explanation based on speech and 'privatization'. But for the moment perhaps we should consider the hostile reading of her sexual largesse as 'licentious charity'. No question, Chaucer is constructing her desires and motives with a knowing audacity that courts moral shock. These self-descriptions in her Prologue are produced with a mischievous jocular exaggeration that befits a person who could 'wel [...] laughe and carpe' in company (1.474); she revels in an exaggeration that mocks critical solemnity. That being so, to resort to a phrase such as 'licentious charity' is to risk becoming the butt of the Wife's playfulness. There might be a comparable risk of tone-deaf response in taking her self-styled sexual 'generosity' as a

---

[37] Lee Patterson, ' "For the Wyves love of Bathe": Feminine Rhetoric and Poetic Resolution in the *Roman de la Rose* and the *Canterbury Tales*', *Speculum*, 58 (1983), 656–94 (p. 680); Martin, *Chaucer's Women*, pp. 70, 96. However, an alternative view links the Wife's sexual generosity with the philosophy of 'plenitude' promoted by the school of Chartres: Ruggiers, *The Art of the Canterbury Tales*, pp. 198–200.

[38] R. W. Hanning, 'Telling the Private Parts: "Pryvetee" and Poetry in Chaucer's *Canterbury Tales*', in *The Idea of Medieval Literature: Essays in Honor of Donald R. Howard*, ed. Christian K. Zacher (London and Toronto: Associated University Presses, 1992), pp. 108–25 (p. 122).

positive invocation of moral language: but it is at least worth considering whether Chaucer genuinely wanted to raise the question why personal physical 'superabundance' should not come under the rubric of liberality.

There is an interesting precedent in the *Decameron* which drives at a similar point about female sexuality, and in that instance Boccaccio arranges for the fictional audience, albeit at first amused, to conclude unanimously in favour. As in 'The Wife of Bath's Prologue', the narrative presents a spirited woman protesting her moral obligation to give away whatever sexual surplus her husband is unable to respond to. This is the tale about Madonna Filippa, who is arrested for adultery but resolves to defend herself with 'the truth'. Her defence is that the law on adultery bears inequitably on women, because women can satisfy more male partners than vice versa. Thus, having satisfied her husband sexually, 'what is she to do with what is left over?' Isn't it better for her to 'present it to a gentleman who loves her' rather than let it 'turn bad or go to waste'?[39] She is implicitly condemning the opposite of good practice in liberality: the stereotype of the niggard as one who hoards food only for it to go off.[40] Such hoarding amounts in medieval moral discourse to a defrauding of those who might otherwise have benefited from it.

True, the moral pleasure taken by both Madonna Filippa and Alisoun in their sustainable bodily largesse would ill survive scrupulous analysis. For one thing, although liberality did not consist only in material goods but in other forms of assistance too, sexual favours are not a medium of generosity that the discourse of liberality normally contemplates. For another, according to strict doctrine Alisoun's body is not hers to give: the lantern-owner in her analogy is her husband.[41] Ethical discourse insists, moreover, that liberality is to be applied in the right way to the right recipients,[42] whereas Alisoun confesses to observing 'no discrecioun' in her choice of recipients (III.622–6). Above all, there is the catch that moralists knew that the characteristic trick of prodigality was to pass itself off as liberality. As we saw in Chapter 1, each vice can be masked

---

[39] *Decameron*, VI.7, trans. McWilliam, pp. 499–500.

[40] Keeping food like this is cited under *nygardschippe*, a subcategory of *Cupiditas*, in *JW*, p. 121; and see Christine de Pizan, *Livre des trois vertus*, III.1, ed. Willard and Hicks, p. 176, trans. Lawson, p. 148.

[41] Giving the light therefore technically constitutes a form of theft, as discussed in Chapter 3 above. Cicero points out that giving as a result of robbing another is not liberality: *De officiis*, I.14, trans. Miller, pp. 47–9.

[42] Aristotle, *Ethics*, IV.1, trans. Thomson, p. 143.

as a virtue: and so, according to Alan of Lille, 'a harlot-like relationship with Prodigality lyingly advertises itself as a tribute to Generosity'.[43] Alisoun's generosity certainly sounds more like prodigality when she later associates herself with Venus's love of 'ryot and dispence' (III.700). Technically, however, even if we were to decide that the Wife of Bath is disguising prodigality as generosity, she would be more worthy in terms of ethical discourse than the miser. Aristotle had already noted that prodigality resembles liberality; that actually the prodigal has the natural inclination towards liberality, and even that a prodigal is distinctly preferable to a miser because 'he benefits a number of people' whereas the niggard 'benefits nobody' (a concession echoed by Aquinas).[44] Hoccleve accordingly identifies prodigality as a more curable illness than avarice.[45] This tipping of the scales somewhat in favour of prodigality is significant when we recall that the Wife of Bath represents mean-minded lantern-owners (her husbands) as 'niggards', as part of her overall characterization of men as a miserly species intent on locking all women and cash away in the safe. At least her natural bent towards liberality benefits somebody.

It is not just that the Wife's prodigality *resembles* largesse. Her attitude conforms in another important respect with that virtue, in that she thinks in terms of 'not withholding': witness her famous suggestion that she 'koude noght withdrawe' her chamber of Venus from a good fellow (III.617–18). A characteristic of largesse, though one which always took it riskily near prodigality, was that true generosity makes it hard to hold back one's goods. Vernacular writers were aware of this, but the point is formally and etymologically made by Aquinas, who explains that *largitas* and *liberalitas* are synonyms on the basis that both signify 'letting go', rather than 'retention'.[46]

The sceptical reader may still be going to have difficulty accepting that this examination of indebtedness to doctrine on liberality in the 'Wife's Prologue' does anything more than confirm that the text mischievously parodies these ethical issues. Is Chaucer through her

---

[43] *The Plaint of Nature*, XVIII, trans. James J. Sheridan (Toronto: Pontifical Institute of Mediaeval Studies, 1980), p. 214. Similarly, the 14th-cent. *Speculum Christiani* explains that 'wast ouerspens is called largys and fredam of hert'; ed. Holmstedt, p. 232.

[44] *Ethics*, IV.1, trans. Thomson, p. 146; Aquinas, *Summa theologiae*, IIa IIae q. 119.3, Responsio, trans. O'Brien, pp. 273–5.

[45] *Regiment*, 4579–92.

[46] 'The bountiful do not hold back but let go'; and, 'when someone lets something go [emittit] he liberates it [liberat] from his care and control': *Summa theologiae*, IIa IIae q. 117.2, Responsio, trans. O'Brien, p. 225.

voice just highlighting with a literary snigger a disproportion between female and male sexual capacities? Or does he more genially characterize what Jill Mann has called the 'inexhaustible credit constituted by female sexuality', invoked by the merchant's wife at the end of 'The Shipman's Tale'? 'Sex has the same careless abundance, the same inexhaustible outpouring, as God's grace', says Mann of that episode.[47]

Before jumping to a conclusion, we still have to take account of something mentioned earlier, namely that the Ciceronian passage which is a matrix for the torch/lantern figure links it with other gestures of liberality: in particular, with giving directions to someone lost, or giving good advice to someone in doubt. It was not necessary to go back to Cicero to know that liberality encompassed counsel or kind advice; this connection was everywhere emphasized in medieval culture. Christine de Pizan generalizes that 'largesse does not consist only in material gifts [. . .] but also in comforting words'.[48] Moral handbooks define charity as the impulse to offer help to another, to counsel or teach someone with whatever 'wit' that one has, to guide others to the right way, or to give and share 'largeliche' what one has from God. This is what St Peter meant by saying that we should share the graces we have received from God with our neighbours, and it is what Cicero meant when he wrote of seeking common profit.[49] Dante enlarges almost lyrically on the magnanimity of good counsel. It offers itself unasked, like a rose that gives fragrance to anyone and not just to a person who comes to smell it. Dante's motto for giving counsel is, as in Matthew 10: 8, 'Freely you have received, freely give.'[50]

That the continuity between material charity and giving advice was commonplace in the late Middle Ages (as indeed it remained familiar to Jane Austen in *Emma*) reveals in a flash the possibility of understanding afresh the relation between the sexual 'liberality' banteringly mooted in the 'Wife's Prologue', and the liberality of counsel which is offered at two points by the old woman of 'The Wife of Bath's Tale'. First, she counsels the knight in his despair of finding

---

[47] Mann, 'Satisfaction and Payment', p. 48.

[48] *Livre des trois vertus*, ed. Willard and Hicks, I.20, p. 78, trans. Lawson, I.19, p. 78. Christine elsewhere reports her father's view that knowledge was a treasure that one could keep giving away, without losing any: *Le Livre de la mutacion de fortune*, I.3, trans. Kevin Brownlee, in *The Selected Writings of Christine de Pizan*, ed. Renate Blumenfeld-Kosinski and Kevin Brownlee (New York: W. W. Norton, 1997), p. 91.

[49] *VV*, pp. 145–6.

[50] *Il Convivio*, IV.27, trans. Lansing, p. 229. *The Wars of Alexander* (4357–61) associates the seminal torch analogy with freely given counsel: ed. Hoyt N. Duggan and Thorlac Turville-Petre, EETS, s.s. 10 (Oxford: Oxford University Press, 1989).

a suitable answer to the question he has been set by the matriarchal court. Incidentally, in this she is certainly helping a person 'lost' like the benighted wanderer of Cicero's text, for she tells the knight at the edge of the forest that 'heer forth ne lith no wey' (III.1001). She offers the prospect of sage advice (old people 'kan muchel thyng', as she puts it (III.1004)). She describes herself as being about to 'teach' him (III.1018) and proceeds to whisper her solution in his ear. (In the version of the story in the *Confessio Amantis*, the ugly old woman intuits that nothing can save the knight 'Bot if thou my conseil have' (*CA*, I.1545–6).) Second, after the knight in the Wife's tale has been obliged to marry the old woman, she counsels him about his prejudices.

Readers tend to suspect that in first communicating in her whisper the secret that will save him she epitomizes negative medieval stereotypes of women as 'incontinent of speech', as 'overflowing mouths'.[51] Alisoun tempts us with that stereotype by introducing a story of Midas's wife, who could not contain the secret that Midas had grown ass's ears. Yet in interpreting this much-discussed allusion we need to remember that Midas was a byword for *avarice*.[52] In her irrepressible urge to divulge his affliction of ass's ears, Mrs Midas partly embodies the antithesis of that avarice: to her it seemed that her knowledge 'swal so soore aboute hir herte / That nedely som word hire moste asterte', and Alisoun comments: 'out it moot' (III.967–8, 980). This un-withholdability should not be written off as sheer indiscipline. Rather, it expresses further what we have just discovered about medieval views of liberality—that it signified a 'letting go' as opposed to 'retention'. (It is rather striking that Hélène Cixous in her well-known piece entitled 'Sorties' has a passage on a woman's liberality, in which she characterizes a verbal dimension in precisely the same vocabulary: 'her tongue doesn't hold back but holds forth, doesn't keep in but keeps on enabling'.)[53] The binding link between 'The Wife of Bath's Prologue' and 'Tale', therefore, is

[51] So Sheila Delany, 'Strategies of Silence in the Wife of Bath's Recital', *Exemplaria*, 2 (1990), 49–69 (p. 51); and Calabrese, *Chaucer's Ovidian Arts of Love*, p. 108.

[52] Midas appears in Gower's section *de Avaricia*, beginning at *CA*, v.141. The construction of negative readings of the Wife of Bath from the interpolated episode of Midas's wife is typified by R. L. Hoffman, *Ovid and the Canterbury Tales* (Philadelphia: University of Pennsylvania Press, 1966), pp. 145–9.

[53] 'Sorties: Out and Out: Attacks/Ways Out/Forays', in *The Feminist Reader*, 2nd edn, ed. Catherine Belsey and Jane Moore (Basingstoke: Macmillan, 1997), pp. 91–116 (pp. 95–7).

that the Old Woman demonstrates liberality with counsel in the tale by deploying the un-depletable resource of words to save the life of a lost fellow human, and this is the beneficial exercise of the quality of generosity hankered after in sexual and economic terms by Alisoun.[54]

However unexpected the link may be to us, counsel was indelibly associated with generosity in medieval moral literature. In *The Book of Vices and Virtues* it is the spiritual Gift of Counsel, vested particularly in the elderly, which is held to dispel the sin of avarice and to promote the virtue of mercy or 'pitee', which people can primarily enact by being 'large and curteis' to each other, as opposed to keeping their purses shut like covetous men.[55] As it happens, this is quite a good description of the efficacy of the elderly woman's counselling of the knight in 'The Wife of Bath's Tale'. Alisoun genders miserliness masculine, not largesse. In an act of redoctrination, she makes a bid to re-gender the ethic of largesse feminine. Through her Chaucer explores polemically an idea that women stand against masculine miserliness in three spheres of life: money, sex, and speech. The sensual largesse in Alisoun is (from a masculine point of view) threateningly unrestrained, but it is a woman's unrestraint that turns out to save the knight's life in the tale.

Of course, as some readers will by now be absolutely desperate to object, there is a contradictory current in Alisoun's self-presentation. Although the generous motives already discussed surface also in her impulsive gift of all her property to her young fifth husband (III.630–1), her 'Prologue' also shows considerable relish in envisaging women's bodies and emotions as marketable goods. Such brash engagement in marketability needs to be read, of course, in the context of a society acutely attuned to dowry negotiation. She talks eagerly of profit and sale and even ransom. The flour having gone (or the 'flower' of virginity having gone), she must sell the bran as best she may (III.477–8). This collides with her view of her sexuality as barley-bread to be given for refreshing five thousand (III.144–6). The notion of herself as refreshment collides in another sense with a perspective which connects her with appetite, or thirst. John Fleming even calls her a 'thirst expert', drawing on her

---

[54] Positive response to the phenomenon of female divulgence of secrets in the tale has hitherto been confined to finding in it a 'community of power': Susan Signe Morrison, 'Don't Ask, Don't Tell: The Wife of Bath and Vernacular Translations', *Exemplaria*, 8 (1996), 97–123 (p. 117); cf. Karma Lochrie on 'gossip' in the Wife of Bath's performance, in *Covert Operations: The Medieval Uses of Secrecy* (Philadelphia: University of Pennsylvania Press, 1999), pp. 56–61.

[55] *VV*, pp. 188–93; cf. *JW* (p. 311), where *largenesse* embraces the gift of 'counseyl'.

'Prologue''s allusions to thirsty women in the Bible and relating her to Ovid's fictional bawd Dipsas (whose name means 'voracious thirst').[56]

All this is a reminder that her 'Prologue' produces emphases of such inconsistency as to build what Arthur Lindley calls a 'haystack of contradictions', and the disconcerting oscillation between generous and appetitive or mercantile impulses is one instance of that.[57] But, whereas the intermittently appetitive or mercantile impulse has been widely noted, neither the full extent of Alisoun's impulse of liberality nor its establishment of a substantial continuity between 'Prologue' and 'Tale' has been well understood. Besides, her tough trade talk constitutes at least in part a survival tactic, adopted in reaction to masculine oppression. The trigger which can switch off that type of feminine reactiveness and enable men to understand women's liberality is a change in men's own perception of women wrought by a woman, as discussed in Chapter 2. It seems that feminine largesse has to save men from themselves.

While there are evidently grounds for a positive ethical interpretation of these aspects of 'The Wife of Bath's Prologue and Tale', just how 'positive' will remain a disputed matter. For one thing, what we have seen is two male writers, Chaucer and Boccaccio, redefining an untameable sexual impetus (something which misogyny fears in women) as a form of admirable generosity. The whole thing could be interpreted as the misogynous trick of the male author: what men cannot own of women's sexuality through conventional doctrines of chastity, they seek to gain 'on the side' by invoking an alternative doctrine of liberality that authorizes women to distribute their surplus urges freely, and blithely ignoring outcomes such as pregnancy. However, as I argue elsewhere, an objection to this sceptical response would be that female bountifulness also seems to be commended by a (presumed) female medieval writer, Marie de France, in the *lai* of *Lanval*. There a woman's material and sexual generosity is pointedly emphasized in order to display deficiencies in Arthurian society. As with the Wife of Bath, the heroine of the *lai* appears to emulate the inexhaustible quality of God's abundance; for when Lanval commits himself to her, she gives a double boon that 'however generously [*largement*] he gave

[56] John Fleming, 'The Best Line in Ovid and the Worst', in Benson and Ridyard (eds.), *New Readings of Chaucer's Poetry*, pp. 51–74 (esp. pp. 61–6).

[57] Arthur Lindley, '"Vanysshed Was This Daunce, He Nyste Where": Alisoun's Absence in the *Wife of Bath's Prologue and Tale*', *ELH*, 59 (1992), 1–21 (p. 9).

or spent, she would still find enough for him', and wherever love might be made, there he would find her, ready.[58] Although this *lai* raises awkward questions about male sexual fantasy, and although it hints that the woman's liberality is a phenomenon somehow incompatible with the cynical state of normative society, the impression nevertheless is that Marie deliberately—and against the prevailing gender construction that we reviewed earlier—genders feminine the principle of largesse of all sorts. As Regula Evitt puts it, 'the woman's "giving gift" establishes a paradigm of concatenating, reproductive generosity'.[59]

The Gendered Risk of Generosity: From Dido to Dorigen

In Chaucer's case it has to be admitted that liberality, where apparent in women, remains an equivocal virtue. It is equivocal, for example, in the foundational case of Dido. Chaucer conceives Dido's fate partly as a tragedy of injudicious generous compassion for her untrustworthy guest Aeneas. Love for him flows from her pity for his desolate and exiled state when he is thrown upon her shores (*LGW*, 1063–5, 1078–9), and pity issues subsequently into abandoned passion when they take refuge from storm in a cave: there 'sely Dido rewede on his peyne' (*LGW*, 1237)—the gullible innocence of her compassionate yielding apparent in the epithet 'sely'. But this 'Legend' of Dido intertwines her queenly munificence with her emotional and finally sexual giving of herself. When we are told at an early stage in their acquaintance that her compassion and 'gentillesse' dictate that 'Refreshed moste he been of his distresse' (*LGW*, 1080–1), already we are not sure (given the double entendres to which this verb is susceptible) whether she will be refreshing Aeneas with material or sexual solace. In what ensues she feasts and hosts him sumptuously, a rhetorical tour de force emphasizing how she showered him with every kind of present to be found in her realm (*LGW*, 1114–25). The narrative sums her up as 'she that can in fredom passen alle' (*LGW*, 1127).

---

[58] *Lanval*, 136–9 and 163, in *Lais*, ed. A. Ewert (Oxford: Blackwell, 1978); *The Lais of Marie de France*, trans. Glyn Burgess (Harmondsworth: Penguin, 1986), pp. 74–5.

[59] 'When Echo Speaks: Marie de France and the Poetics of Remembrance', in *Minding the Body: Women and Literature in the Middle Ages, 800–1500*, ed. Monica Brzezinski Potkay and Regula Meyer Evitt (New York: Twayne, 1997), pp. 77–101 (pp. 95–6). The evidence in *Lanval* is complemented by conspicuous acts of generosity by women in *Le Fresne* and *Eliduc*.

If it is the 'fre', generous nature of Dido's emotions and actions that seems to leave her vulnerable within the terms of this narrative, other narratives confirm the risks of that sort of female generosity where heart and all are freely given.[60] In the case of *Anelida and Arcite* the effect of Anelida's 'fredom' towards Arcite, to whom she commits herself entirely and transparently, is that 'al was his that she hath' (*AA*, 106–7). So utterly dedicated to him is her self-giving that it even limits her conversations with other people to what pleases him (so her 'liberality' is exclusively focused upon him). The poem seems to imply 'Ovidian' criticism of such generosity, or meekness as it is later called on second thoughts. Arcite tires of her and runs off to a new lady who, in pointed contrast, keeps him dangling by a miserly policy of rationing her favours (*AA*, 183–96). It is as if the principle that the betrayed women live by in these texts, that (to adapt Bacon) 'in generosity in love there can be no excess', is a recipe for trouble. None of them manages the prudential model of generosity; none of them is—in the paradoxical phrase used to compliment Queen Cenobia in 'The Monk's Tale'—'large with mesure' (VII.2299). In a way, however, Cenobia is an exception who proves the gendered rule, since the criteria of judgement being applied to her here are those applicable to a monarch. She conforms to princely, not feminine, canons of behaviour.

It is, finally, in the context of this analysis of gendered conventions in the courtly sphere, which represent liberality in a woman (never in men) as a high-risk strategy even if it is something strikingly affecting for readers to experience, that the deployment of the concept in 'The Franklin's Tale' needs to be considered. But the first thing to say about generosity in this tale is that it is a concept remarkably underplayed there, considering (as we saw at the start of this chapter) the prominence given to *liberalità* in both Boccaccian renditions of the story. Chaucer appears to have decided to substitute the somewhat more capacious 'gentillesse' as the superlative virtue in his narrative. Perhaps he knew that the *Decameron* version occurs under the requirement that stories that day must concern actions done liberally or 'magnificamente', and linked the latter to 'gentillesse'? Although his closest options in Middle English for *liberalità* were the nouns 'fredom' or (less exactly) 'franchise' or 'largenesse', he may have felt that none of these quite caught the

---

[60] See e.g. Phyllis, lamenting '. . . I was of my love to [Demophon] to fre' (*LGW*, 2521); and the female falcon incautiously giving her heart 'free' in 'The Squire's Tale' (V.541).

semantic range required to accommodate giving a wife up/giving a prize up/giving payment up. By shifting the focus to *gentillesse*, Chaucer certainly extends the tale's ethical reach.

I mention all this because generosity really makes quite a belated appearance in 'The Franklin's Tale', and that is one reason why it may puzzle the reader there. Lexically, the only foretaste is in Dorigen's pleasure at what she calls the 'large reyne' (v.755) or 'generous rein' that her spouse proffers her when they marry: a suggestive phrase, of course, quizzically implying her sense of generous scope for action, subject to his remote control. Otherwise, although the opening passage mentions liberty and constraint, it does not concentrate on liberality. Where the Aurelius-figure in the *Decameron* relinquishes the lady out of recognition of the husband's *liberalità* in urging that she should keep her word to go to her admirer,[61] Chaucer's Aurelius registers Arveragus's position as one of 'franchise' and (thrice) 'gentillesse' (v.1524, 1527, 1595). Aurelius's own action is described by himself (or by the narrator, depending on the placing of quotation marks) as a 'gentil dede' (v.1543). Eventually he defines the situation more distinctly in terms of generosity as he explains why his scheme has collapsed to the clerk, whom he now owes a huge sum of money: 'right as frely as [Arveragus] sente hire me, / As frely sente I hire to hym ageyn' (v.1604–5). We are at last in the realms of the liberality discourse as applied by the Wife of Bath, user of her instrument according to the New Testament principle we have already mentioned, 'freely you have received, freely give'. Yet the clerk does not pick up on the vocabulary of generosity. Instead he in turn is struck by what he describes as reciprocally 'gentil' behaviour between Arveragus and Aurelius, and wants to demonstrate that a clerk can accomplish 'a gentil dede / As wel as any of yow!' (v.1608–12).[62]

In Boccaccio's renditions (even more so in the *Filocolo* than the *Decameron*) a debate on who best manifested *liberalità* will strike the reader as a logical outcome of strategic verbal anticipation. In Chaucer's rendition it seems to me that, if the reader were anticipating by the end of the tale any question about the characters' relative merits—as opposed to the relative scandalousness of their delusions or of their coerciveness, which critics prefer to debate—it would be a question about who was most *gentil*. Not only, therefore, is the Franklin's closing

---

[61] *Decameron*, x.5, ed. Segre, p. 616; trans. McWilliam, p. 760.

[62] In *Decameron*, x.5 the magician applauds the liberality of the others; trans. McWilliam, p. 761.

question, 'Which was the mooste fre, as thynketh yow?' (v.1622) not
the question most modern readers want to ask, it is also a question out
of alignment with (narrower than) the dominant pattern of conceptual
signals in the text.

Some critics have supposed that it is a question not meant to be
taken seriously but (for example) calculated to expose the Franklin's
shallowness. Such readings detect something irrelevant or tacitly spurious
in the generosity imputed to each character. Arveragus has no right to
be 'fre' with his wife's marital vows and chastity, Aurelius no reason
to think himself generous for relinquishing a 'right' to Dorigen based
on an illegal adulterous promise and on magic, the Clerk no claim to
generosity in forgoing an extortionate payment for illusion-making.[63]
Others are suspicious that the question directs us back from what had
initially claimed to be a somewhat egalitarian view of men and women to
an exclusively male and moreover complacent competition in virtue.[64]
Dorigen, whose own assumptions have been progressively sidelined by
the three males, and from whose perspective their 'generous' acts might
appear to us far from generous, remains the absent 'enigma' of the
story.[65]

Two further readings suggest themselves. One would be that Chaucer
wanted to retain the rounding-off force of the Boccaccian debate
conclusion, even at the cost of some inconsistency with the emphases
created in his own rendition of the tale. He reproduced the Boccaccian
question's phrasing in terms of liberality because *fredom* was sufficiently
a sibling of *gentillesse* for him to get away with it. A second reading, to
which I am drawn, takes Dorigen's own generosity to be implicated in
the Franklin's question, either because she is actually one of the possible
referents of 'Which was the mooste fre?' or because the reader, intuiting
that she is not included as a referent, is fully intended to object that

---

[63] See D. W. Roberston, Jr, 'Chaucer's Franklin and his Tale', in *Costerus: Essays in English and American Language and Literature*, n.s. 1, ed. James W. West (Amsterdam: Rodopi, 1974), pp. 1–26; Alan T. Gaylord, 'The Promises in the *Franklin's Tale*', *ELH*, 31 (1964), 331–65; Pearsall, *The Canterbury Tales*, p. 148.

[64] However, such a sense of masculine solidarity is keener in the *Decameron* version, where husband and ex-lover are (as Robert R. Edwards puts it) 'bound ethically' in their roles in love with the same woman and subsequently become the closest of friends: *Chaucer and Boccaccio: Antiquity and Modernity* (Basingstoke: Palgrave, 2002), p. 171.

[65] Mary R. Bowman, ' "Half as she were mad": Dorigen in the Male World of the *Franklin's Tale*', *ChauR*, 27 (1992–3), 239–51 (p. 247); Nina Manasan Greenberg, 'Dorigen as Enigma: The Production of Meaning and the *Franklin's Tale*', *ChauR*, 33 (1998–9), 329–49.

she should be. The argument for adding her to the list of candidates would be speculative, but not implausible. It would be based partly on her exercise of an impulse of feminine 'fredom' (in the sense, emotional generosity) shared with other Chaucerian courtly heroines. In Dorigen's case the traditional courtly generosity of 'pitee' and love for Arveragus is wrought to an extreme pitch of total commitment.[66] Beyond that there is the larger instinct of charitableness disclosed in her protest to God about the rocks: for, although her stance of protest is morally perilous and the obsessive anxiety from which it derives contravenes ethical wisdom (as will be explained in Chapter 6), the speech certainly expresses a generous concern that the rocks don't conform with the spirit of 'chiertee' (fondness, love) which she assumes God wants to show humanity in creation (v.874, 881). 'Fredom' as generous impulse may also be implicit in her momentary attempt to grant her anguished admirer Aurelius something when he beseeches her love, even if the something confusingly turns out to be meant as nothing.

Such a reading not only permits us to take a cool look at all the men's 'liberality' in this tale, as seems to be warranted, but also potentially to identify in its heroine the quality of womanly 'fredom', the incautious givingness so often explored by Chaucer, as the type of generosity most properly to be admired. Nevertheless, the fact that the 'liberality' motif is relatively underplayed in Chaucer's narrative indicates how much less he was willing than a proto-humanist like Boccaccio to take an interest in the proto-Renaissance fashioning of magnanimity and magnificence. Were we to consider whether it is in fact Dorigen who is 'mooste fre' in 'The Franklin's Tale', we would be recognizing that Chaucer's major interest in generosity was bound up, not with the humanist ideal of 'magnificence', but with his extended interest in how the conflicted ideal of generosity drove women, amidst dramatic narratives of trust and betrayal: how it even drives a Wife of Bath, unwarily giving to her fifth husband—only to regret it—'al the lond and fee / That evere was me yeven therbifoore' (III.630–1).

---

[66] Anne Thompson Lee emphasizes the 'generous and loving integrity' of Dorigen in ' "A Woman True and Fair": Chaucer's Portrayal of Dorigen in the *Franklin's Tale*', *ChauR*, 19 (1984–5), 169–78 (p. 177); David Raybin endorses this, but speculates less convincingly that Dorigen is most 'fre' in something like the word's modern sense: ' "Wommen, of Kynde, Desiren Libertee": Rereading Dorigen, Rereading Marriage', *ChauR*, 27 (1992–3), 65–86 (pp. 81–2).

6

Problems of Patience and Equanimity: 'The Franklin's Tale', 'The Clerk's Tale', 'The Nun's Priest's Tale'

Arveragus's Glad Cheer

A notoriously perplexing moment in Chaucer occurs in 'The Franklin's Tale' when the knight Arveragus tells his wife Dorigen to keep her promise of love to squire Aurelius, after the squire has apparently fulfilled the 'impossible' condition she set for this. Many readers have wondered whether, as Arveragus responds to the crisis, he regresses from an ideal of mutual deference hailed at the start of their marriage, into husbandly coercion.[1] Less often attracting comment, but to my mind just as clamorous for explanation, is the unemotional tenor of Arveragus's initial words during this crisis, as he absorbs the drastic predicament that has been tearfully described to him by his wife:

> This housbonde, with glad chiere, in freendly wyse
> Answerde and seyde as I shal yow devyse:
> 'Is ther oght elles, Dorigen, but this?'
>
> (v.1467–9)

Whatever reaction from Arveragus the reader might have been conjecturing, this was not it. In the face of her desperate news that she seems to be committed to becoming sexually available to Aurelius, Arveragus's ability to preserve 'glad chiere' and respond in 'freendly wyse' sounds a curiously disengaged note. Should it be considered as the verbal equivalent of a reassuring arm around the shoulder? [2]

---

[1] A recent example is Sandra McEntire, 'Illusions and Interpretation in the *Franklin's Tale*', *ChauR*, 31 (1996–7), 145–63.

[2] He 'reassures her of love, reduces the magnitude of the problem': Phillips, *An Introduction*, p. 140. Such a 'reduction' in my view easily strikes us as blandly demean-

Arveragus is complimented by a critic in one Chaucer *Companion* for 'behaving beautifully' in this situation: and is complimented in another *Companion* for responding 'in the idealistic fashion that informs his relationship with his spouse'.[3] Yet the glad cheer risks seeming—if not trivially nonchalant—an insensitive underestimate of the gravity Dorigen herself perceives in her predicament. It takes to an extreme of placidity the non-reproachful reaction to a marital partner's problems that conduct writers sometimes commended.[4] It may also seem to contradict another form of ideal behaviour frequently emphasized by Chaucer, where 'pitee' runs promptly in 'gentil' heart. What is absent is some explicit demonstration of fellow feeling, an empathetic sharing of the woes of a loved one or companion.[5]

Should we suppose that an attempt is being made to project a huge effort of control in Arveragus? Is he suppressing passionate reaction in the interests of resilient optimism? A few moments later the pressure of underlying emotion does *momentarily* gain outlet, for 'he brast anon to wepe' (v.1480).[6] However, interpretation in terms of a strenuous effort of control would be more convincing if it were flagged up as it usually is by Chaucer in other stressful situations. (I am thinking of Troilus steeling himself 'ful manly' so that emotion is not visible in his 'chere' when escorting Criseyde out of Troy (*TC*, v.30–1).)

There are two other alternatives. One is to read Arveragus (with Jill Mann) as simply carrying through his own prior promise not to show

ing. However, there is some precedent for it in the tone adopted by the husband in the *Filocolo* (iv.31): 'I certainly do not want you to kill yourself for this, nor to give yourself a single unhappy moment because of it. It does not displease me at all ...' *Chaucer's Boccaccio*, trans. Havely, p. 158.

[3] Margaret Hallissy, *A Companion to Chaucer's 'Canterbury Tales'* (Westport, Conn.: Greenwood, 1995), p. 201; and Edward Wheatley, 'Modes of Representation', with a discussion of lines 1474–84, in Brown (ed.), *A Companion to Chaucer*, pp. 296–311 (p. 309).

[4] e.g. *The Book of the Knight of the Tower*, trans. William Caxton, ch. 80, ed. M. Y. Offord, EETS, s.s. 2 (Oxford: Oxford University Press, 1971), pp. 109–10.

[5] 'Men seyn, "to wrecche is consolacioun / To have another felawe in hys peyne"', as Pandarus puts it, *TC*, i.708–9; cf. *RR*, 4713–14, trans. Horgan, p. 72.

[6] Kathryn Jacobs emphasizes 'the difficulty of Arveragus's self-conquest, apparent in the grief and frustration that break through his habitual code of submission': 'The Marriage Contract of the *Franklin's Tale*: The Remaking of Society', *ChauR*, 20 (1985–6), 132–43 (p. 134). In Raybin's remarkable view Arveragus '*feigns* "glad chiere" as long as he is able', taking refuge in a patriarchal posture of philosophical detachment: ' "Wommen, of Kynde, Desiren Libertee" ', pp. 68–9.

jealousy in this marriage. In this reading his question means what it says—'is there nothing more serious than this?'—and signals a calm 'relinquishing' of jealous 'interrogation and anger'.[7] The other is to see Arveragus as checking whether Dorigen has told him the whole truth: the position implicitly adopted by him in that case is paternalistic and implies superior quasi-judicial status.[8]

Chaucer registers but does not explain the oddity of the moment because Arveragus's question provokes Dorigen's exclamation, 'This is to moche, and it were Goddes wille!'[9] If he is asking, as one commentator puts it, 'whether committing adultery is all that Dorigen has on her mind', the question is certainly peculiar.[10] Not much is to be gained really by second-guessing the unspoken anxieties of a fictional figure—whether, for example, Arveragus dreads that she may be in love with Aurelius.[11] In any case Dorigen points us to something bizarre about Arveragus's demeanour. And there are indications that this is not a modern difficulty with the passage: early scribes had trouble with it, and particularly with that expression, *freendly wyse*. As Stephen Knight points out, they tried to make it more consistent with their expectations by substituting for 'freendly' words like 'spedely', 'sondry', 'good', 'humble'.[12] Jill Mann has suggested that the adjective is meant to recall the way the tale's opening eulogy of patience links the mutual deference characterizing friendship ('freendes everych oother moot obeye') with the sufferance on which love flourishes.[13] This stretches a slender echo somewhat thin. Arveragus's response is not, for me, about how friends or lovers-as-friends behave. I shall propose instead that what Chaucer is trying to project in Arveragus's good cheer needs to be elucidated by recourse to Stoic ethics. We should associate him, as Barbara Nolan persuasively associates Theseus in 'The Knight's Tale', with the Stoic

---

[7] *Geoffrey Chaucer*, pp. 116–17.

[8] As argued by Derek Pearsall, who engages with concerns I raise here (though not specifically with Arveragus's 'gladness'), in '*The Franklin's Tale*, Line 1469: Forms of Address in Chaucer', *SAC*, 17 (1995), 69–78.

[9] The oddity is not registered in the analogue in the *Filocolo*.

[10] Wheatley, 'Modes of Representation', p. 310.

[11] Greenberg, 'Dorigen as Enigma', p. 340.

[12] 'Textual Variants, Textual Variance', *Southern Review*, 16 (1983), 44–54 (pp. 49–50).

[13] *Feminizing Chaucer*, pp. 168–70. Other critics who urge the relevance of the discourse on *amicitia* include Helen Phillips, 'Love', in Brown (ed.), *A Companion to Chaucer*, pp. 281–95 (p. 287); and Hallissy, *Companion to Chaucer's 'Canterbury Tales'*, p. 201.

ideal of the compassionate person, who relieves those who are in tears, but without weeping *with* them.[14] Such ethical contextualization may lead to a better understanding of the tale's particular exploration of love, and will take us into the heart of Chaucer's conflicted exploration of the values of patience.

It has been usual to focus on *maistrie*, on generosity, liberty, and *gentillesse* as the behavioural determinants of the tale. Just as important, though, are other pointers to conceptual significance in the tale's discourse on patience, following the couple's nuptial agreement from which flows their 'quiete and reste' (v.760). Critics often quote the first part of the discourse for its commendation of personal liberty rather than constraint. The later part trails somewhat, sounds more dully sententious; but it is no mere tendentious embellishment.[15] It is crucial to Arveragus's behaviour and repays attention:

> Pacience is an heigh vertu, certeyn,
> For it venquysseth, as thise clerkes seyn,
> Thynges that rigour sholde nevere atteyne.
> For every word men may nat chide or pleyne.
> Lerneth to suffre, or elles, so moot I goon,
> Ye shul it lerne, wher so ye wole or noon;
> For in this world, certein, ther no wight is
> That he ne dooth or seith somtyme amys.
> Ire, siknesse, or constellacioun,
> Wyn, wo, or chaungynge of complexioun
> Causeth ful ofte to doon amys or speken.
> On every wrong a man may nat be wreken.
> After the tyme moste be temperaunce
> To every wight that kan on governaunce.
>
> (v.773–86)

---

[14] Nolan derives from this observation (Seneca, *De clementia*, II.6.2, *Moral Essays*, vol. 1, pp. 440–1) and from other similar Senecan passages an explanation why Theseus's active compassion (*clementia*) in the *KnT* is generally distinguished from the tearful emotion (the *misericordia*) of those he assists: *Chaucer and the Tradition of the 'roman antique'*, pp. 265–6 and nn. 63 and 64.

[15] For a contrary view of the whole speech as a self-indulgent Franklinesque 'digression', see J. Terry Frazier, 'The Digression on Marriage in the *Franklin's Tale*', *South Atlantic Bulletin*, 43 (1978), 75–85. For more constructive analysis see Robert R. Edwards, 'Some Pious Talk about Marriage: Two Speeches from the *Canterbury Tales*', in *Matrons and Marginal Women in Medieval Society*, ed. Robert R. Edwards and Vickie Ziegler (Woodbridge: Boydell and Brewer, 1995), pp. 111–27.

That patience 'conquers' or *venquysseth* is sheer medieval commonplace. That it achieves what 'rigour' could never attain is, however, a more unusual formulation. In fact Chaucer himself is quite distinctive in using the word 'rigour' (for which 'reddour' would have been the more usual English noun at the time).[16] Probably, as hinted in 'as thise clerkes seyn', he found *rigor* contrasted with sufferance in some existing source on marital harmony. Sermons afforded particular precedent for awareness that the ordinary business of getting on together required a couple to exercise mutual tolerance. The Franciscan Guibert de Tournai preaching in the later thirteenth century commended what he called *dilectio socialis*, a 'love founded on partnership' in which the spouses were 'equals and partners'. In such a relationship it was important that each should be free to criticize, and that each should accept such criticism.[17] A mass of evidence has been dug up by Rüdiger Schnell confirming that preachers across Europe persistently championed patience and considerateness between spouses. Schnell quotes one which explains what each partner gives up in marriage: 'Each parts with freewill and surrenders to the power of the other: the husband must do what the wife wants, so the wife must also do what the husband wants [. . .] they have to give up the will of their own which they once possessed.' Summarizing, Schnell begins to sound uncannily like the Franklin: 'the roles of ruling and obeying are not distributed in a gender-specific way. Husbands and wives are reciprocally dependent.'[18] He demonstrates that *adaptability* is the preacher's dominant recommendation. 'To compromise, to be tolerant, to adapt oneself, to practice forbearance, to be patient, to learn to overlook the other's errors [. . .] all these traits, directed toward both husband and wife, form the core of the behavioral requirements of the discussion on marriage from the thirteenth to the sixteenth centuries.'[19]

---

[16] All other *MED* citations for 'rigor' post-date Chaucer. The word is not found elsewhere in his poetry.

[17] Michael M. Sheehan, '*Maritalis Affectio* Revisited', in Robert R. Edwards and Stephen Spector (eds.), *The Olde Daunce: Love, Friendship, Sex and Marriage in the Medieval World* (Albany: SUNY, 1991), pp. 32–43 (p. 42), citing D'Avray and Tausche, 'Marriage Sermons in *Ad Status* Collections', pp. 114–17. See also Erik Kooper, 'Loving the Unequal Equal: Medieval Theologians and Marital Affection', in Edwards and Spector (eds.), *The Olde Daunce*, pp. 44–56 (pp. 53–5).

[18] Rüdiger Schnell, 'The Discourse on Marriage in the Middle Ages', *Speculum*, 73 (1998), 771–86 (p. 779), citing a late 13th-cent. Bavarian sermon in a Vienna MS.

[19] Ibid., p. 780. He distinguishes the 'discussion on marriage' in sources aimed at the laity generally, from the 'discussion on woman' which dominates other discourses ranging from courtly idealization to 'whether to marry' satires.

In view of these sources it cannot any longer be right to think of the Franklin's plea about marital relationships as something new, as though Chaucer were here achieving a breakthrough. Coming closer to Chaucer's ethical 'auctoritees' and to his vocabulary, it is interesting that the mid-fourteenth-century commentator Robert Holcot picks out from Aristotle an idea that friendship should be natural in marriage, and urges husbands to treat wives with gentleness, not with tyrannical harshness or 'rigour'.[20] But *rigor* can also be found disowned at the start of an exemplum in Seneca's essay on Anger Management from which Chaucer borrowed in 'The Summoner's Tale'. We are told that a certain Gnaeus Piso misguidedly mistook *rigor* for firmness (*constantia*).[21]

Seneca's *De ira* certainly leaves its mark in lines 779–83 of the discourse in 'The Franklin's Tale', lines which urge that one must be tolerant because, for all sorts of reasons, there is no one in the world who doesn't do or say wrong sometime or other. When we are provoked by someone, Seneca argues, we should compose ourselves by reflecting that 'even the wisest men have many faults, that no man is so guarded that he does not sometimes let his diligence lapse, none so seasoned that accident does not drive his composure into some hot-headed action. . .' (*De ira*, III.24.4). A moment later he is repeating—'even the wisest do wrong ['prudentissimi peccant', III.25.2]'.[22] The Stoic wise man was taught, then, to tolerate provocation 'philosophically': that is why in 'The Second Nun's Tale' the Roman official purports not to heed Cecilia's taunts, 'For I kan suffre it as a philosophre' (VIII.489–90).

The Franklin, uttering similar sentiments about toleration of people's inevitable faults, adds a gnomic couplet connecting 'patience' with 'temperance', a virtue he says must be displayed according to the context ('after the tyme') by any person who knows about self-control ('kan on governaunce') (v.785–6). Chaucer is thinking of standard doctrine on the Cardinal Virtues, by means of which 'euery man gouerneth

---

[20] '[. . .] est uxor regenda mansuete, non cum tirannica austeritate vel rigore': Holcot, *Commentary on the Book of Wisdom* (a text widely but not universally thought to have been familiar to Chaucer); quoted in Smalley, *English Friars*, p. 194. Aristotle's glance at marriage as a specific site of friendship was elaborated by Aquinas in his Commentary on the *Ethics*; see Kooper, 'Loving the Unequal Equal', pp. 49–51.

[21] *De ira*, I.18.3, *Moral Essays*, vol. 1, pp. 154–5.

[22] As the *Riv.* note to *SummT*, III.2018 indicates, received wisdom is to suppose that Chaucer knew Seneca's *De ira* only from excerpts in the 13th-cent. compilation, the *Communiloquium* by John of Wales; see Robert Pratt, 'Chaucer and the Hand that Fed Him', *Speculum*, 41 (1966), 627–31. Chaucer's knowledge of the *De ira* seems to me thoroughgoing.

hymself in this world' and thence is enabled to be a 'gouernour' of others too.[23] Such a concern with self-control was a fundamental legacy of Stoico-Christian thought. Seneca asks: 'whom will you more admire than the man who governs himself [qui imperat sibi], who has himself under control [qui se habet in potestate]?'[24]

This ideal of self-rule was so deeply associated with Seneca in the Middle Ages that it is quoted (well, misquoted) as a kind of summation of his teaching in an open book held by a 'philosopher' figure depicting Seneca in a moral and philosophical compendium written in England fifty years before Chaucer.[25] Chaucer very frequently invokes this ideal. In *Troilus* Pandarus asserts that Troilus's self-control especially qualifies him as a safe potential partner for Criseyde: let her think how 'wisely that he kan / Governe hymself' so as to gain admiration wherever he goes (*TC*, II.375).[26] Patently Chaucer invokes the same ethical discourse in the passage in 'The Franklin's Tale'. He ends highlighting not 'patience' as at the start of the passage, but the virtue with which self-control is specifically associated, 'temperaunce'. *Temperantia* (often in Middle English named 'sobrenesse, attemperaunce') meant moderation—a virtue that was reckoned to subsist in *all* virtues while being particularly manifested in 'patience'. It is no coincidence that wrath, of which impatience was a sub-category, could be described in terms of 'mysgouernance'.[27]

Arveragus, then, fulfils Stoic criteria as a self-controlled person whose 'temperaunce' prompts him to promise 'suffrance' in his relationship with Dorigen (v.785–9). But, returning to the crux from which this discussion began, we come nearer to Arveragus's striking *glad chiere* at the moment of crisis when we consider that in Stoic ethics, the overriding criterion of contentment, as of patience and self-control, was that the individual must accept harm or loss or poverty (or indeed good luck) with 'equanimity'.[28] Jean de Meun made a meal of this in formulating the first speech of Reason in his part of the *Roman* as she

[23] *VV*, pp. 122, 124.   [24] *De beneficiis*, v.7.5, *Moral Essays*, vol. 3, pp. 308–9.

[25] Reproduced as the frontispiece to Smalley, *English Friars,* and discussed by her on p. xv.

[26] At *TC*, III.427–9 Troilus's 'governaunce' is implicitly defined as a restraint of 'racle dede' and 'unbridled chere'. At *TC*, III.475–81 Criseyde is duly reassured by the evidence of his self-control in courtship.

[27] *VV*, p. 260

[28] e.g. *Ep.* 9.1–5, *Epistulae*, vol. 1, pp. 42–5; *De constantia*, III.1–5, *Moral Essays*, vol. 1, pp. 54–7. *Patientia* was defined by St Gregory as suffering ills *equanimiter*. *Moralia in Job*, *PL*, 76.183c.

tries to deflect the Lover from the rose-quest. She compares the Lover's tortured passion with the endless anxieties and insatiability of those who subject themselves to fortune by seeking wealth. L'Amant should free himself from the roller coaster of Eros (she says) and emulate 'Socratic' equilibrium, a state of mind that neither gloats over good fortune nor grieves over bad fortune: thus whatever befell Socrates, his expression stayed the same.[29] By following Reason's advice, the Lover will never be distressed ('stressed', even) because nothing that happens will dismay him or upset his equanimity. 'Leave weeping to women and children!'[30] The powerful antithesis in her speech between tortured love and Stoic equanimity reverberates in 'The Franklin's Tale'.

In medieval moral discourse this measured 'equanimity' tends to enlarge, as it were, into something more positive—in fact into gladness. Seneca had already borrowed from Epicure a notion of 'glad poverty' (*laeta paupertas*),[31] but later moralists made a point of identifying gladness as a mark of true patience. They cited a maxim in the writing of Lucan, that patience finds joy in hard times.[32] They modelled both meekness and spiritual fortitude (close ally of patience) in terms of suffering any harm or deprivation 'gladliche', an adverb much insisted on in such contexts.[33] To give one very instructive example, the spiritual gift of fortitude or 'Strength' is typically defined thus: 'forto ber mekly and wyth glad chere gret bodyly harmes, and dyuers sekenes, and losse of goodys'.[34]

'Patience' therefore carries in medieval ethical and moral culture (among other things) a decisive implication of firmly cheerful tolerance of mishaps and harm. Using modern bureaucratic slogans to calibrate the gradations of patience as understood in the Middle Ages, we might say that a patient response to loss or provocation, in order to rate as 'satisfactory', must be an unmoved one.[35] To rate as 'excellent', the response should be positively genial. As Hoccleve puts these gradations in the *Regiment*: 'A good man souffreth wrong and is nat meeved', which is satisfactory (3465); but in a more stirring example of *paciencia*

[29] *RR*, 5812–46, trans. Horgan, p. 90.
[30] *RR*, 6341–79, trans. Horgan, pp. 97–8.
[31] *Ep.* 2.6, *Epistulae*, vol. 1, pp. 8–9.
[32] 'Gaudet patientia duris', *Moralium dogma philosophorum*, *PL*, 171.1034.
[33] *VV*, pp. 82, 132, 186.   [34] *Mirk's Festial*, p. 157.
[35] Thus Gregory defines 'true patience' in the *Moralia in Job* as 'to suffer ills with equanimity and not to be stung with resentment against him who inflicts evil things', *PL*, 76.183c; cited in Hoccleve, *Regiment*, 3459–62.

just after this, we hear of a duke who, when spat upon in the face by a colleague, so far transcended retaliation that he 'lookid foorth in a freendly maneere' (3552). This rates as excellent. Langland thinks along the same lines when he urges that patient fortitude should be 'murie in soule'.[36]

The praise of patience that heads 'The Franklin's Tale' dwells, as we have seen, on sufferance, non-retaliation, the virtue of self-control; but it does not expressly prepare us for 'glad' or 'friendly' or 'murie' resilience—perhaps because, as I have just demonstrated, these further ramifications of the concept were taken for granted. Arveragus's *glad chiere* and *freendly wyse* constitute, according to the ethical standards that were tirelessly promoted at that time, an outstanding, exemplary, controlled response to a damaging situation. For a moment at least, it appears that nothing that happens can dismay him. This is not a matter of behaving like a friend, it is not really about a 'mutuality' in his relationship with Dorigen, it is about exemplary equanimity.[37]

Yet that does not eliminate all objection to such a response. Does the tale imply that something is missing in Arveragus, or not? To clarify this it will be helpful to ponder further how the tale has developed a dynamic around patience, 'temperaunce', and their opposites.

Dorigen herself is clearly represented as prey to exceptionally intense feelings, an intensity that both verifies the depth of her love and disables her from measured or patient acceptance of her husband's absence. There piles up around her a vocabulary of self-damaging emotion. Arveragus's absence 'destreyneth' her; her distress is not merely heavy and 'grete', it is a 'rage' (v.836)—a consuming force (indeed the word designates extreme frustration in love in the *Romaunt of the Rose*).[38] Dorigen is in effect 'slaying' herself; the whole world becomes as nothing to her, except as it emphasizes her fearful deprivation and threatens, in the case of the danger to her husband posed by coastal rocks, to perpetuate it.

Dorigen's catatonic fear has been viewed as a 'passive vulnerability' that 'expresses her femininity'.[39] However, her state primarily clamours

---

[36] In the sketch of the *Spiritus Fortitudinis* given in *PPl*, 'в' xix.295.

[37] It is in the particularities of this Stoic characterization of Arveragus's patience that my analysis differs from Mann's eloquent discussion of that quality in the tale as a 'surrender to "aventure"': *Feminizing Chaucer*, pp. 117–20.

[38] Raisoun finds L'Amant 'in compleynt and in cruel rage' at the walling-up of the beloved rose in a tower to prevent his access: *Romaunt*, 4616.

[39] Crane, *Gender and Romance*, p. 104.

to be read, albeit with empathy, as morally and ethically resonant (and gender-marked in other terms). On the one hand is her desolation, 'rage', heavy affliction; on the other, embodied in her friends' kindnesses and in the sorts of mental resource that they try to reach in her, are potential 'comfort', 'hope', and 'reason'. Ultimately, what with the exhaustion of emotion and the creeping impact of consolation and the non-negotiability of the situation, she 'moste a tyme abyde / And with good hope lete hir sorwe slyde' (v.923–4). Personification looms here and there would be precedent, in the practice of editing certain other medieval authors, for the moral flavour to be sharpened through capitalization: 'And with Good Hope lete hir Sorwe slyde.'

Before hope attenuates Dorigen's anguish, are we to judge that her emotionalism falls short of Stoic standards of the exacting sort that are upheld by Reason in the *Rose* or Prudence in 'Melibee'? When Melibee rampages and cries out at the attack of his enemies, Prudence urges that it is the mark only of a foolish person to display such 'sorwe', and that 'outrageous wepynge' is not consistent with the measured, patient response to deprivation that Seneca would prescribe (VII.979–93). In terms of medieval confessional discourse, Dorigen's state carries further negative resonances. Her misery amounts to a kind of rebellious Ire against what providence has brought her, to which the antidote is Sufferance.[40] Her 'heuynesse' is also reminiscent of a type of 'unpacience' that verges on despair or 'wanhope', against which spiritual fortitude enabling her to 'suffre strongly' would be the necessary remedy.[41] Despair, in 'The Parson's Tale', is a consequence of 'outrageous sorwe' and excessive 'drede' (IX.692), and Dorigen is clearly driven by precisely these impulses into a state of near-despair even if its focus is not, as technically would be the case with Christian 'wanhope', a hopelessness about the state of her own sin.

The focus of her despair is the rocky coastline, which she can only contemplate as a blot on the good of creation in her famous speech of protest against 'eterne God'. *Why* has such an allegedly wise God created 'this werk unresonable' that, so far as she can see, does harm rather than good (v.865–76)? Arguing with God, drawing attention to his apparent

---

[40] *JW*, p. 7. A feminist-psychological reading can come to the same conclusion. Francine McGregor uses the adjective 'rebellious' to describe the various means by which Dorigen expresses her assertive desire for her husband's return: 'What of Dorigen? Agency and Ambivalence in the *Franklin's Tale*', ChauR, 31 (1996–7), 365–78 (pp. 373–4).

[41] *JW*, pp. 112–13.

self-contradictions, she concedes that 'clerkes' produce hypotheses that 'al is for the beste' and that, being no clerk, she cannot fathom 'the causes'. Yet she manages to make the clerkish capacity for such 'argumentz' sound sophistical, whereas her own interposed 'conclusion' (as she scholastically calls it) praying for her husband's safety and the elimination of dangerous rocks, sounds more charitable.[42]

Chaucer withholds comment on this speech. The reader is challenged to fill the gap of signification. On the one hand the questions about the status of destructive evil within the good of creation can be construed as ones that were of serious interest to philosophers of the late Middle Ages. On the other hand some critics think that Dorigen rehearses a kind of primal sin, as of pride, in presuming to doubt God's design.[43] There is no easy escape, at this juncture in the tale, in the supposition that what she is voicing is a pagan, pre-Christian bafflement. Her speech appeals to God using terms of address and descriptors which are indistinguishable from those in contemporary medieval prayer. Despite Minnis's claim that Chaucer is representing Dorigen trying to think like an enlightened monotheistic pagan philosopher, and that it is inappropriate to 'impose Christian standards', it appears to me that she is raising her doubts and seeking reasons at this point against the visible grain of a Christian framework:[44] and this is of a piece with some of the thrust of the tale's express interest in Christianized patience, temperance, and their opposites. Thus she is certainly *not* displaying that first degree of temperance that consists in measured belief in the articles of faith. According to moral theory, such 'mesure' is transgressed by anyone who seeks natural evidence concerning what is above human reason and understanding. The biblical injunction to 'put mesure to thi witt' means not interposing one's own wit in matters of faith, whereas

---

[42] Warren Smith notes that the prayer 'establishes her as a person of pity and compassion': 'Dorigen's Lament and the Resolution of the *Franklin's Tale*', *ChauR*, 36 (2001–2), 374–90 (p. 382).

[43] e.g. Edwin B. Benjamin, for whom Dorigen's questioning of the 'order of the universe' invokes (albeit with delicacy) 'Satanic' imputations of pride: 'The Concept of Order in the *Franklin's Tale*', *PQ*, 38 (1959), 119–24.

[44] A. J. Minnis, 'From Medieval to Renaissance? Chaucer's Position on Past Gentility', *PBA*, 72 (1986), 205–46 (p. 230). There are certainly some 'pagan' flourishes in the tale, but I do not find the kind of sustained pagan ambience that Minnis asserts (e.g. p. 219), drawing on Kathryn Hume, 'The Pagan Setting of the *Franklin's Tale* and the Sources of Dorigen's Cosmology', *SN*, 44 (1972), 289–94. Pearsall more convincingly speaks of the setting as a 'twilight' world like that of *KnT*, part-Christian with pre-Christian touches: *The Canterbury Tales*, pp. 146–7.

Dorigen expressly interposes hers.[45] Again, Dorigen here conspicuously offends against the canons of patience. She is disconcertingly like the wrathful person who remonstrates against God as a result of experiencing setback: one who, when 'god werkyth noght thi wyll', objects that 'god is not ryghtfull'. Dorigen's is a kind of sin of the tongue chiding God, a 'grucchyng' against God that implicitly projects her own desires above God's. It is a 'grucchyng' typical of misgovernance that is linked to wrath—a protest against God in tribulation, that makes the protester sound (as one moralist inventively puts it) like a screeching cartwheel not greased with grace.[46]

Although the 'screeching cartwheel' would be an over-drastic analogy for Dorigen's troubled intervention in metaphysics, the problematic status of her bold posture of questioning, of asking 'why?', was a commonplace of medieval religious thinking. One who believes well—as a sermon-writer puts it—'makythe noon aposayls [challenges] ny questyons why'.[47] There are instructive analogies in the writing of William Langland, for whom such questioning tends to count as a failure in human 'suffrance'. In *Piers Plowman*, the personification Study caustically rebukes inquisitive preoccupation with *why* God allowed Satan's trickery: may those who 'wilneth to wite the whyes of God' have their eyes in their arses—for all was as God willed, 'whatso we dispute' ('B' x.103–30).

Because this Langlandian critique focuses on the alleged intellectual arrogance of secular lords who try to outsmart clerks by questioning the rationale of original sin and thus finding fault with the Creator, it involves rather a different perspective on doctrinal questioning than that in 'The Franklin's Tale'. After all, Dorigen's 'why?' is motivated by the overwhelming personal feeling of desolation in a person confronting a conspicuous danger in the created world. However, the analogy grows closer when Langland's narrator, disillusioned with learning and theology, is represented in a dream-within-a-dream as plunging into spiritual recklessness. In due course he is granted a tour of creation which is intended to bring him back to love of his creator: but instead, he demands to know why all creatures seem to be governed by Reason except humankind. Reason retorts that *why* he puts up with that is not Will's business. God could amend every wrong in a second—but God himself 'suffreth for som mannes goode'. Sufferance is a 'sovereyn vertu'. Will should rule his tongue better, and learn to acknowledge that 'al that [God] wrought was wel ydo, as Holy Writ witnesseth'.[48]

Here the problem of why the Creator should allow apparently negative aberrations in creation presents itself somewhat as it does to Dorigen. By the standards of this Langlandian position, Chaucer is challenging his readers to bring moral criteria concerning sufferance, patience, and temperance to bear on Dorigen's behaviour. Langland's narrator is subsequently told off in no uncertain terms for asking 'why this, why that?' about creation. Only *Kynde* (God as Creator) ultimately knows the 'cause' ('B' XII.217–25). According to Ymaginatyf the human intellect is better employed, not in officiously questioning creation but in discerning from creation—from the birds and the beasts—the moral paradigms that should apply to human life. We must ask, then, whether Dorigen is in blatant moral error when she launches impatiently into presumptuous protest, judges providence in relation to her own well-being (her personal desire for Arveragus), and pitches her wits into the question why God has allowed danger into creation.

The differences between Langland's 'Will' and Dorigen, who both ask 'why?', is that Dorigen is spurred by emotional anxiety whereas Will seems to be implicated in more gratuitous questioning. Nor is there anyone called 'Reason' to point a moral against Dorigen. Chaucer's narrative does not in any crude way present her condescendingly as a woman 'stamping a tiny foot against God' (to borrow an expression from Theodore Roethke).[49] The strategy is more subtle: the reader is brought to recognize that providence and 'fair creation' dramatically exceed the human powers of judgement and prediction from which her protest arises.[50] The rocks seem to her in her emotionally forlorn state unnatural, a 'foul confusion'. She therefore indulges a wish that such rocks should sink out of sight. It is a classic instance of a phenomenon recognized by the Stoics and also contemplated by Boethius: flawed human perception of what is in an individual's best interests—especially (in the Stoic formulation) under the pressure of emotion (*affectus*) which obstructs

---

[48] 'B' XI.367–96; for a brilliant analysis, see Nicolette Zeeman, 'The Condition of *Kynde*', in David Aers (ed.), *Medieval Literature and Historical Inquiry* (Cambridge: D. S. Brewer, 2000), pp. 1–30 (pp. 21–6).

[49] Roethke suggested that this was one of the charges typically levelled at women's poetry: 'The Poetry of Louise Bogan', in *Selected Prose of Theodore Roethke*, ed. Ralph J. Mills (Englewood Cliffs, NJ: Prentice-Hall, 1963), pp. 133–4.

[50] As Smith points out, the clerkish doctrine that 'al is for the beste' even impinges on her speech despite her impatience with it: 'Dorigen's Lament', p. 381.

the judgement.[51] As Arcite puts it in 'The Knight's Tale', regretting the outcome of his release from jail in Greece, 'why pleynen folk so [. . .] / On purveiaunce of God, or of Fortune' when that providence so often gives them something better than they could contrive? 'We witen nat what thing we preyen heere' (I.1251–4, 1260).[52]

So in 'The Franklin's Tale' the disappearance of the rocks, when it seems to occur, prompts Dorigen's horror at the outcome she has previously desired, something she now considers 'agayns the proces of nature' (v.1344–5). That is, the narrative shape, albeit with the assistance of illusion, *proves her to have been* short-sighted, demonstrates the inadequacy of human intellect to determine that providence is 'unresonable'. The 'answer' to her question about danger in creation is therefore (as Priscilla Martin puts it) that she and her husband 'may, without realising it, be in the hands of God';[53] that providence actually mysteriously cares—as, when Arveragus trusts to it ('All may yet be well'), ultimately proves to be the case in the tale. In any case the groundlessness of Dorigen's fears is also quietly suggested by the fact of Arveragus's easy return home. The rocks prove so little an impediment to him that neither they nor any danger in his sea crossing are even mentioned on his arrival home.[54]

This leads us to what is perhaps a further dimension to Dorigen's distress, drawing again on Stoic ethics and contributing the particular sense of spiralling foreboding that makes her such a poignant epitome of human misery. Seneca, as we have seen, tirelessly urges placidity and serenity in the face of fortunes of all kinds. Nothing is worse than to be dragged into *perturbatio*—a weltering sea of emotion.[55] The most genuine pleasure in life is freedom from turmoil, and freedom from

---

[51] Seneca, *De beneficiis*, II.14.1, *Moral Essays*, vol. 3, pp. 74–5, complemented in *Boece*, III pr. 2, along the lines that people know there is a sovereign good but err in their attempts to attain it.

[52] That God's 'prudent purveiance' is often too 'derk' for human wit is asserted in *MoLT*, II.479–83.

[53] Martin, *Chaucer's Women*, p. 128.

[54] See V. A. Kolve, 'Rocky Shores and Pleasure Gardens: Poetry vs. Magic in Chaucer's *Franklin's Tale*', in *Poetics: Theory and Practice in Medieval English Literature*, ed. Piero Boitani and Anna Torti (Cambridge: D. S. Brewer, 1991), pp. 165–95 (p. 169); anticipated by Paul Edward Gray, 'Synthesis and Double Standard in the *Franklin's Tale*', *Texas Studies in Literature and Language*, 7 (1965), 213–24 (p. 214).

[55] 'The man who has been saved from error, who is self-controlled and has deep and calm repose, is free from such perturbation': *De constantia*, IX.3, *Moral Essays*, vol. 1, pp. 74–5.

'anxieties that rack the mind'.[56] The corollary to that is avoidance of groundless fear, a topic to which he devotes the whole of Letter 13. People suffer more in imagination than in reality, he suggests. Even if suffering might be round the corner, one should not 'run out to meet it'. With the help of prudence, one can counter fear resolutely, and perhaps incline to hope after weighing uncertainties carefully.[57] Again in Letter 59, the wise person or *sapiens* is one who remains calm and unshaken. Reaching a state of ideal good depends partly on being 'not harassed by apprehension, through anticipation of what is to come'.[58]

Is not Dorigen constructed in pointed antithesis to this ideal? She is living through something of that stormy life of emotion feared by Criseyde when the latter reflects on the disruptive power of passionate love (*TC*, II.773)—and the manifestation of 'stormy' emotional angst is aptly figured in Dorigen's case as the dread of a loved one's potential shipwreck, apprehension of the hypothetical menace the rocks pose to her husband. In a Christian light her 'derke fantasye' is a mistrust of God's providence; but in an ethical light it is a failure of prudence, a pointless self-embroilment in pessimistic conjecture. She ekes out her sorrow at Arveragus's absence with dollops of grief over potential disaster, a wallowing in sorrow that is acerbically viewed elsewhere in Chaucer's writing.[59]

Dorigen's are understandable human reactions: that is why the moral handbooks spend so much time countering the inclination to protest. But now we might ask, are these morally dubious reactions also *gendered* in this tale? So far as her mistrust of 'purveiaunce' is concerned, there is the implicit mitigating factor that she is at least thinking within a Christian view of monotheistic providence. That is not the case with Aurelius, whose laments and complaints address not 'god' but the pantheon of 'goddes' (v.1030) He prays to Apollo 'the sun', but also invokes Lucina, Neptune, and Pluto (v.1031–79). While Dorigen has the benefit—as it would be perceived in the cultural context of the

---

[56] *De beneficiis*, VII.2.4, *Moral Essays*, vol. 3, pp. 460–1; the ideal is 'peace of mind and lasting tranquillity', *Ep.* 92.3, *Epistulae*, vol. 2, pp. 448–9.

[57] *Ep.* 13.10–12, *Epistulae*, vol. 1, pp. 78–81; echoed in *Ep.* 74.32, 'if folly fears some evil, she is burdened by it in the very moment of awaiting it, just as if it had actually come—already suffering in apprehension whatever she fears she may suffer': *Epistulae*, vol. 2, pp. 134–5.

[58] *Ep.* 59.14, *Epistulae*, vol. 1, pp. 419–21.

[59] Pandarus remonstrates with Troilus, 'Delyte nat in wo thi wo to seche, / As don thise foles that hire sorwes eche / With sorwe', *TC*, I.704–7.

Canterbury Tales—of quasi-Christian horizons, Aurelius is therefore decidedly stuck with paganism. To that extent, while in religious terms the tale may gender female the voice of doubt and protest, it puts one of the complementary male voices more radically beyond the pale in alternative belief.

The reader may on the other hand sense some temptation to form a gendered impression of *emotionalism* in the tale. After all, Dorigen's weeping and sighing at Arveragus's absence is obtrusively tagged by the narrator 'As doon thise noble wyves whan hem liketh' (v.818). This is one of Chaucer's enigmatic throwaway lines, perhaps best interpretable as a false lead momentarily inviting a misogynous suspicion of shallow on-tap feminine emotion, only to catch us out with the subsequent genuine intensity of Dorigen's feelings. In any case, the matching emotionalism of Aurelius seems calculated to avert a simple binary gendering. If anything, Aurelius turns out a worse case of what Seneca would call 'perturbation' than Dorigen. He is introduced as one 'dispeyred' after two years of futile loving; he has been languishing like a Fury in hell (v.943–50). There is the same quality of knowing extravagance in the rhetoric used to present the paroxysms of his young passion as there is in the presentation of Troilus, whose 'fury' of emotional frustration extends to lunging about his room like a dying bull; only Aurelius's passion seems exposed to a narratorial impatience even more devastating than any provided in *Troilus* by Troilus's foil, Pandarus. Rebuffed, Aurelius raves, goes out of his wits, and is put to bed so 'dispeyred' (again: cf. v.1297) as to earn the narrator's flippant disdain: 'Chese he, for me, wheither he wol lyve or dye' (v.1084–6). Aurelius is the faintly ridiculous star of his own Hollywood blockbuster, Torment Furious, in which he hectically outdoes Dorigen's distress; though ultimately his, like hers, can be balanced against salvific Hope—the 'hope of bliss' that dawns when the Orleans magician agrees to help him.

The effect of the narratorial distancing is to force us to register a perspective outside that of the lover, even amidst the lover's extreme emotion.[60] It is not meant to decry emotion altogether. Kolve surely

---

[60] Pearsall sees 'impatience . . . with extravagant emotion' as the passing exasperation of the narrative voice, not as a significant criticism of Dorigen's behaviour: *The Canterbury Tales*, p. 149. This is to understate a dispassionate streak affecting many of Chaucer's narratives. As Nolan says of the Knight's commentary on the antics of lovers, up one minute and down the next like a bucket in a well, Chaucer characteristically infiltrates an anti-passionate 'commonsensical' Stoic view of love's emotion: *Chaucer and the Tradition of the 'roman antique'*, p. 271.

blurs the point when he suggests that Chaucer 'seems to have had only a limited interest in the emotional histrionics of young lovers'.[61] What the tale does is more audacious: it both drives to a limit the emotionalism aroused by love's storms *and* juxtaposes that with a self-discipline that would triumph in equanimity over emotional crisis.

In fact the 'glad chiere' and 'freendly wyse' of Arveragus that in its immediate context seems so perplexing as a response to his wife's trauma, must be read ethically against the tidal surges of emotion and misery that flood around it. Chaucer is articulating the husband's 'pacience' as an attempted optimistic equanimity. Arveragus is—nearly—a copybook Stoic wise person (*sapiens*). He does not 'chide'; he suggests all may yet be well. This is Stoic virtue in action: patience bears inflicted injuries with equanimity. Magnanimity seeks to view potential disaster and affront (for Aurelius has implicitly affronted the husband) with whatever serenity can be mustered.[62] Arveragus's is that heightened version of patience to which the would-be Stoic aspires: not yet utterly oblivious to loss or affliction (hence those tears that he cannot prevent) but able to overcome and heal what 'wounds' he receives. Ideally such patience consists in not *being* injured—being (almost) beyond perturbation in self-composure.[63] In Arveragus's case, he manages to supplement what English moralists would have called 'evenhead' with 'benignite'—which means not only being tolerant and unvengeful, but positively 'merry'.[64] His temperance is what textbooks recommended—it 'pre-empts reproach with cheerfulness ("hilaritate") and readily makes allowances for error'.[65]

The reader is not meant to think such good temper easy, of course. Rather, it requires the highest standards of control or governance, and as Seneca himself would have admitted, the wise person can still feel hurt and pain. 'You must not think that our human virtue transcends nature; the wise man will tremble, will feel pain, will turn pale; for all these are sensations of the body.' In theory the mind in possession of ideal Stoic wisdom does not sag, it aspires to independence from the strokes of fortune. Yet the sensations of the body, and the 'passions' or

---

[61] 'Rocky Shores and Pleasure Gardens', p. 193.

[62] See Seneca, *De ira*, III.5.7 and III.25.3, *Moral Essays*, vol. 1, pp. 266–7 and 318–19; and *De clementia*, I.5.5, *Moral Essays*, vol. 1, pp. 372–3.

[63] Seneca, *De constantia*, III.2–5, *Moral Essays*, vol. 1, pp. 54–7.

[64] *JW*, p. 254. An overriding principle was that virtue 'should be cheerful ... in its acts': Dante, *Il Convivio*, I.8, trans. Lansing, p. 20.

[65] *Formula vitae honestae*, *PL*, 72.26 (my trans.).

affectus lodged in the inferior irrational part of the human soul still make inroads, especially in those (like Arveragus perhaps) who have made great progress in wisdom but not fully attained it.[66] Glad cheer has not eliminated feeling: 'As I may best, I wol my wo endure' is Arveragus's admission of that.

'The Franklin's Tale' goes on to draw our attention away to the issue that the narrator subsequently highlights, namely whether it is stupid of Arveragus to send Dorigen to fulfil her bargain with Aurelius. Critical discussion has been mesmerized by that decision and its consequences, whereas here we have been isolating the problem of the 'gladness' that immediately precedes it. Partly the problem is semantic. The adjective 'glad' has been further reduced in modern English to social triteness ('so glad to see you'): it may be that the modern adjective 'cheerful' better translates and sustains the residual energy of the Middle English word. Chaucer *can* use the word in a bland way: thus when Criseyde is faced with a rainstorm after dinner with Pandarus, she decides that it will be more beneficial to agree to stay overnight 'gladly' with 'a frendes chere' than to put up a show of resistance while expecting to stay anyway (*TC*, III.642). Glad cheer, in this context, is a social form, to be adopted optionally as opposed to other social forms. But a contrasting sense of a weightier significance in the adjective is seen in her own later bidding to Troilus to remain 'glad', as they part after consummating their love (*TC*, III.1513).

The problem is also partly cultural. Stoic equanimity, stretched to these limits in the teeth of traumatic situations, looks unattractively insensitive to a modern society more used to the exaltation of empathic 'caring'. This was a problem for late medieval culture too, as we should pause to acknowledge. The culture was aware of how this aspect of Stoicism had seemed insensitive to St Augustine, whose famous work *The City of God* distinguished Christian from pagan virtue partly on the basis that Stoic serenity or *apatheia* (or what Augustine dubbed *impassibilitas*, 'unpassionability') demanded a degree of insensibility that would constitute a moral defect and would anyway be beyond the reach of ordinary sinful humanity. To the extent that *apatheia* means a life eschewing those emotions that are irrational and 'disturb the thoughts', Augustine admits it is 'a good and desirable state'—but a state more characteristic of eternal life than earthly life. Not to be 'stirred

---

[66] Seneca, *Ep.* 71.29, 74.31, and 75.12 respectively; *Epistulae*, vol. 2, pp. 90–1, 132–5, and 142–3.

or excited by any emotions at all', not to be 'swayed or influenced by any feelings', is to 'lose every shred of humanity' rather than to 'achieve a true tranquillity'. [67]

Chaucer directly challenges us to think these issues through in *Troilus and Criseyde* after Pandarus tries to chivvy Troilus out of his desperation at the prospect of Criseyde's departure from Troy. When Pandarus rehearses clichés about there being more fish in the sea, Troilus is horrified at his friend's seemingly heartless indifference to 'passiones',

> As he that, whan a wight is wo bygon,
> He cometh to hym a paas and seith right thus:
> 'Thynk nat on smerte, and thow shalt fele non.'
> Thow moost me first transmewen in a ston,
> And reve me my passiones alle,
> Er thow so lightly do my wo to falle.

> (*TC*, iv.464–9)

Troilus follows this by swearing his commitment to Criseyde to be so deep that even beyond death in the underworld, he will lament an eternal trauma of separation. Characteristically Chaucer manages to make Troilus both an advocate of the validity of profound human emotion, and an exemplar of theatrical (pagan) emotionalism. Perhaps we are supposed to remember that according to the Augustinian view, life beyond death in the Christian dispensation transcends bleak emotions of the Troilean kind. Certainly elsewhere Chaucer is perfectly capable of giving philosophical Stoic or Boethian aphorisms against passion (just like those caricatured by Troilus) a run for their money against soulful human protest.[68] But he tends to make us very aware, and not unsympathetically aware, that impassioned humans don't *listen* to

---

[67] *City of God*, xiv.9, trans. Bettenson, pp. 564–6, and cf. xix.4. The view of *apatheia* articulated in the *City* was the outcome of a complex evolution in Augustine's relation to Stoicism, as explained by Marcia L. Colish, *The Stoic Tradition from Antiquity to the Middle Ages*, vol. ii, *Stoicism in Christian Latin Thought through the Sixth Century* (Leiden: Brill, 1985), pp. 222–5. See also David Aers, 'Chaucer's *Tale of Melibee*: Whose Virtues?', in Aers (ed.), *Medieval Literature and Historical Inquiry*, pp. 69–81 (pp. 72–3).

[68] 'No man is wrecched, but himself it wene', answers Fortune to a Plaintiff: *Fortune*, 25. (However, Troilus's observation is grounded not in this generalization or its source in *Boece*, ii pr. 4.111–13, but in Seneca's *Ep.* 78.12–13, *Epistulae*, vol. 2, pp. 188–9—as demonstrated by Ayres, 'Chaucer and Seneca', p. 13.)

doctrines of mental resilience. This dialectic is one that is close to the heart of Chaucer's poetry.

In 'The Franklin's Tale' the problem we have identified as the potential insensitivity of Stoicism is compounded by a strategic shortcoming. At the crux, the reader is caught unprepared. So far as the virtue of equanimity is concerned we have had only the clues in the narrator's 'patience'-speech and perhaps a hint that Arveragus rides resolutely or 'magnanimously' above petty emotions, when he has returned to Brittany unconcerned about possible masculine attentions to Dorigen in his absence. Because these clues are somewhat slender, his 'friendly' Stoic resilience at the dramatic crux comes too much out of the blue. As much as the decision that flows from it, this resilience seems deeply problematic. Or to put that another way, Arveragus's resilience (*pacience*), which is what *enables* him to 'cede' Dorigen to another man in the interests of promise-keeping, is problematic, both in itself and in its implicit demand that she herself should sustain the same ethic of resilience in offering her body for the 'love' of squire Aurelius.

Chaucer has overstrained the moral dimensions of this story. I do not think there is any doubt that Arveragus is supposed to be the wise and far-seeing Stoic. That is his first aspiration in his behaviour at the tale's crisis. It is an aspiration for which there is some anticipation in the tale, but which is not well managed at the crucial moment. From here on, the tale retreats into the safer ethical waters of generosity, as discussed in Chapter 5. But 'The Franklin's Tale' is a kind of glorious failure. Chaucer tries to mesh too many conceptual strands at its centre, and the Stoic strand becomes, I believe, awkward in the company it has to keep. There is dislocation (perhaps fruitful and provocative, but dislocation nevertheless) between a Stoic admiration for equanimity and a Christian impulse towards emotional compassion. The gendering of these issues is ambiguous. The tale centres plangent feeling both in Dorigen and in Aurelius, so unless we decide that Aurelius is 'feminized' by his infatuation there is no case for interpreting feeling along simple binary lines. Arveragus in some ways may be closer to appropriating the Stoic vision of the sage than anyone else in the *Tales* except Dame Prudence and Duke Theseus. Yet as the Franklin concedes, his wisdom looks for a while desperately like stupidity. While the outcome of the tale retrospectively validates Arveragus's attempt to conform his personal life to patient equanimity, still it is hard to read of his 'glad chiere' and 'freendly wyse' without wincing.

Griselda's Glad Cheer

An analogous difficulty arises in 'The Clerk's Tale' with Griselda, so I should like to include here some remarks about that tale. The Marquis of that story finally relents towards Griselda, whose womanhood he has been intent on testing, when he sees her unshakeable cheerful forbearance as she offers her best wishes when challenged to appraise the 'bride' who has usurped her place. It is not just her 'pacience' that causes Walter to melt, it is

> Hir glade chiere, and no malice at al,
> And he so ofte had doon to hire offence,
> And she ay sad and constant as a wal . . .
>
> (IV.1044–7)

Looking back in this narrative, we see that right at the start of the marriage, the deal was that Griselda was never to register dissent from Walter, whether verbally or by 'frownyng contenance' (IV.355–6). Consequently when he began to subject her to his tests, it was her 'chiere' or countenance he monitored, and her words he noted, to see if they betrayed any sign of relapse in her (IV.576, 598–601, 708–10). When she complies with his repudiation of her from the marriage, she states that she goes 'gladly' (IV.832). She returns at his bidding in a menial role 'with humble herte and glad visage' (IV.949); states outright that she is 'glad' to act as chambermaid by arranging the rooms for the new bride as he wishes (IV.967); and (the expression is now duplicated within four lines) both goes to meet, and greets, the bridal guests with 'glad chiere' (IV.1013, 1016). Walter's crescendo of torment is met, in fact, with serially cheerful behaviour. It is as though Griselda fulfils what moralists commended as the 'meek' person's relish for ever more humiliating roles: 'the more foul and despitous that a seruice is, the gladloker wole the meke do it'.[69]

---

[69] The fifth branch of meekness, *VV*, p. 138. The spur for the conspicuously iterative motif of Griselda's gladness probably does not come from Petrarch's version of the story, *Epistolae seniles*, XVII.3, which is often thought to be Chaucer's main source but in which there is but one comment on Griselda's 'cheerful look' (*leta facie*); see Thomas Farrell, 'The Griselda Story in Italy', in Correale and Hamel (eds.), *Sources*, pp. 103–29. Rather it is the Boccaccian analogue that supplies comment on the heroine's cheerful expression (*viso . . . leto*, twice, and *lietamente* once): *Decameron*, x.10, ed. Segre, pp. 667, 669; trans. McWilliam, pp. 821, 822, 824.

It is worth reflecting on this for two reasons. One is that the chief critical emphasis on the representation of Griselda has been on her obedience, her self-restraint, the stolid consistency with which she conforms her will to Walter's (qualities partly communicated through the ever-present Middle English adjective *sad*, as was pointed out long ago by Derek Brewer).[70] Too little attention has been paid to the importance—implicitly invoking a Stoic mindset—of the frown-free cheerfulness with which she maintains her role. The second reason is that attending to 'gladness' in her narrative clarifies a contrast with 'The Franklin's Tale'. The betrothal vow to which Griselda commits, never to offer her husband a grudging demeanour, draws attention to itself and yields something like an excess of fulfilment which the reader is brought to recognize as a leitmotif of the story. To an extent, her cheerful equanimity *is* the story. By contrast, in the mutual agreement of Arveragus and Dorigen the 'suffrance' is less provocatively unbalanced; and, the reader has no chance to find out what it means before the crunch comes.

That Griselda should tolerate her husband's nasty decisions seems bad enough to readers. That she should persistently express any kind of good cheer while doing so ratchets up the outrage. Nevertheless I have commented elsewhere on the strategic pro-feminist importance of her voluntary constancy.[71] (The fact that her willed participation in Walter's will is completely unwavering systematically contradicts misogyny's habitual allegation of feminine 'instability'. Conversely, Walter is introduced as a lord who capriciously cultivates the wish of the moment, and his subsequent cruel subterfuges drag him into a mass of inconsistency and lies and arbitrary behaviour. Instability is crucially gendered masculine, not feminine, in this tale.) In the same discussion I briefly suggested that Griselda becomes defined in the text by the oxymoron of pliable steadfastness. Her firmness, that is, has to be demonstrated by resolutely pliant humility in relation to Walter. This paradox, which I called 'the provocative heart of the tale's fascination', will bear more scrutiny here in the context of competing (and gendered) ethical and moral traditions.

In the ethical system that the Middle Ages adapted from antique ethics, patience and perseverance were sub-categories of fortitude. In

---

[70] D. S. Brewer, 'Some Metonymic Relationships in Chaucer's Poetry', in his *Chaucer: The Poet as Storyteller* (London: Macmillan, 1984), pp. 37–53 (pp. 44–51).

[71] Blamires, *The Case for Women*, pp. 164–71.

practice, all three categories tended to flow into each other. Thus, forti-
tude is 'the courage to act in danger without fear, to dread nothing but
shameful things, and to bear bravely with ill as with good fortune'. But
'perseverance' is a virtue 'of remaining firm and stable in pursuit of the
good', whereby someone 'becomes immoveable' and is 'neither broken
by adversity nor made proud by prosperity, and neither frightened by
threats nor bent by promises'. But 'patience' is 'voluntary endurance of
hardships for the sake of honor' characterized by 'not becoming exalted
in good fortune or broken by ill fortune; it bears inflicted injuries with
equanimity'.[72]

From our discussion of Griselda's 'glad cheer' and resolute constancy,
it is clear that she is aligned at the robust end of this amalgam
of virtues. But the definitions also alert us to an element of self-
suppression (to not being inflated by good fortune), and this is where
the gentler, more specifically Christian concept of humility infiltrates
antique fortitude/patience. In fact 'The Clerk's Tale' involves a clear
case of creative manoeuvre between Stoic ethics and Christian morality.
Griselda's 'humility', abasing herself into servitude, is in part a facet of
her patience. But her patience is a facet of a received ethic of fortitude,
Middle English *strengthe*. Because it is quite a stretch from her humility
(shown in extreme deference to Walter's will) to her toughness (shown in
the steely resolve of that deference, whatever is asked of her), the text has
to pursue awkward negotiations between them—none more palpable
than the moment at which the reader is advised not to follow Griselda
in respect of her particular 'humylitee' (IV.1143),[73] even though we are
aware that the narrative has applauded in her the 'humblesse' of women
as something not matched by Job or other men (IV.935–6).

It hardly needs saying that in the Middle Ages humility was indeed
particularly inscribed as a feminine virtue. Women were instructed and
socialized into expecting to practise this virtue: equally the virtue was
demonstrated by reference to examples of wifely abasement. Griselda's
humility will seem less like a 'worst case' example next to the following:

Humility ... must be practiced, first because it patiently endures its troubles; just
as a wife who is mistreated by her husband suffers it patiently so that she may
not cause her husband to become worthy of public shame, and if perhaps, to his
shame, some external lesion from his beating can be seen on her, she carefully

---

[72] *FM*, pp. 618–23, 134–5.
[73] Interestingly changed from Petrarch's advice not to 'imitate the *patience*' of
Griselda: Farrell, 'The Griselda Story in Italy', p. 128.

dissimulates saying she took such an injury elsewhere. In Ecclesiasticus 2 it is said: 'Gold and silver are tried in the fire,' and so forth.[74]

Considered only as a drastic instance of the same phenomenon, 'The Clerk's Tale' has always distressed readers because it seems to validate an abuse of women in which women are required to collude. The tale's ethical and gender positioning is more nuanced than that implies. What remains true, however, is that Chaucer puts the narrative under strain by enlarging the strength of Griselda's will and robust equanimity (an ethical virtue) on the one hand, and by deepening her Christian humility on the other: she has never considered herself to be more than humble servant to Walter, she says (iv.820–4), and, as the Clerk puts it in a nutshell, her spirit was always in 'pleyn' (absolute) humility (iv.926). We are in the presence of a creative disjunction between the ethical and moral inheritance.

Chauntecleer's 'drede'

Finally, what of one of the opposites of patience and fortitude, what of fear? The cross-currents of ethical and moral traditions concerning the status of fear turn out to be even more conflicted, but they can give us a fresh insight even into that graveyard of moral interpretation, 'The Nun's Priest's Tale'. Fear, after all, is a recurrent topic in the tale, what with Chauntecleer's anxiety about his dream, his actual fear of the fox, and Pertelote's disdain for masculine timidity.

From an Aristotelian point of view, fear was a deficiency of spirit productive of cowardice, over-confidence being the contrary excess of spirit, and courage the golden mean. Stoic philosophy had more or less outlawed fear. Seneca was for ever lecturing against what he called pointless fears about the future, against fear of death, against any fear that impeded the capacity to get on contentedly with life.[75] A wise person was to rise unperturbed above the threat of trouble. Fear was one of the 'passions' which afflict everyone but which wise persons must suppress.[76] Seneca even defined absolute freedom as freedom from fear—whether fear of other people or of gods.[77]

---

[74] *FM*, p. 65.
[75] There are examples in *Epistulae* 13, 24, 30, 54, 80, 82, 85, 110.
[76] *Ep.* 85.11–16 and 24–9, *Epistulae*, vol. 2, pp. 290–5, 298–303.
[77] *Ep.* 75.18, *Epistulae*, vol. 2, pp. 146–7.

The powerful condemnatory element in this Stoic thinking on fear (noticed in John of Salisbury's *Policraticus*)[78] could not easily be accommodated into medieval moral analysis. Christianity laid out as one of its foundation stones that fear of God was the beginning of wisdom, 'Begynnynge of wysdam is God to drede' as Hoccleve rendered it.[79] Fear of God was also regarded as a prerequisite for justice.[80] Above all, the first 'gift' of the Holy Spirit was 'drede of God'.[81] Fear was therefore fundamentally positive, since it attested human awe of deity, and—given the potential fear of divine punishment through purgatory or hell—it dissuaded from evil, eroded pride, prompted guilt. Moral analysis of fear found certain types of fear such as fear of privation or of death to be natural and therefore neutral, but detected deadly sin in any fear of losing one's bodily life or one's possessions that resulted in willingness to abandon moral principles. As for fear of hell pains as a motive for spiritual amendment, that was less commendable than fear of angering God and being severed from his love, this being the 'special' holiest form of 'drede'.[82]

However, if fear was in one sense a good 'beginning', it might also in another sense prevent someone from *making* a new beginning. A category of 'unboldnesse' or 'arwenesse' was diagnosed within sloth—'whan a man hath a manere drede to bygynne and dar nout auntre hym'—whereby all the possible reasons for failure are obsessively projected.[83] This sin is called *pusillanimitas* in Latin. Being a state 'full of supposed and imagined perils' which 'loses a sense of purpose',[84] it is a version of the debilitating apprehensive attitude lambasted by Seneca. Now, what is interesting about this is that the medieval moralists deride faint-heartedness, not only as a childish fear like being scared of snails'

---

[78] vii.3, trans. Pike, pp. 223–4.

[79] Psalm 110: 10 (Vulg.), 111: 10 (AV); Hoccleve, *Regiment*, 4852. For a fundamentally positive view of fear, see the section 'Of dradnesse' in *Vices and Virtues: A Soul's Confession of its Sins*, ed. F. Holthausen, EETS, o.s. 89 (London: Trübner, 1888), pp. 58–63.

[80] Hoccleve, *Regiment*, 2479–80.   [81] *JW*, p. 240.

[82] *JW*, pp. 240–2, citing Aquinas's *Summa contra gentiles*. Alastair Minnis and Eric J. Johnson outline the underlying threefold scholastic division of fear into 'natural, culpable and laudable' in 'Chaucer's Criseyde and Feminine Fear', in *Medieval Women: Texts and Contexts in Late Medieval Britain: Essays for Felicity Riddy*, ed. Jocelyn Wogan-Browne *et al.* (Turnhout: Brepols, 2000), pp. 199–216 (pp. 203–4). While indebted to this article, I have found medieval vernacular discussions more instructive in relation to the Chaucerian materials covered here.

[83] *JW*, pp. 106–7; *VV*, p. 27; *ParsT*, x.691, 'drede to bigynne'.

[84] Gower, *Mirour de l'Omme*, 5485–96, trans. Wilson, p. 79.

horns or of hissing geese, but also as a dread of *dreams*.[85] Furthermore, as mediated by Gower in the *Confessio Amantis* this kind of sloth is gendered, for it is defined in terms of the timid person who

> ... hath litel of corage
> And dar no mannes werk beginne:
> So mai he noght be resoun winne;
> For who that noght dar undertake,
> Be riht he schal no profit take ...
> He woll no manhed understonde,
> For evere he hath drede upon honde.

(CA, IV.316–26)

We might first divert to *Troilus and Criseyde* to note that Chaucer applies this vocabulary both to create humour around lovelorn Troilus's apprehensions about his acceptability to Criseyde, and also to contribute a moral thrust to the pressure exerted upon the heroine. In Troilus's case a pattern is created whereby on the one hand Troilus in his 'drede' foresees mountains of impediments, or needs to offer up anxious pleas to every god in the universe; and on the other hand Pandarus, ever the philosopher of practical enterprise, ribs him for being absurdly scared that the man will fall out of the moon and for betraying a 'mouses herte' as if Criseyde will bite him (*TC*, I.1017–25; III.705–37). More insidiously, in the case of Criseyde, Pandarus puts it to her that she must not duck away from the opportunity presented by Troilus's love for her. To pass it by would be to deserve blame for 'verray slouthe'. This understanding of her situation as one requiring initiative, not pusillanimity, is one that she later proves to have internalized (*TC*, II.281–91, 807–8).[86] Pandarus's jibe at sloth illustrates an entirely characteristic Chaucerian move. Often, Chaucer does not so much offer an ethical viewpoint as illuminate how people strategically deploy and manipulate (or become vulnerable to) ethical viewpoints in their daily interactions. Moreover the distinction implied between Troilus and Criseyde is interesting in these instances. It seems that faint-hearted behaviour amounts to a gendered moral defect in the case of the male, but simply to a moral defect in the case of the female. Indeed in a

---

[85] 'That is the drede of here sweuenes', *VV*, p. 27; 'thou faryst as he that hath dreed of his dreme', *JW*, p. 107.

[86] This quasi-moral argument against pusillanimity is elaborated from the merest hint in Boccaccio, *Filostrato*, XLIV.1–2: see *Troilus and Criseyde*, ed. Windeatt, pp. 166–7 and note to II.281–2.

sense Criseyde is being urged to engage in a mode of 'aventure' that takes her beyond safe feminine behaviour. The gendered moral defect more characteristically besetting the courtly female role in the context of courtship would be any failure to show pity or 'routhe', which in Criseyde's case (Pandarus claims) would be implicit in making no response to Troilus.[87]

Playing up Troilus's nervousness in courtship for all it is worth, Chaucer comes close to an emasculation of the prince, but the game is ultimately to enhance the sensitivity and depth of his feelings, not to query his masculinity.[88] Turning now to 'The Nun's Priest's Tale', we shall find the play with similar issues similarly light-hearted, but the tale manages to tie in gendered mockery of fear with other stretching moral questions. Here cockerel Chauntecleer explains to hen Pertelote that he has dreamed of an encounter with an unknown animal (a fox, we realize) that has terrified him (vII.2895, 2906). Pertelote, berating him for betraying a cowardice inconsistent with a 'mannes herte', trivializes dreams as mere trifles ('vanitees') wrought by temporarily unbalanced physiological constitution: let a herbal remedy be taken and all will be well: 'Dredeth no dreem, I kan sey yow namoore' (vII.2969). While elsewhere, in the opening of the *House of Fame*, Chaucer seemingly discloses a deeply erudite curiosity about dreams and their potentially grave significance, the hen's perspective in this tale allies her with the moralists who robustly scorn anyone who is in awe of dreams. Chauntecleer, however, elaborates and melodramatically exemplifies the contrary argument that dreams are 'to drede' and are by no means trifles.[89] He gives an example of two companions about to go to sea. One of them has a dream warning of imminent drowning and proposes delay, but the other scornfully censures him, as if from the 'sloth' handbook, stating defiantly that no dream will frighten him from pursuing his business; dreams are just 'japes', people are always dreaming of owls, etcetera. The first companion, delaying departure, will 'thus forslewthen wilfully [slothfully waste] thy tyde' (vII.3086–96). He sails, and the ship is wrecked.

Although the sloth handbook is here proved misleading by narrative events and Chauntecleer's premonition also will (on this occasion) be

---

[87] '... sith thy lady vertuous is al, / So foloweth it that there is som pitee'; and 'Wo worth that beaute that is routheles!' (*TC*, I.898–9, II.346).

[88] Minnis and Johnson, 'Chaucer's Criseyde', pp. 211–12; Jill Mann, 'Troilus's Swoon', *ChauR*, 14 (1979–80), 319–35.

[89] For 'drede' see vII.2973, 3063, 3109; and for 'vanitee' see 3011, 3091, 3129.

proved right, the reader has a suspicion in any case that the cock's monologue is uttered not so much to stake out a solemn position of deference to dreams as to regain masculine *amour-propre* in front of his partner by outdoing her intellectual resources. He defies his own dream and leaves the perch to get on with his regal sex-life, displacing the effect of his own knowledge with the daring mien and masculine virility ('twenty tyme') that Pertelote has required of him. The consequence of his defiance unfolds to the accompaniment of a self-conscious symphony of allusions to free will, the Fall, women's counsel, and Trojan epic: what it boils down to is that Chauntecleer is seized by the fox, a creature which, on sight, he 'natureelly' fears as his 'contrarie' (VII.3277–90). In this context of instinctual dread, all questions of the morality of fear suddenly seem beside the point. Yet the tale luxuriates, regardless, into more ethical analysis—noting the cockerel's unwary conceit in agreeing to sing for the fox and the fox's moment of unwariness, goaded into letting the cockerel out of its mouth.

Derek Pearsall argues that 'no little nugget of "moralite" which we can hoard away for our better edification' is deducible from this tale: rather, the 'embarrassing surfeit of "morals" we are offered at the end of the tale hints at the inadequacy of easy moralising'.[90] Without damaging the comic texture of the fable it might be retorted that amidst the bunch of morals that the Nun's Priest finally dangles, the warning about the danger of being 'recchelees / And necligent' (3436–7) is neither a red herring nor naïve.[91] In so far as these concepts apply to Chauntecleer rather than the fox, they apply to his descent into rejection of his own premonition. We are in the realms of a phenomenon much in evidence in the *Tales* and studied by Allan Mitchell: 'exemplary morality repeatedly going unheeded'.[92] There is indeed a moral category named 'negligence' and it designates refusal to acknowledge until too late the evidence by which one might have been wary, and refusal to 'lerne to be wys' except—as in Chauntecleer's ostentatious monologue—when it suits one.[93] In light of that type of analysis it might be a bit 'recchelees' of Pearsall to insist so stoutly that there is no moral, since his own words unwittingly underline the relevance of 'negligence': 'the full comedy of

---

[90] *The Canterbury Tales*, p. 237.

[91] Helen Phillips refers to these moralizations as emulating 'the type of simple "moral" given in Aesopian fables' which teases readers to work out more complex meanings: *An Introduction*, pp. 186–7.

[92] Mitchell, *Ethics and Exemplary Narrative*, p. 82.

[93] Gower, *CA*, IV.890–1, 907–9.

the situation [. . .] is that Chauntecleer, for all his eloquence, takes no notice at all of what he says'.[94] And the focus of the cockerel's eloquence, and of Pertelote's contrary advice, is the status of dreams—whether they should be a stimulus for premonitory 'drede' or whether they are of more trifling significance, a spur only for laxatives. Our conclusion must be that the tale's wobbly explorations of 'drede' and 'negligence' manage ingeniously and comically both to confirm and deny negative and positive implications of the state of fear, exploiting with great wit the muddle that is inherent in available traditions and their attendant gendering baggage.

[94] *The Canterbury Tales*, p. 234.

7

Men, Women, and Moral Jurisdiction: 'The Friar's Tale', 'The Physician's Tale', and the Pardoner

Exercise or dubious exercise of jurisdiction is a prominent concept in Chaucer's narratives. Nature exerts jurisdiction over the birds in the *Parliament of Fowls*, Hector over the Trojan parliament (and the fate of Criseyde) in *Troilus and Criseyde*, Fame over her supplicants in *House of Fame*. For examples of figures who manipulate political or ecclesiastical jurisdiction we need look no further than Marquis Walter in 'The Clerk's Tale' or the Pardoner. Jurisdiction, I think, would be a topic able of itself to sustain a book on Chaucer. Here we shall further our interest once again in moral and ethical aspects (particularly gendered aspects) of the subject. Although the *Canterbury Tales* are energized by many instances of indignation about the abuse of jurisdiction, we shall focus particularly on two representations there of victimization of women in the tales of Friar and Physician, which project instructively different resolutions to the predicament of corrupt jurisdiction. While the term 'jurisdiction' will be interpreted somewhat elastically, there is warrant for this in Middle English usage. The *Middle English Dictionary* shows that *jurisdiccioun* had a range of suggestion as wide as, or wider than, the modern word: 'administrative or judicial power, the right to exercise such power, authority under common, civil, or canon law, power in general, authority, control, supervision, extent or sphere of authority, district under someone's authority'. Moreover, the concept was not in Chaucer's time a neutral one: it was increasingly hot property because Wyclif (as we shall see) fanned the flames of an existing and often fractious debate about the balance between civil and ecclesiastical jurisdiction. Arguably the tales discussed in this chapter variously address that debate, though it is more immediately obvious to readers that they stab at the self-confident human ego's capacity to delude itself generally about its own or others' jurisdiction. Underlying such satire, doubtless, are the principles governing medieval theory of kingship: that is, that kings who make law must nevertheless be 'under' the law; and that whoever judges should remember that they themselves are judged in the higher court of God.[1]

'The Friar's Tale': The Efficacy of a Widow's Curse

It is strange how Chaucer criticism has got into the habit of diminishing the significance of the old widow who features in the conclusion of 'The Friar's Tale'. When the summoner stands in her doorway trying to extort money from her on a trumped-up charge of sexual immorality, she curses him to hell, and it works. Hers is therefore a startling intervention, though you would not think so from the way books on gender in Chaucer have completely ignored her. Despite the ostensible efficacy of her curse, critics who do say anything about her are quick to deny her any serious jurisdiction, even at the moment when she seems to exercise some. The present discussion scrutinizes afresh the empowerment of widow Mabel. It will transpire, however, that historical considerations reaching aside from gender lurk in the tale's shaping of jurisdiction. These will necessitate some exploration of the period's controversy concerning lay versus clerical jurisdiction, as well as of excommunication.

Many ironies of 'The Friar's Tale' converge on *jurisdiccioun*, a concept twice brought to our attention early in the tale. An anticipation of this focus can, moreover, be traced back to the pilgrim Summoner's caustic attack on the pilgrim Friar for intervening at the end of 'The Wife of Bath's Prologue'. The image used by the Summoner—flies and friars alike 'falle in every dyssh' (III.836)—is potently suggestive of acts of infiltration and contamination that will be explored in the clashing fictions of Friar and Summoner. Just before 'The Friar's Tale' begins, moreover, the Friar himself has been insinuating that the Wife of Bath has got into somebody else's dish by presuming to bandy *auctoritees* (III.1276–7). Following this blatant bid to reinstate professional male control, the Friar proceeds to a tale expressly concerned with contested jurisdiction in which, paradoxically, an old woman has the final say.

---

[1] 'You who are above the laws, live as a just man under them': Gower, *Vox Clamantis*, VI.8, in *The Major Latin Works of John Gower*, trans. Eric W. Stockton (Seattle: University of Washington Press, 1962), p. 234. *FM* warns, 'you who rule others, remember that God rules you' (p. 503), quoting from Gregory's *Moralium in Job*.

In the tale there is an archdeacon who has 'jurisdiccioun' (III.1319)
under the bishop to punish offences against the church's laws in the
sexual, financial, doctrinal, and sacramental domain (III.1319–20). Part
of the administration of this jurisdiction is delegated by the archdeacon
to a summoner whose task is to track down offenders and issue
summonses on pain of fine or ultimately of excommunication (referred
to as 'Cristes curs', III.1347). Chaucer's pilgrim Friar hates summoners,
and gloats that he himself is outside their remit: summoners have 'no
jurisdiccioun' over *his* order (III.1330). The summoner in the Friar's
ensuing tale is envisaged using his own jurisdiction to operate a vicious
extortion racket even as he exercises the long arm of the church's
terrestrial power.

Chaucer clearly develops the tale's concern with jurisdiction during
the dialogue between the summoner and devil, begun under a thin-spun
pretence that they are fellow bailiffs.[2] On hearing the fiend's real identity
the summoner blithely launches into a notoriously fussy interrogation
about the physical appearance of devils. Whatever the reason—because
he has no conscience and faith, or because he is a hard-nosed spy obsessed
with tricks of the trade and with disguises, the façade of things—the
summoner proves unable to grasp that his own soul may actually be
within (or delegated into) the jurisdiction of his new companion. On
top of that we should surely see the summoner's prattling inquisitiveness
about demonology, 'evere enqueryng upon every thyng' (III.1409), as
trespass into an *intellectual* jurisdiction beyond his competence. He is
turning out to be a fly darting into every dish himself. He embodies an
unanchored inquisitiveness that moralists particularly warned against.
Dante is thinking of people like the summoner when in the *Convivio*
he caricatures the mentally 'capricious' whose minds hop all over the
place, fancying themselves subtle without actually conceiving anything
as it really is: 'uneducated individuals who have scarcely learned the
letters of the alphabet but nevertheless willingly enter into discussions
of geometry, astrology and physics'.[3]

Ian Bishop got this right in his underrated book on the *Canterbury
Tales*. The 'evere enquerynge' summoner is a *curiosus* improperly prying

---

[2] The interchangeability of the roles is attested in the joint condemnation of
'somenors' and 'bailies' who 'somenen and aresten men wrongfully to gete the money
out of his purse': 'The Grete Sentence of Curs Expouned', in *Select English Works of
John Wyclif*, ed. Thomas Arnold, vol. III, *Miscellaneous Works* (Oxford: Clarendon Press,
1871), pp. 267–337 (p. 320).

[3] *Il Convivio*, IV.5, trans. Lansing, pp. 195–6.

into God's business, a type of figure condemned in Ecclesiasticus and in moral handbooks.[4] While the devil is at pains to explain the precise opportunities and limits of the jurisdiction within which God allows devils to operate, the summoner ham-fistedly tries to satisfy his curiosity, tacitly assuming himself to be exempt from the framework of moral and spiritual jurisdiction of which his adversary speaks.

Every reader notices the tale's sardonic accumulation of evidence that the summoner, on top of his foolish assumption of immunity, is represented as out-fiending the fiend in predatory unscrupulousness. While it is perhaps a commonplace of homiletic writing to melodramatize villainy by ranking it worse than the fiend's, I think it worth noting in passing that a particularly analogous usage occurs in a satirical Wycliffite text (perhaps of the 1380s) against the Great Curse (i.e. against excommunication). Worldly clerics are alleged to be trying to destroy lay authority through threats of excommunication, with an abandon (says the writer) not shown by God even against the fiend, 'For God setteth [the fiend] a terme what he schal do and no more', though sometimes allowing the fiend's power to be extended 'to profite of goode men and just ponyschyng of mysdoers'. Priests who presume to curse people to hell for non-payment of a few tithes—a debt of sixpence or fourpence—are worse than fiends of hell: those torment no soul in hell except on account of sin, these (Satan's clerks) 'cursen to helle for a litel temporal dette'.[5]

In line with some analogues for the tale, Chaucer assigns to an old widow the right to precipitate the nemesis courted by the summoner. From the beginning of the tale we have known that the summoner has ridden out 'to somne an old wydwe', 'feynynge a cause' in order to 'brybe' her (III.1377–8). The confrontation itself is delayed by the interlude in which the devil, to the disdain of the summoner, refuses to profit from a carter's impulse to consign his slow carthorses to the fiend. Just before they reach the widow's cottage the summoner pauses in order to gloat that he is about to offer a demonstration of effective extortion

---

[4] Ian Bishop, *The Narrative Art of the 'Canterbury Tales'* (London: Dent, 1987), p. 109. See Ecclus. 3: 22 for the type of rebuke that was trotted out against the *curiosus*: 'Do not seek the things that are too high for you, nor search into things that lie beyond your ken, but rather think about the things that God has commanded, and further about his works do not be curious'; cf. the strictures against such inquiry in *VV*, pp. 132, 150.

[5] 'The Grete Sentence of Curs Expouned', pp. 298, 310. Arnold's dating of *c.*1383 in based on a reference to the Earthquake Council, but allusions to burning of heretics may imply a later date.

technique to his less successful and too scrupulous travelling comrade. In the finale the summoner's taunts and lies work widow Mabel up to a pitch of righteous emotion that triggers her retaliatory 'curse' giving him to the devil. Then, when the summoner insists he is unrepentant in his extortion, there follows the immediate implementation of the curse. The woman's curse, something like (I shall suggest) a maverick lay excommunication, has triumphantly instigated the punishment. Or has it?

The moment when the summoner exclaims that he intends no repentance has been hailed by a chorus of critics as the real mainspring of the tale's conclusion. The argument is that the devil cannot take the soul of an individual simply because another person urgently wishes it: but only if the individual is in sin and impenitent. Chaucer is 'too much a master of divinity', as one 1960s master of divinity (Beichner) puts it, 'to make the curse of an old woman the cause of the devil's seizure of the summoner, even though analogues may treat a curse from the heart as the cause'. This type of response turns Mabel into occasion rather than cause—just a witness for the prosecution, rather than the judge.[6] That her instrumentality might be merely marginal is typically elaborated in a standard article on *entente* in the tale by Passon: 'It is important that "entente" is *not* applied to the old woman here because, in Chaucer's plot, her intention is not really material and will not really effect the summoner's damnation.' For Kolve, in an influential study of the tale, the interim carter episode, not the denouement, is in any case 'the moral and doctrinal centre of the tale'. In Kolve's opinion it is the carter who quintessentially embodies the reader's common humanity in the tale. The widow (this is where his argument creaks) is too old and poor and 'vulnerable' to be an effective representation of that humanity.[7]

Although discussion of the widow's role has recently become more nuanced, it continues to underestimate Mabel. Larry Scanlon, for example, recognizes a momentary awesome power in her. But he claims that Chaucer has crucially ditched the analogues' emphasis on the heartfelt nature of her curse, and even suggests that (because the summoner himself casually invokes damnation just before she curses

[6] Paul E. Beichner, 'Baiting the Summoner', *MLQ*, 22 (1961), 367–76 (at p. 374); and R. T. Lenaghan, 'The Irony of the *Friar's Tale*', *ChauR*, 7 (1972–3), 281–94 (p. 286).

[7] Richard H. Passon, '"Entente" in Chaucer's *Friar's Tale*', *ChauR*, 2 (1967–8), 166–71 (pp. 169–70); V. A. Kolve, '"Man in the Middle": Art and Religion in Chaucer's *Friar's Tale*', *SAC*, 12 (1990), 5–46 (pp. 15, 35).

him) the widow's curse 'as a speech-act' is 'as much authored by the summoner' as by herself.[8] A similarly ambivalent note is sounded by David Wallace. On one hand he is convinced that the widow embodies something numinous that he calls 'the power of the countryside', and detects in her voice a historically inflected note of outraged protest. Yet on the other he still thinks of her as a figure readily 'discarded' by the narrative: 'this is not her story', her function is 'accidental', she is 'used as bait for a man-trap'.[9]

The first point to make in the project of retrieving Mabel from neglect is surely that it is a strange mistake to doubt (as do Passon and Scanlon) the tale's interest in the sincerity and *entente* of her curse. Chaucer has the fiend pointedly test her strength of feeling after she has uttered it: 'Now, Mabely, myn owene mooder deere, / Is this youre wyl in ernest that ye seye?' (1626–7). As confessional sources make clear, *wyl* is a synonym for *entente*: and the site of *wyl* is the *herte*.[10] As we shall see, this matter of the widow's earnestness in pronouncing her curse raises certain questions in relation to the period's institutionalized form of cursing, that is, excommunication.

The second point to make in restoring charisma and authority to Mabel's utterance, reasserting an element of the 'performative' in it, is that widows as a group, plus or minus children, retained in the Middle Ages a generic power to represent what we might call the Return of the Oppressed. This was ascribed to them ubiquitously, but especially through biblical warrant. The moralist Peraldus wrote that God will punish extortioners (*raptores*)

by imprecations and curses spoken at them by widows and children whom they despoil. For the Scripture says that such imprecations are heard out.[11]

---

[8] Larry Scanlon, *Narrative, Authority, and Power: The Medieval Exemplum and the Chaucerian Tradition* (Cambridge: Cambridge University Press, 1994), pp. 153, 155. Robert Myles also downplays Mabel's curse, evidently out of concern that technically she commits a sin if she wholeheartedly curses a person to hell: *Chaucerian Realism* (Cambridge: D. S. Brewer, 1994), p. 115.

[9] Wallace, *Chaucerian Polity*, p. 144.

[10] 'Withoughten veri contricioun of herte mai no syneful [. . .] be saued. Therfore seith the comyn lawe, as autorite witnessith, "the wylle of a man is rewarded, not the werke".' I cite from a Lollard text (the 'Sixteen Points' in Hudson (ed.), *Selections from English Wycliffite Writings*, p. 21), but the writer expressly leans on canon law. For *wyl/entente* as synonyms see *FklT*, v.980–2.

[11] *De avaritia*, pt. ii, ch. 2: cited by Przemyslaw Mroczkowski, '"The Friar's Tale" and its Pulpit Background', in *English Studies Today*, 2nd ser. (1961), ed. Georges Bonnard, 107–20 (p. 119).

Peraldus might be thinking of a verse in Matthew 23: 13 ff., where Jesus publicly attacks scribes and Pharisees who 'devour widows' houses', and forecasts that thereby such oppressors 'shall receive the greater damnation' (Matt. 23: 14).[12] Another powerful biblical site for widows' vengeance is a parable at the start of Luke 18, concerning a widow's pleas against an oppressive judge, who eventually relents. The lesson is that God, even more than this dilatory judge, will defend believers who appeal persistently to him, and he will catch up with their oppressors; widows' imprecations will be heard out. The 'widow' of this passage—as of some others—was taken by some exegetes to be the Church. It is instructive that one Lollard commentator supposed that modern prelates oppress the widow, or Church, even more than the biblical 'judge' could, because modern prelates can 'summone' her 'from oo place to another, to sooke of her moneye [suck money from her]'.[13]

I do not actually see that the widow of 'The Friar's Tale' constitutes a type of the Church, though that equation has been canvassed.[14] Moreover, Chaucer distinguishes her from the biblical 'widows avenged' in that, whereas those widows are the beneficiaries of vengeance taken on their behalf, he invests his widow with an element of active jurisdiction, or quasi-jurisdiction, into which we should now delve. In order to appreciate this fully we need to consider excommunication in and out of the text, and its ill-repute; how a layperson *ought* to respond to the corrupt use of it; what the nature of Mabel's own 'curse' is; and how much it empowers her.

In theory the ecclesiastical courts existed as a means of 'correction', to bring back into the fold those who transgressed in morals or in observance of church obligations and dues. Penance, often involving a degree of public humiliation, was the ostensible mode of correction but could usually be commuted into a fine if one could afford it.[15] Likewise a summons to attend the courts, and the threat of excommunication for non-attendance or for non-compliance with penance, might frequently be bought off. The courts were therefore an engine of income-generation. Gower quips in the *Mirour de l'Omme*, 'behold how our *correctour* is a *collectour* of extortions'—a jingle which comes through unscathed

[12] Paralleled in Luke 20: 47.
[13] *Select English Works of John Wyclif*, vol. ii, Sermon CXCVIII, pp. 186–7.
[14] Tom Hatton, 'Chaucer's Friar's "Old Rebekke" ', *JEGP*, 67 (1968), 266–71.
[15] See Swanson, *Church and Society*, pp. 166–81.

into modern English from the Anglo-Norman.[16] There is no need to add to the abundant evidence collected by Chaucerians confirming the normative nature of the suspicions about corrupt ecclesiastical judicial practices detailed in 'The Friar's Tale'.[17]

Excommunication was the church's chief weapon for enforcing obedience. If the Great Curse of excommunication was invoked, it removed someone from access to all sacraments and the person could be reported to the secular authorities for imprisonment unless they complied with the court's will within forty days.[18] The church's allegedly over-eager resort to excommunication provoked censure from the likes of Gower, whose *Vox Clamantis* protests that when bishops order submission, if there is any resistance 'they quickly curse your souls with a sentence of death'.[19] The author of the treatise *Dives and Pauper* objects that 'buschopys & prestys schulde nout cursyn but for a wol greuous synne and for gret nede'.[20]

Such protest had become routine. Chaucer's 'General Prologue' (I.654–8) follows Gower's *Mirour* in the jibe that the ecclesiastical authorities confuse the soul with the wallet.[21] However, it was quite another thing to contest the underlying validity of excommunication, as the Wycliffites increasingly did in the later fourteenth century. Wyclif's view characteristically focuses on interiority, on absolute individual responsibility for the state of one's soul. He held that people can only excommunicate *themselves*, by their own sin against God. Prelates can do no more than 'affirm' that eventuality, they can only 'bind' one whom God has already 'bound': prelates do not make it happen.[22] Lollard writings followed suit, as can be seen from the 'Sixteen Points', probably late in the fourteenth century,[23] and from the *Testimony of William Thorpe* at the start of the fifteenth. Thorpe, examined by the Archbishop

[16] *Mirour*, 20170–1, trans. Wilson, p. 269.

[17] See esp. Thomas Hahn and Richard W. Kaeuper, 'Text and Context: Chaucer's *Friar's Tale*', *SAC*, 5 (1983), 67–101.

[18] For a contemporary summary of what was involved, see *FM*, v.30, pp. 585–7.

[19] *Vox Clamantis*, III.12, trans. Stockton, pp. 139–40.

[20] *Dives and Pauper*, x.8, ed. Barnum, vol. 1, pt 2, p. 316.

[21] *Mirour*, 20173–96, trans. Wilson, p. 269.

[22] Anthony Kenny, *Wyclif* (Oxford: Oxford University Press, 1985), pp. 49–50.

[23] Point (5) elucidates the Lollard position that 'neither bischoppis curse ne popis curs bynden any man anemptis [in relation to] God, but if that bounde acorde with the bonde of God': Hudson (ed.), *Selections*, pp. 20–1.

of Canterbury, categorically denied that there was any authority in the Bible for any priest to utter the curse.[24]

The time distance between Gower's *Mirour* (*c.*1377) and Chaucer's *Canterbury Tales* (ten or more years later) is in part the distance between a time when jests about the purse being the archdeacon's hell could be made comfortably and a time when—because of increasing official alarm about Wycliffite ideas—they might need more hedging around.[25] Chaucer's 'General Prologue' offers a sort of insurance-clause: 'But wel I woot he lyed right in dede; / Of cursyng oghte ech gilty man him drede— / For curs wol slee right as assoilyng saveth' (I.659–61). While this interjection is commonly read as ironic,[26] it may equally be read as a defensively correct move in an incipiently touchy atmosphere. The affirmation 'curs wol slee' leaves open the latent power of a curse *per se*, divorced from the skulduggery of grasping archdeacons. That would be a point of some consequence for the case of the Friar's widow, towards whom we can now return.

The summoner of the tale is a manipulator of jurisdiction through excommunication as through all else. Against the ignorant, he invokes it as a threat even without a warrant ('Withouten mandement a lewed man / He koude somne, on peyne of Cristes curs', III.1346–8). He is deploying the same scam when he issues his summons to Mabel to be at court next day to answer 'certeyn' (vague) allegations 'up peyne of cursyng' (III.1586–9). Twelve pence, a small fortune, will get her off. He is committing a conspicuous sin of 'raveyne', a sub-category of covetousness, which the moralists associate among other things with extortions by bailiffs, reeves, and church officials from poor men, widows, and children who cannot help themselves.[27]

How ought Mabel to respond? In response to the summoner's initial hammering on her door, and to the raucous insults he utters outside

---

[24] *Two Wycliffite Texts*, ed. Anne Hudson, EETS, o.s. 301 (Oxford: Oxford University Press, 1993), p. 67.

[25] Gower's *Vox Clamantis* betrays more caution, a few years after his *Mirour* and closer to the date-range of the *Gen Prol*: while alleging that 'the purse can wipe out sin', he adds 'I believe it is fitting to bind by the laws of the Church anything in the world that is bound by them with a just cause', III.3–4; trans. Stockton, pp. 122–3.

[26] Following John S. P. Tatlock, 'Chaucer and Wyclif', *MP*, 14 (1916), 257–68 (pp. 261–2), the *Riv.* note declares the ironic reading to be 'now generally accepted'. It is true that 'cursing' and 'absolving' can be found sarcastically paired in Lollard writing: see e.g. 'The Church and her Members', in Wyclif, *Select English Works*, ed. Arnold, vol. III, pp. 338–65 (p. 361).

[27] *VV*, p. 35; *JW*, p. 129.

alleging that she is an old slag shacked up with some priest or friar (a loose end in a friar's tale, that has tickled the critics), she begins with blessings and deferential inquiry: 'God save you, sire, what is youre sweete wille?' (III.1585). The benediction and the emphasis on his will are of course carefully planted here. Protesting her sickness and inability to travel as far as the court, she politely requests a written copy of the charges so as to be able to send a proxy to answer them on her behalf. Her response, to this point, is a model of polite compliance with the emissary of ecclesiastical jurisdiction.

But, faced with his increasingly ruthless manner, with his reckless asseveration (may the foul fiend fetch him if he lets her off), and his nasty ad hoc claim that he has already covered for her adultery in the past, Mabel moves quickly through protestation of guiltlessness to outraged retaliation. The moral handbooks, of course, extol the virtue of obedience to 'the ordenaunce of holy cherch' and to its 'correcyon'.[28] Within the controlling hypothesis that one should submit one's will to those in authority, failure to obey prelates was grievous sin, as commentary on the fourth commandment insisted.[29] This Commandment, 'Honour your Father and Mother', was taken to apply to all sorts of hierarchies. The full discussion in *Dives and Pauper* makes clear that if one were innocent but patiently suffered oppression at the hands of superiors, this was worthy of divine reward. Even superiors who cultivated your money not the safety of your soul should be obeyed in what 'belongs to their office', for that was wiser than resisting abuses that God was permitting. Finally and specifically, even the victim of a wrongful excommunication is counselled to 'suffryn it lowliche for helpe of his soule'.[30] While Lollards denied the efficacy of conventional excommunication, they took over this orthodox idea of a sort of passive-aggressive attitude as the proper response to being excommunicated (as, increasingly, many Lollards were). According to the 'Sixteen Points', anyone unrightfully cursed in God's cause—which means on behalf of Lollard principles—will fare the better for the curse by tolerating it, while the perpetrators of such curses shall be harmed by them.[31]

Mabel's tolerance, however, snaps. She is stung by the summoner into declaring that he is lying, and into consigning him to the devil. Given the shape of the narrative, the spiritual and moral emptiness of the

---

[28] *JW*, p. 270.   [29] *VV*, p. 3.
[30] *Dives and Pauper*, ed. Barnum, vol. 1, pt 1, pp. 340–3.
[31] Hudson, *Selections*, p. 21.

summoner, and Mabel's thwarted attempt to appeal to his humanity, no sane reader will attach the slightest blame to her for abandoning the policy of sufferance. But, what are we to make of her act of 'reverse excommunication'?

First, it may be necessary to insist that it *can be heard as* a quasi-excommunication. To the modern ear, her formulation, 'unto the devel blak and rough of hewe / Yeve I thy body', and her reaffirmation just afterwards insisting that she really means it, 'the devel fecche hym er he deye', like the carter's earlier curse 'the feend yow fecche, body and bones', do not sound in the same league as excommunications (III.1622–3, 1543). Yet both the formidable pronouncement of anathema, and the more familiar and banal utterance of malediction were commonly designated in Middle English by the same simple verb, *cursen*. So, when the narrative tells us how 'the devel herde hire cursen so' (III.1624), it is not possible to distinguish as sharply as we might expect between a concept of malediction and a concept of excommunication.[32] Of course, the actual enunciation of excommunication was couched in a more rhetorically elaborate, formulaic diction. Nor in fact does the formula usually contain specific reference to the devil. Rather, it intones, may X be accursed by God, body and soul, in all circumstances, and may X be damned in death unless he/she repents.[33] 'Giving X's body to the fiend' is a more demotic formulation, though Mabel's conditional 'unless he is willing to repent' enhances the element of continuity between her curse and the anathema proper.[34]

However, if we acknowledge only the anathema ritual itself we miss something crucial. This was the ecclesiastical requirement that parishioners should be solemnly reminded of the clauses of the Great Curse at least four times a year, on specified Sundays and (as the treatise *Jacob's Well* puts it) 'under this form':

Be the auctoryte and powere of almyghty God, fadyr and sone and holy gost [and that of Mary, St Michael, patriarchs, apostles, etc.], we denounce and

---

[32] Lowes, 'Chaucer and the Seven Deadly Sins', pp. 282–5, envisages a more precise verbal distinction than existed. The verb *cursen* is glossed *excommunico, anatematizo* in *Promptorium parvulorum* (*c*.1440). Medieval Latin has more varied resources, including *maledicere*. Verbs also used by Chaucer for simple malediction are *(bi)shrewen* and *chiden*; an associated noun was *malisoun*.

[33] James A. Work, 'Echoes of the Anathema in Chaucer', *PMLA*, 47 (1932), 419–30, pp. 421, 423.

[34] A point made by Work, who cites the characteristic closing formula of the anathema, 'nisi poenituerit et ad satisfactionem venerit', 'Echoes', p. 428.

schewe acursyd in the sentens of the Gret Curs, that is to say, we schewe hem dampnyd and departyd fro God, and fro alle prayerys and suffragys of holy cherch, and fro alle the sacramentys. And we schewe hem to be takyn to the powere of Sathan, the fend, to deth, and to dampnacyoun of body and of soule, tyl thei come to amendement be verry penaunce, and ben asoyled.—Alle tho that wytingly and malyciusly fallyn in ony artycles of the sentence of cursyng, of the whiche I schall schewe summe to you at this tyme, and summe at othere tymes.[35]

This language takes us rather closer to the cursing into the power of the fiend of 'The Friar's Tale', and, although the boredom induced by listening to this formality and the subsequent procession of clauses could apparently drive parishioners to exit the church, the material remained familiar through repetition.

So there are certainly grounds for taking Mabel's utterance as something of a reverse curse, appropriating against her accuser the sacral act of binding which he has threatened her with; but what does this imply about her function, and her jurisdiction? The logic goes beyond the ricochet of poetic justice. A remark on cursing in 'The Parson's Tale' is relevant. The Parson preaches that the effect of malicious cursing 'retorneth agayn to hym that curseth' (x.618–19). This consoling thought has Augustinian backing, in a dictum that was disseminated in canon law: 'as seint Austin seith, ... if any man is cursed wroungfulliche, it schal harme hym rather that curseth'.[36] The widow, therefore, enacts what was perceived as a normative principle of *recoil* against one who misused cursing.

She becomes, however, much more than some kind of inert screen that causes the summoner's malice to rebound on itself. Scanlon has commented on 'the power of this ostensibly disempowered figure to deliver damnation', because in her curse she 'possesses nothing less than the power to bind and loose ... albeit only momentarily'.[37] This part of Scanlon's thesis is right, but it needs to be unpacked. What are the implications of a laywoman's 'momentary' appropriation of executive sacral power, moreover an appropriation that dramatically reinvests the casualized diction of cursing with spiritual efficacy?

---

[35] *JW*, pp. 13–14.
[36] See *Decretum*, pt 2, c. 11, q. 3, c. 87, in Friedberg (ed.), *Corpus*, pt 1, 667; the Middle English version is from the 'Sixteen Points', in Hudson, *Selections*, p. 21.
[37] *Narrative, Authority, and Power*, p. 149.

Various perspectives are possible. Is it a merely concessionary move by the Friar (if indeed we are still conscious of his narrating voice)? In a rural spot 'out of towne' (III.1571), up against a ruthless ecclesiastical mugger, the widow is, as it were, allowed by the Friar to exercise ad hoc charismatic religious power. There had always been a niche in Catholic doctrine for the hypothesis that women might assume exceptional religious powers when society lacked effective moral or spiritual male leaders.[38] Perhaps we are to imagine widow Mabel likewise allowed to assume exceptional powers to make a stand against the corruption of the institution that normally exercises those powers. At the same time she remains safely 'outside', geographically and institutionally: unauthorized except by short-circuit from God, and able to enunciate only a popularized form of excommunication (albeit with considerable impact). Such a female role could be countenanced even in the academic *scole-matere* with which the fraternal orders were associated.

But if that is one perspective, one that affords her space at the cost of neutralizing, perhaps, some of her power, just a slight adjustment of the lens allows us to perceive Mabel's intervention in a more dangerously controversial light. Here we need to recall that Wycliffite polemic protested vehemently that the laity was often morally and spiritually superior to the priesthood placed in authority over it. But how could reform of the church be driven when it was such a self-governing institution? Wyclif himself, a champion of kingship, pinned his hopes for such reform on lay coercion. He 'refused to admit that the clergy are in any way outside the jurisdiction of the king or his officers'.[39] However, in the face of continuing assertion of the immunity of the priesthood to civil justice, and in face of the hegemony of ecclesiastical judgement against dissent, Lollards increasingly projected themselves (Christ's 'trewe servauntis') as being the victims of excommunication perpetrated by corrupt churchmen who arrogantly proclaimed themselves untouchable within their separate jurisdiction.[40]

The whole issue of different jurisdictions was thus in the air—nor was it confined to dissenting voices. Gower objected to ecclesiastics'

---

[38] Blamires, *The Case for Women*, pp. 171–98.

[39] Anne Hudson, *The Premature Reformation: Wycliffite Texts and Lollard History* (Oxford: Clarendon Press, 1988), p. 381.

[40] 'Cursing' and 'jurisdiccion' are discussed one after another in 'The Grete Sentence of Curs Expouned', pp. 295–8. The argument over jurisdiction also features prominently in the 'Thirty-Seven Conclusions' (7th and 11th conclusions) which Hudson thinks possibly aimed at the Lollard knights: *Premature Reformation*, pp. 214–17.

eagerness to hide their sins under the fig-leaves, as he put it, of their profession.[41] How far should the clergy be exempt from the king's and lords' jurisdiction? In what did the spiritual jurisdiction of the clergy consist, and in what manner should they exercise it? Especially inflammatory to the reformers was the exclusive claim of the friars to be subject, under the Pope, solely to their own orders' authority.[42] 'The Friar's Tale' therefore touches a particularly sore nerve when it allows the Friar to boast of this extra level of jurisdictional independence. However, the tale is surely engaging with the wider battleground of jurisdiction—the vexed relationship between moral laypeople and an allegedly immoral clergy—even as it obliges us to think about specific jurisdictions and about curses.

The reformers both championed civil jurisdiction and argued that the ecclesiastical cursings with which they were threatened were risible and presumptuous travesties of God's curse. Thus, a treatise on Church Temporalities (possibly of the late 1370s) notes that senior clerics at court are accustomed to 'blaberen moche of Anticristis curs and [that of] his clerkis' and to fail to speak of the prospective 'curs of God', which the country's lords will risk if they fail to impose Christ's ordinance on the clergy.[43] The same ploy of opposing notional divine cursing to the actual excommunicative practices being wielded against the reformers appears in a satirical commentary on the Articles of Excommunication. Those who falsely excommunicate reformers are described as 'cursed of God', and *this* curse (God's curse on them) is 'evere rightful' whereas 'mannis curs is the wrongful'.[44]

The conclusion of 'The Friar's Tale' has broken away from the Friar-narrator's control towards a radicalism that would actually have been highly provocative to the fraternal orders in the period. The widow, beginning with blessings, salvific welcome, and obedience to her visitor's will, and protesting her neediness and innocence and chastity, epitomizes the superior moral strength of the laity. Being not of lordly position she cannot exert the kind of political power that Wycliffites fantasized about against the corrupt representative of a punitive diocesan organization.

---

[41] *Vox Clamantis*, iii.22, trans. Stockton, p. 155.

[42] See e.g. 'Tractatus de Regibus', in Hudson (ed.), *Selections*, pp. 129–31, which circumscribes the ecclesiastical jurisdiction within an ideal of 'apostolic' austerity, attacks the friars' self-exemption, and urges the overriding authority of civil jurisdiction even in the moral domain.

[43] Wyclif, *Select English Works*, ed. Arnold, vol. iii, pp. 213–18 (p. 217).

[44] 'The Grete Sentence of Curs Expouned', pp. 324–5.

Nevertheless, she can become a voice for God's curse in order to exercise divinely sanctioned lay jurisdiction against what reformers saw as the worst aspects of ecclesiastical authority.

The narrative of her cursing keeps the religious polemic appropriately in play in two ways. First, what she utters is expressly her earnest will, it manifests that inner focus on sincerity of heart that Lollards prioritized. Second, the implication that her earnest will in the matter of cursing is not efficacious on its own—it does not dispatch her oppressor without his co-operation—is also suggestive. Institutional excommunication was objected to by reformers, we have observed, on the grounds that really the individual 'excommunicates the self', cuts the self off from God. A formal curse therefore affirms something that has occurred between the individual and God rather than binding a soul of itself. To me it appears that the summoner has, for sure, systematically 'excommunicated himself' in the course of the narrative—by consorting with the devil, by categorically disowning conscience, by arrogant inquiry into metaphysical 'pryvetee', and ultimately (as every reader notices) by abjuring penitence.

At the same time this is no straightforwardly Lollard narrative. Among other things, the perilous state of the summoner's soul seems to be defined partly by his heedless disdain for being 'shryven' and his contempt for 'thise shrifte-fadres' or confessors (iii.1440–2), whereas Lollards would have seen no peril in such matters, for they disdained confessors and shrift of mouth. Alan Fletcher has cautioned against ready talk of Lollard 'sympathies' in Chaucer, who cultivated a plurality of vision distant from the movement's strident certainties. Discussing 'The Summoner's Tale', Fletcher sees more reason to speak of a complex Chaucerian satire 'with all the bite of a polemic rendered up-to-date by its Wycliffite resonance'.[45]

I am certainly suggesting that the bite of polemic is present in the case of the final curse in 'The Friar's Tale'. The widow, earnestly summoning up the spiritual damnation of an agent of avaricious and intolerant ecclesiastical jurisdiction, who has moreover been observed decisively cutting himself off from God, is in the late fourteenth-century context no mere folktale throwback, and no mere appendage to a drama about repentance either. That she is a woman may perhaps be attributable to the pressure of folktale and sermon exemplum

[45] Alan J. Fletcher, 'The Summoner and the Abominable Anatomy of Antichrist', *SAC*, 18 (1996), 91–117 (pp. 112).

precedent. In the analogues her role, when not assigned to a bunch of villagers, is often taken by a widow.[46] And yet, the allocation of this moral lay triumph to a woman may well consolidate what 'The Wife of Bath's Prologue' has already suggested—a connection between the reformist agenda and female aspiration; in Alisoun's case, through her usurpation of preaching and exegesis,[47] and in Mabel's through assuming quasi-sacerdotal excommunicative functions.

Looking forwards through the architecture of the tales, 'The Summoner's Tale' specifically complements the 'Friar's'. In fact, what we encounter there is a double echo of the assertion of secular over religious jurisdiction seen in 'The Friar's Tale'. In 'The Summoner's Tale' the first level of competition in jurisdiction that is set up involves friars competing among themselves and with the secular priesthood, to achieve spiritual power (along with associated financial leverage) over villagers. The tale's friar sits comfortably in a villager's home that he claims as his own territory. After a magnificently patronizing and hypocritical acclamation of all sorts of powers that he ascribes exclusively to his order, his obnoxious wheedling provokes the famous indignity of Thomas the householder's present of a fart. This retaliation is both personal affront and an implicit lay judgement that the friar's bogus, greedy apostolic mission is worth no more than hot air. The narrative compounds this with a second mockery of the now irate friar when he resorts to the manor house, where against his expectations the lord and his family refuse to apply secular jurisdiction to uphold his cause against the villager. Rather, the corporate response of the household amounts to a comic manorial threat to reinforce and multiply the lay judgement of the fraternal order by organizing (thus authoritatively endorsing) a mock distribution of the villager's windy insult amongst all the friar's brothers. In other words, lay authority takes the part urged upon it by Wycliffite propaganda and refuses to collude with religious jurisdiction against those who are being victimized by religious greed.[48] The complementarity with 'The Friar's Tale' is also neatly gendered. There a widow, now a male householder and a lord of the manor, are instruments of retaliation against bogus jurisdiction.

[46] Peter Nicholson, 'The Friar's Tale', in Correale and Hamel (eds.), *Sources and Analogues*, vol. 1, pp. 87–99 (p. 90).

[47] Alcuin Blamires, 'The Wife of Bath and Lollardy', *MÆ*, 58 (1989), 224–42.

[48] This argument goes much further than the diagnosis of lay usurpation of clerical authority in the tale made by Fiona Somerset, '"As just as is a squyre": The Politics of "Lewed Translacion" in Chaucer's *Summoner's Tale*', *SAC*, 21 (1999), 187–207.

An alternative way of developing the points raised in connection with Mabel in 'The Friar's Tale' would be to observe that the successful appropriation of executive moral jurisdiction by a woman is not a one-off in the *Tales*. Women's talent for jurisdiction is something that Chaucer seems drawn to write positively about. Two examples beg attention. In 'The Clerk's Tale', there is Griselda's statecraft in administering justice whenever her husband is away (IV.430–41). Jurisdiction is again devolved to a woman with (arguably) exceptional results in 'The Wife of Bath's Tale', when the Queen and some of her ladies successfully seek delegated judicial control over the fate of the rapist knight who is otherwise liable to execution under civil law. One thread in Chaucer criticism takes a dim view of this transfer, claiming it is a manipulation of law designed by the Wife of Bath to 'shape a new social structure [of female domination] masquerading as legitimate authority'. Since Guinevere 'subverts hierarchical order by assuming the king's authority, her legal claims of sovereignty and jurisdiction are invalidated'.[49] Apart from appealing in a simplistic way to theories of royal power, this argument has the disadvantage that it misses the socially beneficial and ameliorative outcome of the Queen's experiment. Whatever one thinks of the marital politics of the tale's conclusion, it is clear (as argued in Chapter 2) that the knight's experience under her jurisdiction is educational. An 'amendment' takes place (III.1097, 1106). Although the reader is left wondering whether the wrong against the rape victim herself remains unamended, in respect of the wrongdoer the Queen's mode of justice has found a way to replicate the achievement that is attributed to Griselda—'Peple to save and every wrong t'amende' (IV.441).

Mabel's sudden lurch into eschatological jurisdiction performs a somewhat different kind of avenging justice. She amends wrong in a more drastic way; yet sustains the pattern of a morally and socially responsible exercise of jurisdiction that Chaucer seems keen to assign to women. Mabel is a low-status woman (so far as one can tell) launched like Griselda by unexpected circumstances into holding jurisdiction. In Mabel's case we see more of a retaliatory ethic, exercised to rid society of a parasite and to precipitate the summoner's private doomsday. In some ways her momentary stardom against a cheap mobster in

[49] Robert J. Blanch, ' "Al was this land fulfild of fayerye": The Thematic Employment of Force, Wilfulness, and Legal Conventions in Chaucer's *Wife of Bath's Tale*', *SN*, 57 (1985), 41–51 (pp. 44–8).

a rural backwater, with no one watching except a disguised devil, seems an unpromising context for jurisdiction itself to come under scrutiny. However, from what has been outlined about connections with Wycliffite debate, it seems probable that 'The Friar's Tale' is a significant if characteristically indirect intervention in the hot topic of jurisdiction. It is quite likely that the widow's role amounts to an unconventional and gendered Chaucerian affirmation of lay jurisdiction over ecclesiastical.

Outer and Inner Jurisdiction in 'The Physician's Tale'

Another version of a retaliatory drama focusing on a woman victimized by a corrupt judicial institution (this time civil rather than ecclesiastical) is produced in 'The Physician's Tale'. Here, however, it seems that the victim exerts reformative moral pressure only through self-sacrifice, and questions about jurisdiction raise themselves in a thorny and provocative way. The tale offers puzzling cosmological and other excursions that have foxed critics, to the extent of raising the question 'What is Chaucer doing with the Physician and his Tale?'[50] Literally, the answer is that he is adapting a short lurid Roman narrative which concerns the conspiracy contrived by a false judge, Apius, against the emblematic innocence of a teenage girl, Virginia. Apius conspires to get Virginia into his clutches by fixing a formal plea to be made under his jurisdiction by 'churl' Claudius, asserting that Virginia is Claudius's slave, not daughter to Virginius. The latter, seeing the case go against himself and his daughter, drastically forestalls the prospect of the judge's defilement of Virginia, by beheading her. As we shall see, the structure juxtaposes sites of authority and judgement within an overall design that hints at concentric circles of, as it were, jurisdictions within jurisdictions.

At the centre of the perversion of justice in the tale is the moment in court when Claudius falsely swears ownership of Virginia. This action blatantly constitutes what in Middle English was designated by the term 'fals chalange'. It was a category of sin that encompassed fraudulent plaintiffs (making and contriving false 'billes' and petitions, in pursuit of false judgements) as well as employment of bent witnesses, and corrupt lawyers—in fact all manner of perversions of the course of justice up to and including corruption in judges themselves. False Challenge was identified as a branch of Covetousness on the presumption that

---

[50] The title of an article by Emerson Brown, Jr, in *PQ*, 60 (1982), 129–49.

legal corruption was perpetrated for profit (judges taking bribes from both sides, etc.).[51] It is on the basis of this categorization that Gower incorporates twinned categories of Falswitnesse and Perjurie under 'Coveitise' in his *Confessio Amantis* (v.2859–84).

Gower's text at that point is interestingly germane to the present discussion because his first demonstration of false witness is the story of Achilles and Deidamia, which focuses on the lies of Achilles's mother when she insistently pretends that her boy-child is a girl. She suborns others to swear to this, so that she can get the 'girl' fostered by the father of another girl (Deidamia) in safety, away from warlike masculine pursuits (*CA*, v.2961–3218). The story thus relates the misrepresentation to which a mother is driven by her fears for her son; driven so far as to position him as counterfeit female companion for Deidamia (and indeed he becomes 'a woman to beholde' (*CA*, v.3020)).

I mention this because the concept of counterfeit is so prominent in the introduction of Virginia in 'The Physician's Tale'. We are told it is as though Nature wrought Virginia as the very epitome of her formative power, which no human artist can counterfeit (VI.13, the verb being repeated at VI.18).[52] This finds an echo in Virginia's manner of speaking, described as 'pleyn' (candid), and not obfuscated with 'countrefeted termes' or knowledgeable airs and graces (VI.49–52). The reader is being teased with this vocabulary. As often, Chaucer has arranged for the teller to introduce key discourse with deceptive indirection, in this case a notion of 'counterfeit' that seems at first to be limited to painterly skill in *trompe l'œil* or to an affectation of learned jargon: but the reader needs to hold the vocabulary in mind and recall it at the narrative crisis. There, Claudius brings forward his plea alleging that Virginia is a serf stolen from him when she was a child. Apius initially adjourns for form's sake until Virginius can be summoned to hear this allegation. It is a chilling abuse of jurisdiction by a judge who has fixed the proceedings in advance and who appears the more vicious for this temporary charade of even-handedness. He is counterfeiting

---

[51] *VV*, pp. 35–6; *JW*, pp. 130–1; see also 'fals iuggyng' in *Handlyng Synne*, 5399–5406. The Host responds afterwards to the tale's depiction of a false judiciary. Hornsby has elaborated the procedural accuracy with which Claudius's bill of complaint is presented and the possibilities for subversion identified: *Chaucer and the Law*, pp. 156–8.

[52] The sub-text is that Nature was familiarly personified working at a 'forge' shaping (minting) humans; the concept of 'counterfeit' creation arises by analogy with the production of false coins.

a just proceeding. Since Claudius goes on to declare at the hearing that Virginia is not Virginius's daughter whatever he says (VI.187), Virginia becomes the victim of a trumped-up charge alleging *her* to be counterfeit: she is represented as a knight's counterfeit daughter, who is 'really' someone else's thrall.

Let us draw back to consider what I have referred to as the concentric circles of jurisdiction in the tale. At the start, having mentioned Virginius and his wife and daughter, the tale immediately locates Virginia's beauty within a cosmology of creation. Hence in the outermost circle of jurisdiction is a godlike being, not designated as 'God' in this pre-Christian setting but as the Principal Former. As his deputy, Nature exercises, and takes considerable pride in, a delegated jurisdiction in the sublunar sphere, to fashion creatures and to dedicate them to her 'lord' — Virginia being a superlative example in beauty and virtue.

The ensuing eulogy on Virginia's discretion and moral discipline allows a transition to a further tier of jurisdiction, that of governesses who are often sought out to supervise such girls. Whether their credentials are uprightness or experience, it is governesses' responsibility to protect innocence and not to countenance treacherous vice, as it is also finally the parents' 'charge' in an inner familial circle of jurisdiction to watch over children without negligent softness and punish them strictly lest they 'perisse' by some wolvish attack (VI.99). Perish morally, the Physician probably means, but given that the story will concern a girl's death amidst all the elaborate provisions of familial and every other jurisdiction, here is a specimen of what seems to be quite a rash of unwitting ironies in the tale, to which we shall return in a moment.

The next, paired arenas of jurisdiction will be obvious to the reader. First is that of the corrupt Apius, combining the roles of judicial and political governance ('justice in that toun' and 'governour ... of that regioun' (VI.121–2)) that constitute the institutional focus of the tale. Setting eyes on Virginia he has determined to use the legal system to have her, and this abuse of his jurisdiction is shrilly signalled by the narrator's threefold outburst against 'this false juge' (VI.154–61). The conspiracy is put into action as Apius sits dealing with cases in his courtroom (VI.162–3). In a judgement that waves aside Virginius's expectation of counter-pleading by resort to witnesses or to trial by combat, Apius declares that Virginia shall be transferred into 'oure warde' (VI.201). This plausible and deeply ironic ruse of the lustful judge's 'wardship' of the girl (pending her hypothetical transfer to Claudius) marks the sickening extreme of jurisdictional corruption in the tale; it is a nasty antithesis to the protective wardship ascribed to parents, governesses, and even—in her vigilance against counterfeit—to Nature herself.[53]

But the judge's courtroom is deliberately paralleled with a further, domestic site of judgement: the seat (literally) of familial patriarchal jurisdiction. Virginius sits in *his* hall (VI.207) pondering the legal requirement that will deliver his daughter up to lust. Just as Apius had him summoned to the town court, Virginius 'leet anon his deere doghter calle' before his own seat (VI.208). Just as Apius has given his ruling, so Virginius puts to his daughter his own verdict that she should die by his own execution of her, rather than descend into wretched dishonour as the judge's sexual prey (VI.172, 223).[54] In what is, hitherto, the innermost circle of jurisdiction Virginius in a self-styled act of 'love' despairingly resorts to a private ruling, the use of private manslaughter (as we might term it) to forestall juridical tyranny. Once Virginius has carried out the macabre execution we return to the encompassing civic jurisdiction, since Virginius proceeds to display his daughter's head where Apius still sits in judgement in the official court. Suddenly, materializing from somewhere in response to this horrific denouement, a mass of citizens intervene to bring Apius's plot to a sudden end. This closes the narrative, and although the people's collective action is less politically coherent and prominent in 'The Physician's Tale' than it is in the sources and analogues, there thus remains in the conclusion the shadowy lineament of one further type of jurisdiction, one which might be exercised collectively by the people, able in some utopian republic to detect 'false iniquitee'.[55]

So far our analysis has put a fairly coherent and orderly construction on a narrative which has been thought anything but that by many critics. It has to be admitted that the tale looks like shooting itself in the foot at several points. If (as the Host astringently puts it afterwards) Virginia's beauty 'was hire deth' (VI.297) because it ignited aggressive

---

[53] Saunders, *Rape and Ravishment*, p. 280, notes that wardship thus becomes a cloak for the crime of *raptus*.

[54] What Virginius calls his 'sentence' (VI.224) reverberates with the language expressing Apius's judgement at VI.172, 204. The parallelisms are summarized by Cooper, *The Canterbury Tales*, p. 254.

[55] The argument that Chaucer denudes the story of its political pressure is made by Anne Middleton, 'The *Physician's Tale* and Love's Martyrs: "Ensamples mo than ten" as a Method in the *Canterbury Tales*', *ChauR*, 8 (1973–4), 9–32; and Sheila Delany, 'Politics and the Paralysis of Poetic Imagination in *The Physician's Tale*', *SAC*, 3 (1981), 47–60.

sexual appetite in Apius, is there not an aura of futility to Nature's pride in the formative skills that can create a maiden of such consummate beauty? (And doesn't she create the Apiuses of this world too, and their libido?)[56] Then, the heavy emphasis on adult responsibilities for honest guardianship of children's morals and virginity seems doubly wasted: first because betrayal will come from elsewhere, from the very institution that presides over justice; and second because Virginia is deemed an expert guardian of her own morals. Then, the Roman ethic of 'death-before-shame' that Virginius invokes produces a puzzling reaction in his daughter. I do not mean it is 'puzzling' that, after asking her father directly if there is no alternative (no other 'grace'), she embraces death, tearfully, with filial obedience. What is odd is her last request, to be given some time to lament like Jephthah's daughter. But she immediately faints, which means she loses the one moment of self-expression that she has craved; the anticipated laments are not uttered prior to her death.

Moreover, the Old Testament story to which Virginia refers (Judges 11: 29–40) is one of the most bizarre patriarchal melodramas in the Bible. In return for divine assistance in defeating his enemies, Jephthah vows to God that he will offer up a sacrifice of whatever first emerges from his house on his return. In the event it is his daughter who dances out to greet him. In response to his immediate alarm about the consequence of his vow, she insists that he keep it and sacrifice her, asking only an intermission (which turns out to be two months) during which to 'bewail her virginity'. Virginia's allusion to this story serves to draw ambivalent attention to the extravagance to which daughterly obedience is obliged to stretch. At the same time Virginia does not gain two hours', let alone two months', respite, and the Judaic precedent of lamenting *because* one is to die while still a virgin is utterly incompatible with her situation as she sees it ('"Blissed be God, that I shal dye a mayde!"' vi.248), and indeed is incompatible with the mindset of the whole tale.[57]

---

[56] On these ironies see Hugh White, *Nature, Sex, and Goodness in a Medieval Literary Tradition* (Oxford: Oxford University Press, 2000), pp. 245–6.

[57] The disjunctions befogging the Jephthah allusion were first laid out (but sophist-ically attributed to a dramatization of the Physician's biblical incompetence) by Richard Hoffman, 'Jephthah's Daughter and Chaucer's Virginia', *ChauR*, 2 (1967–8), 20–31. Hoffman notes that exegetes sometimes allegorized Jephthah's daughter as the humanity or body of Christ in his sacrifice; but Jill Mann's later reaffirmation of this connection (*Feminizing Chaucer*, pp. 143–6) overlooks the confusions that beset the allusion.

So 'The Physician's Tale' is sprinkled with oddities, snags, incipient self-contradictions. It has even been thought more or less intellectually broken-backed: that is, modulating awkwardly between a 'Roman' ethic of family honour, an austere Christian celebration of virgin martyrdom, and a late medieval valuation of affectivity.[58] Corinne Saunders puts it in a nutshell: 'the deployment of ideas of virginity, martyrdom and virtue raise expectations that are foiled by the total absence of "grace" '.[59] However, I would venture to say that these snags do not ruin, though they do threaten, the probing of moral jurisdiction that the tale accomplishes. Even at the heart of one of the latent contradictions, one focused in Virginia, lies the key. We saw earlier that the narrator earnestly distances her from that which is counterfeit. Yet, not many lines afterwards, the narrator risks self-contradiction by praising the way she upholds moral discipline through dissimulation—how 'of hire owene vertu, unconstreyned' she would often *feign* illness in order to avoid socializing occasions that might be conducive to flirtatious 'folye' (VI.61–6). Basically she counterfeits a headache in order to secure her maidenly 'shamefastnesse' (VI.55). But this is a kind of dissimulation that is dictated by, and necessary to, those qualities of discretion, temperance, 'mesure', that comprise her disciplined morality. Virginia, I would say, does function as the inner core of moral jurisdiction in the tale. She is the last and most crucial link in the chain. She is the self-regulating individual who voluntarily governs herself in accordance with the whole range of moral and ethical values ascribed to her gender.[60] She is one who 'so kepte hirself, hir neded no maistresse' (VI.106) and she therefore exemplifies perfect jurisdiction over the psyche, perfect Temperance. In a sense this makes her self-contained. Perhaps that is what is exasperating—as totally self-contained people are exasperating—in the episode of her death.

The tale's nest of Chinese boxes of jurisdiction shows Chaucer tentatively developing an interest not unlike that articulated by Gower in the Prologue to *Confessio Amantis* through a concept of microcosm and macrocosm. Gower imagines chain reactions between individual

---

[58] Phillips, *An Introduction*, pp. 146–7.   [59] *Rape and Ravishment*, p. 282.

[60] Here I differ from John C. Hirsh, who argues that 'there simply is no transcendent moral absolute' in the tale: 'Modern Times: The Discourse of the *Physician's Tale*', *ChauR*, 27 (1992–3), 387–95 (p. 388). Denise Baker more appropriately focuses on the embodiment of the cardinal virtue of Temperance in Virginia: 'Chaucer and Moral Philosophy', pp. 246–9, but without deriving an interpretation from that.

humans, the elements, and the cosmos. He writes that according to 'clergie' a human being

> Is as a world in his partie,
> And whan this litel world mistorneth,
> The grete world al overtorneth'
>
> (*CA*, Prol. 956–8)

True, Chaucer does not emulate the completeness of Gower's investment in an abstract Neo-Platonic concept of micro- and macrocosmic continuity, which moreover rather nakedly extols human quiescence for hierarchical political ends. However, in the case of 'The Physician's Tale', jurisdictions are lodged inside each other ('Formere Principal'/Nature/civic court/governesses/parents, fathers/daughter) in a narrative that, like Gower's, looks anxiously down the chain to individual ethical discipline for reassurance in a world where the subversion of individuals can be felt to be utterly corrosive of processes of justice and concord. Both poets ascribe that corrosion to sin.[61] In Chaucer's case, whether as a critique of 'pagan' life or out of hostility to physicians or because he wanted to experiment with bleakness (perhaps sharing the anxiety of others at this period about legal hypocrisy), the optimism of the tale's opening hymn to created human excellence soon collapses. Yet the tale, albeit awkwardly, retrieves something from the bleakness. What it retrieves is not unambiguous. Even so, despite awkward questions begged both by Virginius's action and by a pseudo-'martyrdom' effected in a non-Christian dispensation, there survives relief that the heroine's decisive self-control in committing herself to death does become the catalyst for a purge of those who have made jurisdiction an instrument of vice.

Toying with Jurisdiction: The Pardoner

Linked consciously to 'The Physician's Tale' is the ensuing 'Pardoner's Prologue' and 'Tale', in which the furthest extremity of jurisdictional abuse is visible.[62] In the 'Tale' the three drunken crazies propose a yet

---

[61] The fiend is reported to invade Apius's heart as soon as Apius decides to possess Virginia (*PhysT*, vi.130). In Gower's discourse, it is human sin that disturbs the macrocosm (*CA*, Prol. 918–28).

[62] Continuity is supplied by the Host's reference to Gifts of Fortune, Nature, and Grace (vi.293–7), frequently cited by moralists though usually as beneficial endowments (see *VV*, pp. 13, 19, 133). Another link is the agency of the fiend in both: compare vi.130–2 with 845–50.

more reckless and ignorantly blasphemous travesty of spiritual power when they constitute themselves as a vicious Trinity, 'torturing' Christ's body with their oaths and blundering forth with the objective of killing death. Their mission (never mind that it belongs to Christ) is that 'deeth shal be deed' (VI.708–10), but like the Friar's summoner they have no inkling of the cunning jurisdiction that death can exert over them as a result of their greed.

The moral frisson that this generates is topped off by our acute awareness of the open spiritual recklessness of the tale's speaker, and his own casual attitude to jurisdiction. He tells the company how he uses the pulpit to tout his bundle of papal bulls and proclaim his bogus spiritual jurisdiction to con, defame, and make money. Pure showmanship and a few props enable him to give an impression of having jurisdiction. For him it is all theatre; the doctrine of salvation, sin, damnation is pure means to profit, his clients' souls can wander off picking blackberries for all he cares (VI.405–6).[63] If the summoner in 'The Friar's Tale' cannot seem to get hold of the idea that his extortions in the name of moral law could bring him under the devil's control, the Pardoner yet more blatantly assumes that eschatology cannot touch him since he uses absolution as his plaything: even the apparent admission that 'Christ's pardon is best' amounts only to just another verbal manipulation.[64]

Everything about the Pardoner's performance screams that he is an outright example of atheistic imperviousness to the very beliefs that he manipulates in others, and to the divine jurisdiction he thereby flouts. His excuse, that the moral efficacy of his preaching is immune to his personal vice, quite apart from being highly contentious in the reformist climate of the period, is stretched to breaking point. Performance of spiritual work for profit was, in any case, deadly sin.[65] In his conscious contempt for spiritual jurisdiction he runs the gauntlet of every kind of moral admonition in the confessional literature. But most powerfully, his relationship to the pilgrims exemplifies what was regarded as a particularly detestable characteristic of sin, 'exultation in

---

[63] Phillips points out that the devil traditionally owns blackberries after November: *An Introduction*, p. 151.

[64] There is extensive commentary on this. The relevant lines (VI.916–18) are surely not a heartfelt admission to the Pilgrims, but the Pardoner's quotation of the way he always strategically rounds off his sermons. For a contrary view see Alan J. Fletcher, 'Chaucer the Heretic', pp. 78–80.

[65] *JW*, p. 187.

transgression';[66] or, to give it a vernacular name, 'unschamfulnes'. This, a category of pride, is defined as revelling openly in one's wickedness among the people. The psalm beginning 'Quid gloriaris in malicia?', translated in Middle English as 'Why enioyest thou in thi malice?', is the ulterior text.[67] This psalm goes on to promise such a person destruction by God, along with the people's derision (the righteous shall laugh at him), which offers an interesting supplementary rationale for the pilgrim company's eventual laughter following the tale and the Host's dismissal of the Pardoner.

Social embarrassment therefore duly befalls the Pardoner but not (yet) spiritual destruction. He is as far as Chaucer goes in imagining a certain kind of insouciance in abusing jurisdiction in a spirit of total indifference. The *Canterbury Tales* find great resources variously for satire, pity, and awe in developing the consequences of these evasions and distortions of moral jurisdiction. The Pardoner drives the Host to an explosion of anger that is in its own way another sort of 'curse' to set beside the widow's curse in 'The Friar's Tale'. But the most apt reader response to the Pardoner would seem to be awe. Rolling up into one person the vices of other cynical office-holders, he is the most dangerous because he is loose in the here and now of the pilgrim company.

---

[66] Identified as *elacaio inobediencie* by the contemporary preacher Bishop Brinton: see *The Sermons of Bishop Brinton, Bishop of Rochester (1373–1389)*, ed. Sister Mary Aquinas Devlin, Camden Third Series, vols. 85, 86 (London, 1954), vol. 86, p. 274. I owe the reference to George Kane, but he applies it to the *ShipT* rather than *PardT*: *The Liberating Truth*, p. 18 and n. 78, pp. 30–1.

[67] *JW*, pp. 76–7, citing Ps. 51 (Vulg.), 52 (AV).

8

Proprieties of Work and Speech: 'The Second Nun's Prologue' and 'Tale', 'The Canon's Yeoman's Prologue' and 'Tale', 'The Manciple's Prologue' and 'Tale', and 'The Parson's Prologue'

Near the end of the *Tales*, Chaucer devotes particular attention to different forms of 'bisynesse'—a concept which in moral doctrine signified diligence focused on some beneficial purpose. Its opposite 'ydelnesse' encompassed the modern notion of 'culpable inactivity' but went beyond that to signify any means of passing time to morally questionable ends. Of course, idleness is caught up into the fabric of earlier tales in the collection, too. One pointed example is January, exemplar of 'ese' as we noted in Chapter 3. January's idea of labour or 'werk' is copulation. In his opinion it is a matter for which a sensible workman should prepare well, with suitable virility potions, and to which plenty of time must be allocated. In the event he labours at copulation until dawn, at which auspicious moment for commencing normal work he goes to sleep ('Merchant's Tale', iv.1832–57). However, it is 'The Second Nun's Tale' and 'The Canon's Yeoman's Prologue' and 'Tale' that engage most pointedly in dialectic about work. This chapter explores that juxtaposition further, incorporating comparison with the surprisingly disparate view of alchemy taken by John Gower. In the last tales of the Canterbury sequence the proprieties of fruitful work become intertwined with the proprieties of fruitful language, and we are left wondering what manner of speech, if any, might *not* be 'idle'. There are interesting gender attributions in Chaucer's patterning of these matters. It is a woman who epitomizes verbally and spiritually efficacious dynamism and it is a man who epitomizes empty verbiage conducting obsessional materialistic activity leading to no proper or useful 'conclusion'.

The Second Nun's 'Busy' 'Prologue' and 'Tale'

The first four stanzas of 'The Second Nun's Prologue' raise into cadences of carefully organized poetry a cluster of commonplaces about Idleness that were widely distributed in the moral prose treatises, and they establish a morally resonant frame for the two extant tales of the Eighth Fragment of the *Canterbury Tales*. The Second Nun represents Idleness as nurse of vice and gatekeeper of pleasure,[1] to be remedied by engaging in a contrary 'leveful bisynesse' (VIII.1–5). (That qualifier, 'legitimate' occupation, sets a calculated benchmark for the subsequent tale about alchemy.) One benefit of industrious work is that it safeguards a person against the sudden entrapments of the devil, which threaten to catch out the idle (VIII.6–14).[2] But, the Second Nun goes on, even if one were not motivated to avoid idleness by Christian fear of dying in a state of sin, mere rational thought would suggest the ugliness and barrenness of a state of 'roten slugardye' that produces nothing—no 'encrees'—but merely consumes what others produce (VIII.15–21).[3] And so the speaker (adopting a formula commonly used in the Middle Ages to validate the act of writing) has sustained the common human responsibility for 'bisynesse' by undertaking the labour of translating the Life of St Cecilia to 'putte us fro swich ydelnesse': perhaps using the plural because readers or listeners will themselves repel idleness through the productive act of hearing and meditating on the saint's life (VIII.22–8).

The emphasis on salutary *werk* continues through the rest of this Prologue. Since faith is dead without works, the Virgin Mary is invoked to support the speaker's 'werk' (VIII.64–5, 77, and 84). Then Cecile's name is decoded as a compound encompassing the name of 'Leah', known as an Old Testament epitome of the active life.[4] Hence, among other virtues found to be hidden in the etymology of Cecile's name is 'lastynge bisynesse': she was 'Ful swift and bisy evere in good

---

[1] *ParsT* calls Negligence (sub-category of Sloth) the nurse of harm (x.709), and Idleness the gate of harm (x.713).

[2] On fear of the devil as inducement to occupation see *ParsT*, x.713–16. Jerome's Letter (125.11) to Rusticus was quoted by moralists on the advisability of keeping busy to escape the devil: see *FM*, v.5, pp. 426–7, and *JW*, p. 105.

[3] *FM* emphasizes that the idle live off the labour of others (v.1, p. 410).

[4] Gen. 29: 15 ff.

werkynge' (VIII.96–8, 116). The swiftness and the busyness are again motifs susceptible to degenerative emphases in the case of 'The Canon's Yeoman's Tale'.[5]

The Second Nun's ensuing account of Cecile's life highlights a nexus of ideas intertwined with, and within, the polarity of efficacious work and idleness.[6] We are conspicuously reminded of the deadly sin that her legend opposes, by the way her spouse Valerian, once converted, promises his brother that he will see the invisible crown of Valerian's nuptial chastity if, 'withouten slouthe', he will believe 'aright' (VIII.257–9). In any case, Cecile's every action turns out to be so far from indolence as to be done with near-frenetic enthusiasm. Introduced as one who had 'never ceased' praying during her girlhood (VIII.124–5), she teaches Valerian's brother Tiburce 'bisily' about Christ, and even during her macabre last three days of half-dead torment she 'never ceased' preaching to Rome's believers (VIII.342–3, 537–9). Her indefatigability then turns into a legacy down the ages, because during her martyrdom she has prepared her own house, she says, to be 'perpetuelly' a church (VIII.542–6). The sheer energy of her faith, pitted against increasingly sceptical antagonists, overwhelms first Valerian then Tiburce, whom she sweeps magisterially into sect allegiance as her 'ally', until she finally out-debates (even if she does not convert) the regional Roman official, Almachius. Much of this emphasis on her vigour has been traced before,[7] but what still invites attention is the sheer extent of the penetration of the tale by the discourse concerning Sloth and its remedy of Fortitude, termed 'Strength' in Middle English. I should like to mention in particular three facets of this discourse, namely the motifs of spiritual fortitude, of fear, and of fruition.

The Second Nun does not emphasize Strength, the remedy for Idleness, partly because it is self-evident in Cecile. However, in her elegant introduction she does invoke one of the categories of Strength:

[5] Wenzel explains how 'busyness' was a late medieval addition (popular in English treatises) to the antidotes previously identified for Sloth—fortitude and spiritual joy: *The Sin of Sloth*, p. 89.

[6] Lowes, in his riposte to Tupper, was over-anxious to decentre the tale's (and its prologue's) interest in 'werk' and 'besynesse': 'Chaucer and the Seven Deadly Sins', pp. 288–303. Tupper reasserted the primacy of 'besynesse' in prologue and tale, in 'Chaucer's Sinners and Sins', pp. 83–7.

[7] John Hirsh, for instance, observes that the ostensible religious authority figures in the tale are elderly and lack 'physical vigor, the traditional male resort, which in the tale as a whole is attached rather to Cecilia': 'The *Second Nun's Tale*', in *Chaucer's Religious Tales*, ed. C. David Benson and Elizabeth Robertson (Cambridge: D. S. Brewer, 1990), pp. 161–9 (p. 163).

> Right so men goostly in this mayden free
> Seyen of feith the magnanymytee
>
> (vIII.109–10)

To our ears, the 'magnanimity of faith' is a strange concept; but Chaucer's Parson helps us with it. The first species of Strength is Magnanimity: it signifies great 'corage', a spirit to manage great undertakings against the odds, but not just physically, because such strength must confront the devil's slyness with a matching cerebral force of rational discretion (x.727–33).[8] Cecile exemplifies both facets of sloth-defying Strength. She demonstrates brave spirit when with 'ful stedefast cheere' she consolidates the faith of her converts against imminent beheading, applauding them as Christ's armed warriors who are finishing their battle (vIII.382–7); and she demonstrates cerebral force in her astringent debate with the prefect Almachius. She chops logic with him about guilt and innocence, and when he protests at what he calls her 'proud' language she repudiates the charge, defining her speech as 'steadfast' instead (vIII.474).

Almachius's objection to her militant mode of speech takes us into some gender implications of the tale. From the outset Cecile has responded with what the medieval period would have considered unladylike curtness to her interrogator. In fact she goads him abrasively by declaring him ignorant for starting with two questions in one, and she pours sublime scorn on his claim to exercise power over both life and death. His complaints that she is answering rudely and with 'booldnesse' (vIII.432, 487) are not altogether unwarranted in light of her increasingly insulting vocabulary and her rapid descent from the civil 'ye' to the peremptory 'thou'.[9] We recognize in her the reckless fearlessness of the doomed but righteous dissident, ready to go down blazing defiance at the inquisitor. But in terms of medieval gender norms, what she demonstrates is a transgressive boldness, such as was conventionally outlawed by social and moral codes; for women were not supposed to be 'ful of wordes' and thus 'aperte' or forward, just as they were not supposed to jut boldly about like stags but to comport

---

[8] Compare *FM*, v.37, pp. 618–21: the 'magnanimous' person will 'scorn everything base, profess the truth, and bravely tackle difficult tasks', indifferent (as Seneca suggests) to the comfort of the body.

[9] For a succinct review of these forms, and for a bibliography on the subject, see Pearsall, '*The Franklin's Tale*, Line 1469: Forms of Address in Chaucer', pp. 75–6.

themselves 'loweliche' and modestly.[10] In any case, morally speaking, the only context in which sharp, reproving words might be valid in anyone's mouth was when they were uttered in correction of sin—so long as there was no intent to damage the reputation of the person being corrected.[11] But this 'correction' of sin was expected to be practised mostly by institutionally authorized males (such as the Parson of the 'General Prologue', I.523), and besides, Cecile does actually seem bent on personally insulting Almachius, whom she derides as 'lewed officer' and 'veyn justise' (VIII.497).

Against the powerful gendered code promoting demure female speech, and against the norm of moral anxiety about uttering reproof, the genre of the saint's legend had set up an insulated cultural zone where women could be as belligerently vociferous as they liked in defence of Christianity.[12] Nevertheless, 'The Second Nun's Tale' is distinctly self-conscious in raising these matters of propriety in speech. By answering Almachius's opening question ('What maner womman artow?') with 'I am a gentil woman born' (VIII.424–5), Cecile raises an expectation of *gentil* discourse, only to subvert that in her brusque retorts.[13] Here, therefore, at the start of Fragment VIII is raised afresh and in acute form one of the most pressing and creative issues explored in the *Canterbury Tales*: the appropriateness of speech to its context.

Leaving that on one side for a moment, the second of the tale's topics tacitly related to Sloth is fear. What might be feared, as we saw in her Prologue, might depend on one's religion. This topic is pointedly retrieved when Tiburce lets slip his fear of being persecuted by fire as a punishment for conversion. Cecile answers ('boldly' of course) that while it might be logical to 'dreden' loss of life if there were no other life, her religion finds reassurance in an afterlife (VIII.316–32).[14]

---

[10] *Book of the Knight of the Tower*, ch. xii, p. 27; and *VV*, p. 240. Chaucer acknowledges another gendered ideal of women's speech, which constructs it to be preferably 'pleyn' (straightforward, un-technical, un-complex) in *PhysT*, VI.50–4, and *TC*, II.267–72.

[11] *JW*, p. 99.

[12] See Karen Winstead, *Virgin Martyrs: Legends of Sainthood in Late Medieval England* (Ithaca: Cornell University Press, 1997), pp. 98–111; and Blamires, *Case for Women*, pp. 182–4.

[13] Perhaps as Hirsh suggests her statement of 'gentil' birth also amounts to 'an assertion of power which gives force to her subsequent discourse': 'The *Second Nun's Tale*', p. 166.

[14] The Second Nun is consistent, within superficial inconsistency. In *SNProl*, death is to be feared if it takes a person who is caught in the devil's trap of idleness; in *SNT*, the afterlife is a reason not to fear death, if the person taken is in a state of virtue.

Her boldness here addresses an apprehension in the would-be convert for which one technical moral name was indeed 'unboldnesse': the problem of potential collapse into pusillanimous timidity, a branch of sloth. Both positions—her logic of the afterlife and the logic of Tiburce's anxiety—are to be contrasted with the position projected by Almachius who, when taunted by Cecile, adopts with a flourish the pose of the imperturbable Stoic 'philosophre' (vIII.489–90), which in the heightened spiritual context of a martyr narrative is implicitly inadequate. What should ultimately be feared? Who holds what power over life and death? These are the questions fought over in the narrative of Cecile and in her verbal contest with Almachius, and we have already seen in Chapter 6 how they surface elsewhere in Chaucer, notably in 'The Nun's Priest's Tale'. The prospect of a woman who manifests no *drede* at all in her commitment to Strength constitutes a conspicuous dimension of the gender politics of this tale.

There remains the motif of fruition, the third and perhaps most oblique area of allusion to the discourse of Sloth in 'The Second Nun's Tale'. It is the saintly figure of Urban who supplies the allusion in his emotional prayer to Christ as he contemplates Cecile's conversion of Valerian:

> The fruyt of thilke seed of chastitee
> That thou hast sowe in Cecile, taak to thee!
> Lo, lyk a bisy bee, withouten gile,
> Thee serveth ay thyn owene thral Cecile.

> (vIII.193–6)

Scholars have explored the knowing paradox here in the collocation of 'fruit' with chastity. I am more concerned with the fact that Cecilia's spiritual fruition through her conversion of others is collocated with industriousness (as emblematized by the bee). Moral writings condemned sloth (*accidia*), first because it erodes devotion; and second,

because it bears no fruit of good life. Whence Gregory says, in book 33 of his *Moral Commentary on Job*: 'Willow-trees bear no fruit, and yet they are so green that they can hardly grow dry.' In the same way, slothful people look outwardly green [. . .] but spiritually they are dry and bear no fruit; Hosea 9: 'They yield no fruit.'[15]

---

[15] *FM*, v.4, p. 421.

Idleness, or sometimes Sloth more broadly, was condemned (most particularly in English medieval pastoral writings) as a vice characterized by indulgence in vain pastimes—gambling, playing chess, going to wrestling matches and taverns and so forth instead of performing the duties of devotion or otherwise being active in the worship of God.[16] This was phrased in terms of preferring 'werkys of no profyght' to 'occupacyouns that wern frutefull'. Idle pursuits were of no profit or 'frute' to the soul, they were barren like sand.[17] It is partly to this framework that the hymn to Cecile's 'fruit' makes contrasting reference, and the same vocabulary is invoked when she declares to Almachius that the images of gods revered in his religion are worthless because they 'mowen noght profite' himself or his people (VIII.509–11).

Cecile, therefore, powerfully and stridently, exemplifies an energized militant Christian commitment such as was imagined to have characterized a church fighting for its existence. (The tale's Christians are dissenters whose pristine spiritual energy, as some critics think, forms an implicit reformist critique of what the institutional church was becoming by Chaucer's day.)[18] Cecile exerts herself forcefully, transcends the ordinary proprieties of speech, generates increase in her sect, and though a woman, even seems as much in control of the ostensible male leaders of that sect, who lurk on the fringes of Rome, as they are in control of her. But, as we make the transition from her story to 'The Canon's Yeoman's Tale', it will be helpful to be aware of yet more of the penumbra of ideas surrounding the concept of unfruitful idleness that the Second Nun opposes. Take the analogy between people of idle habits and the barrenness of gravel or sand already mentioned. Influential sermon sources saw an imaginative validity in the comparison, because the un-congealable structure of gravel and sand, an agglomerate of millions of mobile particles, resembled the flitting and inchoate nature of idle thoughts and pursuits, 'varying, discordeng asundre, departyd into dyuerse dyuersite, none hangynge with other'.[19] The imagery associated with Idleness in

---

[16] Kolve, *Chaucer and the Imagery of Narrative*, p. 286; Wenzel, *Sin of Sloth*, pp. 88–90.

[17] *JW*, pp. 105, 228–9.

[18] On the tale as an exploration of the burning issue of the rival powers of church and state see Lynn Staley, 'Chaucer and the Postures of Sanctity', in *The Powers of the Holy*, ed. David Aers and Lynn Staley (University Park: Pennsylvania State University Press, 1996), pp. 179–259 (esp. pp. 194–203).

[19] *JW*, p. 230, citing Chrysostom, *In Imperfecto*, Homily 26. I have emended 'dysirte' to 'dyuersite' in this quotation.

'The Parson's Tale' is different but works to the same end, articulating inchoate diffusion of concentration. The idle person is un-walled, open on every side to devilish suggestion. Idleness is a veritable ship's hull full of a jumble of thoughts, 'jangles', 'trufles', and 'ordure' (IX.713–14). In the polarity of busy fruitfulness on the one hand, and on the other hand a heap of barren inchoate thoughts, we have the essence of the contrast now developed through Chaucer's follow-on of 'The Canon's Yeoman's Prologue' and 'Tale'.

Hectic Idleness in 'The Canon's Yeoman's Prologue' and 'Tale'

It is now a truism of Chaucer criticism that whereas we finally behold Cecile miraculously cool (no sweat at all) in the cauldron that tests her faith, it is profuse sweating that characterizes the Canon, Canon's Yeoman, and even their horses. The sweating turns out to epitomize the effect of their alchemical toil, centred on the furnace. What emerges is that the 'leveful' and 'lastynge' busyness which is the antidote to idleness and which characterized Cecile, gives way in the next tale to a parodic outpouring of energy that is hardly lawful and only a travesty of the spiritual.[20] This was very far from being the inevitable way for a writer of Chaucer's time to think about alchemy, as we shall discover in a moment. But Chaucer's moral analysis is categorically negative and it is constructed carefully out of the discourse of idleness. The Yeoman, letting rip his pent-up discontent once the Canon leaves, repetitively refers to his (and his ex-master's) former 'werk'; but he derides it again and again as profitless labour.[21] This work is a philosophy that yields no 'conclusioun'. The mirage of 'multiplying' precious metal is a futile employment, a labour ('swynk') that deludes, produces no 'avantage', in fact quite the opposite since it deprives any who occupy themselves in it of whatever goods they started with (VIII.730–3). This is a 'craft' in which (unlike, say, that of the smith or the carpenter) one's 'labour is in veyn', since despite all its elaborate attention to arcane processes and despite burning the midnight oil, all the effort

---

[20] See Trevor Whittock, *A Reading of the 'Canterbury Tales'* (Cambridge: Cambridge University Press, 1968), p. 252 for an early recognition that the industriousness depicted in the *CYPr* and *CYT* is misplaced rather than 'leveful'.

[21] Rosenberg explored the oppositional 'werk' in the two tales in his ground-breaking essay, 'The Contrary Tales of the Second Nun and the Canon's Yeoman', p. 282, but without recognizing Chaucer's invocation of Idleness/Sloth discourse in this.

Mowe in oure werkyng no thyng us availle,
For lost is al oure labour and travaille

(VIII.777–81)

In short this is a busyness that leads nowhere, except bankruptcy. No one gains through this trade (VIII.1421). There is therefore hardly a sharper moment of irony in the text than when the fraudulent canon of the 'Tale' encourages the priest who is his victim, on the basis that he will soon see 'How that oure bisynesse shal *thryve and preeve*' (VIII.1211–12, my emphasis). The tale implies that there is an urgency about exposing this folly that can't be entrusted to the vagaries of irony: a coda warns us outright, 'Lat no man bisye hym this art for to seche' (VIII.1442); let nobody 'werken' anything of this sort that is contrary to God's will (VIII.1477).

Alchemical 'work' (even though an element of fascination is recognized in the account of it) is not merely reckoned here an occupation without fruit, it also offers mischievous parodies of the fortitude that Cecile has deployed against such fruitlessness. Where she displays magnanimity (the spirited undertaking of difficult things) in faith, the Yeoman's master too has taken on many a 'greet emprise' that is 'ful hard … To brynge aboute' (VIII.605–7), but to absolutely no avail. Where Cecile rallies victims of persecution, the Canon bucks up his despairing assistants after their pot shatters (VIII.935–7, 945–54) by likening them, absurdly, to merchant adventurers who must take the rough with the smooth. Or again, as the Yeoman puts it, endless outlay coming to nothing would make practitioners distraught almost to madness, were it not that 'good hope crepeth in oure herte' (VIII.868–70). Here the resilience of hope, which might properly relieve the despair that is the extreme consequence of sloth, is misdirected towards engaging once again in an unproductive craft.

Chaucer critics have clarified the further reaches of the parody of Cecilia's spiritual struggle: the way the miracles of her story are echoed in the spurious 'transformations' of metal in the Canon's Yeoman's (or more benignly echoed in the 'conversion' of the Yeoman from belief to scepticism); the way the text parodies the responsive God of her religion, in the elusiveness of the Philosopher's Stone (VIII.862–7); the way the fiend-like alchemist reverses Cecile's missionary effort by corrupting even a priest, using powers that seem capable of mass 'infection' and persecution—'How Cristes peple he may to meschief brynge' (VIII.1072). Critics have commented, too, on the glut of jargon, the insistent materiality of *things* used in the alchemical process whose names the Yeoman pours out. What I should like to add here is the suggestion that this barrage of names of equipment, chemicals, minerals, and assorted physical rubbish, heaped up by the Yeoman in disorganized bursts as his mind flicks through more and more of the alchemical inventory, functions as a correlative to the moralists' caricature of the profitless 'gravel and sand' characterizing idle occupations. This arcane 'craft' and its practitioners can no more attain structured orderliness, it seems, than those 'idle thoughts' caricatured by moralists as grains of sand can hang together rather than 'discording asunder'. The explosive shattering of the alchemical pot, scattering assorted contents like shrapnel into walls and across the floor, dramatically epitomizes fruitless inchoate occupation, and one attended, the Yeoman thinks, by the fiend (VIII.907–17). The fact that the conman alchemist of the 'Tale' is associated with chronic instability—now here, now there, 'so variaunt, he abit nowhere' (VIII.1174–5)—befits the nature of his sin of Idleness as a disintegrative scattering of wits.

Yet the remarkable thing about Chaucer's decision to present alchemy in this way is that his contemporary Gower, from whom he may indeed have taken a cue here, does exactly the opposite. In the *Confessio Amantis*, alchemy, in its original endeavours, is a prime example of a proper busyness to set against Sloth. The Confessor posits that anyone of wit and reason should rightly 'travaile / Upon som thing which mihte availe' since 'ydelschipe' is damnable (*CA*, IV.2331–8). He reflects that those living today are beneficiaries of ancestors whose industriousness long ago invented life's amenities and whose 'besinesse is yit so seene' (*CA*, IV.2346–91).[22] The Confessor catalogues examples such as the plough, alphabets, painting, cloth-making, coin manufacture, but reserves pride of place for alchemical work on metals. He enthusiastically reviews the main points of alchemy, confident that those who 'worked' to develop this 'craft' did so in accordance with nature (*CA*, IV.2457–2509). He acknowledges that whoever begins this 'werk' has to toil scrupulously to attain the Elixir, such is the subtlety of each stage in the process. The nearest that Gower comes to the Chaucerian attack on alchemy as a completely futile occupation is a nostalgic reflection that the original

---

[22] On the background to this concern for practical 'invention' see the section 'Perspective on History: Progress versus Decline', in Rosalind Brown-Grant, *Christine de Pizan and the Moral Defence of Women* (Cambridge: Cambridge University Press, 1999), pp. 154–63; and Blamires, 'Women and Creative Intelligence'.

skill is now all but lost. Consequently diligence does not, as currently practised, produce success, it produces poverty:

> To gete a pound thei spenden five;
> I not hou such a craft schal thryve
> In the manere as it is used.
>
> (*CA*, iv.2591–3)

It is almost as if Chaucer took the first two lines of this to heart and ignored the third.[23] Gower, by contrast, refuses to debunk alchemy: 'The science of himself is trewe' and its earlier exponents are justly famous for their 'besinesse' in the service of virtue and worthiness, even if latter-day practitioners cannot seem to rediscover the thread leading to the natural elixir (*CA*, iv.2597–2625).

A symptom of the reversal wrought by Chaucer in this thinking is that the Latin gloss to this section of Gower's *Confessio* tells us that here the poet speaks against the idle, 'and especially against those who possess gifts of intellect and prudence, but [unlike alchemical experimenters] laze about without producing any fruit by their work'.[24] Chaucer, on the other hand, thinks in terms of frenetic and essentially idle misapplication of gifts of intellect (viii.630). The Yeoman, citing the Aristotelian notion of ethical excess/deficiency, attributes to his master too much wisdom, amounting to a kind of ignorance because a man with 'over-greet a wit' characteristically misuses it (viii.644–9). In pursuing this line of thought, Chaucer has decisively cast the alchemist as an epitome of idle rather than productive occupation. The reasons for this can only be guessed at. Although some critics wonder whether Chaucer's tale bespeaks disaffection with trends towards a profit economy,[25] to me it seems more likely that Chaucer noted both Gower's association of alchemy with industrious labour and his reservation about modern alchemy; reflected on the dissipation of goods and the chicanery that the practice encouraged; and decided to develop

---

[23] There is a flicker of Gower's approach in *CYT*, viii.1396 (people cannot plumb this art '*now-a-dayes*'). It will be seen that I agree with Helen Cooper's view that 'Chaucer's own attitude towards alchemy seems decidedly sceptical', though as she points out 'the Yeoman himself never claims the theory behind it to be false; only that it is impossible to realize in practice, and sinful to try': *The Canterbury Tales*, p. 372.

[24] 'Hic loquitur contra ociosos quoscumque, et maxime contra istos, qui excellentis prudencie ingenium habentes absque fructu operum torpescunt'; gloss at *CA*, iv.2363, ed. Macaulay, vol. i, p. 365 (my trans.).

[25] e.g. Phillips, *An Introduction*, p. 204.

'The Canon's Yeoman's Prologue' and 'Tale' on the 'other' side of the idleness/industry divide.

In the context of Fragment VIII of the *Tales*, the narrative of alchemy also takes on gender implications. Although in 'The Second Nun's Prologue' idleness is momentarily personified as 'she' (VIII.4),[26] the sequence begins by epitomizing spiritually efficacious work in a woman from a bygone era of missionary activity. Conversely the Canon's Yeoman posits a world of the here and now thronged with ostensibly religious males whose activity appears pointless if not destructive. The Yeoman and Canon have at least two companions willing to conjecture why their pot has exploded. In the 'Tale' we then hear of a second canon, the priest whom he dupes, the priest's male servant, and a friar colleague mentioned by the canon: eight men, in all. This male-saturated (and cleric-heavy) environment is interrupted only by mention of the priest's landlady, who lodges him for free on account of his unspecified serviceability to her. This detail merely reinforces how removed women seem to be from the form of idle acquisitive business here projected.[27] Of course, only males would be expected in that culture to access the arcane books involved, and we might need to reckon with a tendency to focus on men in terms of occupations, but on women only in terms of sexual status. Nevertheless the maleness of the environment confirms a contrast wherein it is a man (or perhaps a brace of them—two canons) who epitomize the vice that Cecile eschews, obsessive but 'idle' material activity devoid of fruit for humanity. Recalling the dubious commitment of Nicholas to weather prediction in 'The Miller's Tale' and of the Orléans clerk to magical practices in 'The Franklin's Tale' we may well wonder whether 'idle occupation' is being consciously constructed as a masculine tendency in the *Tales* as a whole.

There remains one more link between the Second Nun's and Canon's Yeoman's contributions to consider, and it is one that will lead us forward to the close of the *Tales*. We have seen how idleness is depicted as the foe to 'increase' and 'fruit'. Speech is meant to participate in the moral imperative of fruition, on the model provided by Christ (in Urban's phrase) as 'Sower of chaast conseil' (VIII.192) and on the model demonstrated in Cecile's zealous teaching. Alchemy, however, speaks

---

[26] Possibly with a side-glance at Oiseuse (Leisure), the demoiselle who controls the gate into the garden in the *Roman de la Rose*.

[27] The detail helps explain how the priest has accumulated ready cash; perhaps it also implies innocent generosity on the woman's part.

a language described as too 'misty' to communicate fruitfully: it is characterized as bird-jabber that impedes the fulfilment of any purpose (VIII.1394–9). Doubtless we are meant to fit this contrast between fruitful and unfruitful discourse in these tales into a larger metaphoric design in the poem as a whole. The Knight was aware as he began his tale of a large 'field' to plough (I.886–7). The Parson will, finally, decline to offer the pilgrims fiction on the approach to Canterbury on the grounds of its inadequate yield: 'Why sholde I sowen draf . . . Whan I may sowen whete?' ('Parson's Prologue', X.35–6). The Host, with sundown imminent, bids the Parson 'Beth fructuous', affirming one last time a generative purpose in their storytelling.[28] In the grander, albeit incomplete, architecture of the *Canterbury Tales*, alchemical babble signals as it were the lowest possible yield from the moral seeding ideally constituted by utterance.

But the Second Nun has problematized speech in other ways. We noted the explicit concern about propriety of speech in Cecile's argument with Almachius, in terms of both his allegation that she speaks aggressively and her sharp allegation that he speaks illogically and inaccurately. There are evolutions of this, too, in the ensuing text. First, the Canon's Yeoman returns us to the morally charged question, when is an insult an allowable insult? He defends his criticism of alchemists by formally invoking the doctrine of correction. He claims he has no intention of 'slandering' religious canons as a body or as individuals, only of correcting what is wrong and making others more wary (VIII.992–9, 1299–1307). The reader, nevertheless, is richly aware of the Yeoman's desire to settle personal scores against the individuals and the profession that he has wasted himself on.[29] So his talk of correction may really amount to another flagrant case of Chaucer's delight in revealing people in the act of putting up moral platitudes to hide under, like umbrellas.

Propriety of speech figures again in the problem of mismatch between the Yeoman's initial (discreet) grand claims about the Canon, and the 'sluttissh' appearance of the Canon's clothing. The Host treats it as a matter of social decorum. How come the Canon is so negligent of his dignity, if his intellectual and material status is as substantial as the

---

[28] The preacher, especially, was obligated to spread the seed of the Word fruitfully: Patterson, 'Chaucer's Pardoner on the Couch', pp. 667–8. On the Host's concern with fruition and procreation see John Plummer, ' "Beth fructuous and that in litel space": The Engendering of Harry Bailly', in Benson and Ridyard (eds.), *New Readings*, pp. 107–18.
[29] Finely investigated by Pearsall, *The Canterbury Tales*, p. 110.

Yeoman has first indicated—'If that his dede accorde with thy speche' (VIII.630–8)? In 'The Second Nun's Tale', the essence of the debate between Cecile and Almachius, similarly, is whether he can back his words with deeds. What the Canon's Yeoman goes on to unveil, though we have to take his account of the doings of both canons on trust, is on the one hand a great glut of words and enticing promises, and on the other no corresponding actions at all: just explosion, sleight of hand, and theft. But the proposition that words should accord with speech rings other bells with the reader, as well as preparing for a full-scale questioning of what speech should say or do (and indeed when speech should say it), in 'The Manciple's Tale'.

On Words Fitly Spoken: Discourses of Manciple and Parson

What concerns us here is, first of all, the 'when' and the 'how much' of speech. The importance in the medieval period of criteria about speaking has recently been demonstrated by medievalists, so there is no need for particular elaboration in that respect.[30] Nevertheless some features of this branch of morality and ethics will bear further emphasis since the moral colouring appears somewhat eccentric by today's standards. The concern for the *timing* of speech is an example. As David Wallace has shown, Chaucer's writings are sprinkled with the phrase 'whan [s/he] saugh [his/hir] tyme'.[31] To some extent this is just a facet of a generalized medieval assumption that there is a right, or propitious, time for doing everything—certainly for major undertakings. To some extent the concern with timing is an effect of the sorts of vaguer gnomic statements about opportune speech that are rehearsed in the wisdom books of the Bible: for example, 'A word spoken in due season [*sermo opportunus*], how good it is'; or 'A word fitly spoken [literally 'at its appropriate time', *in tempore suo*] is like apples of gold in pictures of silver' (Prov. 15: 23, and 25: 11); and, most famously, there is 'a time to keep silence, and a time to speak' (Eccles. 3: 7). To a considerable extent this concern with timing had become a recognized part of the formalized art of speech, a skill that was duly emphasized by its discussion near the conclusion of Albertano of Brescia's *De arte loquendi et tacendi*.[32]

---

[30] See e.g. Wallace, *Chaucerian Polity*, pp. 217–20; Perkins, *Hoccleve's 'Regiment of Princes'*, pp. 12–24.

[31] *Chaucerian Polity*, pp. 232–4, 243, with reference to Prudence's careful interventions in 'Melibee'. See also *FklT*, v.966, 1308; *WoBT*, III.901.

[32] Wallace, *Chaucerian Polity*, p. 218.

To Dante, too, timing was no small matter. He urges in the *Convivio* that 'we should await the proper moment in all our undertakings, and most of all in speaking'. Because astrological dispositions affect the human mind via the body,

> Great discretion must be shown in using or avoiding the use of words—which are, as it were, the seed of our activity—so that they may be well received and fruitful in effect . . . The right moment must therefore be predetermined, both for the one who speaks and . . . the one who listens.[33]

Although Chaucer's works imply an ambiguous attitude towards the reliance on astrological 'election of times' that underpins Dante's point,[34] Chaucer's writings are not sceptical about the need to time one's speaking judiciously. To speak at the moment when one should hold one's peace is deemed a failure of discretion and self-control in the conclusion of 'The Nun's Priest's Tale' (vii.3434–5). *Troilus and Criseyde*, a text rather self-consciously engaged with speech phenomena, shows Pandarus's awareness that the speaker must be sure that the person listening to one's words will have 'savour' in them (*TC*, ii.267–73). Chaucer also goes out of his way in that text to represent Diomede remembering, but ignoring for the sheer challenge of it, one particular injunction against bad timing: Diomede resolves to woo Criseyde even though she appears forlornly in love with another and his speech may therefore be wasted (*TC*, v.785–98).[35]

The 'when' of speech is interwoven with the 'how much', and on the risks of the latter the Book of Proverbs is almost obsessive. Multitudes of words, pouring out of words, unguarded speech and an unrestrained tongue, these are marks of the fool. Brevity of words, carefully meditated speech, suppression of loquacity, restraint of the tongue, these are the signs of wisdom (e.g. Prov. 10: 19, 15: 28, 17: 28). As we saw, one of the Parson's figures for idleness was that of a place with no walls, wide open to the devil. In the Book of Proverbs it is people who can't constrain their spirits by their *speech* who are likened to an unwalled city (Prov. 25: 28).[36] Overall, the Proverbs tend to advocate blanket concealment

---

[33] *Il Convivio*, iv.2, trans. Lansing, p. 151. Dante cites Eccles. 3: 7 and Ecclus. 20: 6–7.

[34] *MoLT*, ii.309–15 and *Riv.* note, p. 860.

[35] Chaucer has expanded the simpler Boccaccian passage at *Filocolo*, vi.10.

[36] The King James translation does not sustain the Vulgate focus on restraint of *speech*: 'He that hath no rule over his own spirit [for 'qui non potest *in loquendo* cohibere spiritum suum'] is like a city that is broken down, and without walls.' The commonplace that the tongue should be 'walled' with teeth and lips appears in *MancT*, ix.322–4.

rather than utterance (e.g. Prov. 11: 13 and 13: 3), because the more folly is characterized by undisciplined outpouring of words, the more intelligence is defined as a holding back (12: 23). The author of the *Book of Vices and Virtues* takes this to heart. Restraint of speech—being glad to be silent, weighing one's words like precious metals before uttering them—is a facet of the moderation wrought by the spiritual gift of Knowledge (*Scientia*).[37] Another spiritual gift is Wisdom (*Sapientia*) and this too, in fostering 'sobrenesse', contributes to moderation of speech. It teaches people to close the 'sluice of discretion' in order to withhold 'the water of folie wordes and outrageous'.[38]

Paradoxically, this withholding is a way of making sure that one's eventual words will properly reveal rather than conceal. The withholding is imagined as a weighing of one's words in the balance of 'trwthe', thus ensuring that 'sothnesse acordeth the entensioun of the herte and the wordes of the mouth togidre, so that the mouth seith but soth as it is in the herte'. Veracity, then, influenced neither by partiality nor profit, becomes the arbiter of utterance and is not finally to be restrained in the appropriate circumstances ('ne schal not a man leue to seie the sothe there that men schulde, and whan need is').[39] Yet this concern that factual truth (*soth*) should be told, subject to appropriate circumstances, is uncomfortably at odds with the more cynical propositions about speech, such as the proverb 'who sayth soth he schal be schent'. In fact it is really at odds with the dominant overall emphasis on restraint and expedience, and it is the latter emphasis that permeates advice on speech in instructional literature, from the elementary (the *Distichs of Cato*) to the more ambitious (the *De arte loquendi et tacendi* of Albertano of Brescia, which may like the *Distichs* have been known directly to Chaucer).[40] As Nicholas Perkins puts it, 'the burden of proverbial wisdom was behind a policy of judicious silence; alternative traditions of truthtelling had to be carefully chosen and subtly deployed to overcome the weight of advice against speaking'.[41]

---

[37] *VV*, pp. 148, 151.   [38] *VV*, pp. 282–3, citing Prov. 17: 14.

[39] *VV*, pp. 283–4.

[40] On the *Distichs* and the proverb about 'soth', see Perkins, *Hoccleve's 'Regiment'*, pp. 13–14. For Albertano's text see the edition in *Brunetto Latinos Levnet og Skrifter*, ed. Thor Sundby (Copenhagen: Boghandel, 1869), pp. lxxxix–cxix. Timing is discussed in the section 'Quando loquendum et dicendum sit', pp. cxvi–cxviii, starting with a flurry of citation from the wisdom books of the Bible. Hoccleve sustains the emphasis on taming the tongue in *Regiment*, 2416–50.

[41] *Hoccleve's 'Regiment'*, p. 17.

The 'when' and the 'how much' of speech, and what truth speech should speak, become the central issues of Fragments IX and X of the *Tales*. In discussing this we need to supplement our earlier discussion (Chapter 1) of 'The Manciple's Tale''s enactment of the metaphorical violence associated with defamation. David Wallace has persuasively argued that the crow in this tale, though taught to 'countrefete' the speech of 'every man [. . .] whan he sholde telle a tale' (IX.134–5), falls short of the *art* of speech.[42] The crow does not speak when it might (it 'seyde never a word' beholding the lovemaking between Phebus's wife and her lover, IX.241). When it does speak, its brutally monosyllabic account of what it has seen, provoking its master Phebus to resort instantly to violence against both wife and crow, betrays ignorance of the principle that a speaker must understand the impact that their speech will have on the hearer.[43]

It is often supposed that Chaucer projects here through the crow the precarious situation of the court poet, even of himself as court poet. That seems to me unlikely. First, 'counterfeiting' has a rather negative resonance in Chaucer's vocabulary. When he wants to describe something like his own verisimilar verbal skill, he speaks (in the 'General Prologue') not of counterfeiting but of 'rehearsing' the words of others. Such rehearsal should be as broad or risqué in vocabulary as is necessary in order not to convey people's stories untruthfully: then comes the slogan, 'the wordes moote be cosyn to the dede' (I.725–42).[44] This is notoriously a smokescreen since, while there are written narratives for Chaucer to rehearse, there are no 'live' performances for him to report. Nevertheless he is surely communicating in a deeper sense the rich range of writing that must be attempted if narrative is to embrace the diversity of human expression. Judged against that criterion, Phebus's crow therefore will not do as an alter ego for Chaucer because its notion of 'telling it like it is' is severely limited to insensitive, raucous, abrasive, gloating exclamation. The crow informs Phebus, with aggressive repetition, that for all his handsomeness, for all his

---

[42] *Chaucerian Polity*, p. 252.   [43] Ibid., pp. 252–3.

[44] The vocabulary about rehearsing stories in order not to be false to the 'mateere' famously resurfaces in the *MillPr*, I.3173–5. The principle that words should accord with actions is seen as a bygone ideal in Chaucer's 'Lak of Stedfastnesse' (3–5). It recalls passages in *Boece*, III pr. 12 ('by the sentence of Plato ... nedes the wordis moot be cosynes to the thinges of which thei speken') and in *RR*, 15158–60. For a provocative, still valuable discussion, see P. B. Taylor, 'Chaucer's *Cosyn to the Dede*', *Speculum*, 57 (1982), 315–27.

musicianship, despite all his vigilance, he has been duped by a complete nobody whom the crow has seen screw his wife on his own bed (IX.248–56).

Chaucer explores here, along with the injurious shafts of defamation discussed in Chapter 1, the logical outcome of adopting a debased notion of what it means to harmonize words and deeds. The tale seems to present a joyless version of the creative enterprise, and it is in this image too that the crow is fashioned. The Manciple parrots the principle that 'the word moot cosyn be to the werkyng' (IX.207–10); but his version of how that applies is that every type of spade must be called a shovel, that vocabulary must not be allowed to euphemize the underlying and shabby truths about people. Differences should be erased. All forms of oppression converge into 'tyranny', and as for high- or low-class women's sexual adventures, 'Men leyn that oon as lowe as lith that oother'; the phrasing of which caustically enacts the levelling-down trajectory that the Manciple is touting (IX.222). We are at the opposite end of the problem of difference that we saw raised in *Troilus and Criseyde*. There, Troilus makes the reader uncomfortable by using fine distinctions, what he calls diversity between things that look alike, to defuse moral implications of Pandarus's behaviour as go-between. Here, the Manciple makes the reader uncomfortable by insisting bitterly that 'difference' of circumstances (IX.212, 225) should *not* be used to make linguistic distinctions that override basic moral equivalence. I do not suppose that either position represents a 'Chaucerian' statement. Democratic instincts may incline us to warm to the Manciple's stance. But his position, self-styled as that of a 'man noght textueel' (IX.235), does indeed spell hostility to textuality, hostility to the writer's interest in lexical diversity. If this is what it means to suit word to deed (all distinction erased, all activity reduced to common denominators of rampant lust and tyranny) then poetry attenuates towards crude monosyllables and we could be left with little but a mean rhetoric of vindictiveness.

It is an expression of the same reductive understanding of speech that affords the protracted banality of the tale's coda, in which the speaker catalogues aphorisms learnt from his mother against 'too much' speaking and against hasty speech. This too is the logical outcome of the hermeneutics exemplified in the tale. Since that hermeneutics leads to plain-speaking belligerence and therefore to retaliation, the preventive must be a retreat into practised silence. Chaucer has imagined speech and 'tidynges' into a dead end—but only as a consequence of a mechanistic view (less subtle than the cumulative view of the *Tales*) of matching deeds with words. He is playing an arch game with readers, one in which, moreover, gender has an unusual part. The crow, which would insist on uttering facts, is male; the voice which conversely would insist on guarding the tongue is reportedly female, the voice of the mother. Chaucer, making the voice of restraint a voice that nevertheless becomes garrulously repetitive, teases us with propositions about propriety, about restraint and unrestraint, detraction and the right use of eloquence, while juggling the gender stereotyping his period usually attached to these propositions.

The *Tales* come to an end in meditation on the questions of propriety and morality in speech that Fragments VIII and IX have increasingly raised. The Parson is concerned as a cleric intent on fruitful discourse to speak no fable, and as a Southerner to speak no alliteration. His contribution is elaborately billed as proper completion—as fulfilment of the Host's plan, fulfilment of the cycle of the day (carefully marked by the descent of the sun and the estimated length of shadows), a knitting-up of the company's festivity. There is perhaps a laconic hint that the pilgrims resign themselves to a *predictable* propriety 'in som virtuous sentence' (x.63). Nevertheless the Parson is asked by the Host on behalf of all to speak fruitfully, at this evening hour, 'in litel space'. This is especially not a moment to waste or 'lose' time, and in theory his tale will be appropriately short. What it turns out to be (all recollection of the company's presence at dusk, riding through a village, quickly evaporating) is an uncompromising and substantial compendium of moral issues with which the tales have taken the liberty of playing. If the Manciple, incited by the Cook's inability to speak, has raised questions in his fable about who should speak, how, and how much, the Parson—whatever reformist nuances may or may not be detected in his words—definitively and decorously fulfils his role as a parson. The fact that he too announces himself as not 'textueel' (x.57) interestingly invites comparison of his mode of discourse with the Manciple's, though it is probably to be read as a rather different self-humbling gesture.

Against the presumed frivolity and accountability of idle speech there is finally placed the strenuous 'propriety' of the Parson's preaching. Indeed it is as though the Parson and his companions have suddenly all been amazingly overcome with a Ciceronian respect for the right thing at the right time, what Cicero calls *ordinis conservatio* ('orderly conduct') when he urges the importance of knowing what is appropriate to each person, circumstance, and age; the importance of understanding the decorum of speech.[45] No doubt the Parson's stern propriety casts a particular retrospective shadow over the 'impropriety' of usurpers or manipulators of preaching among the pilgrims: the Pardoner and the Wife of Bath, not to mention the friar within 'The Summoner's Tale'. If it is the Manciple who eventually makes an issue of when and how someone should speak, it is these others who have previously raised the question. Each threatens (though not without raising productive reformist issues at the same time) a serious destabilization of proprieties.

Whatever may be said about 'The Parson's Prologue' ushering in a 'fruitful' ending which invites critical recollection of preceding contributions such as the Pardoner's, the way in which this Prologue also clamours to be read within the whole edifice of the *Canterbury Tales* is as a concluding column completing a structural arch, of which the balancing column is the 'Introduction to the Man of Law's Tale'. This reading of the work's architecture derives from the degree of parallelism between 'The Parson's Prologue' and that 'Introduction' concerning efficacious use of time. As others have speculated, it seems likely that that 'Introduction' was at some stage envisaged by Chaucer as a starting point for the *Tales*.[46] With its sonorous computation of the date and time by position of the sun and by shadow length (showing it to be ten o'clock on the morning of 18 April), and with the Host's melodramatic wheeling of his horse to address the company, the passage in the 'Introduction' has the portentousness of a major overture. That impression is consolidated by the Host's self-conscious admonition in it against idleness. As we noted in connection with 'The Second Nun's Prologue', literary narration had often been justified as a kind of bulwark against idleness, and writers had contrived endless ways of introducing their works as industrious labour spurred on by desire to defeat torpor.[47] In the 'Introduction to the Man of Law's Tale' the Host urges the pilgrims

---

[45] *De officiis*, 1.40, 1.34, and 1.37 respectively; trans. Miller, pp. 145, 127–9, and 135.

[46] See Carleton Brown, 'The Man of Law's Headlink and the Prologue of the *Canterbury Tales*', *SP*, 34 (1934), 8–35; Charles A. Owen, Jr, *Pilgrimage and Storytelling in the Canterbury Tales* (Norman, Okla.: University of Oklahoma Press, 1977), pp. 30–1, 37. The possibility of this architecture subsists, whichever was written first, *ParsProl* or *MoL Intro*, an issue that remains undecided.

[47] See e.g. the Preface by Hrotsvitha to her Poems and by Hildegard to her *Scivias*, discussed in Blamires, *Case for Women*, p. 193. Kolve contends unconvincingly that the *MoL Intro* does not gesture towards a prefatorial trope when it spurns Idleness, but instead announces a turn from fabliau to more strenuous genres; but he hedges his bets by describing the passage as a 'rebeginning': *Chaucer and the Imagery of Narrative*, pp. 285–93.

not to waste time, conducting a veritable tour de force of tropes on this subject. (Through sleep or through negligence during waking hours, time steals away, as Seneca and 'many a philosophre' have written. Time is like a stream flowing relentlessly downwards from hill to sea, never to be reversed. Once gone, time can no more be retrieved than Maud's virginity, lost 'in hir wantownesse'. The moral is that the pilgrim company must not 'mowlen' (grow mouldy) in idleness, II.32.) In this context the pilgrims' tales acquire a more morally toned rationale than the diversionary function of mirth and 'disport' (helping to shorten the journey to Canterbury) attributed to them by the Host when proposing his scheme in the 'General Prologue' (I.771–82). The tales, rather than functioning to shorten the journey in the sense of relieving its tedium, are cast in the 'Man of Law's Introduction' as a form of productive activity that will use time to positive effect.

One abiding belief about the *Tales* is that in them, every view is made relative. In Grudin's words, Chaucer's is 'an art that potentially liberates all speech. Everything—no matter how authoritative—is tried in the balance. Chaucer offers a way of thinking [. . .] in which all possibilities and points of view receive consideration.'[48] We might say then that Chaucer offers the Parson's perspective as *a* parson's perspective, no more authoritative than a miller's or a prioress's. For sure it is hard to take, for example, the Parson's casual disparagement of rhyme (a skill at which Chaucer works so hard) and of 'fable', as carrying conclusive force. At the same time 'The Parson's Prologue' and 'Tale', like the end of *Troilus and Criseyde*, certainly stages a moral ascent in the eye of its speaker. In the case of the *Tales* the 'ascent', paradoxically, is from narrative poetry to expository prose. As if stung because the Host initially asks him for a 'fable', the Parson promises an ascent from 'fables and swich wrecchednesse' to 'soothfastnesse' and 'vertuous mateere' (x.31–8).

The Parson has in mind the concern expressed by St Paul to Timothy about the potential backsliding of the Ephesians, only too ready to turn from *veritas* (i.e. 'soothfastnesse') to *fabulae* (2 Tim. 4: 4).[49] Those *fabulae* are characterized by St Paul as *ineptae*: trifling, foolish, absurd (1 Tim. 4: 7). There is little doubt that the Parson means to put distance not just between himself and the type of Ovidian fable represented by the story of Apollo and the crow in 'The Manciple's Tale', but between

---

[48] Grudin, 'Credulity and the Rhetoric of Heterodoxy', p. 219.
[49] See also 1 Tim. 1: 4 and 1: 6–7.

himself and any sort of remotely trifling discourse. It is tempting to gloss the Parson's position in terms of moralistic discussion of 'idle words', which constitute the first branch of the sins of the tongue.[50] This tells us that people given to idle words

wirken mochel euele werke whiche that thei beth not war of. First, thei lesen the noble tyme . . . and thei leseth the good that thei might and schulde do, and also thei lesen the tresour of the herte and bryngen it ful of thing that noght is; they openeth the pot, and the flyen gon ynne. Men clepen hem idele wordes, but thei beth not ydel, for thei beth wel dere and ful of harm and wel perilous, as thilke that voiden the herte of al goodnesse and bryngeth it ful of vanite, and wher-of euery man mote yelde acountes to-for God at the day of dom, as God seith in the gospel. It is not a litel thing ne ydel that a man mote yelde acountes of in so highe a court as to-for God and al the baronye of heuene.[51]

Nor is there any escape in literariness. The word may do harm 'though it be fair spoken and wel y-polissched and coloured'.[52] The accompanying categorization of sins of the tongue could, on the strictest application, trawl up quite a few of the *Canterbury Tales*: 'iapes' hook the fabliaux, the Pardoner's monologue is that of a 'vauntour'—but in truth as soon as one looks closely, the 'sins of the tongue' as catalogued are actually quite comprehensively those that the *Tales* invite us to consider critically, because they are so wonderfully articulated and *exposed* in Chaucer's narratives: words, for instance, of disparagement, flattery, false humility, ironic praise, detraction, exaggeration, lying, swearing, oath-breaking, chiding, reviling one's neighbour, menacing, 'grudging' (resisting superiors, or God), 'rebelling' (refusing the advice of others or the Commandments), and blasphemy. Properly considered, this, which is only a selection, is not a list of vain trifles that are constituted *by* the *Tales*, but a list of the stances that are brilliantly and often satirically objectified and problematized *within* the *Tales*, including the fabliaux. Nor can the tales be dealt a moral knockout by the Parson's (and St Paul's) commendation of factual truth or 'soothfastnesse'. How complicated all notions of truth are, is made a recurrent problem in Chaucer's work.

'Idle words' may be the nearest thing to the besetting vice of this Canterbury pilgrimage game, and Chaucer may have been capable (at some stage in his life) of classifying many of his poems as 'vanitees',

---

[50] These were sometimes categorized, after Gluttony, as the second of the 'sins of the mouth', as in *VV*, pp. 54–68.

[51] *VV*, p. 55.   [52] *VV*, pp. 54–5.

including whichever of the *Tales* 'sownen into [tend toward] synne',[53] but most readers, I believe then and now, could legitimately respond that in that case, so-called idle words and vanities furnish the moral as well as imaginative core of his creative output.

[53] As stated in the so-called 'Retraction' appended to the *ParsT*, x.1080–91. For a summary of uncertainties about the status of the Retraction, see *Riv.*, p. 965.

Conclusion

For some critics, it is nothing less than a profound affront to Chaucer to hold that his writings are morally wrought. It amounts to a distortion, produced by the 'deeply conservative' tendencies of a certain type of nostalgic devotee of medieval literature. It is a vice of 'over-reading' to satisfy an anachronistic agenda—'our post-Arnoldian desire for a "moral" Chaucer'. Texts such as 'The Shipman's Tale' and 'The Merchant's Tale' are 'quite devoid of the implicit suburban sexual morality and reflexive piety attributed to Chaucer by those critics who take the *Parson's Tale* to be the key to the *significacio* of each *Tale*'. The key, instead, is to read with the tongue-in-cheek Epilogue of the *Decameron* as a model. It urges the pious to steer clear of the work's risqué stories.[1]

These strictures constitute a rhetorical reaction against moralistic interpretation of Chaucer's fabliaux, in particular. They appear to stem from an underlying either/or mentality, which is quite foreign to the reading methodology of the present book. The notion that we must read Chaucer only as men-of-the-world ('men' because Boccaccio mocks the moral reader in the gender-specific form of 'the *lady* who is forever saying her prayers, or baking pies and cakes for her father confessor') is as narrow as the notion that we must read Chaucer only as slaves to suburban morality, whatever that is. To dismiss 'The Parson's Tale' as a concessionary pious appendage is as pedantic as taking that text as a key to the tales. What readers need are antennae that are alert for a whole spectrum of nuances in Chaucerian expression, whether playful-intellectual, inquiringly philosophical, socially calibrated, lyrical, plangent, devotional, ironic, sardonic, operatically rhetorical,

---

[1] Finlayson, 'Chaucer's *Shipman's Tale*, Boccaccio, and the "Civilizing" of Fabliau', pp. 348, 350. Finlayson cites the suspicion about 'conservative' readers from Spearing, *Medieval to Renaissance*, pp. 20–1. For Boccaccio's remarks see *Decameron*, trans. McWilliam, p. 831.

outrageously comic, witty, ethical, mock-ethical, manipulative-ethical, Christian-doctrinal, or doctrinally subversive, to name a few. The legacy of the excesses of 'allegorizing' readings of Chaucer, based on the false premise that every medieval text expresses either overtly or covertly the conquest of worldly desires by Christian spirituality, may still be giving 'moral' reading of any kind a bad odour for some critics, but it seems time to get beyond those old battle-lines.

The readings in this book have not intentionally neglected pluralistic or sceptical or irreverent dimensions of the writings addressed, but such neglect is a likely incidental effect of my project of elucidating ethical and moral strands and (where possible) the gendering of those strands in the writings. Moreover there does come a point at which critical choices have to be made, and a reader has to decide whether a given narrative is or is not providing awareness of evaluative moral or ethical criteria that affect reader response. 'What Chaucer will seldom do is attach a moral label', observes George Kane: the very difficulty of discerning (let alone making) moral choices is 'part of the representation', and this is the difficulty that Chaucer often signals by 'laying judgement on the reader'.[2] 'The Shipman's Tale', without question, is a test case in that regard. Our analysis in Chapter 4 linked the tale's mischievous focus on what is 'enough' to a norm of contented sufficiency advocated in Stoic ethics, utterly familiar to Chaucer, which Christian morality had absorbed and reinforced as a critique of wealth-acquisition. The tale was seen to *incorporate* this norm. The reading is not, as one critical viewpoint might allege, an *importation* of 'an extratextual norm of rectitude'.[3] In any case such a focus did not inhibit our appreciation also of the tale's witty play with the inequitable transactional ethics of sexuality. Moreover, awareness of Senecan tradition concerning favours led us to fresh insight into a 'digression' in the tale and thence into the tale's whole interest in misrepresentation.

It is Chaucer's incorporation of Stoic (and specifically Senecan) material in his writings that has proved most generative in this book, and to an even greater extent than anticipated. The Stoic cultivation of cheerful equanimity as a bulwark against emotions and afflictions leaves its mark on the characterization of Arveragus in 'The Franklin's Tale'

---

[2] Kane, *The Liberating Truth*, pp. 16–17.
[3] Patterson, *Chaucer and the Subject of History*, p. 362. Distinguishing the 'extratextual' is in any case problematic. Are the accumulated ethical meanings of 'enough', and the moral connotations of phraseology about what God sends, 'extratextual'?

as well as Theseus in 'The Knight's Tale'. In both, that equanimity is pitted sometimes triumphantly, sometimes futilely, against passions whose overwhelming nature can make Stoicism look, at least temporarily, bland, but rarely untenable. (Pandarus in *Troilus and Criseyde* parrots Stoic platitudes facilely at times, for sure, but his practical rationality also serves to anchor Troilus's spinning emotions.) Our analysis of Dorigen disclosed that she betrays ethically culpable fears and emotions, and morally culpable protest: yet her stance exerts also a contrary virtue, for it exudes a moral charitable instinct that complicates the reader's response. In another representation of divergent ethical/moral imperatives, 'The Clerk's Tale' was seen to disconcert us with the conceptual tension between extreme (ethical) fortitude and extreme (moral) humility, to both of which Griselda commits herself. Again, Chaucer's interest in the ethic of measured liberality, its gendering, and the impossible attempt to harmonize it with a Christian model of unbounded generosity, was found to contribute inspiration to 'The Wife of Bath's Prologue' and to connect that prologue with her 'Tale'. January's systematic dedication to guaranteed *voluptas* in 'The Merchant's Tale' betrayed itself both as Epicurean and also as a travesty of ideals of serenity and marital sexuality on all ethical and moral fronts. Perhaps this instance is carefully gendered. At any rate Chaucer eschews the contrary inherited impulse to gender voluptuousness feminine, exemplified two hundred years earlier in *Policraticus*, where the banquet given by Dido to her lover-to-be Aeneas is characterized as a 'feminine' indulgence corruptive of 'masculine' discipline and is said to have been provided with 'a woman's extravagance'.[4] If anything, self-control, particularly in the sense of not giving way to enormities of sensual indulgence, is more comprehensively gendered feminine than masculine in Chaucer's writing, corroborating the Squire's estimate that (in that domain) women are 'mesurable' (v.362). If the Wife of Bath is a notable exception, her excess represents in itself an ethical and moral challenge.

Some other generalized deductions tentatively suggest themselves. Friendship, traditionally considered as an ethical good and gendered masculine, is in Chaucer's writings a very rare commodity. In fact Chaucer critiques homosocial bonding more than he endorses it, a phenomenon that I would connect with the period's fear of social dissolution. Women are excluded from elevated *amicitia*, yet the paradox is that women are seen to work particularly hard to sustain peaceful

---

[4] *Policraticus*, VIII.6, trans. Pike, pp. 323–5.

fellowship. To be sure, women are imagined to be prey to emotions inconsistent with Stoic tranquillity of mind; yet they seem on balance more temperate than men, who go crazy in the thick of their emotions. Men seem to be prolific abusers of jurisdiction (not surprisingly, perhaps, because most jurisdiction is restricted to males). By contrast, when women get the chance to exercise jurisdiction, they mostly do so in morally positive ways.

However, the point of the book is not really to try to reduce the shifting perspectives on gender afforded by the writings into tidy paradigms, any more than the point has been to ossify the elusive accommodations between antique ethics and medieval Christian morality that have been detected. Indeed that is the methodological difference between this project and the type of project exemplified by the analysis of Criseyde's fear in *Troilus and Criseyde* by Alastair Minnis and Eric Johnson. They wish to use the categorical precision derivable from scholastic medieval sources in order to prove that Criseyde's 'drede' is morally neutral because it comes into the 'natural' category of fear. Their technique is to identify the three species of fear that are formalized in scholastic discussions of the subject, then to define the particular Chaucerian case as conforming to one of these sub-categories.[5] I do not disagree that there are instances where Chaucer's narratives appear to invoke some point of moral doctrine (though not generally from the cutting edge of scholastic investigation) more precisely than has been recognized. This book has supplied fresh evidence along those lines. However, to me the evidence suggests that as well as being prepared to avail himself of the more well-worn categories, Chaucer is quizzically sensitive to the latent confusion that characterizes the wider picture of ethical and moral doctrine. Study of Chaucer certainly needs to reckon with the creative engagement in his writings with Stoic elements of antique ethics that were incompletely absorbed into, or recalcitrant within, Christian moral doctrine.

Such study leads, I think, towards a melancholy side of his reputedly benevolent and genial poetry. He seems to have noticed how Stoic discourse sometimes projects its model of ideal serenity as though it were easy of attainment:

we must keep ourselves free from every disturbing emotion, not only from desire and fear, but also from excessive pain and pleasure, and from anger, so

---

[5] Minnis and Johnson, 'Chaucer's Criseyde and Feminine Fear'.

that we may enjoy that calm of soul and freedom from care which bring both moral stability and dignity of character.[6]

Cicero here rattles off (we might protest) a checklist of elemental impulses in life that are, he says, simply to be suppressed in the interests of 'calm of soul'. In Chaucer the attraction of that calm self-control is communicated, as is the attraction of ideal sufficiency. Barbara Nolan rightly suggests that 'The Knight's Tale' identifies in Stoic virtue 'the best that can be hoped for, from a strictly human point of view', that is, from a point of view without benefit of grace.[7] But the prospect of achieving such virtue is made to seem desperately slight within the culture that the poetry generally constructs. The reason is, as we saw Troilus object (seeing indeed *as* an objection what Seneca took to be common sense), that one must be stripped of feelings if the mind is to conquer the pangs of love, or any other emotion (*TC*, iv.464–9).[8] Serenity does not belong on earth. In Chaucer's short dialogue poem about the limits of fortune's power, Fortune herself proclaims that it is 'hevene' not earth that has the 'propretee of sikernesse'; earth 'hath ever resteles travayle' ('Fortune', 69–70). Chaucer's texts keep on registering that desire and love—never mind the rest of Cicero's list—are huge, indomitable forces by which people are constrained into fragile or futile yearnings and relationships, despite any Stoic prescriptions whatever and despite even themselves. 'What meneth this? What is this mystihed?', as the thwarted lover cries (*Complaint of Mars*, 224). And how can 'freedom from care' prevail if friendship and fellowship are constantly threatened by competitiveness and hate, if chicanery attacks us round every corner, if justice is corrupted, if the ostensible guardians of morality grow ever more venal, and if treachery is an ever-present threat?

Can we infer what circumstances of the time drove Chaucer's often melancholic projection of ethical and moral issues? After all, perception of ethics must participate no less in emergent social and cultural processes than do, say, ideas of regional identity or perceptions of social rank.

Scholars have, of course, speculated about the historical embeddedness of certain ethical and moral emphases and their development in the medieval period. For example, a fundamental change in the hierarchical ranking of Sins, which were headed for centuries by Pride as 'chief sin'

---

[6] Cicero, *De officiis*, i.20.69, trans. Miller, p. 71.
[7] *Chaucer and the Tradition of the 'roman antique'*, p. 261
[8] See Chapter 6 above.

until that honour was assigned instead to Avarice, has been explained as a symptom of a 'commercial revolution' from the twelfth to the fourteenth centuries in Europe.[9] If indeed Pride, a vice befitting an era of intensely feudal power structures, was overtaken in importance by Avarice because that was a vice that signalled rising levels of anxiety about the growth of a profit-oriented economy, then the urgency of satire on acquisitiveness in the *Decameron* and the *Canterbury Tales* is not to be reckoned simply as representative of 'traditional' social complaint. To take another example: from the late thirteenth century onwards, writers (including Dante and Chaucer) conspicuously promoted the view that nobility or *gentillesse* is constituted by possession of a nexus of virtues, irrespective of one's origins; or conversely, that a person should earn through virtue the 'noble' status acquired through heredity or other means.[10] John of Wales was urging this in the 1270s in his moral-philosophical handbook *Communiloquium*, which was to be popular in England throughout the later Middle Ages.[11] Historians investigating parliamentary representation in England can help here because their statistics seem to reveal a surprisingly high turnover within the later medieval nobility. Failures in the male line frequently necessitated replacement representatives, introducing 'newcomers' into the nobility in the case of up to one-quarter of this group between 1350 and 1500. So it is possible that discussion of what 'true' nobility meant came to the fore not just because it was always liable to be provoked by eruptions of aristocratic prejudice, but also because it offered a rationale for a social mobility that was distinctly visible in the period's social superstructure.[12]

To come yet closer to the timeliness of Chaucer's incorporations of ethical wisdom, one important factor must be the exponential development of attempts to adjust moral and ethical teachings to practical life in the one hundred years preceding his output. Even the swift emergence of Aristotle's *Nicomachean Ethics* in the thirteenth century is significant here (though Chaucer was to be far less indebted

---

[9] Lester K. Little, 'Pride Goes before Avarice: Social Change and the Vices in Latin Christendom', *American Historical Review*, 76 (1971), 16–49.

[10] The topic is extensively discussed in Dante, *Convivio*, Bk IV. The core of the argument had long been available in Seneca's Letters: *Ep.* 44, *Epistulae*, vol. 1, pp. 288–9.

[11] Jenny Swanson, *John of Wales*, pp. 131–2, citing *Communiloq.* III.3.3. At least 140 MS copies of this text survive; there were five in one Canterbury library alone by the 1360s: Swanson, *John of Wales*, pp. 161–2.

[12] Swanson, *John of Wales*, p. 132.

to it than was Boccaccio). That emergence brooks historicization in ways that extend beyond the simple rationale of 'rediscovery'. Rediscovery presupposes a yawning gap to be filled, and a gap seems to have been there, to judge from the comments of Grosseteste, the theologian responsible for producing a crucial thirteenth-century Latin translation of this book. The friars, he says, were constantly bringing him 'new questions' as they extended the practice of the sacrament of confession. Increasing interrogation of the daily moral life across the whole spectrum of society created, apparently, an appetite for a correspondingly humane but rigorous moral analysis. Access to the whole of an Aristotelian treatise in that area was a godsend.[13]

The fulfilment of this need meant wider and wider education in the requirements of the conscience, as literacy advanced in the next hundred years. A useful crosslight comes from the way the poet of *Sir Gawain and the Green Knight* drew upon Ciceronian and Stoic ethics. Ad Putter attributes the prioritization of temperance and self-control in Gawain's testing in that poem to the dissemination among the nobility of ethical teaching transmitted by clerical compilations, which leaves its mark on courtly romance from quite early in the development of that genre. Hence *Sir Gawain*, elevating integrity in social dealings as an absolute obligation, renders a striking concern for Stoic *honestas*. In Putter's challenging phrase, ethical teachings amounted to 'a means of laicizing conscience'.[14] An 'ethic of introspection' was drawn from the classical tradition, which educated the laity in a 'network of moral imperatives and mutual obligations', at a period when people (not just knightly households I would add, though Putter is thinking especially of them) wanted to understand better the nature of the good life lived amidst worldly concerns: how to negotiate, especially, between spiritual requirements and the ethics of interpersonal relationships.[15]

In Chaucer's case this cultural context conducive to exploration of ethics was particularly enriched by his own concentrated study of the *Consolation of Philosophy* and of Jean de Meun. Above all, though, we recognize in him an inquiring and speculative temperament, one that catches some of the critical spirit of late-century reformism.

---

[13] Alexander Murray, 'Confession as a Historical Source in the Thirteenth Century', in *The Writing of History in the Middle Ages*, ed. R. H. C. Davis and J. M. Wallace-Hadrill (Oxford: Oxford University Press, 1981), pp. 275–322 (pp. 306–7, 310–17).

[14] Putter, *'Sir Gawain and the Green Knight' and French Arthurian Romance*, p. 184; the argument as a whole occupies pp. 152–84.

[15] Ibid., p. 249.

A. C. Spearing suggestively connects what he calls Chaucer's 'speculative freedom' with the questioning stance of Wycliffite polemic.[16] The poet's narratives, questioning why the world is as it is (what is this 'mystihed'?), include a powerful dimension of ethical nostalgia, provoked no doubt by the abuses of power, the vengeful political factionalism, the scandalous state of the church, the social rebelliousness, and the failure of consultative institutions during the last quarter of the fourteenth century. The sense of division and wreckage in society, church, and government appears to have been acute and deep by the 1380s, as we noted in Chapter 1 when discussing fellowship and friendship. Illuminating one major facet of what he calls the 'Ricardian social crisis', Richard Green links the anxiety about *trouthe* in Chaucer's writings with the replacement of an oath culture (a culture of *trouthe*) by a written-contract culture (in effect a culture of verification) that was fast accelerating at this epoch.[17] From the point of view of the findings of the present book, we can describe another antithesis that emerges as a symptom of the times.

The antithesis is this. On the one hand there were the rational, sensitive, manageable-looking tenets of Stoic ethical philosophy—its reassuring headlines of self-control, careful deliberation, contentment with self-sufficiency. These tenets held out optimistic promises: that powerful emotions could be contained, that one could *talk* violent or angry people into a wiser frame of mind, that generosity and clemency were entirely prudent, and that in any instance where reversals or threats or abuse could not be deflected by such means, the victim could ultimately rise above that in an inner bastion of tranquillity. I take it that after perpetrating the joke of presenting himself as an incompetent hack in 'Sir Thopas', Chaucer assigned to himself 'The Tale of Melibee' precisely because it breathes the spirit of Stoic advice, brought to bear on a fictive situation of inflammatory violence. He wanted to 'own' that kind of deliberative, prudential ethic, perhaps also to own up to men's need to listen to women who more often possessed it.

But he lived to see colleagues executed by the Lords Appellant when they took power from Richard II. Neither the Stoic ethic, nor the charismatic moral category of Christian charity overlaying it, survives unscathed in his work. There is too sharp a consciousness (Hugh White calls it a 'bleak conviction') of antithetical human short-sightedness

---

[16] Spearing, *Medieval to Renaissance*, pp. 89–90.
[17] Green, *A Crisis of Truth*, pp. 163, 157–60.

and irrationality and destructive passion.[18] I do not think, as has been mooted, that a 'sense of general moral deficiency' perceptible in his work is rooted in 'the prevalent eschatological obsession of the time'.[19] If anything (a point argued in Chapter 2 in relation to 'The Miller's Tale') Chaucer makes fun of eschatology more than he worries over it. Rather, it is sheer uncontained passions that impede trust in the ethical/moral structures available: it is 'lust volage', defamatory speech, murder—to recall disastrous impulses in 'The Manciple's Tale'—that unhinge optimism. Optimism is restored in the narratives: sometimes by the spectacle of self-inflicted judgements brought upon the vicious; sometimes by conspicuous powers of sufferance; and by benign acts of providence too. But in all this, much of Chaucer's creative attention is devoted to highlighting fissures *between* the ethical and the moral, and (to the delight of the reader) devoted to disturbing the ossified gendering of ethical and moral definition that predecessors had applied. In a cultural climate saturated by moral analysis, Chaucer worked wonders with that analysis.

[18] White, *Nature, Sex, and Goodness*, p. 254.
[19] Kane, *The Liberating Truth*, p. 20.

Bibliography

PRIMARY SOURCES

Alan of Lille, *The Plaint of Nature*, trans. James J. Sheridan (Toronto: Pontifical Institute of Mediaeval Studies, 1980).

Albertano of Brescia, *De arte loquendi et tacendi*, in *Brunetto Latinos Levnet og Skrifter*, ed. Thor Sundby (Copenhagen: Boghandel, 1869), pp. lxxxix–cxix.

—— *Liber consolationis et consilii*, ed. Thor Sundby, Chaucer Society, 2nd ser., vol. 8 (London: Trübner, 1873).

Albertus Magnus, *Opera omnia*, vol. xii, *Quaestiones super de animalibus*, ed. Ephrem Filthaut, O. P. (Aschendorff: Monasterii Westfalorum, 1955).

Andreas Capellanus, *Andreas Capellanus On Love*, ed. and trans. P. G. Walsh (London: Duckworth, 1982).

Aquinas, St Thomas, *Summa Theologiae*, gen. ed. Thomas Gilby, OP, 60 vols., vol. 41, *Virtues of Justice in the Human Community*, ed. and trans. T. C. O'Brien (London: Blackfriars, in conjunction with Eyre and Spottiswoode; and New York: McGraw-Hill, 1972).

—— *The Summa Theologica of St Thomas Aquinas*, trans. Fathers of the English Dominican province, pt iii, vol. 19, *Quaestiones XXXIV–LXVII* (London: Burns Oates and Washbourne, 1922).

Aristotle, *Ethics*, trans. J. A. K. Thomson (Harmondsworth: Penguin, 1953).

—— *Ethica Nicomachea, Aristoteles Latinus*, ed. R.-A. Gauthier (Leiden and Brussels: E. J. Brill and Desclée de Brouwer, 1972).

Augustine, St, *The City of God Against the Pagans*, ed. and trans. R. W. Dyson (Cambridge: Cambridge University Press, 1998).

—— *The City of God*, trans. Henry Bettenson (Harmondsworth: Penguin, 1972).

Bacon, Sir Francis, *The Essayes or Counsels*, ed. Michael Kiernan (Oxford: Clarendon Press, 1985).

Blamires, Alcuin, with Karen Pratt and C. W. Marx (eds.), *Woman Defamed and Woman Defended: An Anthology of Medieval Texts* (Oxford: Clarendon Press, 1992).

Boccaccio, Giovanni, *Decameron*, ed. Cesare Segre (Milan: Mursia, 1984).

—— *The Decameron*, trans. G. H. McWilliam (Harmondsworth: Penguin, 1972).

—— *De Mulieribus claris*, ed. Vittoria Zaccaria, in *Tutte le opere di Giovanni Boccaccio*, gen. ed. Vittore Branca, vol. 10 (Verona: Mondadori, 1970).

Boccaccio, Giovanni, *Concerning Famous Women*, trans. Guido A. Guarino (New Brunswick, NJ: Rutgers University Press, 1963).

—— *The Fates of Illustrious Men*, trans. Louis Brewer Hall (New York, 1965).

—— *Filocolo*, ed. A. E. Quaglio, in *Tutte le opere*, vol. 1 (Milan: Mondadori, 1967).

—— *Teseida*, ed. A. Limentani, in *Tutte le opere*, vol. 2 (Milan: Mondadori, 1964).

—— *Chaucer's Boccaccio*, trans. N. R. Havely (Woodbridge: D. S. Brewer, 1980).

The Book of the Knight of the Tower, trans. William Caxton, ed. M. Y. Offord, EETS, s.s. 2 (London: Oxford University Press, 1971).

The Book of Margery Kempe, ed. Barry Windeatt (Harlow: Pearson, 2000).

The Book of Vices and Virtues: A Fourteenth Century English Translation of the 'Somme Le Roi' of Lorens D'Orléans, ed. W. Nelson Francis, EETS, o.s. 217 (London: Oxford University Press, 1942).

Brinton, Bishop, *The Sermons of Bishop Brinton, Bishop of Rochester (1373–1389)*, ed. Sister Mary Aquinas Devlin, Camden Third Series, vols. 85, 86 (London, 1954).

Brunetto Latini, *Il Tesoretto (The Little Treasure)*, ed. and trans. Julia Bolton Holloway (New York: Garland, 1981).

Buridan, John, *Iohannis Buridani, Quaestiones in octo libros politicorum Aristotelis* (Oxford: Turner, 1640).

Caxton, William, *Caxton's Game and Playe of Chesse, 1474, A Verbatim Reprint*, intro. William E. A. Axon (London: Elliot Stock, 1883).

Chaucer, Geoffrey, *The Riverside Chaucer*, ed. Larry D. Benson (Boston: Houghton Mifflin, 1987).

—— *Troilus and Criseyde*, ed. Barry Windeatt (London: Longman, 1984).

—— *Troilus and Criseyde: A New Translation*, trans. Barry Windeatt (Oxford: Oxford University Press, 1998).

Chrétien de Troyes, *Cligés*, ed. Alexandre Micha (Paris: Champion, 1978).

—— *Arthurian Romances*, trans. D. D. R. Owen (London: Dent, 1987).

Christine de Pizan, *Le Livre de la cité des dames*, ed. Maureen Curnow, Ph.D. dissertation, Vanderbilt University (1975), Xerox University Microfilms (Ann Arbor).

—— *The Book of the City of Ladies*, trans. Rosalind Brown-Grant (Harmondsworth: Penguin, 1999).

—— *Le Livre de la mutacion de fortune*, trans. Kevin Brownlee, in *The Selected Writings of Christine de Pizan*, ed. Renate Blumenfeld-Kosinski and Kevin Brownlee (New York: W. W. Norton, 1997).

—— *Le Livre des trois vertus*, ed. Charity Cannon Willard and Eric Hicks (Paris: Champion, 1989).

—— *The Treasure of the City of Ladies*, trans. Sarah Lawson (Harmondsworth: Penguin, 1985).

Cicero, Marcus Tullius, *De officiis*, trans. Walter Miller (Cambridge, Mass.: Harvard University Press, 1913).

—— *On Duties*, ed. M. T. Griffin and E. M. Atkins (Cambridge: Cambridge University Press, 1991).

—— *Laelius, On Friendship, and The Dream of Scipio*, ed. and trans. J. G. F. Powell (Warminster: Aris and Phillips, 1990).

Dante Alighieri, *Convivio*, ed. Giorgio Inglese (Milan: Rizzoli, 1993).

—— *Dante's 'Il Convivio' (The Banquet)*, trans. Richard H. Lansing (New York: Garland, 1990).

Dionysius (Pseudo-), *The Complete Works*, trans. Colm Luibheid (London: 1987).

Dives and Pauper, vol. 1, pts 1 and 2, ed. Priscilla H. Barnum, EETS, o.s. 275 and 280 (London: Oxford University Press, 1976 and 1980).

Fasciculus Morum: A Fourteenth-Century Preacher's Handbook, ed. and trans. Siegfried Wenzel (University Park: Pennsylvania State University Press, 1989).

Fellows, Jennifer (ed.), *Of Love and Chivalry: An Anthology of Middle English Romance* (London: Dent, 1993).

Florilegium gallicum, ed. A. Gagner (Lund, 1936).

Florilegium morale oxoniense, ed. P. Delhaye and C. H. Talbot, 2 vols., Analecta Mediaevalia Namurcensia, nos. 5–6 (Louvain and Lille: Nauwelaerts and Libraire Giard, 1955–6).

Friedberg, Aemilius (ed.), *Corpus iuris canonici*, pt 1, *Decretum Magistri Gratiani* (Leipzig: Tauchnitz, 1879).

Gower, John, *Confessio Amantis*, in *John Gower: English Works*, ed. G. C. Macaulay, 2 vols., EETS, e.s. 81–2 (London: Oxford University Press, 1900–1).

—— *Mirour de l'Omme*, in *The Complete Works of John Gower*, vol. 1, *The French Works*, ed. G. C. Macaulay (Oxford: Clarendon Press, 1899).

—— *Mirour de l'Omme (The Mirror of Mankind)*, trans. William Burton Wilson (East Lansing: Colleagues Press, 1992).

—— *Vox Clamantis*, in *The Major Latin Works of John Gower*, trans. Eric W. Stockton (Seattle: University of Washington Press, 1962).

Guillaume de Conches, *Moralium Dogma Philosophorum*, PL, 171.1007–56.

—— *Das Moralium Dogma Philosophorum des Guillaume de Conches*, ed. John Holmberg (Uppsala, 1929).

Guillaume de Lorris and Jean de Meun, *Le Roman de la Rose*, 3 vols., ed. Félix Lecoy (Paris: Champion, 1965).

—— *The Romance of the Rose*, trans. Frances Horgan, World's Classics (Oxford: Oxford University Press, 1994).

Hoccleve, Thomas, *The Regiment of Princes*, ed. Charles Blyth, TEAMS Middle English Texts (Kalamazoo, Mich.: Western Michigan University, 1999).

Horstmann, K., '*Orologium Sapientiae* or *The Seven Poyntes of Trewe Wisdom*', *Anglia*, 10 (1888), 323–89.

Hudson, Anne, *Selections from English Wycliffite Writings* (Cambridge: Cambridge University Press, 1978).

Jacob's Well, pt. 1, ed. Arthur Brandeis, EETS, o.s. 115 (London: Trübner, 1900).

John of Salisbury, *Policraticus*, 2 vols., ed. Clement C. J. Webb (Oxford: Oxford University Press, 1909).

—— *Policraticus: The Frivolities of Courtiers and Footprints of Philosophers*, trans. Joseph B. Pike (London: Oxford University Press, 1938).

Julian of Norwich, *A Revelation of Love*, ed. Marion Glasscoe (Exeter: Exeter University Press, 1976).

Knighton, Henry, *Knighton's Chronicle 1337–1396*, ed. and trans. G. H. Martin (Oxford: Clarendon Press, 1995).

Langland, William, *The Vision of Piers Plowman: A Complete Edition of the B-Text*, ed. A. V. C. Schmidt (London: Dent, 1978).

Lydgate, John, *The Fall of Princes*, ed. Henry Bergen, EETS, e.s. 122 (London: Oxford University Press, 1924).

Macrobius, *Commentary on the Dream of Scipio*, trans. William H. Stahl (New York: Columbia University Press, 1952).

Malory, Sir Thomas, *Le Morte Darthur*, ed. Helen Cooper, World's Classics (Oxford: Oxford University Press, 1998).

Marie de France, *Lais*, ed. A. Ewert (Oxford: Blackwell, 1978).

—— *The Lais of Marie de France*, trans. Glyn Burgess (Harmondsworth: Penguin, 1986).

Martin of Braga, *Formula vitae honestae* or *De quattuor virtutibus*, in *PL*, 72.21–8.

Michel, Dan, *Ayenbite of Inwyt, or Remorse of Conscience*, ed. Richard Morris, EETS, o.s. 23 (London: Trübner, 1866).

Mirk, John, *Mirk's Festial, A Collection of Homilies by Johannes Mirkus (John Mirk)*, ed. Theodor Erbe, pt 1, EETS, e.s. 96 (London: Kegan Paul, Trench, Trübner, 1905).

Ovid, *The Art of Love, and Other Poems*, ed. and trans. J. H. Mozley, 2nd edn revised by G. P. Goold (Cambridge, Mass.: Harvard University Press; and London: Heinemann, 1979).

Pearl, ed. E. V. Gordon (Oxford: Clarendon Press, 1953).

Pedro Alfonso, *The Scholar's Guide, A Translation of the Twelfth-Century 'Disciplina Clericalis' of Pedro Alfonso*, trans. Joseph Ramon Jones and John Esten Keller (Toronto: Pontifical Institute of Mediaeval Studies, 1969).

Robert of Brunne, *Handlyng Synne*, ed. Frederick J. Furnivall, EETS, o.s. 119 and 123 (London: Kegan Paul, Trench, and Trübner, 1901–3).

Seneca, Lucius Annaeus, *Ad Lucilium Epistulae Morales*, 3 vols., trans. Richard M. Gummere (London: Heinemann; and New York: G. P. Putnam's

Sons, 1917 [vol. 1, Letters 1–65], 1920 [vol. 2, Letters 66–92], and 1925 [vol. 3, Letters 93–124]).

——*Moral Essays*, 3 vols., trans. John W. Basore (London: Heinemann; Cambridge, Mass.: Harvard University Press, 1928 [vol. 1], 1932 [vol. 2], and 1935 [vol. 3]).

——*Senecae Dialogi*, ed. L. D. Reynolds (Oxford: Clarendon Press, 1977).

——*Seneca: Moral and Political Essays*, trans. John M. Cooper and J. F. Procopé (Cambridge: Cambridge University Press, 1995).

The Southern Passion: Pickering, O. S., 'The "Defence of Women" from the *Southern Passion*: A New Edition', in *The South English Legendary: A Critical Assessment*, ed. Klaus P. Jankovsky (Tübingen: Stauffenburg, 1992), pp. 154–76.

Speculum Christiani, ed. Gustaf Holmstedt, EETS, o.s. 182 (London: Oxford University Press, 1933).

Thoresby, Archbishop, *The Lay Folks' Catechism*, ed. T. F. Simmons and H. E. Nolloth, EETS, o.s. 118 (London: Kegan Paul, Trench, Trübner, 1901).

Two Wycliffite Texts, ed. Anne Hudson, EETS, o.s. 301 (Oxford: Oxford University Press, 1993).

Vices and Virtues: A Soul's Confession of its Sins, ed. F. Holthausen, EETS, o.s. 89 (London: Trübner, 1888).

The Wars of Alexander, ed. Hoyt N. Duggan and Thorlac Turville-Petre, EETS, s.s. 10 (Oxford: Oxford University Press, 1989).

Whiting, Bartlett J. and Helen W., *Proverbs, Sentences, and Proverbial Phrases from English Writings Mainly Before 1500* (Cambridge, Mass.: Belknap Press, 1968).

Wimbledon, Thomas, *Wimbledon's Sermon, 'Redde rationem villicationis tue': A Middle English Sermon of the Fourteenth Century*, ed. Ione Kemp Knight (Pittsburgh, Pa.: Duquesne Univ. Press, 1967).

Wyclif, John, *Select English Works of John Wyclif*, ed. Thomas Arnold, vol. iii, *Miscellaneous Works* (Oxford: Clarendon Press, 1871).

SECONDARY SOURCES

Adams, Robert, 'The Nature of Need in *Piers Plowman* xx', *Traditio*, 34 (1978), 273–301.

Aers, David (ed.), *Medieval Literature and Historical Inquiry* (Cambridge: D. S. Brewer, 2000).

——'Representations of the "Third Estate": Social Conflict and Its Milieu around 1381', *Southern Review*, 16 (1983), 335–49.

——'Chaucer's *Tale of Melibee*: Whose Virtues?', in Aers (ed.), *Medieval Literature and Historical Inquiry*, pp. 69–81.

Ashley, Kathleen M., 'Renaming the Sins: A Homiletic Topos of Linguistic Instability in the *Canterbury Tales*', in *Sign, Sentence, Discourse: Language in*

Medieval Thought and Literature, ed. Julian N. Wasserman and Lois Roney (Syracuse, NY: Syracuse University Press, 1989), pp. 272–93.

D'Avray, David, and M. Tausche, 'Marriage Sermons in *Ad Status* Collections of the Central Middle Ages', *Archives d'histoire doctrinale et littéraire du moyen âge*, 47 (1981), 71–119.

Ayres, Harry M.,'Chaucer and Seneca', *Romanic Review*, 10 (1919), 1–15.

Baker, Denise, 'Chaucer and Moral Philosophy: The Virtuous Women of *The Canterbury Tales*', *MÆ*, 60 (1991), 241–56.

Bartlett, Anne Clark, *Male Authors, Female Readers: Representation and Subjectivity in Middle English Literature* (Ithaca: Cornell University Press, 1995).

Beichner, Paul E., 'Baiting the Summoner', *MLQ*, 22 (1961), 367–76.

Beidler, Peter (ed.), *Masculinities in Chaucer* (Cambridge: D. S. Brewer, 1998).

—— 'Chaucer's *Merchant's Tale* and the *Decameron*', *Italica*, 50 (1973), 266–84.

—— 'Contrasting Masculinities in the *Shipman's Tale*: Monk, Merchant, and Wife', in Beidler (ed.), *Masculinities in Chaucer*, pp. 131–42.

Benjamin, Edwin B., 'The Concept of Order in the *Franklin's Tale*', *PQ*, 38 (1959), 119–24.

Benson, Robert G., and Susan J. Ridyard (eds.), *New Readings of Chaucer's Poetry* (Cambridge: D. S. Brewer, 2003).

Bishop, Ian, *The Narrative Art of the 'Canterbury Tales'* (London: Dent, 1987).

Blamires, Alcuin, *The Canterbury Tales* (Basingstoke: Macmillan, 1987).

—— *The Case for Women in Medieval Culture* (Oxford: Clarendon Press, 1997).

—— 'The Wife of Bath and Lollardy', *MÆ*, 58 (1989), 224–42.

—— 'Crisis and Dissent', in Brown (ed.), *A Companion to Chaucer*, pp. 133–48.

—— 'Refiguring the "Scandalous Excess" of Medieval Woman: The Wife of Bath and Liberality', in *Gender in Debate from the Early Middle Ages to the Renaissance*, ed. Thelma S. Fenster and Clare A. Lees (New York: Palgrave, 2002), pp. 57–78.

—— 'Sexuality', in *The Oxford Guide to Chaucer*, ed. Steve Ellis (Oxford: Oxford University Press, 2005).

—— 'Women and Creative Intelligence in Medieval Thought', in *Voices in Dialogue: Reading Women in the Middle Ages*, ed. Linda Olson and Kathryn Kerby-Fulton (Notre Dame, Ind.: University of Notre Dame Press, 2005), pp. 213–30.

Blanch, Robert J., ' "Al was this land fulfild of fayerye": The Thematic Employment of Force, Wilfulness, and Legal Conventions in Chaucer's *Wife of Bath's Tale*', *SN*, 57 (1985), 41–51.

Bleeth, Kenneth A., 'The Image of Paradise in the *Merchant's Tale*', in *The Learned and the Lewed: Studies in Chaucer and Medieval Literature*, ed. Larry D. Benson (Cambridge, Mass.: Harvard University Press, 1974), pp. 45–60.

Bloomfield, Morton W., *The Seven Deadly Sins: An Introduction to the History of a Religious Concept* (Michigan: Michigan State College Press, 1952).

Blumstein, Andrée K., *Misogyny and Idealization in the Courtly Romance* (Bonn: Bouvier, 1977).

Bossy, John, 'Moral Arithmetic: Seven Sins into Ten Commandments', in *Conscience and Casuistry in Early Modern Europe*, ed. E. Leites (Cambridge: Cambridge University Press, 1988), pp. 214–34.

Bowman, Mary R., ' "Half as she were mad": Dorigen in the Male World of the *Franklin's Tale*', *ChauR*, 27 (1992–3), 239–51.

Boyde, Patrick, *Human Vices and Human Worth in Dante's 'Comedy'* (Cambridge: Cambridge University Press, 2000).

Boyle, Leonard E., OP, 'The Fourth Lateran Council and Manuals of Popular Theology', in *The Popular Literature of Medieval England*, ed. Thomas J. Heffernan (Knoxville: University of Tennessee Press, 1985), pp. 30–43.

Braswell, Mary Flowers, *The Medieval Sinner: Characterization and Confession in the Literature of the English Middle Ages* (New York: Associated University Presses, 1982).

Brewer, Derek, *Chaucer: The Critical Heritage*, vol. I, 1385–1837 (London: Arnold, 1978).

—— 'Some Metonymic Relationships in Chaucer's Poetry', in his *Chaucer: The Poet as Storyteller* (London: Macmillan, 1984), pp. 37–53.

Brown, Carleton, 'The Man of Law's Headlink and the Prologue of the *Canterbury Tales*', *SP*, 34 (1934), 8–35.

Brown, Emerson, Jr, 'Epicurus and *Voluptas* in Late Antiquity: The Curious Testimony of Martianus Capella', *Traditio*, 38 (1982), 75–106.

—— 'What is Chaucer Doing with the Physician and His Tale?', *PQ*, 60 (1982), 129–49.

Brown, Peter (ed.), *A Companion to Chaucer* (Oxford: Blackwell, 2000).

Brown-Grant, Rosalind, *Christine de Pizan and the Moral Defence of Women* (Cambridge: Cambridge University Press, 1999).

Brundage, James, *Law, Sex, and Christian Society in Medieval Europe* (Chicago and London: University of Chicago Press, 1987).

Bryan, W. E., and Germaine Dempster (eds.), *Sources and Analogues of the Canterbury Tales* (Chicago: University of Chicago Press, 1941).

Burnley, J. D., *Chaucer's Language and the Philosophers' Tradition* (Cambridge: D. S. Brewer, 1979).

—— 'The Morality of *The Merchant's Tale*', *Yearbook of English Studies*, 6 (1976), 16–25.

—— 'Chaucer's Host and Harry Bailly', in *Chaucer and the Craft of Fiction*, ed. Leigh A. Arrathoon (Rochester, Mich.: Solaris Press, 1986), pp. 195–218.

Burrow, John, 'The Third Eye of Prudence', in *Medieval Futures: Attitudes to the Future in the Middle Ages*, ed. J. A. Burrow and Ian P. Wei (Woodbridge: Boydell, 2000), pp. 37–48.

Calabrese, Michael, *Chaucer's Ovidian Arts of Love* (Gainesville: University Press of Florida, 1994).

Cixous, Hélène, 'Sorties: Out and Out: Attacks/Ways Out/Forays', in *The Feminist Reader*, 2nd edn, ed. Catherine Belsey and Jane Moore (Basingstoke: Macmillan, 1997), pp. 91–116.

Colish, Marcia L., *The Stoic Tradition from Antiquity to the Middle Ages*, 2 vols., ii, *Stoicism in Christian Latin Thought through the Sixth Century* (Leiden: Brill, 1985).

Cook, Robert G., 'Chaucer's Pandarus and the Medieval Ideal of Friendship', *JEGP*, 69 (1970), 407–24.

Cooper, Helen, *The Canterbury Tales*, Oxford Guides to Chaucer (Oxford: Oxford University Press, 1989).

—— 'The Four Last Things in Dante and Chaucer: Ugolino and the House of Rumour', *NML*, 3 (1999), 39–66.

Correale, Robert M., and Mary Hamel (eds.), *Sources and Analogues of the Canterbury Tales*, vol. 1 (Cambridge: D. S. Brewer, 2002).

Cox, Catherine S., *Gender and Language in Chaucer* (Gainesville: University Press of Florida, 1997).

Crane, Susan, *Gender and Romance in Chaucer's 'Canterbury Tales'* (Princeton, NJ: Princeton University Press, 1994).

Craun, Edwin, *Lies, Slander, and Obscenity in Medieval English Literature* (Cambridge: Cambridge University Press, 1997).

David, Alfred, *The Strumpet Muse: Art and Morals in Chaucer's Poetry* (Bloomington and London: Indiana University Press, 1976).

Delany, Sheila, 'Politics and the Paralysis of Poetic Imagination in *The Physician's Tale*', *SAC*, 3 (1981), 47–60.

—— 'Strategies of Silence in the Wife of Bath's Recital', *Exemplaria*, 2 (1990), 49–69.

Delhaye, Philippe, 'Une adaptation du *De officiis* au xiie siècle: Le *Moralium dogma philosophorum*', *Recherches de théologie ancienne et médiévale*, 16 (1949), 227–58, and 17 (1950), 5–28.

Delumeau, Jean, *Sin and Fear: The Emergence of a Western Guilt-Culture, 13th–18th Centuries*, trans. Eric Nicolson (New York: St Martin's Press, 1990).

Dinshaw, Carolyn, *Chaucer's Sexual Poetics* (Madison: University of Wisconsin Press, 1989).

Edwards, Robert R., *Chaucer and Boccaccio: Antiquity and Modernity* (Basingstoke: Palgrave, 2002).

—— 'Some Pious Talk about Marriage: Two Speeches from the *Canterbury Tales*', in *Matrons and Marginal Women in Medieval Society*, ed.

Robert R. Edwards and Vickie Ziegler (Woodbridge: Boydell and Brewer, 1995), pp. 111–27.

—— and Stephen Spector (eds.), *The Olde Daunce: Love, Friendship, Sex and Marriage in the Medieval World* (Albany: SUNY, 1991).

Elliott, Dyan, 'Marriage', in *The Cambridge Companion to Medieval Women's Writing*, ed. Carolyn Dinshaw and David Wallace (Cambridge: Cambridge University Press, 2003), pp. 40–57.

Evans, Ruth, and Lesley Johnson (eds.), *Feminist Readings in Middle English Literature* (London: Routledge, 1994).

Everest, Carol, ' "Paradys or Helle": Pleasure and Procreation in Chaucer's "Merchant's Tale" ', in Muriel Whitaker (ed.), *Sovereign Lady: Essays on Women in Middle English Literature* (New York: Garland, 1995), pp. 63–84.

Evitt, Regula, 'When Echo Speaks: Marie de France and the Poetics of Remembrance', in *Minding the Body: Women and Literature in the Middle Ages, 800–1500*, ed. Monica Brzezinski Potkay and Regula Meyer Evitt (New York: Twayne, 1997), pp. 77–101.

Farrell, Thomas, 'The Griselda Story in Italy', in Correale and Hamel (eds.), *Sources and Analogues*, vol. 1, pp. 103–29.

Ferster, Judith, *Fictions of Advice: The Literature and Politics of Counsel in Late Medieval England* (Philadelphia: University of Pennsylvania Press, 1996).

Fichte, Joerg O., *Chaucer's Frame Tales* (Tübingen: Narr; and Cambridge: D. S. Brewer, 1987).

Field, Rosalind, 'January's "honeste thynges": Knighthood and Narrative in the *Merchant's Tale*', *Reading Medieval Studies*, 20 (1994), 38–49.

Finlayson, John, 'Chaucer's *Shipman's Tale*, Boccaccio, and the "Civilizing" of Fabliau', *ChauR*, 36 (2001–2), 336–51.

Fisher, Sheila, *Chaucer's Poetic Alchemy: A Study of Value and its Transformation in 'The Canterbury Tales'* (New York: Garland, 1988).

Fleming, John, *Classical Imitation and Interpretation in Chaucer's 'Troilus'* (Lincoln: University of Nebraska Press, 1990).

—— 'The Best Line in Ovid and the Worst', in Benson and Ridyard (eds.), *New Readings of Chaucer's Poetry*, pp. 51–74.

Fletcher, Alan J., *Preaching and Politics in Late Medieval England* (Dublin: Four Courts Press, 1998).

—— 'The Summoner and the Abominable Anatomy of Antichrist', *SAC*, 18 (1996), 91–117.

—— 'Chaucer the Heretic', *SAC*, 25 (2003), 53–121.

Frantzen, Allen, *Troilus and Criseyde: The Poem and the Frame* (New York: Twayne, 1993).

Frazier, J. Terry, 'The Digression on Marriage in the *Franklin's Tale*', *South Atlantic Bulletin*, 43 (1978), 75–85.

Freiwald, Leah R., 'Swych Love of Frendes: Pandarus and Troilus', *ChauR*, 6 (1971–2), 120–9.

Fulton, Helen, 'Mercantile Ideology in Chaucer's *Shipman's Tale*', *ChauR*, 36 (2001–2), 311–28.

Gaylord, Alan T., 'The Promises in the *Franklin's Tale*', *ELH*, 31 (1964), 331–65.

—— 'Friendship in Chaucer's *Troilus*', *ChauR*, 3 (1968–9), 239–64.

Gilligan, Carol, *In A Different Voice: Psychological Theory and Women's Development* (Cambridge, Mass.: Harvard University Press, 1982).

Gowing, L., *Domestic Dangers: Women, Words, and Sex in Early Modern London* (Oxford: Clarendon Press, 1996).

Gravdal, Kathryn, *Ravishing Maidens: Writing Rape in Medieval French Literature and Law* (Philadelphia: University of Pennsylvania Press, 1991).

Gray, Paul Edward, 'Synthesis and Double Standard in the *Franklin's Tale*', *Texas Studies in Literature and Language*, 7 (1965), 213–24.

Green, Richard Firth, *A Crisis of Truth: Literature and Law in Ricardian England* (Philadelphia: University of Pennsylvania Press, 2002).

—— 'Chaucer's Victimized Women', *SAC*, 10 (1988), 3–21.

Greenberg, Nina M., 'Dorigen as Enigma: The Production of Meaning and the *Franklin's Tale*', *ChauR*, 33 (1998–9), 329–49.

Grudin, Michaela Paasche, 'Credulity and the Rhetoric of Heterodoxy: From Averroes to Chaucer', *ChauR*, 35 (2000–1), 204–22.

Hagen, Susan K., 'Chaucer's May, Standup Comics, and Critics', in Jost (ed.), *Chaucer's Humor*, pp. 127–43.

Hahn, Thomas, and Richard W. Kaeuper, 'Text and Context: Chaucer's *Friar's Tale*', *SAC*, 5 (1983), 67–101.

Hallett, Nicky, 'Women', in Brown (ed.), *A Companion to Chaucer*, pp. 480–94.

Hallissy, Margaret, *Clean Maids, True Wives, Steadfast Widows: Chaucer's Women and Medieval Codes of Conduct* (Westport, Conn.: Greenwood, 1993).

—— *A Companion to Chaucer's 'Canterbury Tales'* (Westport, Conn.: Greenwood, 1995).

Hanawalt, Barbara A., *'Of Good and Ill Repute': Gender and Social Control in Medieval England* (Oxford: Oxford University Press, 1998).

Hanning, R. W., 'Telling the Private Parts: "Pryvetee" and Poetry in Chaucer's *Canterbury Tales*', in *The Idea of Medieval Literature: Essays in Honor of Donald R. Howard*, ed. Christian K. Zacher (London and Toronto: Associated University Presses, 1992), pp. 108–25.

—— ' "Parlous Play": Diabolic Comedy in Chaucer's *Canterbury Tales*', in Jost (ed.), *Chaucer's Humor*, pp. 295–319.

Hansen, Elaine Tuttle, *Chaucer and the Fictions of Gender* (Berkeley and Los Angeles: University of California Press, 1992).

Hatton, Tom, 'Chaucer's Friar's "Old Rebekke" ', *JEGP*, 67 (1968), 266–71.

Hazelton, Richard, 'Chaucer's *Parson's Tale* and the *Moralium Dogma Philosophorum*', *Traditio*, 16 (1960), 255–74.

Hill, John, 'Aristocratic Friendship in *Troilus and Criseyde*: Pandarus, Courtly Love and Ciceronian Brotherhood in Troy', in Benson and Ridyard (eds.), *New Readings of Chaucer's Poetry*, pp. 165–82.

Hines, John, *The Fabliau in English* (Harlow: Longman, 1993).

Hirsh, John C., 'The *Second Nun's Tale*', in *Chaucer's Religious Tales*, ed. C. David Benson and Elizabeth Robertson (Cambridge: D. S. Brewer, 1990), pp. 161–9.

—— 'Modern Times: The Discourse of the *Physician's Tale*', *ChauR*, 27 (1992–3), 387–95.

Hoffman, R. L., *Ovid and the Canterbury Tales* (Philadelphia: University of Pennsylvania Press, 1966).

—— 'Jephthah's Daughter and Chaucer's Virginia', *ChauR*, 2 (1967–8), 20–31.

Hornsby, Joseph A., *Chaucer and the Law* (Norman, Okla.: Pilgrim Books, 1988).

Hudson, Anne, *The Premature Reformation: Wycliffite Texts and Lollard History* (Oxford: Clarendon Press, 1988).

Hume, Kathryn, 'The Pagan Setting of the *Franklin's Tale* and the Sources of Dorigen's Cosmology', *SN*, 44 (1972), 289–94.

Huppé, Bernard, *A Reading of the Canterbury Tales* (Albany: State University of New York Press, 1964).

Irigaray, Luce, *This Sex Which Is Not One*, trans. Catherine Porter with Carolyn Burke (Ithaca: Cornell University Press, 1985).

Jacobs, Kathryn, 'The Marriage Contract of the *Franklin's Tale*: The Remaking of Society', *ChauR*, 20 (1985–6), 132–43.

Jacquart, Danielle, and Claude Thomasset, *Sexuality and Medicine in the Middle Ages* (Cambridge: Polity Press, 1985).

Jaeger, S., *Ennobling Love: In Search of a Lost Sensibility* (Philadelphia: University of Pennsylvania Press, 1999).

Johnson, Lesley, 'Women on Top: Antifeminism in the Fabliau?', *MLR*, 78 (1983), 298–307.

Jones, Howard, *The Epicurean Tradition* (London: Routledge, 1989).

Joseph, Gerhard, 'Chaucer's Coinage: Foreign Exchange and the Puns of the *Shipman's Tale*', *ChauR*, 17 (1982–3), 341–57.

Jost, Jean E. (ed.), *Chaucer's Humor: Critical Essays* (New York: Garland, 1994).

—— 'Ambiguous Brotherhood in the *Friar's Tale* and *Summoner's Tale*', in Beidler (ed.), *Masculinities in Chaucer*, pp. 77–90.

Kane, George, *The Liberating Truth: The Concept of Integrity in Chaucer's Writings*, John Coffin Memorial Lecture (London: Athlone, 1980).

Karras, Ruth M., 'Gendered Sin and Misogyny in John of Bromyard's *Summa Predicantium*', *Traditio*, 47 (1992), 233–57.

Kay, Sarah, *The 'Romance of the Rose'* (London: Grant and Cutler, 1995).

Kean, P. M., *Chaucer and the Making of English Poetry*, 2 vols. (London: Routledge, 1972).

Keiser, Elizabeth B., *Courtly Desire and Medieval Homophobia: The Legitimation of Sexual Pleasure in 'Cleanness' and its Contexts* (New Haven: Yale University Press, 1997).

Kelly, Henry Ansgar, *Love and Marriage in the Age of Chaucer* (Ithaca: Cornell University Press, 1975).

Kenny, Anthony, *Wyclif* (Oxford: Oxford University Press, 1985).

Kent, Bonnie, *Virtues of the Will: The Transformation of Ethics in the Late Thirteenth Century* (Washington, DC: Catholic University of America Press, 1995).

Knapp, Peggy A., 'Alisoun of Bath and the Reappropriation of Tradition', *ChauR*, 24 (1989–90), 45–52.

Knight, Stephen, 'Textual Variants, Textual Variance', *Southern Review*, 16 (1983), 44–54.

Kolve, V. A., *Chaucer and the Imagery of Narrative* (London: Edward Arnold, 1984).

—— ' "Man in the Middle": Art and Religion in Chaucer's *Friar's Tale*', *SAC*, 12 (1990), 5–46.

—— 'Rocky Shores and Pleasure Gardens: Poetry vs. Magic in Chaucer's *Franklin's Tale*', in *Poetics: Theory and Practice in Medieval English Literature*, ed. Piero Boitani and Anna Torti (Cambridge: D. S. Brewer, 1991), pp. 165–95.

Kooper, Erik, 'Loving the Unequal Equal: Medieval Theologians and Marital Affection', in Edwards and Spector (eds.), *The Olde Daunce*, pp. 44–56.

Laskaya, Anne, *Chaucer's Approach to Gender in the 'Canterbury Tales'* (Cambridge: D. S. Brewer, 1995).

Lee, Anne Thompson, ' "A Woman True and Fair": Chaucer's Portrayal of Dorigen in the *Franklin's Tale*', *ChauR*, 19 (1984–5), 169–78.

Lenaghan, R. T., 'The Irony of the *Friar's Tale*', *ChauR*, 7 (1972–3), 281–94.

Levy, Bernard S., 'The Wife of Bath's *Queynte Fantasye*', *ChauR*, 4 (1969–70), 106–22.

Lewis, R. E., 'Chaucer's Artistic Use of Pope Innocent III's *De miseria humane conditionis* in the *Man of Law's Prologue* and *Tale*', *PMLA*, 81 (1966), 485–92.

Lindahl, Carl, *Earnest Games: Folkloric Patterns in the 'Canterbury Tales'* (Bloomington: Indiana University Press, 1987).

Lindley, Arthur, ' "Vanysshed Was This Daunce, He Nyste Where": Alisoun's Absence in the *Wife of Bath's Prologue and Tale*', *ELH*, 59 (1992), 1–21.

Little, Lester, *Religious Poverty and the Profit Economy in Medieval Europe* (London: Elek, 1978).

—— 'Pride Goes before Avarice: Social Change and the Vices in Latin Christendom', *American Historical Review*, 76 (1971), 16–49.

Lochrie, Karma, *Covert Operations: The Medieval Uses of Secrecy* (Philadelphia: University of Pennsylvania Press, 1999).

Longsworth, Robert M., 'Privileged Knowledge: St. Cecilia and the Alchemist in the *Canterbury Tales*', *ChauR*, 27 (1992–3), 87–96.

Lottin, D. Odon, *Psychologie et morale aux xiie et xiiie siècles*, 6 vols. in 8 (Louvain: Gembloux, 1942).

Lowes, John Livingston, 'Chaucer and the Seven Deadly Sins', *PMLA*, 30 (1915), 237–371.

Lucas, Angela, 'The Mirror in the Marketplace: Januarie Through the Looking Glass', *ChauR*, 33 (1998–9), 123–45.

McAlpine, Monica, 'The Pardoner's Homosexuality and How it Matters', *PMLA*, 95 (1980), 8–22.

—— 'Criseyde's Prudence', *SAC*, 25 (2003), 199–224.

McEntire, Sandra, 'Illusions and Interpretation in the *Franklin's Tale*', *ChauR*, 31 (1996–7), 145–63.

McGregor, Francine, 'What of Dorigen? Agency and Ambivalence in the *Franklin's Tale*', *ChauR*, 31 (1996–7), 365–78.

Mann, Jill, *Feminizing Chaucer* (Cambridge: D. S. Brewer, 2002); revised edn of her *Geoffrey Chaucer* (London: Harvester Wheatsheaf, 1991).

—— 'Troilus's Swoon', *ChauR*, 14 (1979–80), 319–35.

—— 'Satisfaction and Payment in Middle English Literature', *SAC*, 5 (1983), 17–48.

Martin, Priscilla, *Chaucer's Women: Nuns, Wives and Amazons* (Basingstoke: Macmillan, 1990).

Mertens-Fonck, Paule, 'Le Franklin et la doctrine d'Epicure dans les *Contes de Canterbury*', in *Etudes de linguistique et de littérature en l'honneur d'André Crépin*, ed. Danielle Buschinger and Wolfgang Spiewok, Wodan, band 20 (Greifswald: Reineke, 1993), pp. 273–80.

Middleton, Anne, 'The *Physician's Tale* and Love's Martyrs: "Ensamples mo than ten" as a Method in the *Canterbury Tales*', *ChauR*, 8 (1973–4), 9–32.

Miller, Mark, *Philosophical Chaucer: Love, Sex, and Agency in the 'Canterbury Tales'* (Cambridge: Cambridge University Press, 2004).

Minnis, Alastair, *Chaucer and Pagan Antiquity* (Cambridge: D. S. Brewer, 1982).

—— 'From Medieval to Renaissance? Chaucer's Position on Past Gentility', *PBA*, 72 (1986), 205–46.

—— and Eric J. Johnson, 'Chaucer's Criseyde and Feminine Fear', in *Medieval Women: Texts and Contexts in Late Medieval Britain: Essays for Felicity Riddy*, ed. Jocelyn Wogan-Browne *et al.* (Turnhout: Brepols, 2000), pp. 199–216.

Mitchell, J. Allan, *Ethics and Exemplary Narrative in Chaucer and Gower* (Cambridge: D. S. Brewer, 2004).

Mogan, Joseph J., 'Chaucer and the *bona matrimonii*', *ChauR*, 4 (1969–70), 123–41.

Morrison, Susan Signe, 'Don't Ask, Don't Tell: The Wife of Bath and Vernacular Translations', *Exemplaria*, 8 (1996), 97–123.

Mroczkowski, Przemyslaw, '"The Friar's Tale" and its Pulpit Background', in *English Studies Today*, 2nd ser. (1961), ed. Georges Bonnard, 107–20.

Murray, Alexander, 'Confession as a Historical Source in the Thirteenth Century', in *The Writing of History in the Middle Ages*, ed. R. H. C. Davis and J. M. Wallace-Hadrill (Oxford: Oxford University Press, 1981), pp. 275–322.

Murray, Jacqueline, 'Gendered Souls in Sexed Bodies: The Male Construction of Female Sexuality in Some Medieval Confessors' Manuals', in *Handling Sin: Confession in the Middle Ages*, ed. Peter Biller and A. J. Minnis (University of York: York Medieval Press; in association with Woodbridge: Boydell, 1998), pp. 79–93.

Muscatine, Charles, *Chaucer and the French Tradition* (Berkeley and Los Angeles: University of California Press, 1957).

Myles, Robert, *Chaucerian Realism* (Cambridge: D. S. Brewer, 1994).

Nelson, N. E., 'Cicero's *De Officiis* in Christian Thought: 300–1300', *Essays and Studies in English and Comparative Literature*, University of Michigan Publications (Ann Arbor), 10 (1933), 59–160.

Neuse, Richard, 'Marriage and the Question of Allegory in the *Merchant's Tale*', *ChauR*, 24 (1989–90), 115–31.

Newhauser, Richard, *The Treatise on Vices and Virtues in the Latin and the Vernacular* (Turnhout: Brepols, 1993).

Newman, Barbara, *From Virile Woman to Woman Christ: Studies in Medieval Religion and Literature* (Philadelphia: University of Pennsylvania Press, 1995).

Nicholson, Peter, 'The Friar's Tale', in Correale and Hamel (eds.), *Sources and Analogues*, vol. 1, pp. 87–99.

Nolan, Barbara, *Chaucer and the Tradition of the 'roman antique'* (Cambridge: Cambridge University Press, 1992).

Olson, Paul, 'The *Reeve's Tale*: Chaucer's *Measure for Measure*', *SP*, 59 (1962), 1–17.

Owen, Charles A., Jr, *Pilgrimage and Storytelling in the Canterbury Tales* (Norman, Okla.: University of Oklahoma Press, 1977).

Owen, Nancy H., 'Thomas Wimbledon's Sermon: "Redde racionem villicacionis tue"', *Mediaeval Studies*, 28 (1966), 176–97.

Passon, Richard H., ' "Entente" in Chaucer's *Friar's Tale*', *ChauR*, 2 (1967–8), 166–71.

Patterson, Lee, *Chaucer and the Subject of History* (London: Routledge, 1991).

—— ' "For the Wyves love of Bathe": Feminine Rhetoric and Poetic Resolution in the *Roman de la Rose* and the *Canterbury Tales*', *Speculum*, 58 (1983), 656–94.

—— 'Chaucer's Pardoner on the Couch: Psyche and Clio in Medieval Literary Studies', *Speculum*, 76 (2001), 638–80.

Payer, Pierre, *The Bridling of Desire: Views of Sex in the Later Middle Ages* (Toronto: University of Toronto Press, 1993).

Pearsall, Derek, *The Canterbury Tales* (London: Allen and Unwin, 1985).

—— '*The Franklin's Tale*, Line 1469: Forms of Address in Chaucer', *SAC*, 17 (1995), 69–78.

—— 'Courtesy and Chivalry in *Sir Gawain and the Green Knight*: The Order of Shame and the Invention of Embarrassment', in *A Companion to the Gawain-Poet*, ed. Derek Brewer and Jonathan Gibson (Cambridge: D. S. Brewer, 1997), pp. 351–62.

Peck, Russell A., 'John Gower and the Book of Daniel', in *John Gower: Recent Readings*, ed. R. F. Yeager (Kalamazoo: Western Michigan University, 1989), pp. 159–87.

Percival, Florence, *Chaucer's Legendary Good Women* (Cambridge: Cambridge University Press, 1998).

Perkins, Nicholas, *Hoccleve's 'Regiment of Princes': Counsel and Constraint* (Cambridge: D. S. Brewer, 2001).

Phillips, Helen, *An Introduction to the Canterbury Tales: Reading, Fiction, Context* (Basingstoke: Macmillan, 2000).

—— 'Love', in Brown (ed.), *A Companion to Chaucer*, pp. 281–95.

Plummer, John, ' "Beth fructuous and that in litel space": The Engendering of Harry Bailly', in Benson and Ridyard (eds.), *New Readings of Chaucer's Poetry*, pp. 107–18.

Pratt, Robert, 'Chaucer and the Hand that Fed Him', *Speculum*, 41 (1966), 627–31.

Putter, Ad, *'Sir Gawain and the Green Knight' and French Arthurian Romance* (Oxford: Clarendon Press, 1995).

—— *Introduction to the 'Gawain'-Poet* (New York: Longman, 1996).

Raybin, David, ' "Wommen, of Kynde, Desiren Libertee": Rereading Dorigen, Rereading Marriage', *ChauR*, 27 (1992–3), 65–86.

Reames, Sherry L., 'The Second Nun's Prologue and Tale', in Correale and Hamel (eds.), *Sources and Analogues*, vol. 1, pp. 491–527.

Richardson, Janette, *Blameth Nat Me: A Study of Imagery in Chaucer's Fabliaux* (The Hague: Mouton, 1970).

—— 'The Façade of Bawdry: Image Patterns in Chaucer's *Shipman's Tale*', *ELH*, 32 (1965), 303–13.

Riddy, Felicity, 'Engendering Pity in the *Franklin's Tale*', in Evans and Johnson (eds.), *Feminist Readings in Middle English Literature*, pp. 54–71.

Robertson, D. W., Jr, 'Chaucer's Franklin and his Tale', in *Costerus: Essays in English and American Language and Literature*, n.s. 1, ed. James W. West (Amsterdam: Rodopi, 1974), pp. 1–26.

Roethke, Theodore, *Selected Prose of Theodore Roethke*, ed. Ralph J. Mills (Englewood Cliffs, NJ: Prentice-Hall, 1963).

Rogers, William E., and Paul P. Dower, 'Thinking about Money in Chaucer's *Shipman's Tale*', in Benson and Ridyard (eds.), *New Readings of Chaucer's Poetry*, pp. 119–38.

Rosenberg, Bruce A., 'The Contrary Tales of the Second Nun and the Canon's Yeoman', *ChauR*, 2 (1967–8), 278–91.

Rubin, Miri, *Charity and Community in Medieval Cambridge* (Cambridge: Cambridge University Press, 1987).

Ruggiers, Paul, *The Art of the Canterbury Tales* (Madison: University of Wisconsin Press, 1967).

Salisbury, Joyce, 'Gendered Sexuality', in *Handbook of Medieval Sexuality*, ed. Vern L. Bullough and James A. Brundage (London: Garland, 1996), pp. 81–103.

Saunders, Corinne, *Rape and Ravishment in the Literature of Medieval England* (Cambridge: D. S. Brewer, 2001).

Scanlon, Larry, *Narrative, Authority, and Power: The Medieval Exemplum and the Chaucerian Tradition* (Cambridge: Cambridge University Press, 1994).

Scattergood, V. J., 'The Originality of the *Shipman's Tale*', *ChauR*, 11 (1976–7), 210–31.

Schleusner, Jay, 'The Conduct of the *Merchant's Tale*', *ChauR*, 14 (1979–80), 237–50.

Schnell, Rüdiger, 'The Discourse on Marriage in the Middle Ages', *Speculum*, 73 (1998), 771–86.

Sheehan, Michael M., *'Maritalis Affectio* Revisited', in Edwards and Spector (eds.), *The Olde Daunce*, pp. 32–43.

Siegel, Marsha, 'What the Debate is and Why it Founders in Fragment A of *The Canterbury Tales*', *SP*, 82 (1985), 1–24.

Silverman, Albert H., 'Sex and Money in Chaucer's "Shipman's Tale"', *PQ*, 32 (1953), 329–36.

Smalley, Beryl, *English Friars and Antiquity in the Early Fourteenth Century* (Oxford: Blackwell, 1960).

Smith, Warren, 'Dorigen's Lament and the Resolution of the *Franklin's Tale*', *ChauR*, 36 (2001–2), 374–90.

Somerset, Fiona, ' "As just as is a squyre": The Politics of "Lewed Translacion" in Chaucer's *Summoner's Tale*', *SAC*, 21 (1999), 187–207.

Spearing, A. C., *Medieval to Renaissance in English Poetry* (Cambridge: Cambridge University Press, 1985).

—— *The Medieval Poet as Voyeur* (Cambridge: Cambridge University Press, 1993).

Spencer, H. Leith, *English Preaching in the Late Middle Ages* (Oxford: Clarendon Press, 1993).

Staley, Lynn, 'Chaucer and the Postures of Sanctity', in *The Powers of the Holy: Religion, Politics, and Gender in Late Medieval English Culture*, ed. David Aers and Lynn Staley (University Park: Pennsylvania State University Press, 1996), pp. 179–259.

—— 'The Man in Foul Clothes and a Late Fourteenth-Century Conversation About Sin', *SAC*, 24 (2002), 1–47.

Stokes, Myra, *Justice and Mercy in Piers Plowman* (London: Croom Helm, 1984).

Stretter, Robert, 'Rewriting Perfect Friendship in Chaucer's *Knight's Tale* and Lydgate's *Fabula Duorum Mercatorum*', *ChauR*, 37 (2002–3), 234–52.

Strohm, Paul, *Social Chaucer* (Cambridge, Mass.: Harvard University Press, 1989).

—— *Hochon's Arrow: The Social Imagination of Fourteenth-Century Texts* (Princeton: Princeton University Press, 1992).

Sturges, Robert, *Chaucer's Pardoner and Gender Theory* (New York: St Martin's Press, 1999).

Swanson, Jenny, *John of Wales: A Study of the Works and Ideas of a Thirteenth-Century Friar* (Cambridge: Cambridge University Press, 1989).

Swanson, R. N., *Church and Society in Late Medieval England* (Oxford: Blackwell, 1989).

—— 'Social Structures', in Brown (ed.), *A Companion to Chaucer*, pp. 397–413.

Tatlock, John S. P., 'Chaucer and Wyclif', *MP*, 14 (1916), 257–68.

Taylor, P. B., 'Chaucer's *Cosyn to the Dede*', *Speculum*, 57 (1982), 315–27.

Thompson, N. S., *Chaucer, Boccaccio and the Debate of Love: A Comparative Study of 'The Decameron' and 'The Canterbury Tales'* (Oxford: Oxford University Press, 1996).

Tinkle, Theresa, 'The Heart's Eye: Beatific Vision in *Purity*', *SP*, 85 (1988), 451–70.

Tupper, Frederick, 'Chaucer and the Seven Daadly Sins', *PMLA*, 29 (1914), 93–128.

—— 'Chaucer's Sinners and Sins', *JEGP*, 15 (1916), 56–106.

Tuve, Rosemond, *Allegorical Imagery: Some Medieval Books and their Posterity* (Princeton, NJ: Princeton University Press, 1966).

Wallace, David, *Chaucerian Polity: Absolutist Lineages and Associational Forms in England and Italy* (Stanford: Stanford University Press, 1997).

Watt, Diane, *Amoral Gower: Language, Sex, and Politics* (Minneapolis: University of Minnesota Press, 2003).

Weisl, Angela, *Conquering the Reign of Femeny: Gender and Genre in Chaucer's Romance* (Cambridge: D. S. Brewer, 1995).

Wenzel, Siegfried, *The Sin of Sloth: 'Acedia' in Medieval Thought and Literature* (Chapel Hill: University of North Carolina Press, 1960).

—— 'The Source of Chaucer's Seven Deadly Sins', *Traditio*, 30 (1974), 351–78.

Wheatley, Edward, 'Modes of Representation', in Brown (ed.), *A Companion to Chaucer*, pp. 296–311.

White, Gertrude M., ' "Hoolynesse or Dotage": The Merchant's January', *PQ*, 44 (1965), 397–404.

White, Hugh, *Nature, Sex, and Goodness in a Medieval Literary Tradition* (Oxford: Oxford University Press, 2000).

Whittock, Trevor, *A Reading of the 'Canterbury Tales'* (Cambridge: Cambridge University Press, 1968).

Wieland, Georg, 'The Reception and Interpretation of Aristotle's *Ethics*', in *The Cambridge History of Later Medieval Philosophy*, ed. N. Kretzmann *et al.* (Cambridge: Cambridge University Press, 1982), pp. 657–72.

Wilson, Grace G., ' "Amonges Othere Wordes Wyse": The Medieval Seneca and the *Canterbury Tales*', *ChauR*, 28 (1993–4), 135–45.

Winstead, Karen, *Virgin Martyrs: Legends of Sainthood in Late Medieval England* (Ithaca: Cornell University Press, 1997).

Woolf, Rosemary, 'Moral Chaucer and Kindly Gower', in *J. R. R. Tolkien: Scholar and Storyteller*, ed. Mary Salu and Robert T. Farrell (Ithaca: Cornell University Press, 1979), pp. 221–45.

Work, James A., 'Echoes of the Anathema in Chaucer', *PMLA*, 47 (1932), 419–30.

Zeeman, Nicolette, 'The Condition of *Kynde*', in Aers (ed.), *Medieval Literature and Historical Inquiry*, pp. 1–30.

Index